THE POLITICS OF FORM IN GREEK LITERATURE

Also available from Bloomsbury

READING POETRY, WRITING GENRE
edited by Silvio Bär and Emily Hauser

THE MATERIALITIES OF GREEK TRAGEDY
edited by Mario Telò and Melissa Mueller

THE LIFE OF TEXTS
edited by Carlo Caruso

THE POLITICS OF FORM IN GREEK LITERATURE

Edited by Phiroze Vasunia

BLOOMSBURY ACADEMIC
LONDON • NEW YORK • OXFORD • NEW DELHI • SYDNEY

BLOOMSBURY ACADEMIC
Bloomsbury Publishing Plc
50 Bedford Square, London, WC1B 3DP, UK
1385 Broadway, New York, NY 10018, USA
29 Earlsfort Terrace, Dublin 2, Ireland

BLOOMSBURY, BLOOMSBURY ACADEMIC and the Diana logo are trademarks of Bloomsbury Publishing Plc

First published in Great Britain 2022
Paperback edition published 2023

Copyright © Phiroze Vasunia & Contributors, 2022

Phiroze Vasunia has asserted his right under the Copyright, Designs and Patents Act, 1988, to be identified as Author of this work.

For legal purposes the Acknowledgements on p. x constitute an extension of this copyright page.

Cover design: Terry Woodley
Cover image © *Aristotle with a Bust of Homer*, Rembrandt (Rembrandt van Rijn), Dutch, Leiden 1606–1669 © The Met. Purchase, special contributions and funds given or bequeathed by friends of the Museum, 1961

All rights reserved. No part of this publication may be reproduced or transmitted in any form or by any means, electronic or mechanical, including photocopying, recording, or any information storage or retrieval system, without prior permission in writing from the publishers.

Bloomsbury Publishing Plc does not have any control over, or responsibility for, any third-party websites referred to or in this book. All internet addresses given in this book were correct at the time of going to press. The author and publisher regret any inconvenience caused if addresses have changed or sites have ceased to exist, but can accept no responsibility for any such changes.

A catalogue record for this book is available from the British Library.

Library of Congress Cataloging-in-Publication Data
Names: Vasunia, Phiroze, 1966– editor.
Title: The politics of form in Greek literature / edited by Phiroze Vasunia.
Description: New York : Bloomsbury Academic, 2021. |
Includes bibliographical references and index.
Identifiers: LCCN 2021027048 (print) | LCCN 2021027049 (ebook) |
ISBN 9781350162631 (hardback) | ISBN 9781350162648 (ebook) |
ISBN 9781350162655 (epub)
Subjects: LCSH: Greek literature–History and criticism. | Politics and literature.
Classification: LCC PA3014.P65 P65 2021 (print) | LCC PA3014.P65 (ebook) |
DDC 880.9—dc23
LC record available at https://lccn.loc.gov/2021027048
LC ebook record available at https://lccn.loc.gov/2021027049

ISBN: HB: 978-1-3501-6263-1
       PB: 978-1-3501-9159-4
       ePDF: 978-1-3501-6264-8
       eBook: 978-1-3501-6265-5

Typeset by RefineCatch Limited, Bungay, Suffolk

To find out more about our authors and books visit www.bloomsbury.com and sign up for our newsletters.

CONTENTS

List of Illustrations   vii
Notes on Contributors   viii
Acknowledgements   x

Introduction *Phiroze Vasunia*   1

Part I   Verse (and Some Prose)

1. **Disagreement, Complexity and the Politics of Homer's Verbal Form** *Ahuvia Kahane*   23

2. **Sophocles'** *Antigone*, **Feminism's Hegel and the Politics of Form** *Simon Goldhill*   49

3. **The Aporia of Action and the Agency of Form in Euripides'** *Iphigeneia in Aulis* *Victoria Wohl*   65

4. **Forms of Survival** *Susan Stephens*   83

Part II   Prose (and Some Verse)

5. **The Politics of Informed Form: Plato and Walter Benjamin** *Andrew Benjamin*   103

6. **Plato's** *Seventh Letter* **or How to Fashion a Subject of Resistance** *Paul Allen Miller*   125

7. **Body Politics in Aristotle's** *Poetics* **and** *Rhetoric* *Nancy Worman*   145

8. **Aristotle's Lost Works for the Public and the Politics of Academic Form** *Edith Hall*   161

9. **Politics and Form in Xenophon** *Rosie Harman*   179

Part III   Word and Image

10. **The Politics of Form in Eighteenth-Century Visions of Ancient Greece** *Daniel Orrells*   203

Contents

11   Ekphrasis, Leo Spitzer and the Politics of Form   *Ruth Webb*   237

Bibliography   257
Index   289

ILLUSTRATIONS

10.1 J. J. Winckelmann, *Geschichte der Kunst des Alterthums* (1764), Preface — 205
10.2 Comte de Caylus, *Recueil d'Antiquités égyptiennes, étrusques, grecques, romaines et gauloises* (1752–67), volume 3, frontispiece — 210
10.3 Comte de Caylus, *Recueil d'Antiquités égyptiennes, étrusques, grecques, romaines et gauloises* (1752–67), volume 4, frontispiece — 211
10.4 Comte de Caylus, *Recueil d'Antiquités égyptiennes, étrusques, grecques, romaines et gauloises* (1752–67), volume 5, frontispiece — 212
10.5 Comte de Caylus, *Recueil d'Antiquités égyptiennes, étrusques, grecques, romaines et gauloises* (1752–67), volume 5, title page — 213
10.6 Comte de Caylus, *Recueil d'Antiquités égyptiennes, étrusques, grecques, romaines et gauloises* (1752–67), volume 1, plate 53 — 215
10.7 Comte de Caylus, *Recueil d'Antiquités égyptiennes, étrusques, grecques, romaines et gauloises* (1752–67), volume 1, plate 46.1 — 215
10.8 Comte de Caylus, *Recueil d'Antiquités égyptiennes, étrusques, grecques, romaines et gauloises* (1752–67), volume 1, Greek art chapter vignette — 216
10.9 Comte de Caylus, *Recueil d'Antiquités égyptiennes, étrusques, grecques, romaines et gauloises* (1752–67), volume 2, Greek art chapter vignette — 217
10.10 Comte de Caylus, *Recueil d'Antiquités égyptiennes, étrusques, grecques, romaines et gauloises* (1752–67), volume 1, plate 56.4 — 218
10.11 James Stuart and Nicolas Revett, *The Antiquities of Athens* (1762), General View of Athens — 220
10.12 James Stuart and Nicolas Revett, *The Antiquities of Athens* (1762), Doric Portico — 221
10.13 James Stuart and Nicolas Revett, *The Antiquities of Athens* (1762), bazaar — 223
10.14 Julien-David Le Roy, *Les ruines des plus beaux monuments de la Grèce* (1758), bazaar — 225
10.15 Pierre-François Hugues d'Hancarville, *Collection of Etruscan, Greek, and Roman Antiquities, from the Cabinet of the Hon. W. Hamilton, etc.* (*Antiquités Étrusques, Grecques, et Romaines, tirées du Cabinet de M. Hamilton, etc.*) (1766–7), volume 4, frontispiece — 228
10.16 Pierre-François Hugues d'Hancarville, *Collection of Etruscan, Greek, and Roman Antiquities, from the Cabinet of the Hon. W. Hamilton, etc.* (*Antiquités Étrusques, Grecques, et Romaines, tirées du Cabinet de M. Hamilton, etc.*) (1766–7), volume 2, frontispiece — 229
10.17 Pierre-François Hugues d'Hancarville, *Collection of Etruscan, Greek, and Roman Antiquities, from the Cabinet of the Hon. W. Hamilton, etc.* (*Antiquités Étrusques, Grecques, et Romaines, tirées du Cabinet de M. Hamilton, etc.*) (1766–7), volume 2, vignettes — 231
10.18 Pierre-François Hugues d'Hancarville, *Collection of Etruscan, Greek, and Roman Antiquities, from the Cabinet of the Hon. W. Hamilton, etc.* (*Antiquités Étrusques, Grecques, et Romaines, tirées du Cabinet de M. Hamilton, etc.*) (1766–7), volume 1, Song and Meditation — 232

CONTRIBUTORS

Andrew Benjamin is Distinguished Professor of Architectural Theory at the University of Technology, Sydney (and Emeritus Professor of Philosophy at Monash University, Melbourne). His recent publications include *Towards a Relational Ontology. Philosophy's Other Possibility* (2015), *Art's Philosophical Work* (2015) and *Virtue in Being* (2016).

Simon Goldhill is Professor of Greek at the University of Cambridge and Foreign Secretary of the British Academy. He has published widely on Greek literature and tragedy in particular. His books have been translated into ten languages and won three international prizes. He has lectured and broadcast all over the world, and his most recent publications are *Preposterous Poetics: the Politics and Aesthetics of Form in Late Antiquity* and *The Christian Invention of Time: Temporality and the Literature of Late Antiquity*.

Edith Hall is Professor of Classics at King's College London. She has published more than thirty books, including *A People's History of Classics: Class and Greco-Roman Antiquity 1689–1939* (co-authored with Henry Stead, 2020). In 2017 she was awarded an Honorary Doctorate at the University of Athens and in 2019 Honorary Citizenship of Palermo.

Rosie Harman is Lecturer in Greek Historiography at University College London. Her monograph on Xenophon's historical writing is due for publication shortly.

Ahuvia Kahane studies change, continuity and authority in the ancient world and its relation to modernity. In recent years he has written on 'complexity', 'dynamic systems', time, form and ethical function in Archaic Greece. He is currently completing *Epic, Novel and the Progress of Antiquity* (Bloomsbury) and at work on *Oral Theory, Complexity and Homeric Epic*. Kahane is a Fellow of Trinity College Dublin where he is Regius Professor of Greek (1761) and A. G. Leventis Professor of Greek Culture (2017).

Paul Allen Miller is Carolina Distinguished Professor at the University of South Carolina. He is the former editor of *Transactions of the American Philological Association*. He is the author of *Lyric Texts and Lyric Consciousness* (1994), *Latin Erotic Elegy* (2002), *Subjecting Verses* (2004), *Latin Verse Satire* (2005), *Postmodern Spiritual Practices* (2007), *Plato's Apology of Socrates* (2010) with Charles Platter, *A Tibullus Reader* (2013), *Diotima at the Barricades: French Feminists Read Plato* (2015) and *Horace* (2019). He has edited fifteen volumes of essays on literary theory, gender studies and topics in classics as well as published more than eighty articles on Latin, Greek, French and English literature, theory and philosophy. His *Foucault's Seminars on Antiquity: Learning to Speak the Truth* is forthcoming from Bloomsbury.

Contributors

Daniel Orrells is Reader in Ancient Literature and Its Reception in the Department of Classics at King's College London. He is the author of two monographs, *Classical Culture and Modern Masculinity* and *Sex: Antiquity and Its Legacy* and a forthcoming monograph entitled *Antiquity in Print in the Eighteenth Century*.

Susan Stephens is Sara Hart Professor in the Humanities and Professor of Classics at Stanford University. Her work includes *Ancient Greek Novels: The Fragments*, co-authored with Jack Winkler (1995), *Seeing Double: Intercultural Poetics in Ptolemaic Alexandria* (2003), *Callimachus: The Hymns* (2015) and *The Poets of Alexandria* (2018). Her work has focused on the political and social context of Hellenistic poetry, locating poetic innovation as a response to the bicultural formulation of Ptolemaic kingship. Her current work is on ancient athletics.

Phiroze Vasunia is Professor of Greek at University College London. His publications include *The Gift of the Nile* (2001), *Zarathushtra and the Religion of Ancient Iran* (2007) and *The Classics and Colonial India* (2013). He is the general editor of the series *Ancients and Moderns*, also published by Bloomsbury, and the editor, with Daniel L. Selden, of *The Oxford Handbook of the Literatures of the Roman Empire* (forthcoming). A book on postcolonialism and the study of antiquity is in progress.

Ruth Webb is Professor of Greek at the University of Lille and a member of the research team UMR 8163 'Savoirs, Textes, Langage' (CNRS, University of Lille). She is an expert in Imperial and Late Antique Greek literature, and writes mostly on theatre and rhetoric. She is the author of *Demons and Dancers: Performance in Late Antiquity* (2008), *Ekphrasis, Imagination and Persuasion in Ancient Rhetorical Theory and Practice* (2009) and numerous articles on dance and rhetoric.

Victoria Wohl is Professor at the University of Toronto. She studies the literature and culture of democratic Athens. Her publications include *Love Among the Ruins: The Erotics of Democracy in Classical Athens* (2002), *Law's Cosmos: Juridical Discourse in Athenian Forensic Oratory* (2010) and *Euripides and the Politics of Form* (2015).

Nancy Worman is Ann Whitney Olin Professor of Classics and Comparative Literature at Barnard College and Columbia University. She is the author of articles and books on style, performance, and the body in Greek literature and culture. Her books include *The Cast of Character: Style in Greek Literature* (2002), *Abusive Mouths in Classical Athens* (2008), *Landscape and the Spaces of Metaphor in Ancient Literary Theory and Criticism* (2015) and, most recently, *Tragic Bodies: Edges of the Human in Greek Drama* (2020).

ACKNOWLEDGEMENTS

Earlier versions of many of the chapters in this volume were presented at a conference on 'The Politics of Form in Greek Culture', held at University College London, in June 2016. Those who delivered papers or chaired sessions on that occasion include William Fitzgerald, Edith Hall, Rosie Harman, Ahuvia Kahane, Nick Lowe, Daniel Orrells, Ruth Webb, Tim Whitmarsh, Victoria Wohl and Nancy Worman. The conference was supported by grants from the Department of Greek and Latin at UCL (the A. G. Leventis Fund), the Institute of Advanced Studies at UCL, the Institute of Classical Studies, and the Jowett Copyright Trust (Oxford). Nikita Nicheperovich and Angela Paschini helped expertly with the planning and organization of the event. Happily for this volume, four scholars who did not speak at the conference accepted the invitation to contribute chapters: these are Andrew Benjamin, Simon Goldhill, Paul Allen Miller and Susan Stephens. Alice Wright, Lily Mac Mahon and Georgina Leighton, at Bloomsbury, were ideal editors and put up cheerfully with delays and difficulties at my end. Two readers improved the manuscript by providing helpful criticism on the draft chapters. Christopher Pipe was an efficient copy-editor. Annemarie Schunke offered invaluable assistance with the index. Miriam Leonard provided much-needed help and advice throughout the making of the book. I should like to express my deepest gratitude and appreciation to all these individuals and institutions.

Phiroze Vasunia

INTRODUCTION*
Phiroze Vasunia

I first thought about a volume on this topic when I was reading again the *Theory of the Novel* by György Lukács and *Marxism and Form* by Fredric Jameson, for a series of workshops organized by Tim Whitmarsh, on the 'romance' tradition between Greece and the East.[1] An excellent book, *The Romance between Greece and the East*, emerged out of those workshops, in 2013, thanks to Whitmarsh's efforts, and his work is one reason why the present volume does not extend to prose fiction in the ancient world.[2] On that occasion, I was thinking about the form of the ancient novel – a subject that has been addressed in the last two or three decades, thanks to the inspiration offered by Mikhail Bakhtin's work – but I also began to consider whether the question of form and especially the relationship between form and politics needed to be examined again, not just in relation to the ancient novel but in relation to texts and genres that flourish in earlier periods. How did the turn to New Historicism in the 1990s change the study of form and the situation of form in political and social contexts? How did the much-vaunted return to philology of the next decade renew attention to questions of form, genre and structure? What about the relationship between form and the newly invigorated analyses of gender, race, class and nation? It seemed to me that these were important questions. I was, of course, not alone in thinking so: scholars, in Greek studies and outside, were addressing these issues from the turn of the millennium and have continued to do so into the present.[3] But even as interest in the subject continues to proliferate, explicit reflection on the politics of form seems only now to be developing in Greek studies, and this seems the right time to pull together a few threads and to explore the issues in a little depth.

Jameson, who has written widely about the politics of form, says that form is more important than content, that form is even more political than content. He has made the point in several places, but he tends to avoid ancient art and texts, and one of his clearest expositions of the formal and the political comes in his lecture on modernism and imperialism, which is reprinted in *The Modernist Papers* and where he describes the effect that imperialism has on such authors as E. M. Forster. Jameson writes that imperialism is one of the prime determinants of modernism, of its innovations in style and language and of the break it marks with earlier literary traditions. Imperialism changed the representation and experience of space for those who lived in metropolitan cultures, and it did so, at least in part, by creating and perpetuating an unequal

---

* I should like to thank Miriam Leonard and an anonymous reader for constructive comments on a draft of this introduction.

relationship between those who lived in imperial nations such as England and those who lived in its colonies. Modernism tries to account for the imperialism of the late nineteenth and early twentieth centuries by 'recoordinating the concept of style with some new account of the experience of space, both together now marking the emergence of the modern as such'.[4] In Jameson's analysis, Forster's novel *Howards End* offers a response, on the level of style, to the 'representational dilemmas of the new imperial world system' and to the contradictions of imperial modernity.[5] This is a relatively under-appreciated essay, which complements the more substantial and better-known *Marxism and Form*, but it has potentially significant ramifications for classical scholars interested, say, in the relationship between ancient prose fiction and the contexts of production. If Jameson's first charge to us is to take seriously the content of the form, his second is to show how the concern with form and politics runs through some of the most influential critical thinkers of the twentieth century, from Lukács to Walter Benjamin, to Adorno and Sartre, many of whom also engaged with antiquity in their work. A third challenge he lays down is on questions of gender, sexuality, and the body, and here the challenge is largely by omission since he avoids discussing the topic in the early work on Marxism. On all these points, I think there is an opportunity for classical scholars, a chance for them to add a historical dimension to the study of form, and to draw out the implications of this work further.

One of the salutary effects of Jameson's own work has been to widen the reach of formalist enquiry and to broaden the scope of the politics of form. On this point, Jameson's provocation has been taken up by many scholars outside classical studies including by Caroline Levine in her book *Forms: Whole, Rhythm, Hierarchy, Network*, which appeared in 2015. Levine makes the point that 'attending to the affordances of form opens up *a generalizable understanding of political power*'.[6] That word 'generalizable' is important, but I think we might be circumspect in how we proceed on this matter. Forms and the political are situated, contingent and specific. Different cultures may respond formally in different ways to different political situations, and we need to attend to cultural specificity even if we want to arrive at generalized claims about the nature of form and politics. This is where a focus on Greek culture may be useful – because Greek culture has been deeply analysed in formalistic terms, and because with Greek culture we might perceive the interaction of form and political power in a world, the patterns, orders, distributions and arrangements of which have been intensely studied for generations. But useful, also, because some of the most influential formal systems, whether poetic, artistic or political, have engaged with the ancient Greek in order to arrive at more thorough formulations of themselves. This is to say that the politics of form in Greek culture should be understood as a wide-ranging and even necessary subject for discussion in our time.

We have to face the fact that 'form' is a term of wide semantic range and can be used variously. James Porter writes that 'the Greek critical lexicon utterly lacks any satisfying equivalents for our words "content" or "form": *morphe*, *eidos*, and *schema* do not obviously lend themselves to a juxtaposition with "content" in our sense of the term, nor does a Greek equivalent for "content" readily come to mind'.[7] The modern English term 'form' is itself flexible, but neither in ancient Greece nor in the modern world do writers cease to explore the relationship between what we might term 'form and content'. Simon Goldhill, who is the author of a riveting study on the politics of form in late antiquity, says that form is 'especially labile as a critical term, a shifting and linking way of perceiving'.[8] The term itself can be taken to denote several things: minute details within a text or a line or phrase; genre or another category (such as a dialect, metre, or trope) through which a text can be related to other texts; the metaphysical form of which Plato writes and from which a given text or work of art may somehow descend: or the perceived structure that holds together the content of a work of literature. 'Form' can be a verb or a noun, or, in some contexts, both. For some readers, the term may have more than one of these meanings. An art historian may arrive at a different understanding of form from a literary scholar and draw differently on Kant and Hegel, or Clive Bell, Roger Fry and Clement Greenberg: or the art historian might not so differ from the other, given that some of the best analyses of form, in fact, combine visual culture and textual discussion to an impressive level of sophistication. Perhaps the very elasticity of form, its many meanings, histories, and resonances, makes it so appealing to writers and critics; perhaps its very flexibility is what makes it so easy to use when we talk about things as busy, deep and many-sided as art and literature.[9] Putting forward an account of form as it has been used by art historians, literary scholars and others may therefore be a demanding task, but luckily the interested reader can turn to many treatments of form as it has been defined by critics, at least in the modern period. Goldhill gives an important place to Hegel and Victorian intellectuals in writing that 'the notion of form had become instrumental and normative in the interconnected regimes of literary criticism, religious regulation, social manners and architectural understanding – and even, through the idea of organic form, biological science'.[10] In his book he looks at interactions across genres and also between forms: in our volume, many chapters explore an interesting and productive overlap between genre and form, while others think of form apart from genre and analyse many genres, and indeed many forms, in relation to the political.

The term 'politics of form' is construed in broad and flexible ways, elsewhere as in this volume, and for good reason. Some critics take it to mean that form is the reflection of a contemporary social, historical, or political situation and that an explication of form offers some insight into the nature of such a determinate situation. Some say that form presents a political intervention and even, on occasion, an encouragement to rousing political change such as revolution. Other critics read the relationship between formal and political categories in a dialectical fashion and explore how the two shape each other. Some worry that politics and form are inseparable and that commenting on form is always to comment on politics (and vice-versa), while others fret over the introduction of the political into an aesthetic category which, in their view, should be kept unspoiled. And there are writers who worry that writing about *the politics of form* hollows out both terms and reduces each to its least interesting meaning.[11] This is, no doubt, an opportune moment to say that I do not believe that literature always should be read in terms of politics alone; nor do I believe that a 'political' reading of a literary work necessarily diminishes its textual richness, aesthetic quality or cultural density. Far from it: the most accomplished works of literature and art retain their depth, interest and value precisely because they repeatedly open up to a variety of readings, some of which may well lavish attention on questions of form and ideology.

In ancient Greece, the first sustained reflection on *form* is also the first sustained reflection on *the politics of form*. Reflection on literary form can arguably be found in a range of works from the Homeric epic poems to Aristophanes' *Frogs*, but it is Plato's work that is an influential starting-point for discussion of the subject. Since the crucial passages have been extensively studied, only a brief exposition is called for here. In a famous part of Book 3 of the *Republic*, Socrates turns to 'expression' (*lexis*) and then argues that one kind of poetry consists of imitation (*mimesis*) in which the characters speak in their voices (examples of this mode include tragedy and comedy), another in which the poet speaks in his own voice (*diegesis*; an example of this mode is the dithyramb), and a third or mixed variant in which the poet speaks in his voice and also uses imitation (Socrates refers to epic poetry as an example of this mode). The Socratic preference is evidently for the unmixed, narrative mode of diegesis. Socrates' point is that the guardians of his imaginary *polis* ought not to practise imitation, but if they do imitate anything, they should imitate qualities that are appropriate to them and that can be found in 'the brave, the self-controlled, the righteous', and so forth (395c). Not long after, Socrates also suggests that the poet who imitates all things in different styles, patterns, and rhythms should be sent on his way and not admitted to the ideal *polis*, whereas that poet would be granted entry who imitated good men and 'the patterns (*typois*) for which we legislated at the beginning, when we were trying to educate the soldiers' (398b). Socrates' critique throws a sharp light on mimesis and on the form or mode in which the poet tells stories: the attitude he takes to mimesis leads him to the view that some forms of poetry are more acceptable than others in his ideal city.

Socrates returns to form and mimesis in Book 10 of the *Republic*, where he makes a couple of points that bear directly on the politics of form. Now he appears to be against almost all forms of 'poetry', regardless of metre. Socrates says that 'the only poetry admissible in our city is hymns to the gods and encomia to good men' (607a).[12] To accept other kinds of poetry such as Homer and tragedy into the city is to admit verse that is designed to rouse pleasure in the audience, with the result that 'pleasure and pain will be enthroned in your city instead of law and the principle which the community accepts as best in any given situation'. Poetry, in this perspective, needs to be useful to the *polis*, and poetry that offers no utility to government or the state has no place in the Socratic city at all. Socrates had earlier, in Book 3, made the point that poetry was to be barred from the city because of the problems associated with mimesis; here we see that poetic forms are banned also since they provide pleasure rather than utility.

To be clear, Socrates is not objecting to poetry that gives pleasure: he says he would restore Homer to his ideal city if someone could defend his place in a 'well-governed city' (ἐν πόλει εὐνομουμένῃ, 607c). What he is looking for is poetry that is useful to the city, and if such poetry also happens to give pleasure to the audience, then so much the better.[13] He would happily allow poetry back into the city if someone could defend poetry using any form (lyric, or another metre, or in prose) and could show that poetry aimed not just to give pleasure but was 'useful for government and human life' (ὠφελίμη πρὸς τὰς πολιτείας καὶ τὸν βίον τὸν ἀνθρώπινον, 607d). The issue, for Socrates, is that certain forms of poetry give pleasure to people and enchant them through mimesis to undertake actions that are bad for the city and for themselves.[14]

One reason for the reformulation of the critique in Book 10 is that, since the discussion of poetry in Book 3, Plato has developed the theory of 'forms' or 'ideas'. The theory of forms is complex, but the point I would like to emphasize in this context is that the Platonic 'form' is metaphysical and it is external to the text or object of which it is a form. A couple of implications follow from this theory. One is that form and content can be treated separately since form has a non-material, metaphysical character; the second is that form is a point of origin or a beginning, without which the material manifestation of the object or text could not come into existence, and on both these points the difference is substantial with Aristotle, who offers us the other great constellation of theories from Greek antiquity on form. As S. J. Wolfson writes, 'For Aristotle, form is immanent, emergent, and coactive with its expressive materials – the several cases from which a general typology may be deduced. Platonic form is authorized by transcendent origin; Aristotelian form is realized in process, development, and achievement.'[15]

Both Aristotle and Plato concur that mimesis and tragedy have the capacity to affect and sway an audience, but Aristotle does not hold to the Platonic theory of forms and he frames mimesis in a very different way from Plato: his *Poetics* offers a strong riposte to Socrates' views in the *Republic*. Aristotle thinks of mimesis as innate in human beings and associates it with pleasure. Where Plato is troubled by the ethical, political and social repercussions of art and poetry that involve mimesis, Aristotle makes mimesis a vital part of his analysis of tragedy, of which he is a defender and enthusiast. His definition in the *Poetics* stipulates that tragedy is 'a *mimesis* of a high, complete action' (1449b), and his treatise indicates that for him mimesis is closely connected to learning and understanding: 'poetry is at once more like philosophy and more worth while than history' (1451b). Moreover, Aristotle also suggests, by the introduction of catharsis to his analysis, that tragic poetry has a civic or communal dimension, and it is one that he appears to welcome in the form. Tragedy 'in dramatic, not narrative form, effects through pity and fear the *catharsis* of such emotions' (δρώντων καὶ οὐ δι' ἀπαγγελίας, δι' ἐλέου καὶ φόβου περαίνουσα τὴν τῶν τοιούτων παθημάτων κάθαρσιν): pity, fear, the emotions and their catharsis have a vital role to play in the audience's response to drama. On this reading, Aristotle implies that the pleasure provided by tragedy 'is also of benefit to civic communities' and that the catharsis of emotions that is achieved through tragedy has a social function.[16]

The influence of Plato and Aristotle on the subject of form can be discerned readily in the Hellenistic period at the level of poetic practice and theory. Callimachus, in the third century BC, responds to Plato indirectly if not directly. The narrator's remarks in the *Aetia* prologue, in elegiac verse, about the size and scale of a poem, its delicacy and loudness, the slender Muse and fat sheep, and the cicada and the braying ass can all be read as comments on the politics of form.[17] To turn to a less familiar example, consider Callimachus' use of κακὰ βούβρωστις, a *hapax legomenon* from the *Iliad*, in his *Hymn to*

Demeter. Socrates also cites the relevant passage of the *Iliad* in the *Republic* (379d8). Benjamin Acosta-Hughes and Susan Stephens write, 'Callimachus subsequently includes this by now doubly marked phrase (for Homer and for Plato) in his hymn in such a way that κακὰ βούβρωστις defines not divine whimsy, but retribution for sacrilege, thus imposing moral order onto Homer's random world.'[18] Callimachus thus reframes the Homeric passage in his own hexameters and, as Acosta-Hughes and Stephens demonstrate, repudiates Socrates' concerns about mimesis and poetry in the ideal state. Callimachus was doubtless exceptionally attuned to formal matters, since 'the taxonomic implications of formal criticism would have been significant for his *Pinakes*', and the dexterity he displays in his verses needs to be read in the context of multicultural Alexandria.[19]

The Hellenistic philosophers who write before and after Callimachus show a significant attentiveness to questions of literary form; they reflect an interest in formal criticism (e.g. in word order, syntax, genre, metre, sound, composition) that continues to develop after the fifth century BC and after the dissemination of Aristotle's works.[20] In many respects, these thinkers bear out the programme, set down by Shklovsky and Adorno in their different ways, of not taking form for granted, that is, of 'making form difficult', and they subject the formal features of verse and prose to an intense scrutiny.[21] The philosophers include figures such as Neoptolemus of Parium, now best known for the triad ποίημα-ποίησις-ποιητής and its afterlife in Horace's *Ars poetica*, and Crates of Mallos, who said that a poem should be judged on the basis of its form, especially its sound, and not its content. The philosophers and critics argue and disagree with each other and develop their ideas about form through a subtle and complex idiom. They do not all use the same words for 'form': by the time we get to the Epicurean writer Philodemus, in the Roman era, σύνθεσις ('arrangement') or σύνθεσις τῆς λέξεως may mean 'form', λέξις may mean 'language' but in some instances also 'form', and διάνοια can mean 'thought' – but, again, matters are far more complex than this basic inventory suggests. Philodemus, who draws on and departs from Plato and Aristotle, holds the view that form and content are closely connected and that poetic judgement involves the analysis of both.[22] For Philodemus, language used in a work of literature must be proper (*to prepon*) to the thought or content, so that the content virtually determines the shape of the form – a point that is made regularly by ancient critics.[23] Yet, Philodemus also emphasizes the value of form in poetic judgement and argues that the composer of a poem is responsible 'for the perfection of its form in the smallest detail and the coherence of every detail with larger effects'.[24]

Within Greek studies in the last century, scholars have long been interested in questions of form and politics, but it is arguably true to say that there has been a resurgence of interest in the relationship between form and politics in the last couple of decades or so. Some of this work is not explicitly placed under the heading of form or politics by the authors but nonetheless has contributed to our comprehension of the issues. We have only to think of studies of Sophocles' tragedies and late antique literature by Goldhill, the metrical analyses of Athenian drama by Edith Hall, the political readings of Euripidean plot and structure by Victoria Wohl, and the materialist and post-human investigation of bodies in tragedy by Nancy Worman, to appreciate the extent to which our understanding of Greek drama has grown along these lines.[25] In that sense, developments in the study of Greek culture resemble critical developments in other disciplines: witness the renewed interest in form in modern literatures, art history, music and film studies, for example. What these developments share is an attention to the formal or to the aesthetic and a wariness toward a perceived undervaluing of form in approaches such as New Historicism.[26]

Why Greek studies, in particular, has been marked by a renewed interest in questions of form is hard to explain. One reason may well be that Classics is, not for the first time, acting as a derivative discipline and belatedly following new formalisms that were being explored and refined elsewhere. On this account, Greek studies is jumping on to a bandwagon: on this occasion, however, bandwagon-jumping is not an adequate explanation, and I would not place all recent work into the category. Another reason may be a disaffection, in Greek studies as elsewhere, with New Historicism and the perception that it has undervalued issues of form, aesthetics, beauty, the pleasure of the text and indeed philology. Wohl writes that 'as New Historicism has hardened into an orthodoxy, both in the field of classics and beyond, many have started to worry that in mining the texts for ideological content, it has cast aside important questions of literary form, giving scant attention to the formal structure and poetic language that differentiate a tragedy from, say, a tribute list'.[27] She adds that a consequence of New Historicism has been to turn the literary text from 'the Keatsian urn of New Criticism, self-sufficient in its eternal beauty, into an ornate but ultimately vacuous container of an ideology that itself is thereby reified as its determinate content'.[28] We might broaden out this explanation by substituting for New Historicism a whole range of areas or approaches such as cultural studies, gender studies, race and ethnicity studies, postcolonialism, the critique of ideology and theory. The return to form could now be construed as a kind of forward action, on the part of those scholars who believe in the autonomy of the work of art, or who think that New Historicism is reductive and insufficient to deal with questions of form and aesthetics, or think that it has eroded students' engagement with valuable features of a text such as metre and language. Some of the enthusiasm behind new work on the politics of form even would seem to come from scholars who are sympathetic to New Historicism but who at the same time seek to augment the methods and refine the aims of that approach by the incorporation of formal issues into their work.

We can readily see why the newer formalists would be interested in Greek literature, and especially Greek literature in the period that extends from Homer to the Hellenistic poets. Greek tragedy and comedy are areas where New Historicism has been deployed with a particular facility and enthusiasm and where it continues to be prominently practised. Another factor is formal versatility: the range of metres used in the period is breathtaking, in drama but also outside of the dramatic genres, and the deployment of these metres and the dexterity of the versifiers has rightly attracted the attention of scholars interested in formal questions. Other reasons include the formalized rituals and ritual structures that accompany the performance of poetry, the rituals that accompany religious practice and political life, the creation of aesthetic canons in the period, and contemporary philosophical interest in forms, structures and aesthetics. We can also appreciate why scholars have been so moved as to analyse the politics of form and formal phenomena in Greek antiquity: almost all of Greek literature is composed by 'aristocrats', almost all is composed by men, much of it is composed during periods of political and military upheaval, and an important strand is composed by Plato, who writes stylishly and influentially about the conjunction of forms, poetry and politics in his work. We might add that the cultural status and renown of ancient Athens have made it central to formulations of modernity, so that thinking about the politics of form in the Greek world is also a way of thinking about modernities and self-definitions in modern 'Western' cultures.

We might refer briefly to older explorations of the politics of form within classical studies. Classical scholars are used to thinking about style or word order as inseparable from history, for example, and they habitually suppose that style is connected to social and political matters, i.e. the 'world of the text'. There is a lasting tradition of such work in Greek studies, and we could summon numerous examples from across the twentieth century. Consider the subject of metre and rhythm. As early as 1901, Thomas Dwight Goodell wrote *Chapters on Greek Metric* in which he said, 'Man is not merely a rhythmical animal, as all animals are; he is a rhythmizing animal, as truly as he is a political animal.'[29] In the following year, Walter Headlam wrote about Dorian and non-Dorian metres. For him, 'Wordsworth's ode to Duty, 'Stern Daughter of the voice of God,' or Tennyson's upon the Death of Wellington could not have been written by a Greek except in Dorian metre; to write of ἀρετά or ἀνδρεία in Anacreontic would have been absurd and ludicrous.'[30] In his treatment of Greek metre, published after Goodell's and Headlam's studies, Paul Maas wrote, 'Characters of low social standing (except the Phrygian in the *Orestes*) are never given lines in sung metres but are given instead anapaests, like the Nurse in the *Hippolytus*, or hexameters, like the Old Man in the *Trachiniae*.'[31] Turning to a study written some decades later, we find Peter Rose saying that 'Pindar's formal metrical patterns represent one of the most striking factors (perhaps more significant even than the irretrievably lost music and dance patterns) differentiating his language from the everyday language of the ruling class'.[32] Even in a treatment such as Kenneth Dover's *Evolution of Greek Prose Style* (1997), which is not overtly about politics, the reader comes to see how Dover's careful analysis of prose style has its political dimensions.[33] These examples reminds us that classical scholars have scarcely neglected to join politics and literary form in their work. Hall's recent analysis of the politics of metres in Athenian drama thus exemplifies the new formalism and builds carefully on long-standing reflections on the politics of verse forms.[34]

'Could we ever narrativize *without* moralizing?'[35] The form assumed by Greek prose can also be analysed in terms of its ethical and political dimensions. Think of the traditions of Greek historical prose writing: we shall turn later to philosophical prose and Plato. Every reader of Herodotus, Thucydides and Xenophon comes away from their texts with an appreciation and admiration of their handling of narrative complexity and storytelling skills. Following Northrop Frye and others, Hayden White has pointed out how historical narrative imposes on reality a form, and this form is more often than not the form of a story. The narrative has a beginning, a middle and an end and thus imposes a formal coherence and a meaning on the reality that it represents. This is not to say that historical reality itself exists in a pure or unmediated essence and that it is being somehow distorted by particular historical narratives. But the narrative addresses the desire on the part of the reader for significance, interpretation and closure and is read as a story, a story, that is, which implies a moral and a politics. Moreover, as White writes in his early work, the prose narrative draws its literary force from the type of emplotment deployed in the historical narrative, whether romance, comedy, tragedy or satire, and it is the emplotment no less than the content that structures the response of the reader and informs the text's political and ideological impact. This appears to hold true for relatively early prose writers such as Herodotus and Thucydides, in whose time the genres of tragedy and comedy are being elaborated, as for those writers who are composing their work after the establishment of these literary genres. In White's analysis, the content of the form makes clear that the cleavage between historical writing and ideology is spurious.

Other commentators have interpreted formal elements such as the plot, language and structure of Greek drama in terms of politics. In one sense, this is a tradition that goes back to Aristophanes' *Frogs* and to the contest between Aeschylus and Euripides. Closer to our own time, Jean-Pierre Vernant, who is associated by some with historicist approaches to Greek literature, read tragedy in terms of its relationship to the contemporary political and social situation of Athens. He wrote about the many formal and structural features that make up the genre of tragedy (the language of the protagonists, the songs of the chorus, the mythic setting) and connected these to the world of the democratic city-state. In one analysis, Vernant vigorously chastised Freud for not being alert to the historical specificities of fifth-century Athens in devising his theory of the Oedipus complex; he claimed that Freud's theories were not alert to the evolution and form of tragedy and were built on shaky foundations because they sought to offer general pronouncements on psychological and sexual impulses while ignoring the socio-historical realities of Athens.[36] Other scholars such as Goldhill, Hall, Wohl, Mark Griffith, Peter Rose and Froma Zeitlin have explored the relationship between the genre (including its formal features such as plot, choral song, music, language) and Athenian political and social life.[37] The influence of these writers is apparent in current scholarship on politics and form, as critics venture into new directions and focus on affect, senses and reception.

Newer work on tragedy raises the importance of affect for our understanding of the genre and relates it to questions of form and politics. It is not just pity and fear that the audience feels but a wide range of emotions, and by exploring what these emotions mean and by asking how the forms of the drama shape them, we might arrive at some understanding of the politics of dramatic form. Wohl, for instance, has suggested that 'the relation between aesthetic and political forms is mediated by affect' in Greek tragedy.[38] For her, aesthetic form exerts a real ethical and political impact and it does so through a 'leading of the soul' or *psychagogia*. 'Aesthetic form,' she writes, 'provides a syntax for the imaginary articulation of the audience's real conditions of existence; it "leads the soul" to adopt certain subjective relations to that reality. Ideology is not something that aesthetic form contains, then but something that it *does*.'[39] On this analysis, Euripides' *Ion* does not merely represent ideology but compels its audience to feel the work of ideology and hold up the play for examination. By watching the play and responding to its *muthos* in the theatre, the members of the audience experience its impact at an affectual and intellectual level. Wohl's book, like some of the chapters in this volume, shows how form, politics and affect interact with each other in Greek tragedy and reaffirms that it seldom makes sense to try and read them discretely.

Another way to consider the politics of form is to think not about the internal dynamics of a form but about forms themselves as ideological. As Eagleton puts it, 'aesthetic modes and forms are already in some broad sense of the term ideological'.[40] Literary forms are contingent, and their comings and goings in literary history are ideological. Why forms flourish at a given historical moment, what ideological pressures they bear, why they change into other forms or fade away, are complex and important questions. Rose traces one sequence of formal development in ancient Greece and writes, 'The formal trajectory from epic formulas to choral lyric, trilogy, single play, philosophical dialogue is similarly not intelligible on the basis of a purely internal Hegelian logic of forms.'[41] Rose associates the flourishing of certain genres with material and political life on the ground: economic developments, aristocratic competition and class struggle are some of the factors that determine the rise or fall of particular genres. Explanations for the evolution of genres, therefore, can be sought not just in the dialogue between genres but in historical and societal factors – a point, to be sure, that has been evident to numerous scholars, including some of the most influential readers of ancient texts. Nietzsche may have liked to say of the *Birth of Tragedy* that it paid relatively little attention to the politics of form ('it is indifferent to politics ... it smells offensively Hegelian', he wrote in *Ecce Homo*), but the focus on Socrates and the fifth-century city in his work underscored the political dimensions of tragedy. The point was also evident to critics writing in the Marxist tradition such as Bakhtin. The latter's arguments for the historical origins of prose fiction take account of social conditions and political factors and suggest that, while the ancient novel had its origins in older forms and in the interaction between genres, the emergence of the new genre is shaped by socio-political contexts. This point is worth emphasizing, with the proviso that the relationship between genre and context be understood as fluid and liable to change: one genre might 'perform cultural work that in another period might be done by a different genre or, more intriguingly, by a different product of the culture, such as a myth or a holiday'.[42]

On the relationship between genres, the work of Lukács is more resonant than even that of Bakhtin.[43] Lukács' early work on epic poetry and the novel explores literary fecundity and continuity within a 'political' framework. One genre emerges from another, because of changes in socio-political conditions, but the newer genre continues to bear ties to the older genre: we might almost say, though Lukács' emphasis is on the dialectic, that epic contains the kernel of the novel within it, and that, despite the break posed by the change in historical circumstances, the epic appears to anticipate the novel. The shape of the new genre varies considerably from the old, but this changed shape does not prevent the new form from showing some resemblance to the old. This resemblance can be discerned even though the contexts of literary production have also changed. As Marx hints in the *Grundrisse*, the conditions for epic poetry may vanish, but the form or the genre of epic still continues to manifest itself subtly in later times. The old genre comes to an end; a new genre arises, with a new politics, and a new socio-historical context in which to take root and flourish, but both the old and the new somehow live on and make their way in the world.

No Greek account of form is more important than Plato's, as I said earlier, but the word 'form' corresponds awkwardly with the philosopher's sense of the concept, partly because usage (starting from the Latin *forma*, 'shape') shows a long and supple development, with strong religious overtones, from the Renaissance to the present; these features are true of the word 'form' in English as well as its cognates in the modern Romance and Germanic languages.[44] Even so, Plato wrote dialogues, with the exception of the *Apology* and the largely spurious letters, and why he chose to compose in the dialogue form remains something of an open question. A further issue is the relationship between the politics of the literary forms that Plato crafts and his own theory of forms. The Athenian philosopher uses the Greek words *eidos* (εἶδος) and *idea* (ἰδέα), which are conventionally translated into English as 'form' but raise difficult questions of definition and translation.

The choice of dialogue form has been variously explained, by thinkers from Nietzsche and Bakhtin to contemporary scholars. The end of the *Phaedrus* (especially, 276a–277a) provides some insight into the deployment of the form, as do other parts of Plato's work, even those parts that resemble extended essays rather than dialogues (e.g. the *Timaeus* and *Laws*). Rather than attempt to solve this vexed question in a definitive fashion here, I think we might pay attention to a point to which Longinus makes explicitly in his treatise on the sublime: it was 'above all Plato', Longinus writes, 'who from the great Homeric source drew to himself innumerable tributary streams' and he adds that Plato would not have been so accomplished a philosopher and author if he had not been zealous in competing with Homer for primacy 'like a young champion matched against the man whom all admire'.[45] The philosophical prose work of Plato comes after Homeric epic and is connected to it, but the connection with epic is not loose or casual: it is crucial and defining, as Longinus says, for it is part of Plato's claim to authority and truth that he can use and manipulate Homer in his writings. A similar point is grasped by Nietzsche in the *Birth of Tragedy*. Just before claiming that Plato's work serves as a model for the novel, Nietzsche writes, 'One could say that the Platonic dialogue was the boat on which the older forms of poetry, together with all her children, sought refuge after their shipwreck; crowded together in a narrow space, and anxiously submissive to the one helmsman, Socrates, they now sailed into a new world which never tired of gazing at this fantastic spectacle.'[46] Nietzsche's imagery is scarcely innocent, and when he shows Socrates sailing his raft into a new world, he invites a comparison with Odysseus. Nietzsche implies that the philosopher has displaced the Homeric Odysseus and become the captain of a new prose genre, one that accommodates old verse forms and also rules over them.

By looking backward and forward, Plato both engages with Homer and foreshadows the novelists, and that explains in part why the figure of Socrates was interpreted so ambiguously by Lukács and Bakhtin. Lukács and Bakhtin, indeed, remind us that Plato's work should be situated in its socio-political context as well as in the framework of literary history. Plato's skill in crafting prose would help him in the so-called 'battles of prose', in which prose discourses of philosophy, history, medicine and oratory were beginning to develop and in which intellectuals vied with each other in their claims to truth and wisdom. Moreover, although the precise relationship between the invention of prose and democracy remains a matter of contention, it is worth recognizing that prose begins to flourish in Greece roughly in the era that democracy begins to flourish.[47] For his part, Plato incorporates high and low, verse and non-verse genres, in his prose, and he thus shows in his writings the kind of democratic heteroglossia to which Bakhtin refers. At the same time, Plato's dialogues frequently expose the inadequacies of official Athenian democracy, challenge the political economy of the city-state, and, ultimately, find the city wanting in its condemnation of Socrates. If there is a conflict in Plato's philosophy between democratic form and anti-democratic content, it is often resolved in favour of the latter. We might say, following Bakhtin and Boyarin, that the dialogue form of Plato's work is, in part, a pretence or an illusion designed to hide the monologic thrust of his writings, many of which are anti-democratic in their political stance; but further, as well, that Plato's writings also promote a deeper dialogism (not necessarily in the moments where the form seemingly most reflects spoken dialogue), which is put at the service of the philosophical truths that he is pursuing.[48]

Plato has much to say about the 'form' of beauty in his writings (no other form is mentioned in the *Symposium*, for instance), and he brings us now to the subject of formal beauty. Plato has relatively little to say about the beauty of literature despite his evident interest in beauty and beautiful things and despite the stylistic flair that he displays in long stretches of his compositions. 'Another question matters more than either poetry or beauty does: What leads a mind toward knowledge and the Forms? Things of beauty do so excellently well. Poems mostly don't.'[49] Plato's approach to beauty and literature arguably imposes a separation between the appreciation of literature and the enjoyment of beauty, but in fact his own Greek is ravishingly beautiful, and his deployment of a wide range of literary genres in his own work is undeniable (the *Symposium*, again, and the *Republic* itself show his versatility on this front). By his formal and stylistic brilliance, Plato complicates the substance of Socrates' remarks in the *Republic* and challenges his readers to think at the most profound level about the relationship between poetry and the state. It cannot be the case that literary beauty has no value for Plato. Indeed, the dissonance between Plato's formal, literary beauty and the restrictions placed by Socrates' on the poets remains a problem within the study of ancient philosophy.

Plato's influence may be one reason why some modern philosophical and political thinkers have hesitated to comment on literary beauty; another reason may be the perception that Marx had little to say about the aesthetic qualities of art and literature. Hall writes that critics on the Left have been especially deficient in offering aesthetic criticism or analyses of beauty: 'A true Marxist "aesthetic", facing up to beauty, timelessness, transcendence and sublimity, has always been missing ... The reasons why critics of the Left run away from the concepts of beauty, sublimity and value are that they do not want to endorse a type of language associated with elites, and that "sublimity" and "beauty" have indeed often lain in the contingent, subjective eye of ruling-class beholders.'[50] There is some truth to this view. As Hall points out, however, 'within the various schools of criticism loosely related to "Marxism" there are several promising ideas available'. Lukács, Benjamin, Jameson and Eagleton are examples of critics in the Marxist tradition who have written extensively about beauty, aesthetics and form. Hall herself makes the case for a dialectical reading of Plato and suggests that 'Plato's best writing at the dawn of western philosophy receives its glittering and apparently timeless allure from two such inbuilt tensions: between dramatic dialogue form, rhythmic prose and intimate, chatty colloquialism and between mythic/mystical imagery and rational inductive method.'[51]

We might at this point reflect that an important tradition since at least Kant has regarded the aesthetic as its own domain, as one not dissoluble into something else. We would, then, grant the aesthetic a literary and philosophical capacity rather than see it as contingent, historical, and political, and think of 'the aesthetic realm' as 'the space best suited for a philosophical exploration' of worldly ideologies or as a space from which rigorous ethical or materialist critiques can emerge.[52] On this view, the singularity of the aesthetic experience cannot be interpreted only in terms of ideology, ethics, or politics and should be seen as a specific and integral phenomenon in its own right. This philosophy of aesthetics has been explored by a range of thinkers from Kant, in the *Critique of Judgement*, to Lukács, Adorno, Jameson and beyond, many of whom have certainly offered political readings of literature. Within classical studies, Charles Martindale, drawing on Kant, has tried to repudiate 'the two commonly made objections to aesthetic judgements about artworks (including works of literature), first that they are formalistic (detaching formal features of the work from the discursive and ideological contexts of their use), and secondly that they are really occluded judgements of other kinds'.[53] For him, aesthetic readings are no less valid than political readings, so that the relationship between aesthetics and politics remains an open question. From this perspective, the reading of literature raises a whole series of problems and compels us to think once again of the text, the reader, the relationship between form and content, and the various cultural and socio-historical contexts to which all these might be related, but also, and no less crucially, of the aesthetic experience.

There is far more to say about the aesthetic experience than can be accommodated in this introduction, but we might wish to appreciate the role of the reader or the audience in our discussion of the politics of form. Plato, in the *Republic* but also in such other works as the *Symposium* and *Phaedrus*, and Aristotle, in the discussion of *catharsis* in the *Poetics*, are among the first in the classical Greek and Latin traditions to analyse the experiential dimensions of art and literature, whether written or performed. Following in their wake, we can say that the experience of literary form needs to be understood as a full-scale sensory process, where the reader or spectator engages with a text's materiality, that is, with the ink, wax, stone and papyrus; the sound of syllables, words and music;

the syntax, sentence structure and word order; and the disposition, situation and location of the text or performance. A dazzling array of forms and an astonishing formal complexity are at work when it comes to the experience of ancient literature: this array and complexity make it virtually impossible for us to discern with any precision what is left in and what is left out at various stages in the transmission of the literary work and make it challenging to understand the transformation generated in the receiver by the work.[54] In studying the politics of form in Greek literature, we should pay attention not just to the formal qualities within a text but to the fuller spectrum of formal phenomena that affect the reader's reception of the work and that could potentially transform the reader's person as well.

What is the transformation wrought on the self when the experience of literature is thus conceived? What happens to the receiving subject, who feels and engages with the many forms and formal devices, no less than the content, of the literature? We might answer these questions by turning, like so many before us, to poets such as Sappho, who composed poems (e.g. fragments 2 and 31) in which the effect of love can also be understood as an allegory of the multisensory experience of poetry, or to the many other poets who have explored the synaesthetic nature of verse, from Attar in the *Conference of the Birds* (*Manṭiq-uṭ-Ṭayr*) to the English Romantics ('My heart aches, and a drowsy numbness pains ...') to Baudelaire (*Correspondances*) and others into the twentieth century. Or we might turn to Aristotle, who with his account of *catharsis* gives his readers a theory of affective response that is at once ancient and astonishingly modern. We might, in fact, turn to any number of poets and thinkers in order to formulate our response, but I think it will suffice here, in thinking about our subject, to refer the reader to analyses by materialist critics on the topic since their writings on aesthetics explore precisely the fashioning of the political subject in literary situations of the type we have been considering.[55] As Jameson reminds us, the aesthetic writings of critics such as Lukács show how art that is truly transformative and utopian 'allows us to glimpse the possibility of a subjectivity without privilege and without hierarchy'.[56]

This way of thinking grants to literature and interpretation the ability to *engage* – to move and transform, to motivate and mould. Form is no less important than content in the consideration of politically engaged art, while, for some thinkers such as Adorno, form is even more important than content when it comes to engaged art.[57] The form of the artwork reflects the conditions of its production no less than the content, but frequently the political effect of the form is harder to discern and more difficult to comprehend than the impact of the content. The slipperiness of form makes it a powerful means for challenging, questioning, or breaking down the status quo: because it is indirect and therefore less likely to be understood as threatening; because it achieves its impact slowly and in more subtle ways than the content of the artwork; because it offers a new vehicle for revolutionary content; and arguably because it is less likely than the content to be appropriated and domesticated by powerful existing traditions. One could even argue that openly political content gets in the way of the efficacy of literary engagement: content that is heavy-handed about its objectives appeals to those who already accept the message or meets with denial from those who hold opposing views, whereas formal innovation can be more effective in changing people's political beliefs. The extreme version of this claim would be to say that the political efficacy of the artwork depends on form and that content is irrelevant.

Not all critics insist so vehemently on the primacy of form over content in the realm of political engagement. Even if we were to grant the thesis that everything turned on form and nothing on content, what kind of literature would be ranked among the most engaged? Antiquity seems to offer few if any explicit examples of literary works that engage the world, or transform it on the basis of form alone, despite the claims made by some Hellenistic philosophers. Optatian is the exception who proves the rule, given the forlorn place he occupies in literary history.[58] It is also difficult to assess the direction of change that follows from a form: that is, it is difficult to correlate a particular formal phenomenon with a particular kind of worldly impact. Will the disruption of metrical norms turn the subject into a political conservative or a revolutionary? Is the prose of historical realism in itself likely to move the reader to make demands in the name of social justice? Form by itself would have to work hard to orient the political subject in a particular direction, even when form is a vital factor in aesthetic engagement.

We should return at this point to the difficult question of formal change and innovation and to the relationship that formal innovation bears to social reality. The complicating factors are easy to spell out: no innovation comes out of a vacuum, and the boundaries between creation, innovation, development and evolution are not always easy to draw; the criteria for what counts as innovation are notoriously slippery and vague; and it is hard to link formal changes directly to a particular kind of worldly engagement. Yet, innovation in form is well attested in Greek antiquity.[59] At the level of genre alone, a roll call of the familiar would include epic poetry, 'lyric' poetry, epinician, tragedy, comedy, epitaph and epigram, historiography, oratory and philosophical prose, all of which emerge and evolve before the death of Alexander the Great. Some have explained the emergence of ancient Greek literary forms in political terms or connected the deployment of particular forms to contemporary political developments. To the examples adduced earlier could be added the discussion of Homeric poetry by Richard Janko, or the analyses of epinician verse by Glenn Most, Evelyn Krummen and Leslie Kurke.[60] These accounts are fascinating and learned severally, each in their own way: we also need to acknowledge that work on form and politics needs to be developed further and cut across familiar boundaries of genre or metre. Many literary forms change and flourish in the fifth century BC in Athens, within the same communities, but they do not all relate to extrinsic political factors in the same way. Again, there is the issue of gradation: formal variation can be related to political realities or unresolved tensions in society but also need to be explored and studied at the level of detail since different forms within a single work could be related to different political phenomena. The challenge is of investigating examples small and large, within and beyond the familiar boundaries of genre, and of relating form to socio-political reality across the scale.

Form is not only a register, or a resolution, of the historical or ideological contradictions of society. Literature, and literary form, are far too complex and interesting to be explained or understood only in terms of reference to history. This is why many of our most sophisticated interpreters, including those critics who are inclined to read texts from the perspective of historical materialism or dialectical theory, remain sensitive to formalist technique, aesthetic value, poetic practice and literary language; it is, not incidentally, also why writers such as Lukács, Adorno, Jameson and Eagleton often write in a style that is captivating and consummate – in a prose which, to give Eagleton's description of Jameson's writing, 'carries an intense libidinal charge, a burnished elegance and unruffled poise'.[61] We should think of form as its own thing as well as enmeshed in the world, to see it as both verb and noun, to try to understand what form does and what it knows, and to understand form in the terms of Plato and Aristotle and other thinkers.[62] We need to think, in other words, of form in its complexity, durability, and versatility and to explore form from many perspectives, including the few explored in this introduction.

This volume aims to light up different ways in which we might think about the politics of form and makes no claim to being comprehensive or overly systematic. It is divided into three sections. In the first section (on poetic works), Ahuvia Kahane explains 'rupture' in the linguistic regimes of Homeric figures such as Achilles in terms of formal and thematic complexity; disruptions in language are not 'misuses' but the very condition of politics in the *Iliad*. Simon Goldhill reads *Antigone* as a conflict between the extremism of Antigone and Creon, on the one hand, and other characters' resistance to their demands, on the other; the form of the play questions the delusional heroism and ideological rigidity of the leading characters. Victoria Wohl writes that Euripides, in *Iphigeneia in Aulis*, explores the *muthos* of the plot in such a way as to provide glimpses of alternative ethical possibilities and of a road to an invigorated democratic politics in which agency but also contingency might play hopeful parts. Susan Stephens argues that the poets of Hellenistic Alexandria show literary creativity in inventing, adapting, or renewing genres and that their works can be understood as shaping and responding to the densely complicated politics of their world.

In the second section (chiefly on prose authors), Andrew Benjamin interprets Plato's *Republic* and Walter Benjamin's works to explore the politics of form in relation to a cluster of connected themes such as literary value, the particular and the universal, judgement and knowing, and meaning and presence. Paul Allen Miller argues that the *Seventh Letter* of Plato is aimed at the forming of the philosophical subject and at thinking through a politics of truth and resistance. Nancy Worman suggests that the emphasis on formal unity and purity in the *Poetics* and, to an extent, in the *Rhetoric* leads Aristotle to underplay the value of the gendered body, materiality, and affect and to keep messy democracy at bay, in his discussion of drama. In exploring the politics of obscurantist academic jargon, Edith Hall writes that Aristotle's exoteric writings are more accessible and public-spirited than his esoteric works and that they offer important models for intellectuals in our own day. Rosie Harman analyses form and content in Xenophon's works and shows how seemingly puzzling shifts in style, tone, argument, and theme can be understood in terms of the meaning-making of the text and the construction of ideology.

In the last section, Daniel Orrells examines how eighteenth-century writers argued about the connection between Greek and 'Oriental' forms in art and text and locates these debates within discussions of the relationship between Greece and non-Greek cultures. Ruth Webb writes that ancient (e.g. Theon) and modern critics (e.g. Leo Spitzer) offer contrasting perspectives on ecphrasis (they differ on whether to think of it as formal or formless) but that both groups are nonetheless rooted in political regimes. As these concluding chapters illustrate, early modern and modern explorations of form, in the European tradition, continue to engage with Greek ideas even as they try to arrive at new conceptions of art history, literary criticism and classicism. Understanding the politics of form remains an urgent task for students of ancient Greek literature.

Notes

1. In thinking about form and politics for this introduction, I have drawn on the following: Jameson 1971, 1976, 2007 and 2015; Lukács 1971, 1978 and 2010; Eagleton 1975 and 1990; Adorno 1997; Wolfson 1997; Richter 1999; Leighton 2007; Levinson 2007; Mouffe 2013; Levine 2015; Olson and Copland 2016; Kramnick and Nersessian 2017; and special issues of *MLQ: Modern Language Quarterly* 61 (1) (2000); the *European Journal of English Studies* 20 (3) (2016); *Critical Inquiry* 44 (1) (2017); and *PMLA* 132 (5) (2017). I have also learned much on the subject from the contributors to this volume.
2. Whitmarsh and Thomson 2013. Whitmarsh 2018 offers a stimulating discussion of the form of ancient prose fiction; on which, see also Reardon 1991, Selden 1994 and Grethlein 2017 (for its discussion of Heliodorus' *Aethiopica*).
3. Wohl 2015, Hall 2012 and 2018b, Goldhill 2020.
4. Jameson 2007: 159.
5. Jameson 2007: 164.
6. Levine 2015: 7.
7. Porter 1995: 99. Porter's chapter is a scintillating exploration of 'form and content' in Philodemus' work.
8. Goldhill 2020: xiii. See also the comments on form in the introduction to Rutherford 2012.
9. Leighton 2007: 3.
10. Goldhill 2020: xii.
11. Jarvis 2010: 932.
12. Translations of Plato and Aristotle in this introduction are adapted from Russell and Winterbottom 1972.
13. See Burnyeat 1999: 317–18.
14. From this perspective, Books 3 and 10 of the *Republic* should be read alongside passages from the *Laws*, esp. *Laws* 655c–656a, 658a–659c and 700a–701b. For the *Republic*, see the chapters by Andrew Benjamin and Paul Allen Miller, in this volume, and for the *Laws*, the chapter by Susan Stephens.
15. Wolfson 2012: 497. On the *Poetics*, see the chapter by Nancy Worman in this volume.
16. Hall 2018a: 39.
17. Acosta-Hughes and Stephens 2012, ch. 1, offers an excellent reading of Callimachus' verse in the light of Plato's philosophical work.
18. Acosta-Hughes and Stephens 2012: 20.

19. Acosta-Hughes and Stephens 2012: 30. For the Alexandrian context, see e.g. Selden 1998 and Stephens 2003.
20. Ford 2002.
21. See Porter 1995: 99.
22. In Book 5 of his treatise *On Poems*, Philodemus refers to thirteen earlier attempts at poetic judgement, four of which call for no judgement of content and which he appears to repudiate. See *On Poems* 5, cols. 29–38 (Mangoni), with further details in Asmis 1995: 152–3, who supplies the division into thirteen theories. The Greek text is obscure and admits of other interpretations.
23. Versions of this view can be found in Aristophanes, *Frogs* 1059; see also Aristotle, *Rhetoric* 3.7, 1408a10–11, and Quintilian 11.1.3, with Russell 1981: 130–1, and Porter 1995: 124–5.
24. Armstrong 1995: 232. On Philodemus' poetic theory, see further Asmis 1991 and 1992, Pace 2009 and the introduction to Janko 2000.
25. Goldhill 2012 and 2020, Hall 2012, Wohl 2015, Worman 2020.
26. For discussions of form, style and politics in Greek art, see Neer 2002 and 2010.
27. Wohl 2015: 4.
28. Wohl 2015: 4.
29. Goodell 1901: 64.
30. Headlam 1902: 212.
31. Maas 1962: 53.
32. Rose 1992: 173–4.
33. See e.g. the comparison of Thucydides and Lysias, or the analysis of Xenophon's style in the *Memorabilia* (Dover 1997: 5–10, 154–5).
34. Hall 2006 and 2012.
35. White 1980: 27.
36. Vernant 1981.
37. Goldhill 2012; Griffith 1995; Hall 1997 and 2006; Rose 1992; Wohl 2015; Zeitlin 1985.
38. Wohl 2015: xi.
39. Wohl 2015: 7.
40. Eagleton 2006: xvii.
41. Rose 1992: 372.
42. Dubrow 1990: 269. My thanks to Victoria Moul for the reference.
43. Lukács 1978; Bakhtin 1981.
44. Williams 1983, s.v. 'formalist'.
45. Longinus, *On the Sublime* 13.3–4 (trans. W. Rhys Roberts).
46. Nietzsche 1999: 69.
47. See the discussion in Goldhill 2002. Longinus, *On the Sublime* 44, offers a fascinating discussion of democracy, freedom, literary writing and artistic accomplishment.
48. Bakhtin 1981; Boyarin 2009.
49. Pappas 2020.
50. Hall 2017b: 26.

51. Hall 2017b: 26.
52. Jameson 2015: 7.
53. Martindale 2005: 4.
54. Lukács' early writings on aesthetics are a guide to problems of composition, materiality, sensory experience, and subjectivity and remain of much interest to readers who wish to tackle these issues with conceptual rigour and sophistication: Lukács 1963a, 1963b and 1969; with Jameson 2015.
55. Lukács 1963a and 1963b; on synaesthesia in ancient literature, see also Butler and Purves 2013, which is the first volume in the series *Senses in Antiquity*, edited by Shane Butler and Mark Bradley.
56. Jameson 2015: 27.
57. Adorno 1997. On Adorno and form, see the thoughtful analysis of Rush 2009.
58. Squire and Wienand 2017; Goldhill 2020: vii–xii.
59. And the subject of comment: on the origins of tragedy, see e.g. Aristotle, *Poetics* 1448b–1449b, and Horace, *Ars poetica* 274–84.
60. Janko 1991: 38; Most 1985; Kurke 1991; Krummen 1990.
61. Eagleton 1981: 60.
62. Leighton 2007: 27–8.

PART I
VERSE (AND SOME PROSE)

CHAPTER 1
DISAGREEMENT, COMPLEXITY AND THE POLITICS OF HOMER'S VERBAL FORM
Ahuvia Kahane

Introduction

One of Milman Parry's greatest achievements was to have initiated a broad debate about the nature of Homeric diction and the meaning of its basic form.[1] Yet Parry's groundbreaking argument also had the effect of 'depoliticizing' formulaic diction.[2] Emphasis on systematic rules, on compositional utility and on the 'grammar' of traditional oral diction was matched by the reduction of semantic resonance of individual formulae to 'essential ideas'.[3] Furthermore, as already understood by Milman Parry's son, the young Adam Parry, the issue was not simply semantic detail but the basic form of Homer's traditional linguistic medium and its function in relation to society and thought:[4]

> The formulaic character of Homer's language means that everything in the world is regularly presented as all men (all men within the poem, that is) commonly perceive it. The style of Homer emphasizes constantly the accepted attitude toward each thing in the world, and this makes for a great unity of experience. Moral standards and the values of life are essentially agreed ... The unity of experience is ... made manifest to us by a common language.

The problem was at its most distinct in the disillusioned figure of Achilles, 'the one Homeric hero who does not accept the common language, and feels that it does not correspond to reality'. Parry explains:[5]

> The poet does not make a language of his own; he draws from a common store of poetic diction ... Neither Homer, then, in his own person as narrator, nor the characters he dramatizes, can speak any language other than the one which reflects the assumptions of heroic society ... Achilles has no language with which to express his disillusionment.

Of course, differences of opinion seem to be the very substance of Homeric poetry.[6] The whole point of Adam Parry's brief essay was thus to try to argue that Homer's politics were more than just a veneer and that Achilles can, in fact, express his disillusionment in epic words. As Parry says:[7]

> He [Achilles] does it by misusing the language he disposes of. He asks questions that cannot be answered and makes demands that cannot be met.

It is not surprising that many readers found Parry's argument unsatisfactory. His practical discussion was sparse and his focus on broad elements of rhetoric misplaced. As Michael Reeve, for example, noted in an early response, 'neither an unanswerable question nor an impossible demand is by its nature a misuse of language ... that is, of traditional vocabulary'.[8] Richard Martin, who provides a detailed survey of the history of this debate, agrees, as indeed have many of the scholars who attempted to resolve this difficulty and, more broadly, to characterize difference and semantic resonance in Homeric diction.[9]

Of course, for a long time now scholars have been modifying, qualifying, adapting and challenging Milman Parry's formulaic arguments.[10] Yet with very few exceptions, all scholars, oralists, neoanalysts, students of traditional thematic and mythological 'pathways' of epic, students of intertextuality and allusion, of poetic subjectivity and intention, narratologists and even scholars who study Homer without paying specific attention to the question of phraseology allow for the fundamental 'traditional' character epic diction and its references, whether in the form of fixed inherited patterns or as meaningful individual divergence from traditional form and thought.[11]

Here, then, is the essence of our problem. Homer's world is a world of language: In the larger scheme of things and despite epic's narrative quarrels and disagreements, so long as we acknowledge the shared traditional frame of this language, it seems that we remain within the 'rules', conventions and expectations of a single speech community and therefore, in essence, outside the realm of true difference and of a politics of epic form in which different views can actually be heard (we will explain this idea further below).

The gist of Adam Parry's original question is perhaps deeper, more troubling and in essence a matter of both political philosophy and linguistic method: Can the language and thought of Homer's epic ever exist 'politically', outside of its own traditional hexameter form? Can Homer's discourse exist *both inside and outside* its own linguistic-political system?[12]

In this chapter I want to argue that such a 'topological' existence is possible and that politics are indeed inherent in Homer's language. It nevertheless seems to me that the current debate has reached a point of saturation and that something of a change of tack is required.[13] The problem, as I will argue, has been made more difficult to resolve by, on the one hand, a common understanding of the idea of politics that is at least partly complicit with existing order and, on the other hand, an adherence to certain underlying principles of language as a set of rules. In search of an alternative, I shall first adopt a different approach to 'the political' and to the idea of dissent, guided largely by the influential work of contemporary philosopher Jacques Rancière and by some of his comments, both general and, more specifically, on Homer. As a corollary, with regard to language, I shall follow a usage-based argument concerning alternative principles of grammar and diction pioneered by such scholars as George Lakoff, Charles Fillmore and

William Croft and more recently developed by Adelle Goldberg, Michael Tomasello, Joan Bybee and others. I will, in addition, draw on important usage-based studies of so-called 'complex adaptive language systems' by Diane Larsen-Freeman, Nick Ellis, Lynn Cameron and Caroline Kramsch and other linguists. What binds these arguments about political philosophy, linguistics and complexity together and stands at the core of this essay is a methodological rethinking of the place of the unpredictable, the exceptional and thus the free and the 'political' within otherwise well-ordered formal systems.

When our basic problems and methodological alternatives have been clarified, we will apply them to some prominent examples of diction in Homeric verse. We will try to uncover some of the 'political' usage of Τὸν/Τὴν δ' ἀπαμειβόμενος προσέφη . . ., one of Homer's most common and widely discussed formulaic constructions.

The sum of these efforts, to put it plainly, is to try to demonstrate that exception exists as an integral component of the formal rules of language, that Homer's diction does indeed resides both *inside* and *outside* of the system of Homeric verse and thus that a politics of epic verbal form is possible.

Politics and the political

It might seem that the existence of struggles over power, resources and authority in the Homeric poems and thus of politics in Homer is given, and that the rest is merely a matter of highlighting the contents of such disputes or, in terms of diction, their precise verbal form.[14] This assumption, I would like to suggest, only masks the true problem of politics.

Consider a musical analogy: Bach's monumental *Matthäuspassion* brings together many conflicting characters and positions: Jesus, Pilate, Judas etc. Yet together the different elements of Bach's oratorio clearly represent the canonical practice of early eighteenth-century Protestant German culture. They figure and indeed enshrine a common theological and 'political' experience within a highly recognizable, unified harmonic framework. Such formal recognition performs an ideological function. In a deep sense, Judas and Pilate are as much a part of the canon as Jesus himself. The *Passion* contains no 'exceptions', no political or theological 'others'.

We could argue that Homer's narrative also seems to mark a distinct 'apolitical' common experience. Recognition of this shared aspect of the poems can be traced back, for example, to Vico's *Scienza Nuova* (1725) or indeed much earlier, to classical antiquity itself (see, e.g., *Greek Anthology* 16.295, 297, 299) and to the idea that Homer represented 'the whole of Greece'.[15] Even more pronounced were statements commonplace among scholars at the time when Adam Parry was writing his essay. Moses Finley, for example, in his most famous work *The World of Odysseus*, says:[16]

> The heroic code was complete and unambiguous, so much so that neither the poet nor his characters ever had occasion to debate it. There were differences of opinion . . . but these were either disagreements over matters of fact or tactical alternatives.

Finley makes his point without apology:[17]

> The basic values of [Homeric] society were given, predetermined, and so were a man's place in the society and the privileges and duties that followed from his status.

For a long time, classical scholars have, of course, criticized, indeed sometimes dismissed or derided such views.[18] But were Finley and others like him simply led on by blind dogma?

At issue, I suggest, is the philosophical question of political subjectivity.[19] In the *Iliad*, both Agamemnon and Achilles are scepter-wielding (σκηπτοῦχοι), Zeus-nourished (διοτρεφέες) noble (ἄριστοι) rulers (βασιλῆες).[20] They are in some ways equal political agents. It was precisely the general function of such states of agency that Hannah Arendt, for example, considered, partly through comments on Homer's epic, in her most famous philosophical essay, *The Human Condition* (published in 1958, very shortly after Finley's book and Parry's article) in the course of her wide-ranging attempt to salvage the idea of politics and political agency from the ashes of the Second World War. Committed, complex and influential, Arendt's argument nevertheless almost unintentionally exposes deeper 'political' problems.

Among other things, Arendt pointed to the concept of *archê*.[21] 'To act', she says, 'in its most general sense, means to take an initiative, to begin (as the Greek word *archein*, "to begin", "to lead", and eventually "to rule", indicates), to set something into motion.'[22] From this perspective, as philosopher Jacques Rancière recently put it, 'the order of *praxis* [in the Arendtian context – "action"] is an order of equals who are in possession of the power of *archein*, that is the power to begin anew'. In this sense, Homeric kings are equally able to take an initiative, to begin, to lead, to rule and thus to be free. Arendt's series of equations of political agency and freedom, Rancière says, 'finds its equivalent in the movement that engenders civic equality from the community of Homeric heroes'.[23] Achilles and Agamemnon seem to be 'equals ... in their participation in the power of *archê*'.[24] Indeed, let us note, the dispute between these heroes is only possible on the premise of their shared agency and equal status as political subjects. Whether they act in accordance with the heroic code or are disillusioned by it, these heroes and others, and even the Homeric narrator himself and perhaps his Muses too must thus be viewed as sharing in the same community of values. Beyond Book 18 of the *Iliad*, Achilles and Agamemnon, much as they detest each other and although their personal objectives and motivations differ, are reconciled to action within the bounds of common objectives and a single community. In this sense, as Rancière argues, their equality points to a fundamental state of agreement. We seem to be veering back towards 'differences of opinion' within what is otherwise a 'predetermined' order of privileges and duties.

The problem of viewing such relations politically in Homer is, however, more severe. It is only by recognizing the fullness of the problem, that, as we shall see, an alternative perspective can begin to emerge.

As Rancière argues, the state of civic co-agency between Agamemnon and Achilles and the kind which Arendt invokes in her argument for political action also accommodates a more fundamental state of inequality. 'The first witness against [Arendt's] Homeric idyllic', he says, 'is Homer himself.'[25] Rancière here invokes the narrative of the Greek army's near-revolt in Book 2 of the *Iliad* and the manner by which Odysseus suppresses the challenge to Agamemnon's authority by the renegade Thersites.

It might be useful to briefly remind ourselves of the main elements of this important scene. Agamemnon has decided to test the army's resolve. He suggests that the Greeks should all go back home (2.10–41). This move nearly backfires when the Greeks enthusiastically embrace the proposal and make ready to sail (147–54). At the last minute, guided by Athena, Odysseus intervenes. He walks round the Greek camp, reminding each man of his duty and of station in life. 'Listen to those who are better than you … you are of no account in either war or the council … the rule of many is not good. Let there be one king only' (200–6):

> δαιμόνι᾽ ἀτρέμας ἧσο καὶ **ἄλλων μῦθον ἄκουε,**
> **οἳ σέο φέρτεροί εἰσι, σὺ δ᾽ ἀπτόλεμος καὶ ἄναλκις**
> **οὔτέ ποτ᾽ ἐν πολέμῳ ἐναρίθμιος οὔτ᾽ ἐνὶ βουλῇ·**
> οὐ μέν πως πάντες βασιλεύσομεν ἐνθάδ᾽ Ἀχαιοί·
> **οὐκ ἀγαθὸν πολυκοιρανίη· εἷς κοίρανος ἔστω,**
> **εἷς βασιλεύς,** ᾧ δῶκε Κρόνου πάϊς ἀγκυλομήτεω
> σκῆπτρόν τ᾽ ἠδὲ θέμιστας, ἵνά σφισι βουλεύῃσι.

Strange man, sit and be quiet and listen to the speech of other men who are better than you, you unwarlike weakling of no account either in war or in the council. Not all of us Greeks can here be kings. It is not good to have many kings, let there be one king, one ruler only, to whom the crafty son of Kronos gave the sceptre and the law, to rule over his people

Only Thersites, a lone voice of dissent, rises up to speak (2.212–20):

> Θερσίτης δ᾽ ἔτι μοῦνος **ἀμετροεπὴς** ἐκολῴα,
> ὃς **ἔπεα φρεσὶν ᾗσιν ἄκοσμά τε πολλά** τε ᾔδη
> μάψ, ἀτὰρ **οὐ κατὰ κόσμον, ἐριζέμεναι βασιλεῦσιν,**
> ἀλλ᾽ ὅ τι οἱ εἴσαιτο **γελοίϊον** Ἀργείοισιν ἔμμεναι·
> **αἴσχιστος δὲ ἀνὴρ ὑπὸ Ἴλιον ἦλθε·**
> φολκὸς ἔην, χωλὸς δ᾽ ἕτερον πόδα· τὼ δέ οἱ ὤμω
> κυρτὼ ἐπὶ στῆθος συνοχωκότε· αὐτὰρ ὕπερθε

> φοξὸς ἔην κεφαλήν, ψεδνὴ δ᾽ ἐπενήνοθε λάχνη.
> ἔχθιστος δ᾽ Ἀχιλῆϊ μάλιστ᾽ ἦν ἠδ᾽ Ὀδυσῆϊ·

> Thersites, a man of unmeasured speech, alone scolded, he knew within his heart many disordered words, purposeless and lacking in beauty and order, by which to contest the authority of kings, but all that he knew would raise a laugh from the Argives. He was the most shameful man who was to have come to Troy, bandy-legged and lame of one foot. His shoulders were bulging over his chest and squeezed together. And above a pointy head with a whispy shag growing on top. He was most hated by Achilles and Odysseus.

Thersites is 'the most shameful man to go to Troy'. He knows many words by which to 'contest the authority of kings' yet he is ἀμετροεπής, a man whose speech is 'unmeasured' and 'un-metrical', 'lacking all beauty and order', as unfit for the heroic life as it is for *epos*, the hexameter form itself.[26] Thersites' purpose is as 'ridiculous' as his looks. He is a 'bandy legged', 'lame' hunchback. His head is 'oddly pointed', his hair 'thin and woolly'. Homer's phrenological hermeneutic is clear: ugly form matches illegitimate political thought. In the verses that follow, Odysseus reminds this upstart of his place in society (2.246–64) and beats him into submission.

Reading this scene, Rancière says:[27]

> Against the garrulous Thersites – the man who is an able public speaker despite the fact that he is not qualified to speak – Odysseus recalls the fact that the Greek army has one and only one chief: Agamemnon. He reminds us of what *archein* means: to walk at the head. And, if there is one who walks at the head, the others must necessarily walk behind. The line between the power of *archein* (i.e., the power to rule), freedom, and the *polis*, is not straight but severed.

The example of Thersites, Rancière argues, illustrates a common state of affairs. In Homer (as indeed often elsewhere), we find a curiously stable yet unequal distribution of political subject positions:[28]

> In order to convince oneself of this, it is enough to see the manner in which Aristotle characterizes the three possible classes of rule within a *polis*, each one possessing a particular title: 'virtue' for the *aristoi*, 'wealth' for the *oligoi*, and 'freedom' for the *demos*. In this division, 'freedom' appears as the paradoxical part of the *demos* about whom the Homeric hero tells us (in no uncertain terms) that it had only one thing to do: to keep quiet and bow down.

The force of Thersites' submission and exclusion is, let us add here, vividly illustrated by use of his epithet ἀμετροεπής. The word places him outside of epic diction and politics.[29] Yet of course whether ἀμετροεπής is traditional or the product of an individual poet who is adapting this tradition, it fits perfectly within a single, tightly organized system of hexameter language and thought. This could be viewed as an act of political sleight-of-hand. Suspending the disjunction between meaning and form we also co-opt inequality into the good social order of Homeric epic.[30]

The point is this: A 'stable' distribution of unequal roles, if it is maintained, if it is shared, willingly or unwillingly, precludes the possibility of 'political' action. As Rancière says:[31]

> The logic of *archê* presupposes a determinate superiority exercised upon an equally determinate inferiority.[32]

Can we, then, ever escape the absence of politics? How can the voice of those who disagree or are excluded from speech by the system itself be heard? The problem relates, not merely to Thersites or to Achilles, but more broadly to Homer's women, servants, slaves and strangers and to all other characters 'who are not counted either in battle or in council' (*Il.* 2.201–2; cf. *Od.* 1.358 etc.) and who are thus 'of no account',[33] it also relates to the Trojans and to all of epic's 'others', indeed, as a matter of principle, to individual poets, real or implied, working within the Homeric poems and within the performance traditions of epic song.

Here, let me suggest is where Rancière's argument as it appears in the 'Ten Theses on Politics' and throughout his writing points to a way forward. 'What is specific to politics', Rancière suggests, 'is the existence of a subject defined by its participation in contraries. Politics is a paradoxical form of action.'[34] As he says:[35]

> Politics is a specific break with the logic of the *archê*. It does not simply presuppose a break with the 'normal' distribution of positions that defines who exercises power and who is subject to it. It also requires a break with the idea that there exist dispositions 'specific' to these positions.

Thus,[36]

> Politics is by no means a reality that might be deduced from the necessities leading people to gather in communities. Politics is an exception in relation to the principles according to which this gathering occurs ... Politics exists as a deviation from this normal order of things. It is this anomaly that is expressed in the nature of political subjects, which are not social groups but rather forms of inscription that (ac)count for the unaccounted.

Gabriel Rockhill, one of Ranciere's many critical exponents, provides a succinct explanation:

> In its strict sense, politics only exists in intermittent acts of implementation that lack any overall principle or law, and whose only common characteristic is an empty operator.

The Politics of Form in Greek Literature

Politics and indeed a politics of aesthetics thus requires 'a specific regime of speaking whose effect is to upset any steady relationship between manners of speaking, manners of doing and manners of being', what Rancière sometimes describes as 'democratic disorder of literariness'[37] or, in literature, a special kind of 'mute' language (*la parole muette*) that breaks the bonds of its own framework, which is equally open and available to all, a kind of hieroglyphic sign whose meaning cannot be reduced to an outside interpretive law.[38]

In his writing, Rancière often identifies such 'mute' language with certain aspects of modernity, modern literature (especially Flaubert) and modern art (for example certain films by Godard and others).[39] But Rancière no less associates aspects of this regime with, for example, the kind of dumb 'childlike' speech of Homeric poetry whose readings were pioneered in modernity, for example, by Giambattista Vico.[40] 'Childlike' here becomes, not a patronizing progressionist term of praise for historically early 'innocence', but one – turning the Viconian reading into an unexpected virtue – that marks the potential for political freedom and equality.

The purpose of our essay, of course, is not to explore Rancière's philosophical poetics or judge his historical analyses, nor to consider his arguments about modernity, but rather to see whether the fundamental principle of a politics of aesthetics which he uncovers can usefully point us in the direction of a political reading of Homer's verbal art. It is, then, to the analysis of language, to linguistics and to the practical possibility of speech which ruptures the logic of tightly organized hexameter diction that we must now turn.

Language and linguistics

Adam Parry died in a motorcycle accident in 1971, well before the publication of most of Rancière's work which, in any case, he is unlikely to have read.[41] Parry may not have succeeded in giving a full account of Achilles' language of disillusionment, but his argument for the political 'misuse' of language seems to have independently pointed to a linguistic application of the principle of 'rupture' necessary for 'intermittent acts of implementation that lack any overall principle or law' and thus for a language of Homeric politics.

To ensure that we consider the implications of this idea in their full rigour, I want to turn to a more technical linguistic perspective. Can a language system break its own rules and thus permit or enable 'free' expression? Methodologically, this problem can be described in two closely related ways. The first concerns the relation between the rules of grammar and the meaning of words. So long as meaning conforms to formal grammatical rules, it must appear to be confined to its own form, bound, in this sense, to repeat analogous constitutive elements of the system. The second, related problem concerns the structural relationship between expressions that follow grammatical rules, their variants and what we might call true exceptions. So long as we are dealing with systematic variants (no matter how infrequent or 'unique') of a formal pattern, the idea of language that 'misuses' language and thus of the politics of form remains an illusion.

Methodologically, it is difficult, let me suggest, perhaps even impossible to solve this problem, especially when it comes to Homer's highly patterned formal diction, within the frame of what are otherwise widely used approaches to language and linguistics that share the premise of common, often abstract, sometimes algorithmic frameworks of 'deep' linguistic rules. Thus, for example, classical Greek and Latin grammars which are still in common use in school and university language-teaching emphasize abstract paradigms of declension (of nouns, pronouns, adjectives and participles), conjugation (of the verb) and syntactic structure (e.g., conditionals, subordinate clauses, indirect discourse etc.). *Mutatis mutandis,* the Sausseurian idea of *langue* as the underlying structure of language and *parole* as its divergent application incorporates a like hierarchy. Much twentieth-century structural linguistics, as developed by Noam Chomsky and others, employs the same principles. Indeed, Chomskyan linguistics take the idea of the methodological primacy of algorithmic grammatical structure separate from lexical values and semantics much further by suggesting that the abstract rules of grammar are genetically hard wired into the human brain and largely precede linguistic use.[42]

Of course, in their different ways, many such approaches to grammar also acknowledge variation on the 'surface' of discourse, at the level of *parole,* for example, where the formal laws of grammar are applied, re-applied and adapted by individual language-users and communities to the contingencies of specific lexical items, idioms, morphological and phonological traditions, to performance situations, social contexts, roles and subject identities. Thus, the king and the poet speak with courtly eloquence while the beggar and the prostitute speak the language of the gutters and so on. Indeed, the multitude and the rabble, the uneducated and the poor may sometimes even speak 'ungrammatically'. Nevertheless, we could argue, it is precisely these linguistic differences at the surface that define, judged by the standard of grammatical rules, the deeper, 'rightful' relative places of the king-as-king and the beggar-as-beggar in the hierarchy of the kingdom. This of course, is the linguistic corollary to the arguments made by Moses Finley and *mutatis mutandis* by Jacques Rancière when they point to differences of opinion rather than true politics. The general premise of paradigmatic approaches to language, we must again stress, is that different registers bind the privileged, the disillusioned and the disenfranchised, within a single, common language whose underlying grammatical essence is uniform and in this sense apolitical.

In order to pursue the argument for political language and especially for a politics of epic hexameter diction, as Adam Parry saw it, as a language of 'misuse', we need a different kind of linguistic regime, one that (as a matter of methodological principle) is free from predefined grammar and which can express dissent. The change required is far-reaching, though its roots can, in fact, be found in longstanding work in semantics, pragmatics, discourse analysis and in yet earlier studies of language.[43] It has, however, been much more distinctly developed in several strands of usage-based (sometimes known as cognitive functional) linguistics, construction grammar and especially the study of complex dynamic language systems which have been put forward over the last thirty years or so. Here, let me suggest, we have a method to suit the needs of a political analysis of verbal form.

Already in 1987, in his influential *Women, Fire and Other Dangerous Things*, George Lakoff, for example, had argued for an essential 'continuum between the grammar and the lexicon'.[44] Contrary to many algorithmic approaches to grammar, Lakoff made the dramatic assertion that grammatical structures were '*motivated*, and in many cases even *predicted*, on the basis of meaning'.[45] Work by his contemporaries Charles Fillmore, William Croft, Talmy Givón, William Hopper and others and, more recently, by Joan Bybee, Adelle Goldberg, Michael Tomasello and many other linguists, cognitive psychologists, students of developmental linguistics and of language acquisition has helped expand and establish both detailed empirical support and the theoretical foundations of arguments of this type, which turned around conventional relations between formal linguistic patterns and thought.[46]

As Michael Tomasello, for example, has recently put it, 'the fundamental reality of language is people making utterances to one another on particular occasions'. Grammar is thus always epiphenomenal, in other words 'derivative' – it is not a set of independent, abstract laws which define language by objective standards. The engine driving language development is communicative meaning, not form:[47]

> When people repeatedly use the same particular and concrete linguistic symbols ... in 'similar' situations, what may emerge over time is a pattern of language use, schematized in the mind of users as one or another kind of linguistic category or construction. As opposed to linguistic rules conceived of as algebraic procedures for combining symbols that do not themselves contribute to meaning, linguistic categories and constructions are themselves meaningful linguistic symbols – since they are nothing other than the patterns in which meaningful linguistic symbols are used to communicate.

Formal paradigms of Greek and Latin grammar, Sausseurian models and their conception of *langue* and *parole* and modern generative and other algorithm-based grammars emphasize, as we have noted, the primacy of abstract (or underlying) linguistic structure and, importantly, have less interest in the process of symbolization and in meaning.[48] In contrast, usage-based linguistics argues that grammar and grammatical constructions are never devoid of semantic content or communicative function which, indeed, shapes the evolution of grammatical form.[49] The formal rules of language are thus inherently driven by the expressive needs of users.

Of course, with use, certain formal patterns of diction are likely emerge. Michael Tomasello, for example points out that 'loose and redundantly organized discourse structures will, over historical time congeal into more tightly and less redundantly organized constructions'.[50] Yet, as he and other usage-based linguistics stress, exactly the same fundamental cultural-historical forces and communicative needs that generate linguistic utterance and produce patterns in the first place are also the forces that, over time, can change and rearrange these patterns, often through a process known as *reanalysis*.[51]

Language formation thus entails the inherent potential for to-and-fro change, interaction and mutation.[52] The essential process that drives change is nevertheless simply repeated utterance and the re-application of expressions in new and different contexts by means of some form of what we may call analogy.[53] Indeed, among psychologists and linguists it is generally recognized that 'the talent for analogical reasoning constitutes the core of Human cognition' and that analogy is 'the core component of linguistic competence'.[54]

While sets of analogous examples may share some consistent element of form or communicative thought, these will always be affected by any number of complex interactions with specific other sets of contingent circumstances or with individual contexts and will thus in some ways be different.

If we allow that that the fundamental constructive principle of grammatical language is communicative function and that grammatical form is in essence epiphenomenal, it follows that neither the meaning of individual examples nor any set of examples, regardless of the formal attributes which may link it to other examples or sets of examples or to larger wholes, is predetermined by an overall principle or law. Individual expression, exceptionality and the potential for 'rupture' of the rules are thus formulated in the most rigorous sense as inherent features of traditional but necessarily complex linguistics system. Where linguistic rupture is part of the system, so is the potential for politics as Rancière, and we, have defined them.

Before we move on to see how such ideas are applied to the diction of Homer, we need to stress the importance of interaction to the 'freedom' of the linguistic system. In recent years, linguists have provided considerable impetus to such arguments drawing both historically and conceptually, on the study of complex, interactive phenomena in the exact and natural sciences, as well as in mathematics and logic.[55] As Diane Larsen-Freeman and Lynn Cameron, for example, explain in *Complex Systems and Applied Linguistics*:[56]

> [Complexity] does not merely mean complicated. Although the agents or components in a complex system are usually numerous, diverse, and dynamic, a defining characteristic of a complex system is that its behaviour emerges from the interactions of its components.

Complex linguistic behaviour, both in general and as we shall see in Homer's diction too, arises necessarily from repeated usage and interaction in otherwise highly organized but open systems. Interaction can generate diversity that *exceeds* predictable results. Claire Kramsch and other linguists stress:[57]

> Because the systems are open what arises may be in nonlinear relation to its cause. In other words, an unexpected occurrence may take place at any time . . . Complex 'systems' have no distinct boundaries; they exist only because of the fluxes that feed them, and they disappear in the absence of such fluxes. One could therefore say that a complex system is dynamic rather than static; it exists only in the interaction between things and is therefore not itself a thing.

Complex linguistic systems[58]

> operate under conditions that are not in equilibrium [i.e., they are not static]. When you learn one additional piece of knowledge, this new knowledge doesn't just add itself to the other things you acquired previously. The equilibrium you thought you had reached in your prior state of knowledge gets disrupted as one new piece of knowledge reconfigures the whole picture.

This, let us suggest, is precisely the linguistic framework that we need to support a politics of Homer's verbal form.

Complexity, rupture and formulaic diction in Homer

At least some general recognition of the importance of usage for our understanding of Homeric verse is attested, even in fairly early work. Already in 1960, Albert Lord pointed out that:[59]

> When we speak a language, our native language, we do not repeat words and phrases that we have memorized consciously, but *the words and sentences emerge from habitual usage*. This is true of the singer of tales working in his *specialized grammar*.

Other scholars, for example T. G. Rosenmeyer, had acknowledged that 'the bard regards his poetic phrase as indistinguishable from poetic substance'.[60] Gregory Nagy, in an argument first put forward in 1976, had suggested that traditional themes can motivate formulae which in turn motivate metrical form (rather than the other way around) – an essential principle which nevertheless emphasises conformity to traditional thought rather than exceptionality and freedom of expression.[61] In 1991, Bakker and Fabricotti had argued for the semantic relation between metrically fixed core elements and semantically resonant peripheral diction in Homeric epic.[62] Revising this essay in 2005 and citing Givón, Hopper and other early exponents of usage-based approaches, Bakker pointed out that 'grammar is not a constraint but a set of *emergent* rules that make purposeful expression and communication possible'.[63] In 1994, in *The Interpretation of Order*, I myself stressed that 'the study of patterns is, to a point, an investigation of *usage*' and argued that 'certain repetitions of formal features of grammar and metre ... have semantic and consequently literary significance'.[64] Here, semantic potential is exposed although the study may not have sufficiently stressed the phenomenological primacy of semantics. More recently, Bakker in the epilogue to his 2013 book on the *Odyssey* considered the formation of epic patterns driven by communicative interaction and routinized use and argued for the 'interformular' potential of specifically defined traditional diction as meaningful repetition, though he was reluctant to accept 'likelihood of allusion or quotation'.[65] Here again, the semantic freedom of diction over its form and the potential of individual meaning is perhaps insufficiently stressed. A longer and more technical attempt to redefine repetition in Homeric diction in terms of usage-based grammar was put forward by Chiara Bozzone, who, following Goldberg's notion (above) of constructions as 'learned pairings of form and function' has proposed that we should indeed think of formulae as inherent carriers of meaning.[65] Two years later, Cristóbal Cánovas and Mihailo Antović in an edited book entitled *Oral Poetics and Cognitive Science*[67] had also suggested that construction grammar and oral formulaic theory can be viewed as 'congenial approaches', as did Hans C. Boas in the same volume.[68] Finally, starting with semantic and poetic arguments and focussing precisely on a discussion of allusion in Homeric epic, Bruno Currie has briefly (and non-technically) invoked usage based linguistics in his argument, stressing the relation between allusive potential and traditional (epic) art. Currie cites linguists Michael Barlow and Suzanne Kremmer: 'the linguistic system is built up from . . . lexically specific instances, only gradually abstracting more general representations'.[69]

Studies of this type underscore some of the methodological principles of semantic readings of Homeric diction, but they often depend rather heavily on the dynamics of pattern and systematic variation and do not, by and large, provide a systematic methodological account of the prospect of 'rupture' and exceptionality which, as we have seen, is at the core of the argument for the politics of epic form. It is this exceptionality in Homeric diction that we must now consider.

Let us take as our example one of the most common and familiar instances of patterned usage in Homer. Consider speech introductory verses that begin with the formula Τὸν/ Τὴν δ' ἀπαμειβόμενος προσέφη... (//→hepth.) and end with typical noun-epithet formulae denoting the protagonists of Homer's poems and other familiar characters, all attesting to the same analogous form [Nom. (C hepth.→//)]:[70]

πολύμητις Ὀδυσσεύς // 'resourcefull Odysseus') – 5x *Il.*, 45x *Od.*

πόδας ὠκὺς Ἀχιλλεύς // 'swift footed Achilleus') – 12x, only in *Il.*

κρείων Ἀγαμέμνων // 'the ruler Agamemnon' – 5x, only in *Il.*

ξανθὸς Μενέλαος // 'fair-haired Menelaos' – 4x, only in *Od.*

κρατερὸς Διομήδης // 'mighty Diomedes' – 2x, only in *Il.*

Τελαμώνιος Αἴας // 'Telamonian Ajax' – 2x, only in *Il.*

κορυθαίολος Ἕκτωρ // 'helmeted Hector' – 1x, in *Il.*[71]

Πρίαμος θεοειδής // 'godlike Priam' – 1x, in *Il.*

νεφεληγερέτα Ζεύς // 'Zeus gatherer of clouds' – 8x *Il.*; 6x *Od.*

Milman Parry lumps together a large number of formulae of the type Τὸν/Τὴν/etc. ... προσέφη/μετέφη ... ('to him/her replied ...') including Τὸν/Τὴν δ' ἀπαμειβόμενος προσέφη ... ('to him/her said in reply ...') arranged in paradigm form, under the same 'essential idea' of 'X spoke to him in a certain tone or with a certain gesture' (which Parry does not otherwise differentiate semantically).⁷² This translation is predetermined, indeed is only possible if we extract the speech-introductory construction from its specific usage contexts and, to begin with, follow Parry's paradigmatic definition of the formula ('a group of words regularly used under the same metrical conditions to express an essential idea').⁷³

Now, of course, we almost always interpret meaning relationally – i.e., in relation to other things we know, say and hear – through analogy, etc. But the point of a usage-based approach is that such relations are contextual, not abstract, and that the basis of such relations is meaning while abstract form is epiphenomenal. Homer's language system, like all others, 'exists only in the interaction between things and is therefore not itself a thing'. Language is a 'complex' system in the technical sense, and as such it retains overdetermined, unpredictable elements not pre-defined by form, let alone by one single type of form. One can certainly, as one does, repeat existing expressions and create new ones by analogy, but analogy – as indeed Milman Parry himself recognized – is not a fully predictable process.⁷⁴ One can never fully state or assume the 'traditional referentiality' or 'interformular' function of a formulaic expression in Homer. Rather, tradition acts as a stochastic set of doorways which may look similar, but which open onto different corridors and rooms: 'the equilibrium you thought you had reached in your prior state of knowledge gets disrupted as one new piece of knowledge reconfigures the whole picture'. We may, of course, first encounter larger contextual sets and make certain assumptions about these. But our assumptions will always be modified by narrower and yet narrower sets of examples, each of which will cause a forking, a redefinition or a fragmentation of meanings, ultimately reaching unrepeatable unique contexts. In practice, the more we acknowledge the complex makeup of contexts, the more we are likely to find 'non-linear' free expression and difference.⁷⁵ Given the complexity of interaction between juxtaposed formal patterns, we cannot replicate the exact function of the same formal pattern twice.

Commenting on the general function of the formula Τὸν/Τὴν δ' ἀπαμειβόμενος προσέφη … Adrian Kelly rightly says:⁷⁶

> This responsory hemistich signals a disagreement between characters and it is differentiated semantically from the 'to him replied' (τὸν δ' ἠμείβετ' ἔπειτα) unit in representing an increased determination to assert the speaker's intention and/or status in a situation. This disjunction need not stem from actual disagreement … or the immediate context, and the speaker may only feel that the statement is inappropriate or reveals an inappropriate attitude … perhaps requiring modification or extension.

Already here, we begin to see some contextual semantic reanalysis of the meaning of this expression relative to the Parryan idea of 'X spoke to him in a certain tone'. Yet, as we shall see, the 'disagreement' that seems to be embedded in Τὸν/Τὴν δ' ἀπαμειβόμενος προσέφη … requires further qualification. To expose the politics of this formula we need to take a closer look at its usage. The closer we look, the further away we move from any single, abstract shared pattern and the more a 'politics' of diction will emerge.

For a start, let us look again at the selection of speakers which Τὸν/Τὴν δ' ἀπαμειβόμενος προσέφη ... introduces and the place and role, the political 'subject positions' which these speakers hold in the specific narratives of each poem. The selection is significant and *exclusive*. Of the heroes, only Achilles and Odysseus (the poems' protagonists), Agamemnon, Menelaos, Diomedes, Ajax, Hector are so introduced, and of the gods Zeus (οὗ τε κράτος ἐστὶ μέγιστον) alone. In other words, only a certain class of dominant figures who by virtue of their position in the narratives of the *Iliad* and *Odyssey* have the privilege and power to express disagreement and assert their intention or status, seem to be introduced by the Τὸν/Τὴν δ' ἀπαμειβόμενος προσέφη ... Such classifications are not absolute – the whole point is that situations affect meaning[77] – but the formula does exclude other speakers, most of whom do not share such privilege. This is not to suggest that Τὸν/Τὴν δ' ἀπαμειβόμενος προσέφη ... is the only way of asserting determination or status. But it does mean that in the case of this particular prominent expression Parry's paradigmatic 'essential idea' and even Kelly's more nuanced description elide exclusion and interpret the formula within the framework of a shared (and necessarily coercive) verbal experience.

To understand the meaning of the formula more accurately we nevertheless need to turn Kelly's description upside down. We need to make a methodological u-turn. Τὸν/Τὴν δ' ἀπαμειβόμενος προσέφη ... is not a formula that *signals* disagreement as an abstract form. Rather, it is a form of expression, a group of words, whose function is *signalled* in context by the disagreement of specific speakers who have the privilege of doing so.[78] This formula, in other words, is an expression that is defined by Odysseus, Achilles, Zeus etc., and by a political class-distinction.

Starting from usage, then, a better interim translation of Τὸν/Τὴν δ' ἀπαμειβόμενος προσέφη ... might be something like:

> A particular Homeric hero who possesses the privilege of asserting his intention or status in words, a privilege which is denied to other figures, exercised this privilege within a particular narrative context and said ...

Needless to say, this translation is unwieldy to the point of being unusable, though, we must stress, even it is merely temporary, since each individual instantiation of the formula could, as a matter of principle, further redefine and fragment its meaning: separating, for example, Zeus' divine might from mortal privilege. Language often follows general formal patterns but the meaning of those patterns, and even their form, as the linguistic study of complex adaptive systems suggests, is constantly renegotiated in context.

More importantly for us, the difficulty (as above) in neatly and concisely capturing the meaning of the formula is proof of its political potential as an 'intermittent act of implementation'. It is difficult to co-opt the cumbersome formulation we have given above and thus a fixed 'meaning' of Τὸν/Τὴν δ' ἀπαμειβόμενος προσέφη ... into a stable illusion of shared experiences. The unwieldy meaning of the formula suggests that the traditional language of Homeric verse, despite, indeed *because* of its shared form, is *not* a closed system of values and thoughts, *not* a language whose meaning is constrained by pre-existing rules and by extension by political codes. Instead the formula 'ruptures' language.[79]

A complete, fixed description of the meanings of Τὸν/Τὴν δ' ἀπαμειβόμενος προσέφη ... is, as readers must now appreciate, methodologically not possible and it is undesirable too. Consider however, in brief, some further aspects of the analysis and, for example, some of the characters who are excluded from being introduced by the formula. Not least among these is Thersites, who, of all Homeric characters is the one who tries, and most prominently fails, to assert his dissenting view and his status.

In reductive technical terms, a formulaic expression *Θερσίτης + (- x//) or *(- -) + Θερσίτης// [Nom. (C hepth. →//)] , that is to say, either an expression which begins with the nominative of Thersites' name and runs on to the end of the verse or in which the verse ends with Thersites' name, is certainly possible. Of course, unlike the great heroes Thersites has no 'proper' epithet, unless we regard the *hapax* ἀμετροεπής 'unmeasured speech' (2.212), ἀκριτόμυθος 'of undiscerning speech' (2.246), φολκός 'bandy-legged' (- -) or χωλός 'lame' (- -) (2.217) as potential epithetic forms.[80] But localization of the metrical shape (C - - -) of Thersites' name at the hepthemimeral caesura is extremely rare and using his name at this position would have forced, not simply a *versus spondaicus* (a hexameter verse where the fifth foot is a spondee, not a dactyl), but an exceptional (hepth. - - - - x//) metrical sequence. Likewise, - - - // is extremely rare and, of course, the name Θερσίτης, attested only once in the nominative, is never used in verse-terminal position.[81] Thus, Thersites' political exclusion is, we might say, reflected in the formal potential of his name.[82]

The epithet ἀμετροεπής suits him, let us now suggest, not because his speech is unmetrical, but because it describes (uniquely) the usage of his name, 'The Bold/Rash One',[83] which is itself 'bold' and 'rash' relative to the heroic convention and which ruptures, for example, the language of Τὸν/Τὴν δ' ἀπαμειβόμενος προσέφη.... In other words, the usage of Thersites' name disrupts what we might call 'the shared language of consensual epic disagreement' and therefore, as if by some verbal topology, points to some potential for substantive dissent from *within* epic language itself.

Thersites does, of course, speak briefly (2.225–42), introduced by a different, anomalous speech-introductory verse which does not include his name. This speech introduction clearly marks his exclusion as a man 'of no account'. Yet it also marks him out *in hexameter* as a speaker *of hexameter* and thus, paradoxically, in *de facto* discursive terms as someone who acts on equal terms with all speakers in Homer, as someone who is, literally, 'accounted for' (2.224):

αὐτὰρ ὃ μακρὰ βοῶν Ἀγαμέμνονα νείκεε μύθῳ·
But he, shouting loudly, scolded Agamemnon in speech,

The narrator can describe Thersites as an illegitimate, deformed and derisible speaker. Odysseus can chide him with words and silence him with blows of the sceptre. Yet no amount of mockery or violence can take from Thersites his subversive introduction or the account of his speech. Here, it is epic itself that ruptures its own language *by* its language and begins to express the kind of politics which, it seems to me, all readers otherwise sense it contains. A paradigmatic formulaic analysis will unite the many discursive anomalies associated with Thersites and his illegitimate status as a speaker, thus eliding both into a static consensus within a single discursive and political system of unequal subjects. In contrast, a usage-based analysis allows us to mark out diction and status. *Thersites' exclusion is precisely what empowers him to speak 'outside' of the diction and the verbal consensus.*

Let us take this type of analysis a step further by looking at other, intersecting sets of contexts and other forms of rupture. Thus, for example, no reader will fail to note that Τὸν/Τὴν δ' ἀπαμειβόμενος προσέφη … excludes female characters. All of the figures introduced by this formula are male.

Women are, of course, prominent speakers in Homer.[84] Furthermore, many female name-epithet formulae suit the metrical slot from the penthemimeres to the end of the verse. These include λευκώλενος Ἥρη, 'Hera of the white arms', (22x, *Il*. only), πόδας ὠκέα Ἶρις, 'swift footed Iris', (9x, *Il*. only) and above all γλαυκῶπις Ἀθήνη, 'grey eyed Athena', (*Il*. 28x; *Od*. 50x). Here the politics of exclusion become even more distinct than in Thersites' case. The noun-epithet formulae of Hera, Iris and Athena are always used in verse-terminal position. From a formal-paradigmatic perspective, feminine noun-epithet formulae of this type seem like natural complements to the … ἀπαμειβόμενος προσέφη speech-response pattern. They require only a minor alteration to the grammatical gender of the particle. Yet the feminine-gendered speech-introductory variant *Τὸν/τὴν δ' ἀπαμειβομένη προσέφη … is never used in Homer or anywhere else.[85] Nor, indeed, in Homer, is ἀπαμειβομένη otherwise attested: The inflection of the participle ἀπαμειβόμενος is grammatically 'defective', and this, as often elsewhere with defective paradigms, is the result of semantic forces and societal circumstances.[86] It grammaticalizes the exclusion of female speakers (even Athena!) from some speech-acts that express disagreement 'to him/her in answer [she] said …' and assert a speaker's intention or status.[87] We may thus wish to modify our previous attempt to translate the formula Τὸν/Τὴν δ' ἀπαμειβόμενος προσέφη … and add: 'A privileged speaker, *not a woman*, said …', and so on.

There are, needless to say, abundant examples of feminine noun-epithet formulae introduced by other, formally similar variants of speech-response verses such as Τὸν/τὴν δ' ἠμείβετ' ἔπειτα …, 'then to him/her replied…', and related verse types.[88] Mapping the semantics of these – especially from a usage-based perspective – would requires a very large separate study. But as, Adrian Kelly notes of Τὸν/τὴν δ' ἠμείβετ' ἔπειτα …:

> This response formula connotes the emotional perturbation of a respondent resulting from the remembrance of a past injury or action which impinges upon a

current intention or activity. The recollection need not actually be expressed by the respondent speaker, for it can also be introduced by the prior speaker, nor must it necessarily be something of great antiquity. Indeed, the speaker may actually react to something just said as a source of his perturbation.

Certainly male speakers (Achilles, Agamemnon, Zeus etc.) are also introduced by Τὸν/Τὴν δ' ἠμείβετ' ἔπειτα..., but the idea of 'emotional perturbation' is, let me suggest, part of a framework of communicative meanings signalled by Homeric gender perceptions and the exclusion of women from war and words.[89]

Once we begin to acknowledge the 'muted' contours of excluded feminine speech in Homeric diction, we may begin to recognize the gendered politics embedded in even the most common and most familiar components of Homer's formulaic verse. In this essay, we have, of course, so far looked only at very small number of possibilities. But we need to stress again, the closer we move to smaller subsets and individual examples, the more fragmentation, mutation and rupture are revealed.[90] Furthermore, sets and subsets never overlap in full: The set 'feminine characters', for example, does not fully overlap with the set of 'excluded characters' etc.[91] Partially-overlapping sets necessarily interact with each other in complex, unique and unpredictable ways. The 'traditional referentiality' of formulae is thus constantly reanalysed and modified.

Let me offer one final illustration of the semantic potential of Τὸν/Τὴν δ' ἀπαμειβόμενος προσέφη...

Following earlier observations by Norman Austin, Egbert Bakker has recently noted that the noun epithet πολύμητις Ὀδυσσεύς is most commonly used in speech introductory contexts (in 62 or 63 if we count inclusively out of 66 instances). Of these, Τὸν/Τὴν δ' ἀπαμειβόμενος προσέφη... is particularly frequent (50x).[92] Bakker thus argues that Odysseus' name-epithet formula, metrically conditioned by the first part of the verse, leads to the 'epiphany' of Odysseus, 'the man full of *mētis*, precisely and almost exclusively when he takes to the floor in order to speak'.[93] 'The resulting highly formulaic lines,' he says, 'are not so much ready-made ways of saying "and Odysseus answered him" as the performance of a recognizable verbal ritual that is the tradition's coding of a frequently recurring poetic need.' 'Epic grammar', Bakker says, 'codes best what epic poets do most'.[94]

These observations illustrate one aspect of the usage of the speech introductory grammatical construction Τὸν/Τὴν δ' ἀπαμειβόμενος προσέφη, construed, in this case, a character-based poem-specific set. Let me stress, however, that the formula's function is, in fact, far more in flux and indeed *conditioned by* (rather than *conditioning*) its name-epithet supplements and their specific usage. The form is 'recognizable', but the need that defines it is made up of the semantics of contingent use.

The privileged male figures introduced by Τὸν/Τὴν δ' ἀπαμειβόμενος προσέφη (Odysseus, Achilles, Agamemnon, Menelaos, Diomedes, Hector and Zeus) share various formal analogous attributes. Yet, as even orthodox formalists must allow, Homer's characters are not mere clones. Each figure has its own persona, appearances and narratives. Zeus is an immortal god. Agamemnon and Diomedes do not share Odysseus' *polymetic* verbal cunning. Likewise Achilles, though he is a hero of deep understanding, is characterized, not by Odyssean trickery, but by direct, impetuous action and emotion.

In his great response to Odysseus in book 9 of the *Iliad*, Achilles is introduced by the familiar formula (9.307):

Τὸν δ' ἀπαμειβόμενος προσέφη πόδας ὠκὺς Ἀχιλλεύς·

Here too, we could argue, an epiphany is affected. Yet the responsive 'epiphany' in 9.307 clearly eschews all *mêtis*. Indeed, it introduces more than an expression of simple disagreement. As we discover in the following verses, Achilles seems to reject the very principle of semiosis (9.312-13):[95]

ἐχθρὸς γάρ μοι κεῖνος ὁμῶς Ἀΐδαο πύλῃσιν
ὅς χ' ἕτερον μὲν κεύθῃ ἐνὶ φρεσίν, ἄλλο δὲ εἴπῃ.
For hateful to me as the gates of Hades is the man
who hides one thing in his heart and says another.

For Achilles, the gap between what exists in thought and the verbal signifier is as hateful as death. And it is none other than the narrator, epic's wordsmith, who says so, *in hexameter verse*. This, we should recognize, is not simply a matter of truth and lies. Short of direct telepathic communication, the gap between thoughts and spoken or written words is the condition of all language *qua* its function as a system of signs. The implication here is that Achilles seeks transparent expression of thought, unhindered by verbal form. He thus seems to refuse language itself.

Achilles does, of course, speak the language of heroes with great eloquence. Yet apparently to him such language, *qua* language is little more than hateful 'noise' which on its own (presumably even if it is mighty and 'unbroken', cf. the narrator in *Il*. 2.490: φωνὴ δ' ἄρρηκτος 'an unbreaking voice') ruptures the expression of true thought.[96] Achilles' tragedy, we might say, is that he himself is precisely the creature of language he hates. But this tragedy is no less than the triumph of Homeric poetry as politics.

Conclusion

Unlike Thersites, Achilles is never described as ἀμετροεπής, a *hapax legomenon* which we could nevertheless now use to describe, not the veil of a political illusion, but the true 'political' *parole muette*, an emblem of the politics of form in Homer's verse. It marks speech that does not fit the logic of *archê* and words that are, on the one hand, not 'well formed' (ἄκοσμά; οὐ κατὰ κόσμον) but, on the other, not noise, words which fit the hexameter perfectly but have an exceptional 'un-epic' meaning, a meaning which is 'at odds with [their own] metre'. Indeed, ἀμετροεπής may even point to the transcendent speech of the Muses who, after all, 'have been everywhere and know everything' (*Il*. 4.485). The Muses' endless speech – which can never be contained by the finite words of any mortal poet or by rigid metrical form – must by definition take *everything* and *everyone* into account, including the disillusioned, the malformed, the excluded and the silenced.

Regardless of how and to what depth we choose to explore the use of Homer's highly structured diction, it is clear that patterns and repetitive verbal forms are *not* the tradition's way of regulating meaning, values or thought. Quite the contrary, *repetition is the form of change*. The medium of shared form serves, not as a benchmark or a ruler, but as the stage for performing specific needs and perspectives. The point, from a hermeneutic and methodological perspective, we must stress, is *not* that different contexts produce variation, though inevitably they do. The point rather is that different contexts produce systematic *complexity* in which the juxtapositioning of thematic and formal components preclude, the possibility of saying the same thing twice with the same words. In this sense Homer's diction is, we might say, nothing but an 'empty operator'. It 'misuses' its words as a matter of systematic necessity, generating verbal difference, producing semantic exceptions which diverge from abstract, formal relations and laws. This divergence, we may now conclude, is the condition of politics, the point at which we leave Finley's uncompromising, pessimistic view of the heroic code and look to the politics of dissensus in the diction of Homeric verse.

Notes

1. There is no useful way of summing up the bibliography. Recent discussions, e.g., in Bouvier 2015; González 2013; Montanari, Rengakos and Tsagalis 2012; Friedrich 2011; briefly Russo 2010 (cf. Russo 1997), Elmer 2010 and Foley 2010 (with further references). See further below n. 10 and discussion in Kahane 2018. For current research see *Oral Tradition*, http://archive.oraltradition.org/bibliography/. Edwards 1986 and 1988 and J. M. Foley 1985 gave an indication of the size of the debate decades ago.

2. 'Certainly the view that the *Iliad* is not critically reflective dates from at least the time of Plato. But the argument was given a different theoretical basis by Milman Parry's insight, and Lord's continuation of the work, that not only did the *Iliad* arise from oral composition but the method of "composition *during* oral performance" imposed a structure on Homeric verse that emphasized the functionality, more than the interpretability of Homeric language' (Hammer 2002: 6). See Parry 1956 (discussed below) and responses in Reeve 1973; Claus 1975; Nimis 1986; Scully 1984; Hogan 1976; Friedrich and Redfield 1978; Messing 1981; Martin 1989 (who surveys earlier literature); Mackie 1996. More broadly, for debates over ideology and power among individuals and groups in Homeric epic and epic see recently Solez 2012; Rose 2012; Redfield 2011; Osborne 2009; Scafa 2008; Christensen 2007; Hammer 2002, Hammer 1999, Hammer 1998. Hammer 1997; etc. The bibliography in Hammer 2002 is useful. Nevertheless, as we shall argue below, much of this work sidesteps the fundamental problematics of either politics and political subjectivity or 'form' and representation, or both.

3. For use of the term 'grammar' with reference to traditional epic diction, see Meillet 1923: 61; for Parry's use of the term, see Foley 1988: 9; for Lord, see Lord 1960: 65 'The poetic grammar of oral epic is and must be based on the formula'; Austin 1975: 79–80 (with some qualifications); useful discussion in Foley 1988; Schein 2016 [1998].

4. Parry 1956: 3–4. Cf. Elmer 2013a and Elmer 2015 who points to 'discrepancies' in the usage of formulae, accountable by different approaches of performers to the tradition: 'The Iliad

affirms that, in spite of any apparent contradiction, its words fundamentally mean what they say ... Odyssey, by contrast, embraces contradiction as a way of capturing all sides of its central hero's complex character, and as an expression of the Odyssean principle of "declaring one thing and concealing another in one's heart". This suggests a degree of freedom within the tradition which, as we shall see, is compatible with the theoretical argument developed in our essay. Nevertheless, both Parry's argument and our own are based on the assumption that divergence is particularly important in the *Iliad*.

5. 1956: 6.
6. I do not consider the relation of Homeric poetry to external historical politics in this essay. See briefly comments in Hammer 2002: 20–6.
7. 1956: 6.
8. Reeve 1973: 194; cf. Martin 1989: 152–3.
9. See Martin 1989: 148–61. See also in n. 2, above.
10. Already M. Parry 1971: 313 suggests that '[t]here are *more general types of formulas*, and one could make no greater mistake than to limit the formulaic element to what is underlined [as formulaic, in the analysis pp. 301–2]'; Russo 1997: 259–60: 'The word formula proved to be a poor thing, hopelessly inadequate to cover the different *kinds* of formulaic realities in Homeric diction. And it is reasonable to assume that the talented traditional poet would always have been capable of some non-formulaic, original language'; cf. Russo 2010. Recent contributions to the debate that address the formal/technical divide, e.g., in Bakker 2013 ('interformularity'); Bierl 2012; Bozzone 2014 ('constructions'); Burgess 2001, 2006, 2012 ('meta-Cyclic' poetry); Čolacović 2006, forthcoming ('post-traditional' poetry; see also Danek 2005); Currie 2016 (formula and allusion); Danek 1996, 1998, 2002; Finkelberg 1990, 2002, 2003, 2004 ('meta-epic' verse); also Finkelberg 2015; Friedrich 2007 (interpreting exceptions to economy); Nagy 2015; Montanari, Rengakos and Tsagalis 2012 (orality and Neoanalysis); Kullmann 2015); Schein 2016 [1998], 2016; Tsagalis 2008, 2011; 2014 ('intratraditionality'); also Foley's notion of 'traditional referentiality' 1991; 1999 (for which cf. Lord 1960: 148; Danek 2002; Bozzone 2014: 46–9, Currie 2016: 4–9); Bakker 2001; Balling and Madsen 2003; and other essays in *Trends in Classics* 2.2 (2010) (on epic diction and hypertext).
11. See, e.g., Martin, an exemplary analyses, which nevertheless relies on structuralist conceptual frameworks of pattern and variation (following Leech 1985) and assimilates such classic terms as 'syntagmatic' and 'paradigmatic' to discuss relations amongst examples and sets (Martin 1989: 164 and n. 43 invoking, tellingly, Ducrot and Todorov for definitions). For the methodological difficulties, see below.
12. My discussion should be read against the background of broad recent discussions about form and especially its relation to politics. See, e.g., Levine 2015 (31: 'When we think of form, we think of a containing wholeness, which in turn calls up frightening models of political control and totality ... Does a formalist reading practice always necessarily entail a valuing of containment and exclusion?') with responses by Bozovic, Brown, Clune, Hammer, Long, McPherson, Nersessian, Sandler and Serpelli and further references in *Papers of the Modern Languages Association* 32 (2017); Kramnick and Nersessian 2017, with responses by Levine, Eyers, Levinson and Love and further references in *Critical Inquiry* 44 (2017). Jacques Rancière's work on the politics of aesthetics stands at the centre of another broad contemporary debate over the meaning of form.
13. See, e.g., Finkelberg 2012: 63: 'In recent decades, the number of scholarly publications on matters of formulaic analysis has sharply decreased, and the enthusiasm with which the essentials of oral formulaic theory were discussed in the 1960s has given way to expressed fatigue and a defensive, if not apologetic, attitude.' Burgess 2015: 97: 'Since the Homeric

Question will never be fully resolved, there is surely a point where prolonged speculation gives poor returns for the effort ... It would be a shame if the Homerist – or the author on introductory books on Homer – did not move on to other subjects.'

14. See above, n. 2.
15. See Most 2005; Porter 2004.
16. 1956: 126–7 (1st ed. 1954). Cf. also, e.g., Bowra 1961.
17. 1956: 128. For a different perspective, which is close in substance but views consensus as a core value of tradition, see, e.g., Elmer 2013b.
18. See, e.g., Osborne 2016: 66–8 on the heroic code and 73: 'It is tempting to wonder whether the greatest influence of *The World of Odysseus* was not its impact on Finley's own career.'
19. See Rancière 2010: 150, explained below.
20. σκηπτοῦχος: Schmidt *s.v.* LfgrE; Σ D *Il.* 1.279: σκηπτρόφορς –for φέρω as display of authority, see Ready 2010. διοτρεφέες: Σ D *Il.* 2.660 – royal authority comes from Zeus.
21. 1958 Ch. V ('Action') and esp. 'The Disclosure of the Agent in Speech and Action', 175–80.
22. 1958: 177.
23. Rancière 2010: 29–30.
24. Rancière 2010: 30. For this idea, see also, e.g., Finley 1956: 127-8. Arendt plays down the element of 'rule' in *archein*. See, e.g., 1958: 32: 'To be free meant both not to be subject to the necessity of life or to the command of another *and* not to be in command oneself. It meant neither to rule nor to be ruled.' Rancière rightly exposes the elisions of such equality; see 2010: 27.
25. Rancière 2010: 30.
26. Kirk (1985: 140): 'a polished piece of invective'. Martin 1989: 146–7: the 'deficient' style of Thersites' words matches his character which is 'repugnant to the elite'. See n. 29 and below. For Thersites, see Rosen 2007 and Rosen and Díaz 2003; Marr 2005; Stuurman 2004; Raaflaub 2004; Schmidt 2002; Kouklanakis 2001; Nagy 1997; Mackie 1996; Lincoln 1994; Lowrie 1991; Postlethwaite 1988; Rose 1988; Thalmann 1998; Thalmann 1988; Ahl 1984; etc. See especially Marks' (2005) important argument about the possible 'equality' of Odysseus and Thersites.
27. Rancière 2010: 30, opposing Arendt's position.
28. Rancière 2010: 30.
29. 'By Iliadic standards', Thersites' speech is 'unmetrical' (1989: 147). The word ἀμετροεπής is not mentioned in extant scholia and is otherwise rarely discussed (Dion. Hal. *Rh.* 11.8.5; Pollux, *Onom.* 6.146.3; Ariston. *De Signis* 22.281.3). Cf. *Il.* 3.215 ἀφαμαρτοεπής; Busch in LfgrE *sub voc.*
30. Rancière's response to the problem often depends on such disjunction. Cf. Kahane 2007.
31. Rancière 2010: 30.
32. Cf. Finley 1956: 123–4:

> Homer spoke for the aristocracy, from the opening line of the *Iliad* to the final sentence of the Odyssey. But what does that tell us? Does it mean, for example, that he is not to be trusted whenever he puts an idea or sentiment on the tongue of a Thersites or a Eumaeus? To answer that question in the affirmative would be to imagine a society in which aristocrats and commoners held two completely contradictory sets of values and beliefs, a society such as the world has never known. Beyond a doubt there were two standards in certain spheres of behavior, with respect to the ethos of work, for example, or in the protection of rights. Odysseus' employment of the sceptre offers a fine symbol ... The scepter, any scepter, was not only the symbol of authority; it was

also the mark of *themis*, of orderly procedure, and so it was given to each assembly speaker in turn to secure his inviolability, as when Menelaus rose to challenge Antilochus. Against Thersites, however, it was a club, for Thersites was of those 'who are not counted either in battle or in council' [*Il.* 2.201–2].

Finley the Marxian critic may have read Rancière's later work (see below, n. 41), but would have probably dismissed it as vehemently as he did Arendt's (see Beard 2016: 186).

33. The term 'unaccounted-for' is important in Rancière's thought; see, e.g., 2010 32 on Homer's *anarithmoi* (not in Homer, but see *Il.* 2.202: οὔτέ ... ἐναρίθμιος)
34. Rancière 2010: 29, 'Thesis 2'.
35. Rancière 2010: 30, 'Thesis 3'.
36. Rancière 2010: 35, 'Thesis 6'.
37. Rancière 2010: 158.
38. Rancière 2010: 157–9 and elsewhere. Extended discussion in Rancière 1996.
39. See Rancière 2006.
40. See Vico 1985: 66, *Axiom* XLIX (209). Rancière 2010: 160–1 says

    This new idea of mute writing had been pioneered by Vico, when he set out to upset the foundations of Aristotelian poetics by disclosing the character of the 'true Homer'. The 'true Homer' was not a poet in the representational sense, meaning an inventor of fictions, characters, metaphors and rhythms. His so-called fictions were no fictions to him, for he lived in a time when history and fiction were mingled ... His metaphors bore witness to an age where thought and image, ideas and things could not be separated. Even his rhythms and metres reflected a time where speaking and singing were interchangeable. In short, Homeric poetry, the essence of poetry, was a language of childhood. It was, Vico said, similar to the language of dumb persons.

41. Rancière's work first came to prominence in 1968 in his contribution to Althusser's *Lire le Capital* (*Reading Capital*).
42. See briefly Tomasello 2003: 5. For Greek and Latin Grammar, *id.* 17–18; For Chomsky (invoked, e.g., in Nagler 1974 – an important early work on the formula), see *id.* 2–3, 96, 102, 248, biology – 284; for De Saussure *langue* and *parole*, (admittedly a more complex case; invoked, e.g., in Finkelberg 2012: 82; Nagy 2012: 27–30), see *id.* 12. Currie 2016: 227 and n. 2 rightly objects to the Sausseurian framework.
43. Already in work by Franz Bopp (1816); W. von Schlegel (1818) and W. von Humboldt (1825) and perhaps most importantly, later, in the work of Antoine Meillet, Milman Parry's teacher (1912). For discussions of early work, see Kuryłowicz 1965; Givón 1971; Hopper and Traugott 2013. For Meillet 1912, see comments in Lehmann 2015: 1; Hopper and Traugott 2013: 22).
44. Lakoff 1987: 465.
45. Lakoff 1990: 463, cf. 465.
46. See Bybee 1985, Bybee 2006; Givón 1995; Croft 2001; Tomasello 2003; Goldberg 2006; Hoffmann and Trousdale 2013.
47. Tomasello 2003: 99. Cf. 17–18 on paradigmatic approaches.
48. See also above, n. 42.
49. Cf., e.g., Fillmore, already in an early essay (emphatic small caps in the orig.): 'MEANINGS RE RELATIVIZED TO SCENES' (1977: 1).
50. Tomasello 2003: 14 citing Traugott and Heine 1991 and Hopper and Traugott 1993.

51. Eckhardt 2006: 4–5; cf. Tomasello 2003: 15–17; Beckner and Bybee 2009. Cf., e.g., Fillmore, above, n. 49.

52. Cf., e.g., Kramsch 2002 on linguistic 'ecosystems'.

53. 'The notion of resemblance/similarity is thus crucial for forming natural categories. And it is also crucial for defining the process via which category membership – and eventually also the prototype itself – is extended. This process is called metaphor or analogy.' Givón 1984: 17; cf. Meillet 1912.

54. Blevins and Blevins 2009: 2; cf. Kuryłowicz 1965; Penn, Holyoak and Povinelli 2008; Raimo 2003. Analogy was recognized already in antiquity (see Law 2003; Duso 2006; Castello 2008). Universal/formal approaches to grammar often dismiss the process: 'analogy is simply an inappropriate concept in the frst place', Chomsky 1986: 32. For Milman Parry's very important views, see below, n. 72.

55. Non-technical overview in Byrne and Callaghan 2013. Linguistics: Larsen-Freeman 1997; Ellis and Larsen-Freeman 2009; Larsen-Freeman and Cameron 2008; Beckner and Bybee 2009; Kramsch 2012; For science, see, e.g., chemist Ilya Prigogine (Nobel prize, 1977) and physicist Gregoire Nicholis (Nicolis and Prigogine 1989: 3):

> At the end of this [the twentieth] century, more and more scientists have come to think, as we do, that many fundamental processes shaping nature are irreversible and stochastic; that the deterministic and reversible laws [of, e.g., Newtonian physics] describing the elementary interactions may not be telling the whole story. *This leads to a new vision of matter, one no longer passive, as described in the mechanical world view, but associated with spontaneous activity.*

56. Larsen-Freeman and Cameron 2008: 1.

57. Kramsch 2012: 11–12.

58. Kramsch 2012: 12.

59. Lord 1960: 36; further references in Kahane 1994: 16. For Lord, cf. also Bozzone 2014: 13; Cánovas and Antović 2016a: 84.

60. Rosenmeyer 1965: 297.

61. Nagy 1976: 256. Cf. Nagy 1992: 34 and comments in Kahane 1994: 45–6; cf., also, e.g., Fränkel 1975: 31–2: 'Verse and content ... were combined with complete plasticity'; Kirk 1985: 19: 'The cola are a reflection of sentence-articulation as predisposed by a permanent rhythmic pattern.'

62. Bakker and Fabricotti 1991. For the dichotomy, largely avoided in usage-based approaches and construction grammar, see Christiansen and Chater 2016: 227–40. In the context of Homeric diction, see Boas 2016: 110: 'unlike many other theories of grammar, CxG [Construction Grammar] does not make any theoretical distinctions between different areas of grammar such as core and periphery'.

63. Bakker 2005: 21. Cf. Givón 1979 and Tomasello 2003: 14 who cites him: 'Today's syntax is yesterday's diction'.

64. Kahane 1994: 15.

65. Bakker 2013: 9. Bakker's emphasis on traditional links rather than specific points of allusion bears some resemblance to Burgess' arguments about intertextuality and phraseological 'pathways'; see Burgess 2012, esp. 168; Burgess 2010: 212 n. 5: 'specific poems are not referenced, rather, epic "pathways" are "indexed"'.

66. Bozzone 2014: 4, citing Goldberg 2006; cf. Bozzone 2010.

67. Cánovas and Antović 2016a; see also Cánovas and Antović 2016c and Cánovas and Antović 2016b.

68. Boas 2016.
69. Currie 2016: 227 citing Barlow and Kemmer 2000: iiiv-ix. See further in Kahane 2018; Kahane 2019. For usage-based linguistics and Greek and Latin more generally, see Mocciaro and Short 2018.
70. Full data and lists of examples in the *Chicago Homer* (Kahane, Mueller, Berry et al.).
71. Parry and others certainly thought an expression can be regarded as formulaic within the epic tradition even if in its exact form it appears only once within a given poem. See discussions in Lord 1995: 122; Bynum 1987.
72. Parry 1971: 15–16. For Parry's paradigmatic presentation as a reflection of his methodology, see Kahane 2018.
73. Parry 1971: 13, 272.
74. Parry regarded analogy as 'perhaps the single most important factor for us to grasp if we are to arrive at a real understanding of Homeric diction' (Parry 1971: 68. Cf. Edwards 1986: 202). Yet he says, for example, in the context of exceptions to the law of formulaic economy (Parry 1971: 176):

> This operation of analogy, the power of which is attested by each artifice of epic diction, is too powerful to stop once it has created a metrically unique formula. In the bard's mind, there will always be an association between the words of one unique expression and another, and thus, by analogy, he will draw from two unique formulae one which will repeat the metre of an already existing formula.

For an extended discussion of this essential (but insufficiently acknowledged) observation see Kahane 2018.

75. Compare M. Parry on the 'juxtaposition of formulae', Parry 1971 202–21.
76. Kelly 2007: 281.
77. See, e.g., Fillmore, above, n. 49.
78. Even formalized representations of locution reduced to mathematical notation (e.g., Searle and Vanderveken 1985) acknowledge the dependency of form on contingent circumstances. The speech act 'I now pronounce you husband and wife', for example, has no performative illocutionary force unless the speaker is a priest. Simply saying these words does not make the speaker a minister ordained to conduct a legally binding marriage.
79. This is a very general argument, of course. It relies on (a) the theoretical argument of usage-based approaches and (b) the highly repetitive nature of this speech-introductory formula. If the most traditional and frequent formulaic expressions 'rupture' language, then *a-fortiori*, less common and more unique expressions would do so. Extensive, systematic empirical demonstrations of this argument would, of course, be of advantage, but must await a longer study.
80. Thersites 'is the only character in the *Iliad* to lack both patronymic and place of origin' (Kirk 1985: 138).
81. - - - ending Heph. (pos. 7): 0.6% (*Il.*), 0 (*Od.*); at the verse-end (pos. 12) 7.1% (*Il.*), 11.3% (*Od.*) (O'Neill 1942: 144 tab. 14); *versus spondaici*: 4.6% (*Il.* and *Od.*) (O'Neill 1942: 159 tab. 38).
82. See Kahane 1994 for related arguments about the semantics of the metrical usage of other proper names.
83. Cf. Kirk 1985: 138.
84. Cf. recently Minchin 2006; Fletcher 2008; Rousseau 2015.

85. Cf. Beck 2005: 33–4 and appendix II, 284–5; Beck 2012; De Decker 2015: 188–91.
86. 'Paradigms can be defective, in which case one or more forms are missing for certain words. Usually such gaps are well motivated on logical grounds (although the details of that logic might be language-specific). So, for example, verbs denoting weather phenomena like Czech *prset* "rain" tend to lack first- and second-person forms, and some modal and stative verbs like Czech *moci* "be able" and *trvat* "last" might not have imperative forms; nouns denoting masses and abstractions sometimes lack plurals' (Janda 2007: 645).
87. Some conceptions of the process of grammaticalization assume reduced semantic functions ('semantic bleaching'). Usage-based approaches begin with symbolic usage and thus assume the potential for semantic development within different forms (already in the work of Lakoff, Fillmore and others in the 70s and 80s; see Bybee 1985, Bybee 2006; Givón 1995; Croft 2001; Tomasello 2003; Goldberg 2006) and the process of 'semantic reanalysis'. As Eckhardt (2006: 4–5) explains, evidence from the last decades suggests semantic gain in reanalysis where earlier studies (e.g. Meillet 1912) tended to associated grammaticalization with a weakening of semantic functions. See also Tomasello 2003: 15–17; Beckner and Bybee 2009; Hoffmann and Trousdale 2013: 305–7 (sect. 23.2).
88. Τὸν/τὴν δ' ἠμείβετ' ἔπειτα completed by θεὰ γλαυκῶπις Ἀθήνη 7x; βοῶπις πότνια Ἥρη 5x and θεὰ λευκώλενος Ἥρη 1x, breaking economy, both forms in *Il.* only; θεὰ Θέτις ἀργυρόπεζα 3x and Θέτις κατὰ δάκρυ χέουσα 1x, both forms in *Il.* only; φιλομμειδὴς Ἀφροδίτη 1x; Διώνη, δῖα θεάων 1x; ποδήνεμος ὠκέα Ἶρις 1x; περίφρων Πηνελόπεια 4x, *Od.* only; φίλη τροφὸς Εὐρύκλεια 1x. Cf. *Il.* 8.484: Ὣς φάτο, τὸν δ' οὔ τι προσέφη λευκώλενος Ἥρη. Full mark-up of repetition and variants in Kahane, Mueller, Berry et al. There are a few instances of the simplex participial form ἀμειβομένη followed by προσέειπεν. Nevertheless, examples of ἀμειβομένη appear only in the *Odyssey* and only four times (4.234, 4.706, 19.214, 19.252), all verse terminal (… ἀμειβομένη προσέειπε(ν)//) and, significantly, without the proper name of the female speaker in the same verse. These examples describe the poem's two strong, cunning women, Helen and Penelope. Otherwise, there are two instances of the fem. pl. -αι, at *Il.* 1.604 and *Od.* 24.60, both of the Muses.
89. See Rousseau 2015.
90. Mutation, let us stress, in evolutionary biology (see Gould 2002; Eldredge and Gould 1972; discussion in the context of ancient literature in Kahane 2013) and elsewhere assumes unexpected, arbitrary change ('error', 'exception'), not an algorithmic process.
91. For a diagrammatic description see Kahane 2005.
92. Complete lists of examples, statistics and references in Kahane, Mueller, Berry et al. and the paper concordances.
93. Bakker 2013: 163. Cf. Austin 1975: 28–9.
94. Bakker 2013: 158–9 and 163. Cf. Tsagalis 2014: 394–8.
95. *Il.* 3.13 is, unique, but the previous line is famously reiterated by none other than the Odysseus who, spinning lies for gain in his own poem, says (*Od.* 14.156–7):

> ἐχθρὸς γάρ μοι κεῖνος ὁμῶς Ἀΐδαο πύλῃσι
> γίνεται, ὃς πενίῃ εἴκων ἀπατήλια βάζει.
> Hatful to me like the gates of Hades is the man
> who, giving way to poverty, tells lying tales

96. For the distinction 'noise' (*phônê*) vs. 'speech' (*logos*), see Aristotle, *Politics* 1253a and Rancière 2004a. The distinction has deeply affected modern discussions of political philosophy, including Foucault, Agamben etc.

CHAPTER 2
SOPHOCLES' *ANTIGONE*, FEMINISM'S HEGEL AND THE POLITICS OF FORM
Simon Goldhill

The proposition of this chapter is that the multifold critical interpretations of Sophocles' *Antigone* since Hegel have been fundamentally flawed, precisely because they have not appreciated what this volume calls the politics of form. Indeed, it will be argued that the very recognition of the form of this play, and its consequent privileged place in the comprehension of the genre of tragedy, has misrecognized its own political investments in a damaging way. As a small sop against the overweening and thus immediately suspicious suggestion that pretty well all modern critics have misunderstood the play at an essential, formal level, I should offer the immediate personal palinode that I include my own published interpretations in this history of systematic error.

Of course, my aim here cannot be to catalogue and criticize in detail and in full what is an unmanageably large set of critical work. I will be focusing rather on the line of argument about political conflict that stems from Hegel and also at the more recent feminist engagements with the play that also find their starting point in Hegel. A grounding thesis for what has become a very well-known and extended debate about how the *Antigone* speaks to civic and familial justice is that the form of the play revolves around the opposition of Antigone and Creon, expressed by Hegel as a clash of right and right. Now, Hegel's exposition has certainly been challenged, as we will see, both by those who have seen in Creon's and Antigone's positions a dangerous extremism rather than a simply a proclaimed right, and by those who wish to redraft his opposition especially in terms of gender and familial politics. But these critiques leave untouched the grounding thesis that the play's form is structured around the opposition of Creon and Antigone. It is this grounding thesis that I set out to challenge.

To begin, however, we need some background, concerning Hegel on the one hand and, on the other, the effect of Hegel on the critical tradition of interpreting Sophocles' *Antigone*. There are three uncontentious starting points that stand behind my argument here, but which need at least lapidary exposition.

The first starting point is that Hegel is the most influential figure in making the telling of history integral to the making of political theory.[1] The subject of nineteenth-century historicism has been obsessively worked over in recent scholarship. For Reinhart Kosselleck, a new sense of history and of a person's relation not just to the past but to the experience of time takes shape from the middle of the eighteenth century onwards.[2] A string of brilliant analyses have explored this in different ways: from Ruskin's recognition of how the speed of a train changes a traveller's relation to the world, through geology's recognition of the abyss of time, to the historiographers' move from stadial to evolutionary historical modelling.³ For my purposes in this chapter, I would stress that the telling of Greek history has a particular place in this sea-change. George Grote's *History of Greece*, published in twelve volumes between 1846 and 1856, is paradigmatic. E. A. Freeman, the Regius Professor of History at Oxford, summing up the Europe-wide reaction to it, wrote that Grote's work was 'one of the glories of our age and country' and 'to read the political part of Mr Grote's History is an epoch in a man's life'.⁴ Ancient Greece was constructed in the Victorian genealogical imaginary as the origin of western culture (along with the Bible) – for Matthew Arnold, the great guru of cultural evaluation, Hellenism and Hebraism provide the matrix in which all culture is to be understood⁵ – and to tell the history of Greece is thus to engage in contemporary politics. Reading Grote's politicization of Greek history, for Freeman, was 'an epoch in a man's life': it was defining of the political self. Grote was a radical, and his history set democratic Athens as opposed to authoritarian Sparta as the pinnacle of political achievement in antiquity, a model of freedom which was the bedrock of its artistic and philosophical achievements. Grote's history is not merely liberal in its political persuasion, but also firmly Whiggish in its historiography: culture developed for him in an evolutionary progression from Homer through to democracy and beyond to Christianity, with a steady growth in ethical appreciation, a sense of duty, and a political will embodied in political systems. Hegel's idealization of Greece was equally foundational: a Philhellenism based on genealogy and idealism. Ancient Greece was an ideal towards which all modern thought looked. The discussion of what Hegel makes of *Antigone* must be articulated within this framework of a particular heightened historical sense that the history of Greece, the history that starts with Greece, is an essential factor in the self-understanding and self-definition of modernity's politics.

My second starting point is that the post-Kantian German Idealists and Hegel above all are obsessed with Greek tragedy as the pre-eminent aesthetic model through which politics finds expressive, artistic form – to the extent that the *Phenomenology of Spirit* has rightly been called a 'tragic text', which has a 'tragic conception of truth', and a dialectic that is 'structurally tragic'.⁶ With the German Idealists, philosophy underwent a tragic turn.⁷

The German Idealist turn towards tragedy and the tragic as a privileged aesthetic mode made tragedy, and Greek tragedy in particular, the site where aesthetics, politics and history are most intimately intertwined. So for Hegel, building in particular on Schelling, tragedy, as George Steiner comments, is a 'testing ground and validation for the main tenets of his historicism, for the dialectical scenario of his logic and for the central notion of consciousness in progressive conflict'.⁸ In Hegel's project, tragedy is a prime means of challenging Kant and developing his own sense of the historicity of ethics, and its relation to what could be called collective, normative values, and to the compulsions under which a human subject works. This is a process, in short, which goes to the heart of Hegel's understanding of a human self-consciousness that is divided against itself – and yet can progress through this division and its transcendence.

Now, in his historicizing teleology Hegel strives to construct a universalizing view of the family and of the state as abstract and general principles – for which the *Antigone* is a central case – but it is through his insistence on conflict as the essence of tragedy that Hegel's model continues to have an impact on modern criticism, and on feminist thinking in particular – not just in his articulation of a clash of systems of belief, but also in the internal conflicts of the ethical agent in a historical context. Hegel's tragedy is a doorway to rethinking Kant's notion of the subject – and his determination of the subject divided against itself has proved especially fertile ground for feminist argument. The power of German Idealism's response to Kant, then, is that 'tragedy and the tragic' become a way of exploring the central questions of human freedom, political autonomy, self-consciousness and ethical action. Tragedy is not just a literary exemplification of theory, but a means of comprehending the self as a political, psychological and religious subject. Tragedy, in short, is a route to the self-definition of modernity.

It is crucial for my argument here that in this construction of the tragic there is a heightened and particular focus on the individual as the locus of tragedy: the heroic individual. For Schelling the individual hero is 'the only genuinely tragic element in tragedy'.[9] This is because it is in the individual that we can see the tension between inner freedom and external necessity that makes tragedy such a powerful representation of the *Sittlichkeit* of humans. So Schelling writes – in lines that made a huge impact on Hegel: 'This is the most sublime idea and the greatest victory of freedom: voluntarily to bear the punishment for an unavoidable transgression in order to manifest his freedom precisely in the loss of that very freedom, and perish amid a declaration of free will.'[10] This is a shocking account of human action: suffering for a transgression that is unavoidable becomes, through a willing acceptance of the punishment, a gesture of free will, asserted as it is lost. The Christian overtones (and Romantic Weltschmertz) here are clear enough – and this all becomes part of Hegel's idea of how the individual and society interact. I shall be particularly interested to trace what happens to this suffering individual hero in feminism's Hegel.

It will be no surprise – this is my third starting proposition – that in this pursuit of understanding the ethical and political subject, Sophocles' *Antigone* is *the* tragic text for Hegel. George Steiner's book, *Antigones*, has traced in lavish detail the impact of Hegel's use of *Antigone*, and as much as *Antigone* helped Hegel express his abstract, general ideas of the family and the State, so too his reading of *Antigone* has been deeply influential on how the play is understood today. Let me very briefly rehearse what Hegel has made so familiar. Hegel argues that the play dramatizes a clash of competing duties and commitments. Creon, the king, justifies his actions from the beginning of the play by means of an appeal to the State. In Jebb's lovely Victorian prose: 'If any makes a friend of more account than his fatherland, that man hath no place in my regard . . . nor would I ever deem the country's foe a friend to myself; remembering this, that our country is the ship that bears us safe, and that only while she prospers in our voyage can we make true friends.'[11] For this reason, he honours with burial Eteocles who died fighting for the city, but denies burial and denigrates Polyneices, who led an army against his own city – though both men are brothers, sons of Oedipus and siblings to Antigone. Throughout the play, Creon justifies his ethical and political decisions as motivated by the demands of State.

By the same token, Antigone insists on burying her traitor brother because he is of the same blood, the same family as herself, and justifies her action by appealing to the immutable ties of kin. For Hegel, her turn to the law of the family is a demonstration of what is right: 'True ethical sentiment consists just in holding fast and unshaken by what is right, and abstaining altogether from what would move or shake or derive it.'[12] Antigone for Hegel is a heroine of ethical action. Yet, it is often forgotten, though not by Miriam Leonard in her superb discussion of the place of Greek in modern French thinking, that his description of Antigone opens into an analysis of family relations, which explores what the divine law of the family is.[13] The position of the daughter in this scheme of things is difficult. Unlike Lacan, Hegel is very keen – 'of course', you might be tempted to say – that there is absolutely no sexual desire between sister and brother, and that the heroine is completely pure. But, he also insists that the daughter cannot be a full ethical subject, because she cannot be fully self-conscious as a female and a daughter, of her own ethical commitment: 'She does not become conscious of [the nature of ethical life [*sittliches Wesen*]], and does not actualize it, because the law of the family is her inherent implicit inward nature, which does not lie open to the daylight of consciousness, but remains inner feeling and the divine element exempt from reality.'[14] A woman's 'ethical life is not purely ethical', he declares, as if in a straight genealogy back to Aristotle.[15] But because a sister's relation to a brother is not marked by sexual desire,[16] but by ethical similarity (unlike a woman's relation to her husband), 'The loss of a brother is irreparable to a sister, and her duty towards him is the highest.'[17] So although Antigone cannot quite be a full ethical subject, none the less she is motivated by the highest duty. Her duty to her brother clashes with Creon's duty to the State.

Thus for Hegel, Sophocles' *Antigone* dramatizes the clash of right and right – the duty to the state and the duty to the family – and as such represents the inner division of self-consciousness in its tragic journey towards transcendence.

So much by way of a framework for Hegel, then: Hegel is deeply influential on nineteenth-century political thinking within the tradition of German Idealism by virtue of his heightened historical consciousness, by virtue of his tragic modeling of conflict as integral to historical and ethical self-consciousness, and by his privileging of Sophocles' *Antigone* as a demonstration of the conflicts at the heart of political self-consciousness, and the consequent crisis of ethical action. It is the overwhelming legacy of this Hegelian analysis that I wish to disrupt.

Now – as we turn to trace the effect of Hegel's project – it would be hard, I think, to find *any* modern interpretation of the play that did not rehearse Hegel's drive towards the polarization of heroic individuals, each committed to their own strong sense of duty. There are some obvious underpinnings for this position. Polarization is a default rhetoric of Greek expressivity, which invented *men* and *de*, 'on the one hand, on the other hand', as a structuring principle of argument.[18] It is, what's more, a commonplace of Greek thinking that the household and the state, *oikos* and *polis*, are the two defining frames of social life, which can produce the significant tensions of competing demands.[19] The oppositions of male and female, state and family, are reasonable places to start any discussion of Greek political thinking and its inheritance. But before I turn to feminism's specific engagement with Hegel's *Antigone*, it is worth pointing out how modern criticism has not just followed Hegel but significantly qualified his declaration that the play dramatizes a clash of right and right.[20] Creon, after all, is not merely a careful exponent of political responsibility, but a figure who rapidly is exposed as a rash tyrant, whose commitment to his own laws leads his son to accuse him of being a fine ruler of a desert island. His is an extreme and over-committed stance which results in him being destroyed by the loss of the very family he tried to subordinate to the state. At the end of the play, he is crushed in despair by the death of his wife and son, and the collapse of all he valued. Similarly, Antigone may argue for the family, but, as we will see, she viciously dismisses her sister, loves her dead brother over any living ties, and acts out the etymology of her name, which means 'opposed to generation'. By dying she destroys the future of the very family she claims to uphold. That is, *Antigone*, in modern critical eyes, has become not so much a simple if devastating clash of right and right but rather a conflict between two positions which start in reasonable commitments, but each of which becomes distorted into extreme and overcommitted positions that are self-destructive. *Antigone* picks up what is perhaps the most repeated subject of Sophoclean drama: that is, the negotiation of the extreme figure, who goes too far, in both transcendence and transgression; and by doubling the figures of such extremism and setting them to clash with each other, constructs a new dynamic of exploration of the consequences and engagement of social normativity and its precariousness.[21] It is also worth noting that all too many modern performances, adaptations and versions of *Antigone*, have repressed any such extremism in Antigone's position, and allowed her opposition to state authority to emerge as a heroic political ideal, praise that goes back at least to Victorian scholarship's construction of pious Sophocles.[22] As we will see, both the recognition of the extremism of Antigone's and Creon's positions – their self-assertion and over-commitment – *and* the way in which this can be drafted as a heroic political ideal, will turn out to be indicative performances of what I am calling the politics of form. Yet the crucial point for my argument is that while these critics have insisted on Antigone's and Creon's extremism (and this has become the standard interpretation now), what remains is the assumption that the structuring principle of the play – its form – is to be understood as a political clash of the two individuals, Creon and Antigone.

In recent years, however, some of the most trenchant and far-reaching scholarship on *Antigone* has come from an explicitly feminist tradition, and this has become the most significant and politically insistent engagement with the Hegelian tradition. Again, what follows should be understood as a lapidary framework for the challenge to the inherited view of conflict and opposition I am leading towards, rather than as a comprehensive doxography.[23]

A reasonable starting point in what will turn out to be a long, and distinguished list of reflections through *Antigone* on the family and the state, female subjectivity and political ethics, is the work of Luce Irigaray.[24] Irigaray focuses on Antigone's lack of ethical self-consciousness in Hegel's account. She stresses how the difficult place of Antigone within Hegel's categorizations of gender act as a challenge to the very polarization he seeks to maintain. This is part of her general argument which sets out to 'question again the foundations of our symbolic order in mythology and in tragedy, because they deal with a landscape which installs itself in the imagination and then, all of a sudden, becomes law'.[25] *Antigone* is a stay of the symbolic. Because *Antigone* is part of the history of political thought, it must be reread. My first point, then, simply enough, is that retelling, or re-analyzing, the *Antigone* is part of political theory's commitment to changing thinking. Tradition is not just handed down, but remade at every announcement of tradition, and the inheritance is there to be redrafted, no longer as patrimony but as a refusal of the law of the father.

Following on from Irigaray, a host of feminist thinkers have continued this process of refashioning. Indeed, many of the most distinguished writers who identify as feminist theorists in particular, have had their go at *Antigone*. This is not the place for a full history of such redraftings, many and complex as they are, but I do want to focus to two of the most influential recent engagements, both of which are intensely aware of the complexity of reading Sophocles' play with and through Hegel, namely, Judith Butler's *Antigone's Claim* and Bonnie Honig's *Antigone, Interrupted*. I have already criticized both Butler and Honig specifically with regard to the place of Antigone's sister, Ismene, and thus the notion of sisterhood in their understanding of Sophocles' play; my aim here is to move towards fundamentally re-grounding the nature of this debate (including my own contribution to it) and to open a new question about the politics of the Hegelian legacy of the heroic individual.

Irigaray, according to Judith Butler, for all her radical critiques of the symbolic, is still in line with Hegel because she, like Hegel, 'articulates a prepolitical opposition to politics, representing *kinship as the sphere that conditions the possibility of politics without ever entering in to it*'.[26] That is, woman, as Irigaray indeed writes, is 'the guardian of the blood'. 'Both she and it', writes Irigaray, 'have had to use their substance to nourish the universal unconsciousness of self; it is in the form of *bloodless shadows* – of unconscious fantasies – that they maintain an underground subsistence'.[27] This repression can erupt and threaten to lay waste to the community, to turn it upside down, which is the hope that womanhood would demand the right to effective action. Irigaray wants to find *a place to think from*, which she describes as the place where 'blood's autonomous flow will never re-unite again'.[28] For Butler, however, this leads to a string of questions. Can kinship exist, she wonders, without the support and mediation of the state? Can there be the state without the family as its support and mediation? She reminds us that Antigone's family is the incestuous family of Oedipus (something Hegel scarcely considers), and the familial origin too of the legitimacy of Creon's rule. For Butler, Antigone's act of resistance produces 'the social deformation of both idealized kinship and political sovereignty'.[29] Against the sort of idealism Hegel and his followers produce – and she includes Irigaray in that roll-call – Butler aims to uncover the messy performativity of Antigone, to find a precarious and questioned space between kinship and the reigning systems of cultural intelligibility:

> Antigone represents not kinship in its ideal form but its deformation and displacement, one that puts the reigning regimes of representation into crisis and

raises the question of what the conditions of intelligibility could have been that would have made her life possible, indeed, what sustaining web of relations makes our lives possible, those of us who confound kinship in the re-articulation of its terms?[30]

Butler's agenda is to claim the re-articulation of kinship terms as a performative act of resistance, a politics that is acted out. She wants to make Antigone not a hero of pure desire and ethical rectitude as lauded by Hegel, nor the guardian of blood as a form of eruptive jouissance – the very reverse of Hegel – as lauded by Irigaray, but a heroine of the marginal, transgressive, precarious, othering, disruptive force of questioning. A model for her own position, in short.

Now I have no doubt that the *Antigone*, from indeed its first word, does explore what is shared – the fundamental question of kinship. Its first word is precisely *Ô koinon*: 'O shared'/ 'common', and the play goes on to dramatize bitterly the tensions of belonging in the Oedipal family and in the competing demands of what is shared expressed by the duties of family and state, in their distorted extremisms of Creon and Antigone. As I have discussed elsewhere, it is marked that Antigone herself finds it almost impossible to use the first person plural – 'we' – and, especially when talking to her sister, repeatedly reverts to the singular and divisive 'you and I' – or indeed as she tellingly puts it , 'you and me – I mean me' (*Ant* 31–2),[31] For all the language of sharing and commonality, for all the proclamation of the duties to the collective of the family, Antigone finds it very hard to make a link with anyone.

It is fascinating to see how Irigaray repeats Antigone's dismissal of Ismene. She writes: 'Ismene seems indisputably a "woman" in her weakness, her fear, her submissive obedience, her tears, madness, hysteria – all of which are met with condescending scorn on the part of the king. Ismene is consequently shut up ... with the other women.'[32] Irigaray, associating herself with Antigone, dismisses Ismene as a mere woman in contrast to Antigone 'who does not yield to the law of the city, of its sovereign, of the man of the family'.[33] There is no doubt who the hero is here. Butler follows a similar line. For her Antigone is 'not quite a queer heroine' – something devoutly to be admired – but her example gives rise to a form of critical intervention that is celebrated because it challenges normative heterosexuality in the form of the family.[34] Ismene is repressed in Butler's account too, despised as no more than a weak foil to Antigone's strength. It is striking that neither Irigaray nor Butler consider why Antigone, in order to defend her brother's rights of burial, is made to reject her sister. Neither Irigaray, nor Butler, has any qualms in following Antigone in this gesture.

The point is a simple one. In finding Antigone to be a feminist heroine of resistance, both Irigaray and Butler, as I have argued in more detail elsewhere,[35] repeat the gesture of Antigone in rejecting Ismene as a mere woman. They act out Antigone's claim. They dismiss sisterhood in the name of a new sense of gender and belonging, but do not discuss or reflect on this founding gesture of dismissal. Like Hegel, they look at brother–sister relations, but ignore the sister–sister bond (and Derrida has discussed at length how such a move in Hegel makes his analysis of the family divided against itself[36]). They do not recognize the self-isolating stance of Antigone who is, as the chorus scorn, *autonomos*, 'someone who marches to her own rules', someone who puts the self above the community, someone who can say 'I' but not 'we'.

It is precisely in response to this problem that Bonnie Honig offers her readings of *Antigone* culminating in her book *Antigone, Interrupted*.[37] Indeed, Honig attempts to reclaim not merely Ismene but the bond between Antigone and Ismene for a valued and lauded model of sisterhood. She is absolutely explicit about her agenda. She wants to discover a sense of agency that can escape from the binarism and aggression of Creon – and indeed of Hegel: 'As [Antigone and Ismene] act in agonistic concert, they hint at an alternative politics, and an alternative to Hegel's dialectic.'[38] In holding out 'agonistic concert' as an ideal, Honig praises 'agonistic mutuality, pleasure, care, rage, cooperation and rivalry'.[39] How does Honig get to find such an idyll in the interaction of Antigone and Ismene? Reading against the grain of the play, Honig argues that the first burial of Polyneices is actually conducted by Ismene alone, although she said all through the play so far that she would not even help. Antigone's willing confession to the burial is, insists Honig, defending her sister against accusation. When Ismene later claims to have taken part in the burial – and Antigone and everyone else treat her as merely over-emotional – this too is Antigone desperately trying to save her sister from her own punishment. The sisters are, according to Honig, really loving, and the arguments between them are just what happens within a family, and should be seen as subordinate to the profound care Antigone actually shows. Antigone is a heroine of the dissimulated protection of what matters, not of outspoken challenge to authority. For some, this has proved to be a creative (mis)reading, and depending on how sophisticated and engaging an image of sisterhood you think this offers, it is possible to see it as an attempt to direct modern obsession with the play away from the politics of opposition towards a politics of mutuality.

Both Butler and Honig take Antigone as a hero of the play, and laud her individual, heroic act of political resistance, in Butler's case in the name of recognizing a transgressive potential within traditional kinship ties, and in Honig's case, in the name of a more traditional familial bond between sisters. Both engage with the powerful patriarchal legacy of Hegel, and both privilege Antigone's claim beyond a symmetrical clash of right and right, with a careful eye to the dynamics of precarity, a politics of interpersonal caring, an exploration of what it means to share. Both offer powerful and significant critiques of Hegel. Yet, in the second half of this chapter, I want to argue that both Butler and Honig also share with Hegel an uncontested commitment to a form of heroism that Sophocles' play also challenges. It is here where the politics of form has been misrecognized and where, consequently, the politics of critical engagement has been insufficiently articulated.

My argument is simple – but far-reaching. The central structuring opposition of the *Antigone* – its form – is not the opposition of Creon and Antigone, but the opposition of Creon and Antigone on the one hand, and all the other characters on the other. It is an opposition between extreme commitments (and the distortions, violence and consequences of such extremism) and the attempts to escape from the gravitational pull of such positionality, its failures, hopefulness, and ordinariness. As we will see, this apparently simple opposition structures the play, but is far from straightforward not just in how it is dynamically explored through the narrative of the drama but also in its political purchase – the way in which the audience or the critics become engaged by it. The introduction of the third actor, associated with Sophocles, is integral to this structuring. So, too, the tension between the collective of the chorus and the individual actor (basic both to modern and German Idealism's understanding of the dynamics of tragic drama) is turned via this triangulation into a particularly supple and dynamic form by Sophocles. The *formal* elements of drama and the form of the play's argument are mutually informing.

As has been noted long ago, although the play is known by the title *Antigone*, its structure of action circles around Creon, rather than Antigone or even the opposition of Antigone and Creon.[40] After the prologue's conversation between the sisters, Creon's entrance and self-defining political speech, the king has four *agones*, first with the guard, second with Antigone (introduced by the guard), thirdly with Haimon, fourth with Teiresias. The play ends with his reaction to his wife's silent suicide. Antigone is led to her death half way through the drama, and there is no discussion (as in *Ajax*, say) of what to do with her corpse: the retrospective discussion of how she should be evaluated is tied up with the treatment of the corpse of Polyneices (who is buried before they go to release Antigone) – both cases seen as failures of the king's judgement. Her funeral procession scene with the chorus dramatizes also their ambivalence about her behaviour. Antigone's opposition to Creon is indeed the matter of the play, but it is dramatized as much through the king's response to others who broach the subject of Antigone with him, as with Antigone herself. Antigone speaks fewer than 200 lines.

The individual character with the next largest number of lines (more than Haimon, Teiresias or Ismene) is the guard – who plays next to no role in either Hegel's interpretation or in the work of Butler or Honig. But he is no mere functionary, although he is, of course, crucial to the functioning of the plot by bringing the news of the first burial and then capturing Antigone after the second burial, and bringing her before Creon. His role is made possible only by the use of a third actor, of course, and demonstrates most vividly how this formal element of drama is absolutely integral to how the play expresses its structure. The guard, although not named, is finely characterized, with a mixture of homespun wisdom, broad comedy and clumsy self-expression. His interaction with Creon is telling. He is most concerned with his own survival and the pattern of his everyday life. His fear of Creon leads him to dramatize his hesitations about coming on stage, and to articulate his desire to get off stage as quickly as possible (223–6, 329–30). While he speaks he lives, and his diversionary self-justifications enrage Creon and are ignored entirely by Antigone with silence. He is a figure whose self-interest runs through all he says, but this self-interest – in contrast with Antigone – is no more than survival and the avoidance of any disastrous punishment. He declares at the end of his first scene that there is no way he will be seen ever coming back to the palace (329), but immediately after the first stasimon he does come back, with Antigone, marking how things change (388–96), and that, despite his oath, here he is again. Unlike Creon and Antigone, he is prepared to shift and change his mind opportunistically in the pursuit of the avoidance of difficulty. As so often with Sophocles, the three actors are used to create a complex, triangulated dynamic, where the fierce commitment to a single course adopted by Creon and an equally fierce resistance to it from Antigone – in both cases to the point of self-destruction – are set not only against each other but also against the opportunistic, flexible self-preservation of the guard, caught against his will in the cross-fire of the king and his niece. The guard is a crucial foil to the argument of Creon and Antigone.

Ismene provides perhaps a more complex response, not least because she is more intimately tied into the familial story. In the prologue, shocked by Antigone's plan, she indeed reminds her sister of the family history and its disastrous inheritance (49–56). *Phronêson*, she introduces the summary, which could be glossed as 'reflect with wisdom and learn from the following ...'. She reminds her sister that there have been already three disasters: first their father's bloody suicide; second their mother hanging herself; and third their brothers slaughtering each other on the same single day. Thus they are the only two remaining. She adds that they are also women, and that the power is with the rulers (61–3). In the face of Antigone's scorn and determination, Ismene continues to remind her sister not to act against the will of the citizens (78–9), that she is frightened for her sister (81), and that Antigone should at least try to do the act in secret. Antigone dismisses all such concerns, and rejects her sister bitterly. The linguistic separation of the *ego* and the *su*, 'I' and 'you', is dramatized in a dynamic of failed assimilation and hesitancy, set against obdurate certainty.

Ismene's final lines of the scene are famously ambivalent (98-9):

ἀλλ᾽ εἰ δοκεῖ σοι, στεῖχε. τοῦτο δ᾽ ἴσθ᾽, ὅτι
ἄνους μὲν ἔρχηι, τοῖς φίλοις δ᾽ ὀρθῶς φίλη.

If that is your decision, go then. But you should know that
You are crazy to go – though rightly caring to your cared ones.

Ismene appears to have been overwhelmed and concedes: if this course of action seems right to Antigone, she should go. But she immediately retreats from any imprimatur: to go, she is certain, is to be crazy – lacking the sense or caution Ismene has been enjoining. But, in another swerve of feeling, Antigone's madness is immediately set against another judgment which is hard to translate. Antigone, declares Ismene, is also properly *philê* to her *philois*, that is, she is properly performing the moral obligations of someone tied by bonds of kinship and care. This is usually taken to mean that Ismene recognizes that Antigone's behaviour is motivated by a desire to observe kinship ties with her brother, and thus can be valued as proper – and that is how I have translated it above. Ismene is torn at the end by her double recognition that Antigone is both right and wrong, both committed to her family and at the same time beyond the norms of restraint and sense.

These lines prepare us for Ismene's second scene, where once again Sophocles has constructed a triangulated scene of layered dynamics of power and emotion. Ismene runs in to interrupt the *agon* between Creon and Antigone with the claim that she did the burial herself. Again, Antigone dismisses her, and with increasing cruelty. When Ismene asks how she will live without her, Antigone merely sniffs, 'Ask Creon. You are his kin' (549–50). Now Creon throws back at her her previous accusation to Antigone of madness: 'I declare that one of these children is now turning out mad, the other was like that from birth' (561–2). It is clear that Creon does not believe Ismene has anything to do with the burial (771) as Antigone also declares (538–9), but has had her good sense (by which he appears to mean submissiveness (531)) corrupted by associating with Antigone (565). As the guard triangulates the opening of this scene, Ismene is a foil to the argument at its close. Unlike the guard, desperate to get off stage and out of the firing line, the previously hesitant Ismene, who raised so many questions against Antigone's decision, now wants to join her cause – but is equally excluded – and impotent. She is dragged from her caution by the force of the opposition of Creon and Antigone, but repelled by them from its intense centre, and left useless.

Ismene, like the guard, will survive the play, but silenced and ignored. Antigone, as she rejects her sister's offers of help out of hand, contrasts herself to Ismene precisely in terms of survival: 'Save yourself; I do not begrudge you your flight' (552); 'You chose life; I death' (555). Yet, Antigone demands to be seen as the last member of the family (895), as if Ismene is no more, or of no account. Ismene's caution has had no effect on the course of the action. She has failed to convince Antigone to change her plans, and failed to convince Creon to include her in her sister's punishment. The contrast between Creon and Antigone, on the one hand, locked in an increasing hostile fight, and Ismene, on the other, excluded both for her caution and for her lack of it, is eloquent. She asks, καὶ τίς βίος μοι σοῦ λελειμμένηι φίλος;, 'If I am deprived of you, what life, what life of care [*philos*] is there for me?' The play itself offers a silent answer to this question.

Haimon's response to Creon is different. He enters, after Antigone and Ismene are removed, with words of reconciliation and care. His first words are 'Father, I am yours' (635), a mark of belonging far from Antigone's oppositional stance. He replies to his father's speech about political order and social control with his own politically charged speech about the principles of compromise. He develops his case with a set of familiar images. The unbending tree is destroyed by the storm, the branch that bends survives; the sailor who knows to slacken the sail before the squall does not sink. Yet the scene descends rapidly into a stichomythic exchange of brutal counter-attack and rejection, which turns to mutual, angry accusations of senselessness – and Haimon fleeing the stage. As the messenger later reports, he ends up threatening his father with a sword before killing himself over the body of Antigone. The choral stasimon, which follows this scene, sings of passion and its power: they recognize – and the audience may or may not share this view – that the young man was motivated by desire and anger, beyond any argument about social order. *Eros*, as Thucydides knew too well, is a force in political decision making, but one which distorts perspectives, fosters violence.[41] Their retrospective judgment on the scene is also prophetic: the man who promoted compromise, kills himself – an uncompromising act if ever there were one.

There are at least two ways that this scene enacts the opposition between the extreme commitments of Creon and the attempts to find a place elsewhere from which to address conflict. First, it dramatizes how the language of compromise is not enough. Just as Ismene's attempt to persuade Antigone to temper her actions meets with emotional dismissal, so Haimon's attempt to establish a space for compromise is bitterly rejected by Creon as an argument in support of his enemies. The language of compromise has no purchase on extremism. But second the scene also shows what happens when the emotionally fragile young man comes into the orbit of the extreme stance of Creon. The non-exclusive, non-extremist compromise figure is pushed into a position of aggressive exclusionary extremism. Where Ismene in her emotionally overwrought return to the stage tried to join herself to Antigone in a misplaced and rejected gesture of sympathy, Haimon ends his life in suicide after a violent gesture towards his father. Like father, like son? Or perhaps the political point is about how hard it is to resist extremism without imitating its violent certainty.

Haimon's suicide anticipates and prompts Eurydice's suicide. She has only nine lines. In the final scene of the play, she comes on stage to hear the messenger's account of the death scene of her son over the corpse of Antigone. She listens in silence and exits – to commit suicide, as we discover. The results – again – of extremism are extreme. Eurydice is also the sort of familial collateral damage that Creon – and Antigone – fail to factor into any of their decisions, based as they are on their own projection of self. The effects of Creon's commitment go beyond the boundaries of what he can imagine – or control.

Teiresias is a particularly fascinating figure for the picture I am drawing. He advises Creon with the same word Ismene had used to Antigone: *phroneson* 'reflect with wisdom and learn from the following …' (1023). He announces that the dead body of Polyneices is polluting the land of Thebes, and that the king should – a resonant phrase, this – 'yield to the dead and do not goad the destroyed', ἀλλ᾽ εἶκε τῶι θανόντι, μηδ᾽ ὀλωλότα / κέντει (1029–30). Creon's response is violent and angry – again there are mutual accusations of corrupt motives and poor wisdom – and the seer responds with equally violent prophecies of destruction for Creon's house. As soon as the seer leaves, however, now the chorus remind the king that Teiresias has never been wrong before and the king, terrified, agrees. He seeks advice from the chorus about what to do, and the scene ends with him exiting to put right what he has done wrong. It will, of course, be too late. Teiresias, a figure who is outside the normal boundaries of humanity, with the gift of omniscient prophecy, none the less intervenes too late to save Creon from self-destruction: the language of undoing and saving which runs through the intensely hopeful and even regretful words of the king as he exits, is richly ironic.[42] Teiresias adds the authoritative voice of the divine into the play's narrative, but if the correct treatment of the corpse seems now to be clearly asserted, the problem of dealing with the extremism of a Creon or an Antigone remains. The chorus – who have ineffectually attempted to temper both Creon's and Antigone's perspective throughout the play – mediate Teiresias' authority in order to change Creon's stance in this scene, as they have helped the audience to reframe their understanding of the action through the generalizing frame and search for complex motivation in each of the stasima. Yet they too, finally, can make no difference to the unfurling of disaster.

Sophocles dramatizes how difficult it is to deal with extreme commitments. Both Antigone and Creon start from a reasonable place – the importance of obligations to the state or the family – but both take these starting positions to such an extreme form of commitment that self-destruction is the result of their clash. Extremism becomes self-refuting in its self-destructiveness. Antigone and Creon clash in mutual hostility and rejection – but no one who suggests any compromise or change can make a significant difference. And the clash between the extreme pairing of Antigone and Creon, and all the other characters of the play structures the drama's narrative through its sequence of scenes of dialogue and triangulated debate. Each scene sets figures of compromise in failed opposition to Creon or Antigone, and even the *agon* of Antigone and Creon is framed and interrupted by the guard and Ismene at its end and beginning. The guard's fear and opportunism allows him to survive and escape the destructiveness of the palace – into obscurity, anonymity and silence. Ismene fails to dissuade her sister, and when she offers her intense emotional sympathy, she is rejected by both Creon and Antigone. Although Ismene survives, Antigone announces herself as the last of the family, and Ismene's question about what her life could hold in the future is treated with silence by the narrative. Like the guard, she disappears. Haimon attempts to regulate his father's extremism – and ends up pulled into the same pattern of violent certainty, which concludes in suicide, the most extreme failure of the language and practice of compromise. Teiresias can appeal to authority beyond the human – but his interventions are too late: the consequences of extremism outlive the extremist's remorse. The stain of causality spreads – to Eurydice, whose very presence in the play comes as a surprise, but whose death emphatically seals the demonstration of Creon's lack of control. Even the chorus who do intervene to change Creon's mind, do so too late and without any ability to effect the unfurling of disaster. The central structuring opposition of the play is not, then, the local argument of Antigone and Creon, fundamental though this clash is to the play, but the opposition between extreme, distorted, self-destructive commitment, and compromise, self-protection, resistance to conflict.

Yet it is crucial that this is not a hierarchical opposition. The play does not simply promote compromise as the response to extremism (in an *avant la lettre* liberal gesture of political decency). *Antigone* does not leave room for the exigencies of negotiation or the search for the middle ground. Sophocles' profoundly tragic vision of politics sets extremes against each other in self-destructive hostility – but the alternatives are all hopeless too, whether it is the collective observation and misplaced intervention of a chorus, the misplaced sympathy of Ismene, the uncontrolled response of Haimon, the emotional despair of Eurydice, or even the religious authority of Teiresias. Between self-destructive opposition and inevitably failing intervention, there is no adequate path. This is an extremely depressing political vision, where ethical commitments and obligations distort into self-destructive certainty, and the response to such self-destructiveness is ineluctably insufficient.

As such, the play is vicious to its audience. The temptation is so strong to take up one character's stance: to find the heroism of Antigone and celebrate it; to insist on the doomed grandeur of Creon; to fall back on the authority of the divine with Teiresias; to hope for compromise with Ismene; to get away unharmed with the guard; to retreat to the platitudes – or the magnificence – of the chorus' search for a language of compromise. But the play reveals the shortcomings of each and every one of the characters and their stances. It leaves us nowhere comfortable to go. The play even insists that if you come to realize what you have done wrong and want to change it, the consequences are already in motion and unstoppable. The play's negativity is so strong that it is perhaps easy to understand – though not to sympathize with – the myriad of performances that seek to make Antigone a heroine – even a saint – whose resistance to the state's authority is taken as unproblematically good in ethical terms, however destructively it ends. Antigone has been made to speak for the oppressed, the abused, the violently mistreated, with whom we *should* feel sympathy and extend care. Yet when a positive message of care and sympathy is drawn from the *Antigone*, I question whether the harsh wonder of Sophocles' labour of the negative is not being turned to a too comfortable story of what is already known and valued. Should we not hear Antigone's rejection when she says 'you and me, I mean me'? Even when feminist theory rewrites Hegel (as is absolutely necessary) to celebrate Antigone's resistance and the resistance to Hegel, is not the dangerous lure of heroic commitment, as Sophocles articulates it, being underestimated?

To interpret *Antigone*, indeed, is to engage with a politics of form. To read the form of the *Antigone* as a clash of right and right, embodied in the political stances of the figures of Creon and Antigone, is to commit to a particular logic of political conflict, based on the opposition of obligations to the state and the family, as expressed in the gendered language of the family and the violent enforcement of duty to the state. This is a history of political thought through *Antigone*, at the head of which stands Hegel. Contemporary criticism has resisted Hegel's authority in two ways. First, by insisting that to see the play as a clash of right and right is to fail to recognize that Creon and Antigone both enact extreme rhetorical positions and practices that distort any starting principle into a self-destructive, self-assertive extremism: a clash of extremisms not rights. This is part of a critique of idealism in politics, given more robust conviction by the recent histories of extremism, idealism and self-destructiveness in contemporary politics. Second, feminist criticism has resisted by insisting that Hegel's very construction of his ideal of the family and thus his ideal of Antigone as a figure represents a complicit patriarchal conceptualization of gender roles within the family that needs critique and indeed political intervention. This is part of a feminist critique of the mobilization of gender within society, a critique which has utilized notions of performance, history and transformation to see in the potential for redrafting the myths of patriarchy (and *Antigone* prime amongst them) a political intervention of continuing urgency: the *Antigone*'s explorative and forceful language of what is common or shared, the precariousness of care, the violence of interpersonal motivations, marks out a territory of social normativity which remains of pressing concern.

Yet this chapter has argued that while both of these thoroughgoing critical engagements with Hegel's tradition are necessary as critiques of Hegel, such readings wholly misread the politics of form in the *Antigone*. The central structuring of the play should be understood to be the contrast between the paired extremisms of Creon and

Antigone, and the other characters' attempts to escape from or resist or redirect the gravitational pull of these figures. A bleak politics emerges where extremism clashes self-destructively with extremism, but attempts to engage positively with such extremism – through negotiation, persuasion, avoidance – in different ways end up as ineffectual and self-deluding. To focus on the conflict of Creon and Antigone as the major focus of the play is not just to under-read the contribution of some characters to a story, but to allow oneself to be lured into the gravitational pull of the politics of heroism – at the expense of strategies of resistance to such distorting extremism, equally dramatized in this play. Or how we conceive of the politics of form for *Antigone* is itself part of the politics of form – how we form and are formed by politics. How stories form and are formed by politics – as the continuing role of *Antigone* in contemporary feminist political argument reveals. The *Antigone* could thus be called one of the most insidious reader traps of world literature. There is no reading it without commitment to a politics of form – and without being exposed by one's commitment.

I have asked elsewhere whether we can read *Antigone* without Hegel.[43] I would now phrase that question as: can we read *Antigone* without re-establishing the grim oppositional logic of self-assertion and certainty, the violent politics of autocratic thinking, the insidious lure of taking an argument to its conclusion in extremism? Without, that is, rehearsing the politics of form that Hegel and those who have responded to Hegel, within Hegel's framing, have insisted upon. Perhaps the most pertinent and difficult act of resistance that *Antigone* calls us towards is the resistance to the certainty of ideological proclamation, and to comprehend the politics of form that sets Ismene, the Guard, Haemon, Eurydice and the Chorus as alternatives to the opposition of grandly self-destructive heroism. To ask whether Antigone or Creon is right or more right or 'the hero/ine' is to misrecognize how the play sets their self-destructive argument in a frame that offers an alternative if constantly failing positionality – and to become complicit with the violence that produces the alternative's failure.

Notes

1. See from a huge bibliography Inwood 1983; Kelly 1969; McCarney 2000; Pinkard 2002; Pippin 1988; Taylor 1975.
2. Kosselleck 1985; see also Kosselleck 2002; Fritzsche 2011.
3. Exemplary are Rudwick 2005; 2008; Schivelbusch 1980; Burrow 1981; Bowler 1989; Melman 2006.
4. Freeman 1856: 172: see Turner 1981: 213–62.
5. Anderson 1965; Carroll 1982; Collini 1994; de Laura 1969; Gossman 1994, Leonard 2012.
6. Eagleton 2003: 41; Beistegui 2000: 28; Eagleton 2003: 41.
7. I have discussed this in more detail with regard to Oedipus in Goldhill 2014; see also Goldhill 2012: 137–65.
8. Steiner 1984: 21.
9. Schelling 1989: 254; see Barth 1991.

10. Schelling 1989: 254; See Schmidt 2001. For the implications of this focus on the individual and the status of the chorus, with specific reference to Sophocles, see Goldhill 2012: 166–200.
11. Jebb 1900.
12. Hegel 1967: 452.
13. Leonard 2006, with the background of Leonard 2005.
14. Hegel 1967: 476.
15. Hegel 1967: 477.
16. Hegel 1967: 475: 'They do not desire one another'.
17. Hegel 1967: 477.
18. Lloyd 1966.
19. Goldhill 1986: 88–106, with further bibliography.
20. For examples from a long bibliography, see Goldhill 1986: 88–106; Segal 1981; Nussbaum 1986; Blundell 1989; Foley 2001: 172–200; Griffith 1999 – all with further bibliography.
21. See the seminal Knox 1964; with the equally seminal redrafting of Winnington Ingram 1980; both are influential on Segal 1981 and Whitlock Blundell 1989, who have deepened this understanding of Sophocles.
22. See Sourvinou-Inwood 1989 for a strong expression of the negative view of Antigone's decision; Foley 2001: 172–200 is more nuanced.
23. For examples, see Benhabib 1996; Butler 2000; Dietz 1985; Elshtain 1982; Elshtain 1989; Hartouni 1986; Holland 1998; Honig 2013; Mills 1996; Saxonhouse 1992; Söderbäck ed 2010; Zerilli 1991.
24. Irigaray 1985, on which see Whitford 1991; Chanter 1995; Leonard 2006.
25. Irigaray 1985: 2.
26. Butler 2000: 2.
27. Irigaray 1985: 225.
28. Iriagray 1985: 226.
29. Butler 2000: 5.
30. Butler 2000: 24.
31. Goldhill 2012: 31–2.
32. Irigaray 1985: 217–18.
33. Irigaray 1985: 218.
34. Butler 2000: 72.
35. Goldhill 2006.
36. Derrida 1997.
37. Honig 2010, 2011, 2013.
38. Honig 2011: 63.
39. Honig 2011: 64.
40. Kitto 1961 offers an influential version of this argument.
41. See Wohl 2002.
42. As discussed in full in Goldhill 2012: 13–37.
43. Goldhill 2012: 249–63.

CHAPTER 3
THE APORIA OF ACTION AND THE AGENCY OF FORM IN EURIPIDES' *IPHIGENEIA IN AULIS*[1]

Victoria Wohl

This paper considers action and agency as problems of dramatic form in Euripides' *Iphigeneia in Aulis*. Aristotle's famous definition of tragedy as a *mimēsis* of a *praxis*, an imitation of an action, makes *praxis* both the content of tragedy and its formal essence. *IA* not only imitates *praxis*; it explores the very conditions of possibility of *praxis*. It also, and more urgently, explores the conditions of its impossibility. What happens when action becomes impossible? What happens to tragedy? And what happens to the *prattontes*, characters who exist solely in order to carry out the *praxis*? In pursuing these questions, *IA* situates action between *ēthos* (dramatic character and ethical agency) and *muthos* (the story, the myth, and the formal structure of the dramatic plot). The play sets action and agents in a tension that exposes the limits of individual agency but also grants a surprising agency to the dramatic form itself. The *muthos* can make things happen when individual characters cannot. The play explores the agency of form, moreover, through its own dramatic form: through the structural tension between *ēthos* and *muthos*, between the characters' ethical reversals and the teleological necessity of the plot and the inherited myth. In so doing, it invites us to understand *praxis* not as the product of an autonomous ethical subject, but precisely as an effect of form, a conclusion with important political implications for an Athenian audience facing their own crisis of *praxis* at the end of the fifth century.

For Aristotle, 'the *muthos* is the first principle and, as it were, the soul of tragedy' (*Po.* 1450a38–9). It is *muthos* – by which he means the arrangement of incidents into a coherent whole – that constitutes the 'significant and complete action' (*praxeōs spoudaias kai teleias*, *Po.* 1449b24–5) that is tragedy's *telos*.[2] *Muthos* is thus for him the 'form' of tragedy in a technical sense: it provides not only the essential nature of the action but also the immanent force that enables its realization.[3] That formal potential is actualized with the help of the other 'parts' of tragedy – character, diction, thought, spectacle and music – but can produce effects even in their absence: a well-constructed *muthos*, Aristotle claims, will produce fear and pity in its audience even if they do not see the incidents (*Po.* 1453b3–7). The claim is no doubt hyperbolic – and hardly a recipe for exciting theatre – but it emphasizes the *dunamis* that plot bears in Aristotle's view: its immanent power is so great that it can operate even without the *energeia* of performance. *Ēthos* is decidedly secondary (*Po.* 1450a39). It is not dispensable, since action must be performed by agents, who will necessarily have a certain character and thoughts (*Po.*

1450a17–23): these determine the quality of the action but do not make it happen. Aristotle explains the relation between *ēthos* and *muthos* by a comparison to painting: *muthos* provides the form; *ēthos* merely fills in the colour (*Po.* 1450b1–3).[4]

Euripides anticipates Aristotle's analysis of *ēthos* and *muthos* in his innovative deployment of these formal elements: in *IA*, as throughout his plays, Euripides uses tragic form to think about tragic form and its political implications.[5] *IA* problematizes the relations among the genre's defining formal elements, *ēthos*, *muthos* and *praxis*. The play struggles to root *praxis* in the will of an individual agent, but that effort fails. The moment of decision, which should convert *ēthos* into action, instead becomes a point of blockage, *aporia*, even madness. Instead, practical efficacy is discovered in the dynamic structure of the tragic plot. *IA*'s tension between *ēthos* and *muthos* resonates with modern debates over structure vs. agency as the 'first principle and soul' of action, including and especially political action. Theories ranging from Marx's economic determinism to Saussure's structural linguistics to Foucault's productivity of discourse have granted determinative force to impersonal networks, processes, and forms. Such theories, combined with post-structuralism's many-fronted assault on the autonomous voluntarist subject, have precipitated a certain crisis of agency, an erosion of the traditional belief that action originates in the will of an individual human agent. Contemporary thinkers have responded by re-evaluating the relation between structures and agents and seeking a third way between what Diana Coole terms 'the alternatives of unrealistic voluntarism or paralysing fatalism'.[6]

Coole's alternatives neatly encapsulate the dilemma staged over and over again in Greek tragedy. In tragedy, as Jean-Pierre Vernant famously argued, an archaic notion of daemonic agency coexists in tense equilibrium with a fifth-century legal understanding of personal intention and responsibility.[7] The tragic protagonist must act, and is held accountable for his actions, within a web of forces beyond his control: the will of the gods, ancestral curses, fate. *Ēthos* and *daimōn* are both antithetical and inextricable, and tragic agency is staged as a perennial question: 'to what extent is man really the source of his actions?'[8] *IA* asks precisely this question. It does so, moreover, with an urgency imposed by its own historical crisis of agency. The final years of the fifth century, as I shall suggest at the end of the paper, witnessed a breakdown in the democracy's traditional paradigm of political agency and a loss of faith in the ability of the average citizen to generate effective political action. *IA* offers an ambiguous response to this crisis. In this play individual agents are too weak to accomplish the *praxis*, dramatic or political. If that *praxis* is nonetheless accomplished, it is thanks not to the vacillating and impotent political leaders nor to the extraordinary self-sacrifice of Iphigeneia (an act, I shall propose, that paradoxically evacuates agency) but instead to the autonomous force of the play's formal structure, its *muthos*. Structure prevails where agents fail.

But if *IA* suggests the insufficiency of the voluntarist subject to the demands of action, it is not ready to give up entirely on the agent, for all his *aporia*. Instead, that *aporia* is shown to be definitive of the very form of action within the play's dramatic temporality. Whereas Aristotle views dramatic action from a position of analytical retrospection from which it can be declared 'significant and complete', *IA* stages action in its unfolding:

the drama takes place in the aporetic present tense of *acting*. This is the 'ongoing present' Lauren Berlant describes: that moment in which the event – the action – is still finding the form that will come to define it, in hindsight, as a *teleia praxis*.⁹ That formal *telos* is not inscribed from the start, as it is for Aristotle, but emerges over time and within time, and the duration of its emergence is characterized by uncertainty, openness, *aporia*. This aporetic unfolding of the act-in-process occupies a middle ground between the 'unrealistic voluntarism' of an autonomous ethical agent and the 'paralysing fatalism' of a *telos* predetermined by the myth and plot – a space of practical indeterminacy essential to democratic politics. In staging this present moment of acting and its uncertain relation to the *telos* of action, *IA* suggests that *aporia* is not so much a *failure* of agency as in fact a *mode* of agency and the enabling, as well as the disabling, condition of democratic politics.

Iphigeneia in Aulis begins in *aporia*.¹⁰ It is just before dawn in the Greek camp; all is still due to the 'silence of winds' (10). This lack of wind creates a literal *aporia*: the Greeks can find no *poros*, no path, out of Aulis. They cannot sail; they cannot get to Troy and fight the war that will guarantee Greek freedom and rule. The oracle they hope will break the *aporia* instead doubles it:

Κάλχας δ' ὁ μάντις ἀπορίαι κεχρημένοις
ἀνεῖλεν Ἰφιγένειαν ἣν ἔσπειρ' ἐγὼ
Ἀρτέμιδι θῦσαι τῆι τόδ' οἰκούσηι πέδον,
καὶ πλοῦν τ' ἔσεσθαι καὶ κατασκαφὰς Φρυγῶν
θύσασι, μὴ θύσασι δ' οὐκ εἶναι τάδε.

The prophet Calchas responded to us in our *aporia*
to sacrifice Iphigeneia, my child,
to Artemis who inhabits this place,
and there will be sailing of ships and the razing of Troy
if we sacrifice; if we do not sacrifice,
these things do not happen.

IA 89-93

What starts as a simple demand – 'sacrifice Iphigeneia' – becomes an alternative between two grammatically parallel but mutually exclusive 'more vivid' futures: sacrifice, and the mission will sail and succeed; don't sacrifice, and it won't (cf. 358–9). In place of a singular divine imperative, Calchas offers the Greeks two *poroi*, but these only produce a new *aporia*, a choice between two impossible alternatives.

The structure of the oracle proposes that the path out of *aporia* lies in the decision of the individual agent, and the play does everything to highlight this ethical focus. The goddess does not demand that Agamemnon sacrifice his daughter, as in other versions of the myth, but that he decide whether or not to sacrifice her.¹¹ The binary structure of this choice is reiterated throughout the play's opening scene. Before the drama even begins Agamemnon had written to Clytemnestra telling her to bring their daughter to Aulis on the pretext of marriage to Achilles. But he has spent the night writing new letters only to toss them away, 'nearly mad from *aporia*' (40–1, cf. 108–10). The opening scene ends with him sending another letter, telling Iphigeneia not to come. The Greeks' objective *aporia* becomes subjective as Agamemnon tries to choose between the oracle's two *poroi*. That ethical *aporia* is in turn literalized in the double letters and in the cross-roads – *poron skhiston* (144) – at which Agamemnon has his servant wait to intercept his wife and daughter.

The prologue's aporetic alternatives anticipate the myriad changes of mind – *metabolai* – that are this play's most conspicuous formal feature.[12] Agamemnon has changed his mind once before the play begins. He will change it again in the next episode after a heated *agōn* with his brother Menelaus, who will also change his mind in the course of the scene. Their *metabolai* set the stage for Iphigeneia's shocking reversal: after first begging for her life she does an abrupt volte-face and offers herself willingly for sacrifice. Aristotle condemns this as ethical inconsistency (*to anōmalon*), for, he notes, 'the woman who supplicates is nothing like the later woman' (*Po.* 1454a32–3). Even Artemis may change her mind (if the play's ending is authentic) and save Iphigeneia at the last minute from the sacrifice she had herself apparently demanded. The two mutually exclusive futures laid out by the oracle, the double *poroi* out of *aporia*, the many changes of mind: these reiterated binarisms situate *IA* within what Jacques Derrida (following Kierkegaard) terms the 'madness' of the instant of decision.[13] We might contrast Aeschylus' *Oresteia*, a key intertext throughout this play. There the sacrifice of Iphigeneia is described in a vivid but compressed flashback (in the parodos of *Agamemnon*) and the whole trilogy is an attempt to work through its tragic aftermath. *IA* is concerned less with the consequences than with the decision itself. Here, the decision *is* the drama and the play is an exploration of the madness that decision produces and requires. That madness is thematized in the play. To sacrifice his daughter would be madness, Agamemnon says again and again (136–7; cf. 389, 876–7, 1256), but that is what he does. It would be mad to choose death over life, says Iphigeneia (1251), but that is the choice she finally makes. This madness structures the play's action: with its constant reversals, the play itself, like its protagonist, is 'nearly mad from *aporia*' (41–2). Madness even infects the text: the *IA*'s countless interpolations and structural oddities appear like symptoms of thematic *aporia* manifested on its textual body.[14] These textual *aporiai* turn the reader into an Agamemnon, choosing at every moment which lines to sacrifice and which to save – a truly madness-inducing endeavour.

Aporia is thus the play's subject and its substance. Out of the madness of this *aporia*, something must be done or not be done. That is the choice the oracle presents and the stakes are high. They are high for Agamemnon. Euripides stages the general's moral dilemma with an almost lurid sentimentality, showing his love for his daughter and hinting at the bitter homecoming that awaits him if he kills her. But the stakes are also high for the audience, who have come to watch the sacrifice of Iphigeneia. If Agamemnon decides not to do the deed, will this still be a drama (a 'doing')? Can a tragedy be the *mimēsis* of a non-*praxis*? Form risks dissolving into non-form, as we shall see, as

Agamemnon's choice threatens to unwrite the very play, and with it the entire familiar Iliadic tradition on which it is based. Both the audience and the play itself presuppose a mythic reality in which Iphigeneia ultimately will have been sacrificed. Given the apparent inevitability of its outcome we might wonder how genuine Agamemnon's choice really is. And yet this mythic necessity merely underscores the play's insistence on Agamemnon's decision. For the play to work emotionally – for there to be any drama in this drama – we have to believe that Agamemnon could actually choose not to sacrifice Iphigeneia. Without that belief, the *praxis* might be *teleia* but it would not be *spoudaia*, significant or meaningful. The oracle's binary alternatives thus set *muthos* and *ēthos* in tension from the start. They force the agent to choose what to do; but that choice risks negating the action of the plot, leaving us with *prattontes* but no *praxis*. The play as a whole will unfold as an attempt to work through this paradox, and in this way to move from *aporia* to action, from nothing – no wind, no war, no play – to something: a *praxis* or at least its imitation.

The structure of *IA*'s opening scenes thus isolates and dramatizes the present instant of decision. How is that decision to be made? In *IA* there are no social institutions of deliberation. The Greek army is a powerful force, as we shall see, but it does not form a collective body that could debate and decide on behalf of the whole. Nor is there a divine *boulē* to which one could refer the question. There is no suggestion here, as there is in Aeschylus, that the demand of Artemis is part of Zeus' larger plan. With no theological nor political superstructure, the decision falls entirely upon Agamemnon. '*Ti drasō*' he cries, 'What am I to do? What *poros* will I find and where?' (356). His choice of action – *draō* in the 'deliberative' subjunctive – offers the only *poros* out of *aporia*. In order for something to happen instead of nothing it must be willed by an individual.

Starting from that premise, the play's central project is an attempt to suture *praxis* to *prattōn*, to root action in the will of an agent. This will turn out to be surprisingly difficult. The play's long first episode stages an *agōn* between Agamemnon and Menelaus, who has intercepted the second letter, the one telling Iphigeneia not to come, and reviles his brother for his reversal. He represents Agamemnon as driven by a hidden will to power. 'You were eager to lead the Greeks to Troy, in appearance not desiring it, but consenting in your wishes' (τῶι δοκεῖν μὲν οὐχὶ χρῄζων, τῶι δὲ βούλεσθαι θέλων, 337–8). In this compressed line, a contrast between seeming (*tōi dokein*) and wanting (*tōi boulesthai*) replaces the usual dichotomy of seeming and being (*to dokein* and *to einai*): wanting thus assumes the weight of reality, as well as the force of desire (*khrēizon*), while the awkward near-pleonasm of *boulesthai thelōn* doubles down on volition. A similar hypostasis of the will drives Menelaus himself. Why did he intercept the second letter? Agamemnon asks. 'Because wanting was chafing me. I was not born your slave' (ὅτι τὸ βούλεσθαί μ' ἔκνιζε· còc δὲ δοῦλος οὐκ ἔφυν, 330). On the one hand, will is an assertion of the autonomy proper to a free man. On the other hand, it exerts a pressure of its own, beyond considerations of status or honor: it chafes (*eknize*). This verb, often used of *erōs*, turns the will itself into a quasi-corporeal drive, an itch that must be scratched.[15]

The itch of will is traced to familiar sources: lust and ambition. Agamemnon's wanting is rooted in *philotimia* (342). *Philotimia* is the desire for honor that was presumed to motivate public figures in democratic Athens; it provides an easy explanation for the impetus behind political agency.[16] But here *philotimia* also erodes agency, rendering it inconstant and opportunistic. Power made Agamemnon 'change his character', charges Menelaus (*metabalōn allous tropous*, 343; *tous tropous methistanai*, 347; cf. 363). 'He thinks crookedly, one thing now, another in the past, another in the future' (332). The same *philotimia* that explains his decision makes that decision capricious and unstable. The will-to-power is itself weak-willed. And Agamemnon denies even this feeble volition: he depicts himself as an unwilling leader (84–6).[17]

If Agamemnon is driven by ambition, his brother is motivated by shameless lust for an unfaithful wife (385–7). To his own inconstancy, Agamemnon opposes the irrational constancy of *erōs*. Am I mad (*mainomai*) if I have changed my mind for the better? he asks. No, you are mad, you who have lost an evil wife and want to get her back (388–90). The choral ode that follows builds on this theme of irrational passion. Beginning with a prayer for protection against the 'mad goads' (*mainomenoi oistroi*) of violent Eros (543–7), it traces the Trojan conflict back to the mutual love-at-first-sight of Paris and Helen (584–6). Its punning on *erōs* and *eris* (582–9) posits *erōs* as the original cause of the war, echoing Agamemnon's accusation. But in fact Menelaus' *erōs* is no less inconstant than his brother's *philotimia*. When he finally realizes what he is asking Agamemnon to do, he declares himself prepared to renounce Helen: I can always get another wife, he says (585–8). When the going gets tough, Menelaus is willing to give way on his desire, and the choral ode, with its mad goads of love, merely emphasizes this. For these characters, desire is weak and uncommitted, strong enough to get them into their aporetic situation but not to get them out of it.[18]

The pursuit of motives thus stalls out in an agential dead end. *Erōs* and *philotimia* serve as virtual synonyms for volition, but neither proves strong enough to explain, much less to motivate, *praxis*. Instead of a voluntarist agent, the author of decision and action, we discover a fundamental ethical passivity. Consider Agamemnon's second change of mind, when he decides (once again) to kill his daughter. Despite the lengthy *agōn* debating the issue, despite the numerous arguments made pro and contra, this decision feels oddly unmotivated.

οἴμοι, τί φῶ δύστηνος; ἄρξωμαι πόθεν;
ἐς οἷ' ἀνάγκης ζεύγματ' ἐμπεπτώκαμεν.
ὑπῆλθε δαίμων, ὥστε τῶν σοφισμάτων
πολλῶι γενέσθαι τῶν ἐμῶν σοφώτερος.

Alas, what am I to say, wretched as I am? Where shall I start?
What yokes of necessity I have fallen into!
The *daimōn* came over me
so as to outsmart my schemes by far.

IA 442–5

The critical moment is marked by an allusion to the parodos of Aeschylus' *Agamemnon*. There, after weighing the equally 'heavy fates' of killing his daughter or abandoning his troops, the king finally 'put on the yoke-strap of necessity, blowing an impious reversal of mind, unholy, unsanctified, from which he changed his mind so as to dare everything' (ἐπεὶ δ' ἀνάγκας ἔδυ λέπαδνον φρενὸς πνέων δυσσεβῆ τροπαίαν ἄναγνον, ἀνίερον, τόθεν τὸ παντότολμον φρονεῖν μετέγνω, *Ag.* 218-21). For Aeschylus the moment of decision is an ethical paradox: it is the instant when the agent actively assumes necessity as his own volition. Within the constraints of *anankē*, he makes an active choice.[19] By contrast, Euripides' Agamemnon is an accidental agent. He has fallen (*empeptōkamen*) into *anankē*'s bonds. The verb is grammatically active (as in Aeschylus) but the action bespeaks a lack of intentionality: *empiptō* is more usually used of events or states that befall an individual, like illness, passion, disaster or madness.[20] Aeschylus' Agamemnon decisively assumes his fate; Euripides' falls haplessly into his. And he didn't even fall: he was pushed. The *daimōn* 'came over him' (*hupēlthe*, 444). His decision is a concession of defeat: the action done by him becomes an action done to him. In place of Vernant's tense equation between *ēthos* and *daimōn*, here the *daimōn* seems just a transparent excuse for ethical impotence. It is an outsourcing of agency: the *daimōn* made me do it.

The same is true for *anankē*. Agamemnon concludes: 'I have arrived at necessary fate: to accomplish the bloody death of my daughter' (ἀλλ' ἥκομεν γὰρ εἰς ἀναγκαίας τύχας, θυγατρὸς αἱματηρὸν ἐκπρᾶξαι φόνον, 511-13). But Menelaus questions this necessity: 'who will force you to kill your daughter?' (513). And well might he ask, for *anankē* is remarkably opaque in this play.[21] It has no theological grounding, as we have seen; the oracle's command is never represented as part of some larger divine scheme. Perhaps it amounts to no more than luck or random chance, as the difficult phrase *anankaias tukhas* in 511 suggests. Or maybe it refers to human compulsion. This passage comes at the end of the *agōn* with Menelaus and we might imagine that Agamemnon has yielded reluctantly to the force of his brother's persuasion, as he had once already before the play even began (89-98). 'I give myself to you. Yours is the power,' he tells his brother (472). And yet no sooner does he put himself under his brother's *kratos*, than Menelaus, moved by Agamemnon's suffering, reverses his formerly adamant stance. His brother hands over responsibility to him; he hands it back: 'let me have no more share in the oracle,' he says; 'I hand my share over to you' (498-9). The Atreidae's twin *metabolai* leave Agamemnon's decision under-motivated: he yields to his brother's demand at the very moment that his brother relinquishes that demand.

From this perspective, *anankē* starts to look less like a constraint upon agency than a desperate excuse for the renunciation of agency. The passage quoted above (442-5), which starts with the bonds of necessity, goes on to lament the unhappiness of the well-born (446-50). This theme runs throughout the play, starting in the prologue where Agamemnon envies his old slave for his life of safe obscurity (16-23). In a symmetrical inversion of Menelaus' accusation of his secret will to power, Agamemnon dreams of renouncing not only the burdens of leadership but ethical agency altogether. He wants someone else to decide for him. 'Conquered in every way' by the situation (745), this Greek commander longs to be compelled, to delegate volition to some overwhelming necessity, to abdicate agency and be the *daimōn*'s slave. *Anankē* is not the cause of agential failure, then, but its solution: it allows Agamemnon to make a decision and, at the same time, disown it, to act without committing to being the agent of that act. If in the *aporia* of the play's opening we seem in danger of having *prattontes* but no *praxis*, at the end we appear headed for a *praxis* without *prattontes*.

If the *muthos* succeeds, then, if it manages to represent a 'significant and complete *praxis*', it will be despite the characters not because of them. The play labours to ground action in *ēthos*, but the site of ethical agency turns out to be empty, too frail to bear the burden of initiating the *praxis*, much less bringing it to completion. With its mad *metabolai*, *ēthos* cannot produce a clear path of *praxis*. All it can do is keep returning to its founding *aporia*, asking *ti drasō*? over and over – a *poros* that leads nowhere.

And yet, the *praxis* does ultimately succeed. The play does manage to get where it's headed, and while the episodes are marked by *aporia* and *anōmalia*, the overall structure of the drama is relatively unitary, even teleological. At the start a decision is made to sacrifice Iphigeneia. At the end she is sacrificed. This *praxis* unfolds with a curious autonomy from its *prattontes* and their agonies of indecision. It operates as a kind of structural fatality, a necessity not theological but formal, in Aristotle's sense, an expression of the formal structure of the *muthos*, both the plot and the myth, as it develops from potential to realization.

This formal necessity is signaled in the prologue by the agency of the letter.[22] Before the play began Agamemnon had made up his mind to perform the sacrifice and had sent a letter calling Iphigeneia to Aulis. The first episode shows him indecisive again, his *metabolai* literalized in the writing and unwriting of new letters. At the end of the scene he sends a second letter reversing his decision. But even as he is agonizing over his choice, changing and rechanging his mind, off-stage the first letter is wending its way toward its goal. A letter, as Lacan says, always reaches its destination.[23] This one does so despite Agamemnon's vacillations and despite his second letter, intercepted by Menelaus. While the second letter precipitates the violent *agōn* between the two brothers (314–33), the first renders that *agōn* void: Iphigeneia is already there. Indeed, it voids the entire ethical crisis of the first half of the play, with all its *aporiai* and reiterated *metabolai*. The language of *desis* and *lusis* surrounding the letters (110; cf. 38) associates them with the plot as it moves toward its resolution, irrespective of the decisions of its agents.[24] On the one hand, the letters written and unwritten are symptoms of Agamemnon's ethical *anōmalia*. On the other hand, they represent a kind of automatism of the *muthos*. The play has made up its mind even if the characters have not.

The formal agency first materialized in the letters is later embodied in the Greek army. When Agamemnon is asked what *anankē* will force him to kill his daughter he names 'the whole assembly of the Achaean army' (514). This shadowy collective has no actual presence in the play: it is never represented, directly or indirectly, on stage. Instead, it emerges as a figment of Agamemnon's imagination, both compensation and justification for his ethical weakness. Urged on by the *philotimia* of the demagogue Odysseus (527), the soldiers are enflamed with mad lust for the mission: 'some Aphrodite raged in the Greek army' (1264; cf. 808). This lust, as Agamemnon imagines it, impels them to extraordinary action: if he refuses to perform the sacrifice, he says, the army will kill him and Iphigeneia; if he tries to flee, they will pursue him back to Argos, where they will kill his daughters and lay waste to his land (528–35, 1267–8). This paranoid fantasy – unparalleled in any other treatment of the myth – projects Agamemnon's weakness as the mob's menacing strength. Greece compels him to carry out the sacrifice 'whether I want to or not' (κἂν θέλω κἂν μὴ θέλω, 1271). He is a slave to the mob (τῶι τ' ὄχλωι δουλεύομεν, 449–50; cf. 517, 1012, 1269).

The *okhlos* is thus another name – like *daimōn* or *anankē* – for Agamemnon's ethical vacuity and a symptom of his agential failure.[25] But this paranoid hallucination also figures the teleological drive of the plot. Agamemnon is unable to act; the Greek army is nothing but action, pushing – and pushing him – irresistibly toward the sacrifice. While the play offers various traditional rationales for the expedition (glory, profit, vengeance), the army's passion for war is presented as pathological (*nosei*, 411), a mad passion (*memēne d'Aphroditē*, 1264) and 'terrible *erōs*' (808). It is pure agential impulsion. That impulsion grows stronger as the play progresses. It exerts pressure from off-stage, as the fantasied army becomes a real lynch mob that threatens to stone Achilles as he tries to protect his bride (1345–68). Like the letters, then, the mob figures an impersonal agency that overruns the characters in its drive toward the *telos* of the *teleia praxis*. That *praxis* will be not only complete (*teleia*) but also perfect (*teleia*) when, in the final scenes, the slogan of 'Greece mighty and free' emerges to quell our doubts about the moral validity of this war and to lend its ideological sheen *ex post facto* to the murder that allows it to proceed (1378–1401).

The same formal impetus inscribed in the letters and incorporated in the army is at work in the play's language as well. Euripides revels in the grim ironies of the familiar tragic trope of marriage-to-death: Iphigeneia will soon be leaving him, her father tells her; she will take a solitary journey and live in another house far away; the preliminary offerings to Artemis are being readied, etc. (460–1, 667–90, 716–24, 1110–16).[26] Agamemnon uses the linguistic overlap between marriage and death to conceal his plans. But this ambiguous language also ensures that – regardless of those plans and independent of them – beneath the sentimental domesticity of the wedding plot-line the sacrifice is proceeding steadily toward its *telos*. Thus when Agamemnon speaks of *proteleia* (718), which can refer to the sacrifices preliminary to either war or marriage, the word bespeaks his deliberate decision to sacrifice his daughter and his scheme to keep this from his wife. But it also speaks to the mythic necessity that will eventuate in the girl's death (*prothuma*, 1310). Not only does it evoke Aeschylus' description of Iphigeneia's sacrifice (Aes. *Ag.* 65); it also recalls the zeal of the Greek soldiers, first for the girl's wedding (*protelizousi*, 433) and later for her blood. The linguistic ambiguity of the word – its *poros skhistos* leading toward marriage or death – places it at the crossroads between two mutually exclusive outcomes. But this ambiguity is in fact a hollow irony, for *proteleia*'s *telos* has already been determined: one path is already the road not taken and the sign pointing toward it is merely misdirection. To that extent, the play's ironies are themselves ironic, simultaneously underwriting and overwriting the characters' plans.

A similar irony structures the play as a whole through its counterfactual intertextuality. In *IA* Clytemnestra appears, against all expectation, as a loyal and loving wife, a respectable woman concerned to preserve social proprieties and her own unblemished reputation. This decorous queen hints darkly at the homecoming Agamemnon can expect if he kills their daughter (1171–84): 'Do not force me to become a bad wife to you!' she beseeches him (1183–4). Like Calchas' oracle, Clytemnestra lays out two alternative paths, and imagines a future in which her villainous character, so familiar from Aeschylus, will become a mere might-have-been. If by sacrificing his daughter Agamemnon turns this Clytemnestra into *the* Clytemnestra, Aeschylus' anti-heroine, then by not sacrificing he would unwrite the *Oresteia*. But Euripides' constant references to Aeschylus' trilogy not only imply that this could not happen; they remind us that it has already not happened. The *Oresteia* exists, and it exerts its pressure on the action right until the end, when Clytemnestra predicts the 'terrible struggles' Agamemnon will undergo upon his return to Argos (1455).[27] The ironic language of the play and its Aeschylean intertext thus work together, one within the text, the other from without: they point toward alternative endings only to ironize them and drive the action toward its inevitable conclusion in the accomplishment of the deed that they proclaim a *fait accompli*.

This structural irony operates most obviously, and its teleological drive most forcefully, in the often-noted tension between the play's episodes and its choral odes.[28] *IA*'s structure of *metabolē* presents ethical choice as unconstrained; it insists that Agamemnon could actually choose not to sacrifice his daughter. But the choral odes presuppose the outcome of this free choice. While Agamemnon dithers in the aporetic present of deciding, the odes are set in a future-perfect temporality in which that decision will already have been made. The parodos, an ekphrastic celebration of the mustered Greek forces, bestows in advance the *kleos* of a victory that will be possible only if Iphigeneia will have been killed. The Greek soldiers are already in this first song the Homeric heroes that Iphigeneia's death will enable them to become. In the ode's visual idiom, the Trojan War is already an aestheticized fetish object, obscuring the painful labour of volition, both Agamemnon's and Iphigeneia's, that produced it.[29] The choral odes that follow return obsessively to the war's contingent origins: the marriage of Peleus and Thetis, the divine beauty contest, the fateful meeting of Helen and Paris. And yet, these contingent beginnings are already pregnant with their inevitable end: full of Homeric vocabulary and Iliadic allusions, they unfold within a mythic reality in which Troy has already fallen. The odes thus take for granted the completion of a *muthos* that the play's ethical agents treat as open and undecided. Whatever choices are being made or unmade in the play's dramatic present, the odes advance an action that must happen because it has already happened: it is already inscribed on the tablets of the muses (798–9).[30]

The tension between *ēthos* and *muthos* thus produces a double futility. On the one hand, if action really is ethical – if *praxis* originates in the free choice of a *prattōn* – then the play risks unwriting itself. If Agamemnon chooses not to sacrifice Iphigeneia, the odes, with their Iliadic sensibility, would evaporate before our eyes. The *Oresteia* would vanish and *IA* itself evanesce: the play would become an imitation of the action of its own formal dissolution. On the other hand, if the Trojan War really is inevitable, as the choral odes suggest, then Euripides' insistence on the ethics of the act is disingenuous at best, and sadistic at worst. The characters' hard-won *metabolai* are meaningless: they may be engaging to watch, but they can accomplish nothing within the world of the play itself. *Ti drasō?*, cries Agamemnon, his deliberative subjunctive voicing the madness of ethical deliberation. But from the perspective of the *muthos*, that *drasō* is not an aorist subjunctive but a future indicative: his anguished 'what shall I do?' is what he *will* do. In doing it he becomes the agent not of his own act but of a formal necessity that plays out through him. The *muthos* dictates the lines of action. All the rest, as Aristotle says, is just colour.

The play's tension between *ēthos* and *muthos* would seem to be resolved with Iphigeneia's voluntary self-sacrifice.

οἷα δ' εἰσῆλθέν μ' ἄκουσον, μῆτερ, ἐννοουμένην·
κατθανεῖν μέν μοι δέδοκται· τοῦτο δ' αὐτὸ βούλομαι
εὐκλεῶς πρᾶξαι, παρεῖσά γ' ἐκποδὼν τὸ δυσγενές.

Hear what thoughts have come over me, mother,
as I have been reflecting.
I have resolved to die. I want to do this
with glory, rejecting everything ignoble.

IA 1374-6

Iphigeneia's intervention has the suddenness of a *deus ex machina*.[31] Like a *deus ex machina* it appears to miraculously resolve all the play's *aporiai*, not only the *aporia* of the fleet's immobility, but also her father's aporetic response to it. With Iphigeneia's self-sacrifice the play seems finally to find the ethical well-spring of action. The sacrifice is not imposed by any external necessity; there is no *daimōn* nor yoke of necessity. Instead Iphigeneia's *praxis* emerges from her own *ēthos*, the result of her own reflection (*ennooumenēn*, 1374), resolution (*dedoktai*, 1375), and will (*boulomai*, 1375). That she had refused the sacrifice before accepting it only emphasizes the fact that this is her decision to make. That ethical choice aligns with and enacts the formal necessity of the plot. Through her choice, the winds will blow, the Greeks will sail, the war will be fought and won. The language of *kleos* in this passage recalls the parodos, with its anticipatory glorification of the Greek soldiers as Homeric heroes. Iphigeneia assumes that mythic vision as her own ethical imperative: her glorious act will actualize the perfect future of the ode's future perfect. The *praxis* will have been completed: the play will turn out to have been the imitation of an action after all, and not just of *aporia*.

So the play's letter reaches its destination, hand-delivered by this unlikely agent. Iphigeneia's decision would seem to finally align *ēthos* and *muthos*, allowing both to progress together toward the *telos* of the *teleia praxis*. If Iphigeneia breaks the play's ethical paralysis, however, she does so only by negating ethical agency altogether. Her volition seems to make good her father's lack of volition: 'I give myself voluntarily (*hēkousa*) for sacrifice on behalf of all Greece' (1554–5). But in doing so it figures him –

as he had figured himself – as a passive agent: 'he killed me involuntarily (*akōn*) on behalf of Greece' (1456). With her quasi-divine act of will, all her father's agonies of indecision, all his unsent letters and *metabolai*, are rendered irrelevant. There is an action, but Agamemnon does not have to act; a decision is made but he doesn't have to make it. His wish to outsource agency is finally fulfilled. He gets his *praxis* without the burden of being its *prattōn*.[32] Thus Iphigeneia's miraculous act does not cure the agential impotence the play stages but instead sublates it. She becomes the (literally) vanishing mediator between *prattōn* and *praxis*: thanks to her extraordinary intervention action can happen without an ordinary act of will.

Moreover, Iphigenia's self-sacrifice also sublates without resolving the *aporia* at the heart of action, the 'madness' of the moment of decision. Iphigeneia's self-sacrifice is represented as a strong act of volition, a choice freely made. And yet there is something here that doesn't quite work. Iphigeneia's *metabolē* is not fully convincing; hence Aristotle's charge of *anōmalia*: 'the woman who supplicates is nothing like the later woman'.[33] It is not for want of justification. Iphigeneia offers myriad explanations for her decision: the freedom of Greece, her own *kleos*, the goddess' demand. But none of these justifications answers the one, incontrovertible, reason she earlier offered for refusing the sacrifice:

ἓν συντεμοῦσα πάντα νικήσω λόγον·
τὸ φῶς τόδ' ἀνθρώποισιν ἥδιστον βλέπειν,
τὰ νέρθε δ' οὐδέν· μαίνεται δ' ὅς εὔχεται
θανεῖν· κακῶς ζῆν κρεῖσσον ἢ καλῶς θανεῖν.

One concluding argument will prevail over all.
This is sweetest for mortals: to see the light.
The underworld is nothing. He is mad who prays
to die. Better to live badly than to die nobly.

IA 1249–52

The compelling force of the life instinct makes her change of mind feel under-motivated, even as it is over-motivated. 'I should not love my life too much,' she says weakly (1385). But even Achilles is unconvinced: 'death is a terrible evil,' he repeats (1415), and holds open the possibility that she might change her mind again on the very altar (1424–30). In this instant, the plot's teleological drive becomes a death drive that operates through the character, eviscerating her pleasure and her very attachment to life ('this is sweetest for mortals: to see the light'). For all the play's efforts to align *ēthos* with *praxis*, there is still a lingering *aporia*, an internal dehiscence between agent and act at the very moment the agent voluntarily chooses that act. The mysterious impulse that emerges in that gap to force a decision can be experienced only as an instance of ethical *anōmalia*, even madness. 'He is mad who prays to die,' she says (μαίνεται δ' ὅς εὔχεται θανεῖν, 1251). Yet this, in the end, is precisely her prayer.

Thus the heroic act that should redeem *ēthos* and ethical agency instead enacts a deathly *Handlungstrieb*. The *muthos* operates behind the characters' backs, as it were: it bypasses their deliberations and sweeps aside their hesitations, which subsequently appear as so many mad anomalies in a psychic coherence lent them by the plot itself. Proceeding towards its *telos* with the characters or against them, the *muthos* is indifferent to their struggles of will and their counterfactual desires. Indeed, it is indifferent to their very life or death. The derangement of the text makes it impossible to know whether the play ends with Iphigeneia being led to her certain death or with a messenger speech announcing her miraculous last-minute salvation. Even without that (probably spurious) final speech, the tradition holds both paths open and leaves us wondering whether Iphigeneia in fact dies at the end or not.[34] But in a sense it doesn't matter: either way the sacrifice is performed. The *praxis* is complete. *IA* is (as Aristotle prescribes) the *mimēsis* of a significant and complete action, the sacrifice of Iphigeneia.

What should we make of this efficacy of tragic form and evanescence of *ēthos* within the historical context of Athens at the very end of the fifth century? *IA* was produced in the Spring of 406/5 under dire circumstances: the city was impoverished, the people starving and desperate. The end was near – Athens would surrender to Sparta less than a year later – and it seemed that the Athenians themselves could sense it. In these terrible straits, the Athenians sought a saviour. We hear in Aristophanes' *Frogs* of their longing for Alcibiades: maybe he could be enticed back from Persia to save them? *Frogs'* own solution is only slightly more improbable, as Dionysus descends to the underworld to bring back a dead poet to save the city.

The fantasy that the city will be saved by some super-agent – be it a humanized god, a resuscitated poet, or even a real individual like Alcibiades – suggests a crisis of political agency. It indicates a loss of faith in the everyday agency of the average citizen, one of the ideological cornerstones of Athenian democracy. That traditional model of democratic agency can be seen, for instance, in Aristophanes' *Acharnians*. That play shows how the hero's humble desire for peace drives him to a decision that generates political action. The *dikē* of the polis, in this comedy, rests not in the institutional structures of democracy (which are shown to be corrupt or ineffectual) but within the *ēthos* of the individual, Dikaiopolis. *Acharnians* proposes that any engaged citizen can take action to end the war; in *Frogs*, performed twenty years later, it will take a god. The difference between the two plays measures what we might see as a shift in the balance between structure and agency within democratic Athens, as the individual human agent comes to seem inadequate to resist the impersonal impetus of the war.

IA, as we have seen, stages this collapse of the traditional model of political agency. Its aporetic action and mad *metabolai* evacuate the voluntarist subject as the site of ethical agency and well-spring of *praxis*. Iphigeneia's miraculous act, far from resolving the crisis, instead perpetuates it. If this maiden is the saviour the Athenians of 405 were seeking, her intervention shows that this fantasy of salvation comes at the expense of real political agency. She saves the Greeks from *aporia*, but also from the need to make their own *poros* out of it – from the need to decide and to act on that decision. Her heroic act preempts heroic action. Thus all the glory of the war will redound to her: she – not her father nor the Greek soldiers – will be 'Troy's city-conqueror' (1476, 1512); she, not they, will 'bring victorious salvation for Greece' (1473–4). The Iliadic *kleos* of which the chorus sings in the parodos will ultimately be hers alone (1383, 1504). Her act also preempts political action. The formula for official polis resolutions in classical Athens, *dokei tēi boulēi kai tōi dēmōi* ('it seems best to the Boulē and the demos'), rooted political efficacy in the decision of the demos and its will (*boulē*), as instantiated in the Council (Boulē). Iphigeneia's resolve appropriates this language of political resolutions, replacing the demos' will and decision with her own: 'I have resolved to die (*katthanein men moi dedoktai*) and I want to do this with glory' (1375–6; cf. 1422). Her exceptional, anomalous intervention replaces and displaces the everyday deliberation and decision-making, both individual and collective, that constituted real political agency in democratic Athens.[35]

The play might be read, then, as a despairing renunciation of the belief that individual volition is sufficient to carry through political *praxis*. And perhaps such despair was warranted. No one did save Athens, neither Alcibiades nor Dionysus nor the dead Euripides. And yet Athens survived. What preserved it in the end, though, was not any individual but the institutional structure of the democracy itself – not an ethical agent but a political form. *IA* suggests that form can effect *praxis* when *prattontes* cannot. Athens' own history bears this out, as the formal structure of the *politeia* preserves democracy and 'saves the city', as Aristophanes would have it. That agency of form is instantiated – it is itself formalized – in the fourth century's shift toward a more institutional and constitutional mode of democracy.[36] In the fourth century, laws were regularized, codified and archived; the justice of the city came to be seen as residing in the fixed distribution of powers and offices, not in the *ēthos* of the individual citizen. The civic stability and practical efficacy that individual agents could no longer sustain were rediscovered in the agency of institutional forms. Euripides anticipates this shift in his meditation on the efficacy of dramatic form. His play offers a grim vision of this formal efficacy, as a young girl is murdered not so much by her weak-willed father as by the structural necessity of the *muthos*. The historical example of Athens suggests a more optimistic reading: structures endure even when individuals fail, and they provide a framework within which individuals will find new opportunities for action.

And yet, if Euripides does anticipate an emerging 'formalism' within Athenian politics, that anticipation can be seen only in comfortable retrospect, from the other side of the devastating end of the war. *IA* denies us the comfort of that retrospective position. It unfolds, as we have seen, in the chaotic present tense of a situation within which the event – both the sacrifice of Iphigeneia within the play and the end of the war outside it – has not yet found its definitive form. The 'significant and complete action' the play stages may be clear in hindsight: from that vantage point the *teleia praxis* assumes the teleological necessity that Aristotle ascribes to *muthos* – the inevitable realization of a potential immanent within its form – and that we saw staged as *muthos*' autonomous agency within the play. This is the perspective of the audience: for us, secure in our post-Oresteian, post-Iliadic reality, the *praxis* is complete and comprehensible, 'the sacrifice of Iphigeneia'. But for all Agamemnon knows, in the messy midst of things, the *praxis* may turn out to be the non-sacrifice of Iphigeneia: for him the situation has not yet achieved its final form and there is nothing inevitable to that formal *telos*.

This double temporal perspective thus presents two contradictory views of the action. It also presents two contradictory views of acting and its *aporia*. From the *ex post facto* perspective of the completed *muthos* the characters' *aporia* can appear only as ethical failure, as I have argued, and the vacillations it induces as an *anōmalia* marring the plot's perfect wholeness. But viewed as they view it, from within the 'unfolding activity of the contemporary moment',[37] the characters' *aporia* appears not as the evacuation of agency but in fact as a mode of agency, perhaps the only mode of agency available to them in the desperate opacity of the moment. From this perspective, their *aporia* represents a way of preserving a space – or perhaps better a time – for reflecting and deciding, against the teleological pressure of a *muthos* for which the decision has already been made. Holding open the possibility of counterfactuality, of deciding otherwise, *aporia* is an assertion of will precisely in the form of indecision. In staging the characters' extended equivocation and undermotivated *metabolai*, Euripides preserves a moment for ethical agency against the determinism of *muthos*. He proffers *aporia* itself as the equivocal middle ground of agency between Coole's 'alternatives of unrealistic voluntarism or paralysing fatalism'.

By problematizing the relation between *muthos* and *ēthos*, then, and holding open a gap between acting, in all its contingency and uncertainty, and a completed action, *IA* installs *aporia* at the very heart of *praxis*. Ethical *aporia* is not extraneous or incidental to the play's *praxis*, mere color added as an afterthought to a drama already complete and perfect in itself. Instead, *aporia* is part of the colorful essence of the *praxis*, part of its immanent form. And it is precisely in that *aporia*, finally, that *IA* preserves a *poros* for democratic politics. For if the becoming-event of a situation – its formalization – opens new possibilities for future political agency (as Athens' history suggests), the *aporia* of agents in the present moment creates the conditions of that becoming. Their *metabolai* may not be able to precipitate *praxis*, but they can hold open a space for its formal unfolding and a possibility, however slight, that the form it ultimately takes might be something other than the familiar stories already inscribed on the tablets of the muses. This is the space of democratic politics in its present-tense indeterminacy, a space where individual *prattontes*, precisely through their *aporia* and *anōmalia*, might actually rewrite the plot.

Notes

1. It is my pleasure to thank Phiroze Vasunia for organizing the conference from which this paper emerged and the conference participants, especially Nancy Worman and Iakovos Vasiliou, for engaged discussion. I am also grateful to Phiroze Vasunia, Erik Gunderson and Alex Purves for helpful comments on an earlier draft of the paper and to Sean Gurd for an invitation to participate in the Classical Association of Canada panel at which I first tried out the argument presented here. A different version of this argument can be found at Wohl 2018.
2. ὁ μῦθος τέλος τῆς τραγῳδίας, *Po*. 1450a22–3. Belfiore 1984 highlights the distinction between *ēthos* and *muthos*; cf. Jones 1962: 11–62. Halliwell 1998: 138–67, by contrast, emphasizes Aristotle's 'agent-centred view of drama' (146) and the close connection between *ēthos* and *praxis*. As I will suggest at the end, *IA* supports a reading of tragedy (if not of Aristotle) in which *ēthos* is an essential element of the *praxis*.

3. See Lear 1988: 19, 39–40 on form as *dunamis* aiming at its own actualization. A stress on the immanent dynamism of form, which I adopt from Aristotle, differentiates my approach from the more structuralist formalism of Levine 2015, for whom forms (singularly and in combination) offer affordances for agents but do not themselves exhibit agency.
4. A similar priority of action over agent also holds in Aristotle's ethical thought: see Vasiliou 2011. Aristotle's formalism of affect (minus its psychagogic teleology) has been brilliantly revived by Brinkema 2014, for whom affect inheres in aesthetic forms detached from any subjective origin (author or character) or endpoint (spectator).
5. I make the case for the wider claim in Wohl 2015.
6. Coole 2005: 125. See Deleuze and Guattari 1983, Deleuze and Guattari 1987 (on assemblages), Latour 1996, Latour 2005 (on actor-network theory) and Bennett 2010. My reading of the agential force of the tragic *muthos* has been influenced by these thinkers' insistence on the emergent efficacy of material and immaterial forms.
7. Vernant 1988a; Vernant 1988b.
8. Vernant 1988b: 46. On this question, see also Williams 1993.
9. 'A situation occurs that becomes event as it becomes form, in the ongoing present out of which are refracted near pasts and near futures': Berlant 2008; and cf. the more extensive discussion at Berlant 2011. In emphasizing the situation over the event, Berlant articulates her debt to and difference from Alain Badiou, for whom the event – both its meaning and its being – is constituted only retroactively.
10. 40–1, 55, 88–9; cf. 537; Luschnig 1988: 1–20. All translations are my own. I follow Diggle's text, in full awareness of its problems. Apparently unfinished at Euripides' death, the text of the *IA* is especially troubled, with many interpolated lines, passages and perhaps even whole scenes: see Mellert-Hoffmann 1969: 91–155; Stockert 1992: 63–87; Gurd 2005. I do not weigh in on specific textual issues, but since my argument concerns the overall structure of the play, I believe it stands even if any given scene or passage I discuss is determined to be spurious.
11. Dowden 1989: 9–19; Stockert 1992: 50–62; Michelakis 2006: 21–9.
12. See especially Gibert 1995: 202–54. Cf. Knox 1966; Chant 1986; Burgess 2004; and the useful chart at Lush 2015: 224. Forms of *metabolē* recur in the play (343, 363, 500, 1101). Torrance 2013: 44–6 proposes that the word, which Euripides is the only tragic poet to use, is a metapoetic term of art.
13. Derrida 1992: 26; cf. Bennington 2011 on the recurrence of this phrase throughout Derrida's work. This 'madness' is necessary if a decision is to be truly just and not merely the automatic repetition of existing rules or laws: hence Derrida's insistence that justice is an 'experience of aporia' (Derrida 1992: 16). See further Derrida 1995: 26–8, 78. Sacrifice (including Abraham's sacrifice of Isaac) is one of his primary examples.
14. Jouan 1983: 24–30 lists the formal anomalies; Gurd 2005 theorizes them.
15. On the language of will in the two lines see Stockert 1992: 288 and 293 ad loc. On the itch of desire see esp. Pl. *Gorg.* 494c-e.
16. See, e.g., Thuc. 2.65.7, 8.89.3. The word occurs frequently in Plutarch's political biographies. See further de Romilly 1965.
17. Cf. 520, 527, where Agamemnon attributes *philotimia* to Calchas and Odysseus: *philotimia* glosses without explaining political will.
18. Snell 1983. The characters are thus unethical as Lacan defines the term: they always and immediately give way on their desire (Lacan 1992: 311–25). On *erōs* in the play see the comments of Michelini 1999: 51–2.

19. On the decision of Agamemnon in Aeschylus as a crisis of agency see Lloyd-Jones 1962; Nussbaum 1986: 25–50; Vernant 1988a: 71–7; Williams 1993: 132–6. Mastronarde 2010: 236–7 compares the two scenes. Euripides alludes to this passage again at the end of the play: 'It is terrible if I dare these things and terrible if I don't' (1257–8; cf. *Ag.* 206–11). By that time, however, the decision has already been made.
20. LSJ (s.v. 3). We find this usage at *IA* 808: δεινὸς ἐμπέπτωκ' ἔρως. Contrast Agamemnon's use of the grammatically active but semantically passive formulation at 137: αἰαῖ, πίπτω δ' εἰς ἄταν. Compare ὑπῆλθε at 444, another verb often used, especially in tragedy, 'of involuntary feelings' (s.v. LSJ II).
21. Cf. 395, 761, 1183, 1219, 1327, 1409; Wassermann 1949; Siegel 1981: 261; Michelakis 2006: 57; Stockert 1992: 329: 'Ananke bezeichnet mehr den Zwang der konkreten Situation als ein allgemeines Prinzip.'
22. See Lacan 2006, where the movement of the letter in Poe's 'The Purloined Letter' illustrates the determination of the subject by the 'insistence of the signifying chain' and the corresponding 'ex-sistence' of the unconscious. If the unconscious is the trace within the subject of the autonomous processes of the signifying chain (as Lacan argues in the introduction to that seminar, Lacan 2006: 33–48; cf. Fink 1995: 14–23) then we might say that the agency of form, in the sense that I am discussing it here, constitutes the characters' unconscious, an unconscious (as I will suggest below) that they can experience only as a kind of madness.
23. E.g. Lacan 2006: 18, 30.
24. Torrance 2013: 159 reads the letters metapoetically: the first symbolizes established tragic myth; the second, Euripides' attempt to rewrite it. This is part of a broader argument (Torrance 2013: 158–65) that the play's tension between individual action and the mythic tradition is a self-conscious reflection on 'the challenges of tragic *mythopoiēsis*' (161). See further Zeitlin 1980's seminal study of the tension between myth and dramatic action in Euripides' *Orestes*.
25. Lush 2015 views the army as 'the principal determinant of the trajectory of *IA*'s events' (222), though he sees the characters' vacillations as a response to, not the etiology of, the army's power.
26. On the trope in general see Rehm 1994, and in *IA*, H. P. Foley 1985: 68–78.
27. The force of the reference would be even stronger if, as many believe, the *Oresteia* was restaged at the end of the fifth century. The audience would also be aware of this inevitable outcome from Agamemnon's posthumous narrative in *Odyssey* 11. Sorum 1992 argues that the conflict in *IA* between the human dilemmas of the dramatic fiction and the inevitability of the traditional myth nullifies human action. She views the myth not as an actant alongside and in tension with the agency of the characters but rather as a static constraint upon the freedom of dramatic action (542).
28. See, e.g., Walsh 1974; H. P. Foley 1985: 78–84; Stockert 1992: 418; Sorum 1992.
29. On the visuality of the parodos see Zeitlin 1995.
30. The reference to the *deltois Pierisin* at 798–9 casts doubt on the story of Helen's swan-ancestry. But though the *muthoi* may be fictional they are still effective: regardless of Helen's parentage, the Trojan War will in fact play out precisely as the chorus imagine in this ode. I discuss Helen as a locus of tragic counterfactuality in Wohl 2014.
31. Jouan 1983: 24. Iphigeneia's change of mind has been much discussed: see, for example, Knox 1966: 229–32; Siegel 1980; Lawrence 1988; Luschnig 1988: 105–9; Sansone 1991; Rabinowitz 1993: 38–54; Gibert 1995: 222–52; Burgess 2004: 51–4; Mastronarde 2010: 238–40; Lush 2015: 232–7.

32. The paradox is nicely illustrated in the image of Agamemnon at the sacrifice but turned away, his eyes covered with his robe (1550). The moment is famously captured in a panel from the House of the Tragic Poet in Pompeii, probably based on a fourth-century Greek original. Platt 2014: 222–31 analyzes the rhetoric of *ēthos* in this image. Of course, Euripides does not let Agamemnon off the hook entirely: his daughter may absolve him of responsibility but his wife does not and we know that she will make him pay.

33. *Po.* 1454a31–3. Funke 1964 supports Aristotle's charge; contra Mellert-Hoffmann 1969: 9–91. We might think of this *anōmalia* as a surplus of *ēthos* over the requirements of the *muthos*, that is, an incoherence not only within the character but also between character and plot.

34. There are perhaps hints of the tradition of Iphigenia's salvation in the final paians in praise of Artemis and the girl's ambiguous reference to 'another life and fate' (1507–8). On the final odes, see Weiss 2014.

35. Thus I disagree with those like Markantonatos 2012 who see Iphigeneia's self-sacrifice as a positive model for political engagement. For a nuanced treatment of the politics of Euripides' sacrificial virgins see Roselli 2007.

36. Ostwald 1986; Wolin 1994. Cf. Wohl 2015: 140–1. This more 'formalized' *politeia* was, of course, the context for Aristotle's formalist analysis of tragedy.

37. Berlant 2011: 4. Her word for this 'sense of the present' is 'impasse' (Berlant 2011, 4), a literal translation of *aporia*.

CHAPTER 4
FORMS OF SURVIVAL
Susan Stephens

Modern theorists of genre usually focus on prose forms, especially various permutations of the novel, because unlike epic or lyric, the novel is not yet canonized; rather its forms are still evolving within contemporary cultures. In addition, by virtue of its large-scale narrative, the novel situates its action within a fictive reality that constructs its own social formations. Critical analyses can then 'read' these narrative constructs in various ways to explore their dialogic engagement with previous forms, to expose their underlying contradictions, projections of wish fulfillment, or to consider the hegemonic forces that underpin their creation (activities that are not mutually exclusive). Fredric Jameson is a leading exemplar of this kind of criticism. But in *The Political Unconscious* he questions the validity of 'those modes of formal or stylistic, purely textual analysis which are generally strategically limited to lyric poetry', on the grounds that they project as universals of human experience features that are in fact culturally conditioned and ignore the historically specific nature of their own critical practice. He opts instead for forms of rewritings that lend themselves to the types of analyses outlined above. For Jameson such analyses (which he labels 'strong') are dialogic because they would 'seek a latent meaning behind a manifest one' or 'rewrite the surface categories of a text in the stronger language of a more fundamental interpretive code'.[1] Even if we do not accept his explicit and totalizing Marxist philosophy of history as our 'interpretive code', Jameson's reservations about the modes of analysis operative in lyric poetry are valid when considering the scholarship on Hellenistic genres.

Unlike the novel, most ancient poetic genres are no longer being written; they originated in oral performance (epic, lyric, and choral drama); they have historically agreed upon exemplars and trajectories; and their modes of analysis often leave their textual subjects distanced from a wider social and political discourse about the value/meaning of literary production that Jameson would embrace. Although New Historicism has provided mechanisms for analysing genres as embedded in and thus capable of dialogic engagement within ancient socio-political frameworks,[2] critical work on Hellenistic poetry has, in the main, continued along formalist lines of criticism and, even more than that of archaic and classical genres, would appear to fall outside of the parameters that might qualify it for 'strong' analyses.

Modern critics still tend to identify Hellenistic genres with exclusivity, ambiguity, and learned allusion. This habit of mind has led to a generation focused on 'tradition' versus 'originality', whose interpretive tool of choice has been intertextuality, the exploration of the ways in which verbal imitation of the products of earlier literary ages (Homer, lyric, tragedy, comedy) have been repurposed and combined by subsequent poets. While, in principle, intertextual analysis could yield 'strong' readings or dialogic engagement with earlier forms, in practice it has led to the privileging of what came before, enabling scholars to concentrate on a slender range of familiar texts (especially Homer) and to adduce differences in genre, meter, and dialect without contextualizing the reason for this apparently obsessive desire for *aemulatio* or *variatio*. Belatedness hovers over the whole enterprise, as if having literary predecessors necessarily reduced the creative juices and consigned this later poetic practice to a second-tier status. Of course, it is possible to construe this critical stance as a conscious rejection of engagement with the political, in reaction to those scholars who read the poets of Hellenistic courts as panderers to power, a viewpoint that was obviously conditioned by the cooptation of creative art and artists by Fascist and Communist regimes of the last century. But neither the aesthetic retreat from nor the unexamined disdain for the politics of Hellenistic poetry much advances our understanding of their creative moment.

If we do not want to pre-judge Hellenistic genres before we begin, it is necessary to find an approach outside of the parameters of current discourse that allows us to assess the traditional forms in which these poets wrote and the new forms that they devised within their contemporary culture. Caroline Levine's recent critical study, *Forms: Whole, Rhythms, Hierarchy, Network*, deliberately sets out to bridge formalist/ historicist/ Marxist gaps by juxtaposing formal elements of the literary imaginary with formal elements found in human social constructs and in the natural order and thus focusing on their similarities. Her overarching category of 'forms', she tells us, can 'constrain', 'differ', 'overlap and interact', 'travel' and 'do political work in particular historical circumstances'.[3] More importantly she turns to the concept of 'affordances' borrowed from design theory to articulate the variety of unexpected results that various formal constraints enable.[4] In her final chapter she analyses *The Wire*, a television series in which 'a great many social, political, natural, and aesthetic forms encounter one another'. This holistic analysis of how forms collide provides a discursive model applicable not simply to texts but to the contexts in which Hellenistic poetry evolved.[5]

In what follows I have borrowed from her articulation of a 'new formalism' in a deliberately schematic way to explore three different aspects of the intersection of the political and the aesthetic in Hellenistic poetry: (1) the physical reification of genres that resulted from an imperial decision to create the Alexandrian library, a space where scholars determined the generic representatives of the archaic and classical poetry that we have inherited; (2) the literary categories in which the Hellenistic poets composed; and (3) the role of Wilhelm Kroll's assessment of Hellenistic genres as *Kreuzung der Gattungen*. Hellenistic poetic composition was a matter of contemporary practice, while the activities of the library and Kroll's verdict were acts of reception: Hellenistic reception of an archaic and classical past and an early twentieth-century reception, in turn, of Hellenistic poetry as occupying a transitional space between the poetic production of Classical Greece and of Augustan Rome. These activities are not innocent of each other; the practice of organizing and cataloguing previous Greek literary texts influenced the compositional strategies of Hellenistic poets, and what they produced in turn prompted Kroll's choice of an interpretive model, namely that of Gregor Mendel's experiments with hybridizing plants, in modern terms 'cross-pollination'. The effect of these two discrete receptions, ancient and modern, has been to overshadow the creative imaginary that was Hellenistic poetic production as a space in which social, political, and aesthetic values converged.

Hierarchy

> Hierarchies arrange bodies, things, and ideas according to levels of power or importance. Hierarchies rank – organizing experience into asymmetrical, discriminatory, often deeply unjust arrangements.
>
> Levine 2015: 82

Before turning principally to the poets of early Alexandria, I want to consider the critical assumptions about ancient genres that condition our understanding of Hellenistic practice. Within the mainstream of modern classical studies genres that are formed in oral and performance practices are privileged over those that come to be written, with the result that a focus on formal features of performance (or the lack thereof) occludes what may be important social and political continuities between earlier poetry and what the Hellenistic poets choose to compose. This is not to dismiss the necessary role that genres and their specific conventions played in encoding a set of communal expectations, so much as to argue for a greater flexibility in thinking about generic practices and to make allowances for what has not survived. This last is a particularly pernicious problem, since our literary data sets have significant lacunae for most of the ancient Greek-speaking world between the seventh and fourth centuries BC. Even when we seem to be on more solid ground, in talking about lyric, de facto, we are talking about the nine poets canonized during the Hellenistic period – Sappho, Alcaeus, Alcman, Stesichorus, Ibycus, Pindar, Bacchylides, Simonides and Anacreon. For only one of these – Pindar – have more than a handful of poems survived intact, and we do not know if his production is typical or unique. It is also is wise to remember that 'Sappho' and even 'Pindar' have been constructed from ancient and modern critical judgements.[6]

What has survived of poetry originally intended for performance represents a fraction of what must have actually existed. The loss is especially significant for understanding regional poetics outside of a few places, most obviously Athens. For Hellenistic poets this has created a significant obstacle to evaluating their relationship to their immediate poetic predecessors, since none of these poets were Athenian, and most came from Ionic or Doric speaking regions whose local traditions are now lost. For example, in 'T. S. Eliot and the Alexandrians' Paul MacKendrick, remarking on what he calls the 'cultivated pedantry' of the Alexandrian poets, states that they 'wrote in the broad Doric of the choruses of tragedy or Alcman's lyrics, as distant from them in time as Pope from Chaucer'.[7] It is easy to arrive at this verdict if you overlook historical specificity. Callimachus was Cyrenean, a very old Doric-speaking city that traced its origins to Sparta. Theocritus was from Syracuse, also Doric speaking. A high proportion of the

Greek immigrants to Alexandria were Doric speaking. Dismissing these dialect choices as archaic imitation or gratuitous displays of recherché learning actually obscures important Hellenistic contexts. In fact, the use of Doric seems occasionally to have been a consciously political act since the Ptolemies prided themselves on a Macedonian heritage that could be marked by elements of a Doric dialect.[8]

Plato began a trend that relegated musical practices in his own and, de facto, later times to a second-tier status. In the *Laws*, his Athenian interlocutor famously argues:

> [In the good old days] our music was divided into its own various genres and types (διῃρημένη ... κατὰ εἴδη τε ἑαυτῆς ἄττα καὶ σχήματα): and one form of song was prayers to the gods, they were called 'hymns' by name; and the opposite of this was another form of song – and someone might call them 'lamentations' – and paeans were another ... In this way they also arranged these and others; and it was impermissible to blend one form of song with another (τούτων δὴ διατεταγμένων καὶ ἄλλων τινῶν οὐκ ἐξῆν ἄλλῳ εἰς ἄλλο καταχρῆσθαι μέλους εἶδος.) ... Later, poets were introducers of unmusical lawlessness (τῆς ἀμούσου παρανομίας); ... gripped by the pleasure principle, they blended (κατεχόμενοι ὑφ' ἡδονῆς κεραννύντες) lamentations with hymns and paeans with dithyrambs, imitating tunes for the *aulos* with those for the *kithara*, and mixing all kinds together (πάντα εἰς πάντα ξυνάγοντες).[9]

Plato's concerns are with poets who innovate on supposedly traditional forms by importing melodies and rhythms associated with one generic type into another. In inveighing against this compositional practice he creates the impression (dubious at best) that at one time 'pure' generic forms did exist. Moreover, in this often-quoted passage his notion of genre is formal; he expresses no views on thematic or other stylistic considerations that might be relevant. Elsewhere he singles out various moments in epic and drama that are not suitable for imitation on moral grounds, but those are complaints not about genre, but mimesis. It is obvious from these animadversions in the *Laws* that poets did not share his reservations about generic purity, namely that each genre had a 'correct' musical form. This is confirmed by what survives of late fifth- and fourth-century lyric, in which considerable formal (modal, linguistic, and stylistic) experimentation was taking place, not coincidentally because performance was moving toward professional musicians who performed at much higher technical levels than traditional citizen choruses.[10]

If Plato made poetic genres conform to his theory of forms, Aristotle promoted a biological theory of genres, of growth, maturity and decay that has proven seductive for modern critics, particularly when writing about the Hellenistic period. But neither Plato nor Aristotle was engaged in purely aesthetic or poetological debates. In essence theirs was a competition for who should best advise the polis: the poet or the philosopher.[11] The difference between the two perspectives is crucial – poets were employed or commissioned by the tyrant or the polis to write for choruses and public performance on a regular basis. What they wrote necessarily encoded the values of the society in which they performed, and formal and stylistic changes in what they wrote over time both influenced and reacted to contemporary circumstances. Philosophers could at leisure analyse and critique, but theirs was a retrospective project. As Glenn Most has observed, Aristotle's *Poetics* divorced tragedy from its ritual and political contexts in creating a universalized definition of the 'tragic', which in turn has influenced modern reception of the ancient genre.[12] This kind of philosophical analysis reifies one kind of model – of growth, perfection and decay – to the exclusion of others; but equally it may encourage an essentialist theory of genre, as each form must be a separate and identifiable species.

Theorists of classical genres focus on performance and performance traditions, because so much of what survives from the archaic through the classical period (seventh to fourth centuries BC) depended on polis-sponsored events, such as Athenian tragedy and comedy; or hymns, dithyrambs and paean choruses either within the city state or sponsored by the city state for performance at Panhellenic shrines like Delos or Delphi. In contrast, criticism of Hellenistic poetic practice has been systematically uncoupled from performance. Genres born in performance and cult are now viewed as exclusively 'literary', mannered and etiolated experiments at the end of a tradition. Despite attempts like that of Alan Cameron to argue for a multitude of venues (some new, others traditional) where works of Hellenistic poets continued to be performed – they continue to be regarded as poets of the book, for whom writing bore a closer analogy to a laboratory experiment than lived practice. This is an argument still current: Stephanie Ann Frampton writes recently in *Eidolon*:

> Within a generation or two of its founding, the Library was firmly established as a stage for recherché learning in the face of expanding koine; famously the home of 'cloistered bookworms in the chicken-coop of the Muses' (in Robert Barnes' now lapidary rendering of Timon of Phlius, Diels Frag. 12), the library was, as Peter Bing writes, an 'instrument that facilitated the emergence of a privileged circle of learned readers – a tiny elite, to be sure'.[13]

The Hellenistic poets undoubtedly wrote at a moment of transition between performance as the primary mode of poetic dissemination and the enticements and/or opportunities of greater permanence that writing and the library presented, but performance did not end. In respect to poetic production and practices, early Hellenistic courts functioned analogously to earlier tyrants' courts and to city-states. The crown not only supported poets, but festivals proliferated to which poetic events were attached.[14] The Ptolemies actively supported dramatic production, and several of the playwrights who constituted the so-called Pleiad were connected to the Alexandrian library.[15] Callimachus wrote the majority of his poems in well-established genres – hymns, paeans, epinicia, threnody, iambic – and all of them could have been performed within venues supported by the Ptolemaic court.[16] Theocritus wrote hymns, encomia and epithalamia, and may have composed for competition.[17] How we think of these particular exempla depends on how we construct their relationship to earlier genres. Do we consider them part of an organic continuum of poetic growth and transformation, particularly as it accommodates itself to the lack of a citizen chorus? Or do we regard these poets as altogether different, retreating from the public functions of the poetry that had preceded them as they continued to compose in now outmoded forms and only for 'a privileged circle of learned readers'?

The unspoken assumption of this latter reception, originating in the nineteenth century, is that the literature produced within a democratic Athens is inevitably superior to that of an imperial court (the same problem, of course, obtains for Roman poetry[18]). As a result the products of what is imagined to be a pure Greek culture must be superior to whatever a Hellenistic age could produce. Johann Gustav Droysen is usually invoked as the first to render this crucial verdict on the Hellenistic age.[19] For him Alexander brought about a new world in which Greek culture was disseminated (and diluted) by virtue of his conquest of the eastern Mediterranean. But for Droysen the resulting *Mischkultur*, in true Hegelian fashion, led to a religious syncretism from which grew the positive formation of Christianity. Quite clearly related to the notion of *Mischkultur*, is the important formulation of the classical scholar, Wilhelm Kroll, who argued that Hellenistic poetic genres were the result of *Kreuzung der Gattungen*. The connotations of the German word ranges from 'contamination' to 'blending', with inevitable consequences for reception. For a century Hellenistic poetic genres (*Gattungen*) have been regarded as the product of *Kreuzung* – either an unconscious promiscuity that resulted from the *Mischkultur* of Alexandrian Egypt or deliberate, bookish experimentation, as this new breed of scholar poet, like Mendel in his laboratory, spliced and diced the generic genome to produce new forms.[20] Instead of viewing these generic transformations as normal, if not inevitable once writing became more embedded in Greek culture, as affordances of greater generic potential, the scholarly embrace of *Kreuzung* in tandem with Plato and Aristotle's reification of forms, have stripped Hellenistic genres of their vitality and consigned them to 'the chicken coop of the Muses'.

Bounded Wholes

> This chapter takes its lead from the long traditions of thought that seek to link aesthetic, philosophical, and political domains by way of the bounded whole.
>
> Levine, Forms, p. 27

Genres are bounded wholes, containers that can be both constraining and enabling. As it happens, the act of placing something within a container is a literal description of the cataloguing work of the Alexandrian scholars, whose decisions both constrained and enabled the Greek generic forms that were transmitted to future generations. The newly acquired lyric poem must first have been identified by author – not always a transparent task when external tags (σίλλυβοι) were frequently lost – and deposited accordingly into the appropriate container, an upright hollowed cylinder, a κιβωτός (*capsa*, in Latin) or book box. In this environment, the impulse to connect texts with an author guaranteed survival; rolls of anonymous lyrics have not come down to us. Next, each poet's works must then have been sorted into genres, e.g., hymn, dithyramb, paean, threnody, epinician, epithalamium. Sorting was based, probably in the first instance, on formal criteria (e.g., metre, dialect, syntax), but topical criteria were also invoked, e.g., whether a poem was for Apollo (paean) or Dionysus (dithyramb). Disputed cases illustrate the process: Callimachus and Aristarchus disagreed over the genre of Bacchylides 23: the former opting for paean on the grounds that it contained the paean refrain, which would seem to be a formal criterion; the latter thought it a dithyramb on the basis of narrative content.[21] Inevitably, the process of cataloging necessitated decisions that have had consequences for later generic theorists.[22]

These scholars and their numerous minions who read aloud, copied and did the grunt work of moving and storing rolls[23] engaged in their tasks because of a political act, and an act that was very much a product of a *Mischkultur*. The first Ptolemy, who at the death of Alexander gained control of Egypt, established a line of kings and queens that lasted three hundred years. He did not succeed by happenstance so much as by a strategic set of decisions that allowed him to pose as pharaoh in the traditions of old Egypt as well as a monarch in the mode of the kings of Macedon or the tyrants of Sicily. Ptolemy began his rule in Memphis, the capital of old Egypt where the high priesthoods of Ptah were particularly instrumental in extending his power. When his court moved formally to the newly established city of Alexandria, probably around 312 BC, the city itself was in the process of being built. Among its earliest establishments was a library, to which the crown attracted individuals who acted collectively to acquire and organize the production of earlier Greek writers.

The *Letter of Aristeas* credits Demetrius of Phaleron with being instrumental in the Library's establishment[24] and classical scholars have long cited Aristotle's library and the influence of the Peripatetic school of philosophy as the model that the Ptolemies followed.[25] But as Kim Ryholt has observed:

> The inspiration for [the library's] creation is usually sought in the Greek world and there alone. There is, however, very limited evidence of institutional libraries in the Greek world before the Hellenistic era. By contrast, Egypt had a millennia-long tradition of temple libraries, and one that is well documented.[26]

He refers to the Houses of Books associated with the great Egyptian temples, one of which was in Memphis. Within these establishments Egyptian scholar-priests copied, annotated, commented on, and preserved a wide variety of texts. The Alexandrian library bears an uncanny resemblance to these local structures. In its creation it served several agendas: as a visible repository of earlier Greek literature it could be a source of pride and familiarity for Greeks who migrated to an alien place; it could attract leading artists from around the Mediterranean; it could send a signal to Egyptian elites that Ptolemy was operating as a pharaoh by building a familiar type of establishment within his new capital city; and finally it was an act of cultural imperialism. An anecdote now recorded in Galen makes this clear: Ptolemy III supposedly set out to acquire copies of the most famous and idiosyncratic literary products of Athens, their dramas, official copies of which were kept by the state. Ptolemy arranged for the rolls to be sent to Alexandria to be copied, posting ten talents as bond. In the event, he kept the originals and forfeited the money.[27]

The story is improbable; it would have been cheaper than ten talents to copy the plays in Athens, but it does send a signal that literary supremacy had passed from one city to another. A similar point is made in one of the recently discovered epigrams of Posidippus: a lyre, carried by a dolphin, migrates to Alexandria to be dedicated in Arsinoe's temple.

> To you, Arsinoe, this lyre, which was made to sing
>   by the poet's hand, a dolphin like Arion's
> brought to you from the wave . . . crossing the high sea . . .
>   with the voice of a nightingale.
> Accept this dedication, Brother-loving one
>   as an offering of the temple-guardian.[28]

Arion of Lesbos was a famous archaic poet said to have been the inventor of the dithyramb and also of tragedy. According to legend, he was saved by a dolphin from death at the hands of pirates and deposited on the shores of Corinth where he graced the court of the local tyrant, Periander, with his music.[29] The lyre carried by a dolphin evokes this past world of lyric poetry. Its migration to a new location in Alexandria and at a temple of Arsinoe II indicates a very early awareness of the Ptolemies' sponsorship of the arts. It is also possible to infer from the object (a lyre) that Posidippus has in mind a living lyric tradition migrating to the court, not exclusively earlier lyric texts destined for inclusion in the new library.

Rhythms

> One the one hand . . . historically minded critics recognize and appreciate the artifices of periodization; on the other, they not only depend on conventional period categories, but explicitly reinforce them.
>
> Levine, Forms, p. 55

Greek performative genres are first visible from the end of eighth century BC. Their emergence coincides with the rise of city-states, hero cult, the widespread worship of the Olympic pantheon headed by Zeus as divine king, the Delphic oracle, and the Olympic games. While Greece never formally unified, these commonalities, reinforced by language, conferred a sense of cultural identity that remained more or less intact until the conquest of Alexander in the late fourth century BC (332–323).[30] The poetry of Homer and Hesiod is thought to have been significant in transmitting these values throughout Greek speaking poleis.[31] But the political organization of the post-Alexander world was no longer that of the small city-state: it was characterized by the rise of a few monarchies centered in non-Greek lands. The kingdom of the Ptolemies, for example, was located in the new city of Alexandria, and its residents were drawn from a variety of both Greek and non-Greek places. In this world the Homeric poems held sway within the educational system, but their heroic codes in service of a war of Greeks against Trojans (non-Greeks) were less relevant in a world of empires, mercenary soldiers, and proxy wars. For this new world Apollonius composed an epic that now occupies a secure place in the canon between Homer and Vergil. The *Argonautica*, as much as Vergil's *Aeneid*, is a generic response to its precursors as well as an adaptation of the epic form to a new political environment. Apollonius' Argonauts, who are a collection of young adventurers from diverse Greek cities, circumnavigate the whole of the Greek *oecumene* as it was known in 240 BC, travelling from west to east in books 1–2, then north to south in book 4; as they do so, they reprise at various moments the route of Xenophon's Ten Thousand, but in reverse (book 2), that of Odysseus through western Italy and Sicily (book 4), and that of Pindar's Argonauts in *Pythian* 4 through Libya (also book 4).[32] In contrast to the Homeric poems, the *Argonautica* constructs itself as a pre-Iliadic narrative of the events that inevitably led to the post-Iliadic Greek settlement of Libya in North Africa (and by extension, Alexandria).

The story of Jason and the Argonauts, already recounted in Pindar and Herodotus, belonged to the foundation myth of Cyrene.[33] Apollonius tells this story at the end of book 4, when the *Argo* and its crew are stranded in the Syrtes of Libya. As they carry the *Argo* for twelve days across the marshes to the sea, they encounter Triton, who gives them a clod of Libyan soil and a prophecy. They are to throw the clod into the sea and from it will arise an island. In the fullness of time, their descendants will, from this island, migrate (that is, return) to North Africa. The clod itself, a piece of the North African littoral, is a promise to future generations of Greeks of their entitlement to this land.[34] The dynamics of the *Argonautica* reflect the world of the Ptolemies at the same time that they undermine the values of the Homeric past. Jason and his crew behave like Alexander's quarrelsome generals on the one hand and like the displaced mercenaries of Xenophon's *Anabasis* on the other.[35] There is no secure Hellenic centre to their world or homelands on behalf of which they fight. When battles do occur, they are confusing and pointless: in contiguous sequences the Argonauts engage in mutual slaughter with their hosts, the Doliones, as a result of mistaken identity, then with the Bebrycians after Polydeuces had dispatched their king Amycus in a boxing match.[36] These Homerically marked moments in Apollonius' epic consistently call into question the values of his predecessor at the same time that his characters serve notice on the emerging empire of the Ptolemies. All of them carry baggage from the classical past that they will not escape, and thus serve as object lessons, or perhaps omens of the dangers that could await the new regime of the Ptolemies.[37]

Callimachus' hymns have a similar dynamic as they adumbrate a future that is post Panhellenic, not just in values, but also in location. Four of Callimachus' hymns are in dactylic hexameter and clearly share space with the Homeric hymns in form and content. Within them he constructs a new divine world order for the Ptolemies. In his first hymn, Zeus, who is born in Greek Arcadia, is moved over the course of the poem to Alexandria, where he is heralded as the divine avatar of Ptolemy.[38] In the *Hymn to Apollo*, who sits at the right hand of Zeus, Callimachus interweaves an aesthetic manifesto with praise for the patron deity of his ancestral city of Cyrene (in North Africa); Apollo disdains impurity in all of its forms, especially poetry.[39]

Callimachus treats the twin children of Leto and Zeus respectively in his Artemis and Delos hymns: the former ends with the establishment of the cult of Artemis at Ephesus, a location that was renamed in honour of Arsinoe II (the daughter of Ptolemy I) by her first husband, Lysimachus of Thrace. The Delos hymn ends with the establishment of Apollo's cult on Delos, a location central to Ptolemaic interests, and a praise of Ptolemy II for his defeat of the Gauls.[40] In these two hymns Zeus embraces Artemis and Apollo and their mother, Leto, at the expense of his wife Hera.[41] Thus Callimachus tacitly constructs a new divine family – Zeus, Leto, Artemis and Apollo – who mirror historical circumstance: Ptolemy I put aside his first wife Arsinoe I in favor Berenice I.[42] But more importantly, it reformed the old Panhellenic order: in the Zeus hymn, for example, the old center of Greece (Delphi) is relocated to Crete[43] and Hera and Ares (so divisive in the Homeric poems) are displaced in favour of divinities imagined as presiding over civic order, healing and the arts.[44] In this way Callimachus mirrors Posidippus' epigrams on the new aesthetics and expectations for the Ptolemaic court.[45]

If Apollonius' *Argonautica* and Callimachus' *Hymns* work within and against earlier poetic genres, Theocritus' pastoral poetry stands at the beginning of a new one. 'Pastoral' now refers to a generic form with a long historical tradition. It may also refer to a cluster of formal features: shepherds and the like who, within a fecund landscape (the so-called *locus amoenus*), engage in song, usually to cure the pangs of unrequited love. This latter pastoral incorporates a set of dependable binaries: rural and urban; simplicity and sophistication; innocence and decadence that have been deployed across other genres including drama and the novel. Pastoral is today used even more broadly to include 'any literature that describes the country with an implicit or explicit contrast to the urban'.[46] Theocritus heads the tradition, with his series of short hexameter poems, now called idylls. But however rustic their *mise en scène*, his poems are sophisticated and urbane productions – a seeming contradiction that lies at the heart of pastoral and continues to colour its reception. Vergil in his rereading of these poems is generally credited with the next phase – the explicit contrast of the rural with the urban – and with it the sensibility that the former was threatened by the latter. If pastoral could idealize country life as either a critique of or escape from the decadence of urban life, the apparent mannerism of its conventions has led to charges of emotional vacuity and posturing. But it has also joined common cause with ecocriticism, as scholars look to literature to understand the complexity of human connections to natural world. Theocritus' oeuvre partakes of this concern.

In addition to the poems that Theocritus characterizes as βουκολιάζειν, what are now the canonized elements of pastoral surface in more than one of his non-bucolic works. In particular they are connected to his poems on the Ptolemies: *Idyll* 15, an urban mime centred in early Alexandria that features an Adonis festival sponsored by the queen (Arsinoe II), and *Idyll* 17, an encomium of Ptolemy II Philadelphus. In both of these idylls, the ripeness of nature (sans shepherds) is linked to the virtues of the good ruler, an association that is inverted in *Idyll* 16, for Hiero II of Syracuse, a ruler whose landscape has been devastated by war. Taken together these poems suggest that pastoral at its inception was not a poetry of nostalgia or of escape from urban decadence,[47] so much as part of an exploration of the relationship of the ruler to the prosperity of the natural order, an order that, not coincidentally, is linked to the writing of poetry:[48]

> Countless lands and their countless tribes of men,
> aided by the rain of Zeus, bring their crops to ripeness,
> but none produces as much as the Egyptian fields do
> when the Nile inundates and breaks up the soil,
> and none has as many towns with skilled mortals.
> ... In peace his people ply their trades.
> ... No foe comes by land having to raise the battle cry
> in villages not his own, no foe leaps from his swift ship
> onto the shore and harries with armed violence the herds of Egypt.
> So great a man is enthroned on those broad plains,
> ... fair-haired Ptolemy.
> No man comes to the sacred contests of Dionysus
> knowing how to lift up his clear sounding song without receiving a gift
> worthy of his craft. And the interpreters of the Muses
> sing of Ptolemy in exchange for his benefaction.
>
> *17.77–81, 97–103, 112–116*

Affordances

> To capture the complex operations of social and literary forms, I borrow the concept of affordances from design theory ... a term used to describe the potential uses or actions latent in materials and designs.
>
> *Levine, Forms, p. 6*

If the activities of the Alexandrian Library led to the canonization of genres, the need to organize individual poems into larger units afforded the invention of the poetry book. As Alessandro Barchiesi has pointed out, the very act of organizing, for example, Pindar's discrete epinicia on Olympian victories into a roll was to privilege the first poem and to invite the reader (subconsciously or otherwise) to invest the whole with meanings that flowed from the contrasts and juxtapositions of the sequencing of individual odes.[49] The recently discovered roll of epigrams by Posidippus of Pella makes clear that the narrative potential resulting from arrangement and enjambment of shorter poetic texts was an early adaptation of the Alexandrian poets.[50] Posidippus' poetry book may usefully be viewed through Levine's notion of forms: epigrams are containers that constrain and enable – the discrete form of the poetic unit (whole) encapsulates a specific event that can be exploited in terms of a time frame (rhythm), political, religious, or social hierarchies (networks), at the same time that it refuses to participate in one explicit narrative. Over the course of the roll Posidippus stages the movement of valuable objects, of people, and of political power towards Alexandria, and Alexander and the Ptolemies are visible or latent in every section. Within this frame the empire of the Ptolemies, the lives of insignificant men and women, the aesthetics of the miniature, the realities of war, and human strategies to ameliorate their social conditions are given equal space, and competing priorities. Luxuries and abundance flow towards the land of the Ptolemies at the same time they reveal the danger and risk inherent in their acquisition: a war may bring luck to kings in one epigram or it may devastate a town or an individual family in another; gods may respond to prayers or humans misread their intentions; an aesthetics of realism can be introduced via a fine statue of the poet Philitas (not coincidentally the tutor of Ptolemy II) or also give us the gruesome image of skeletal man debilitated from snakebite. Precious stones flow towards the centre to delight the senses, but natural disasters may arrive as well to threaten personal and civic destruction. Previously, critics have been reluctant to impute to Hellenistic authors this blend of aesthetics and politics, but this new find requires us to acknowledge that Alexandrian poetics was, from the beginning, intimately connected to imperial power.[51]

Callimachus' *Aetia* is doubtless a related and even bolder experiment, enabled by the same principle of interlocked short narratives to confront the reader with multiple hierarchical structures, temporalities, and competing social arrangements without endorsing any one. The poem is now fragmentary, but its general contour is not in doubt: at least fifty 'explanations' (*aitia*) of social phenomena have been organized into one long elegiac poem (between 4,000 and 6,000 lines) with an underlying temporal movement from a pre-Iliadic world to contemporary Alexandria. The *Aetia* fits no generic model – it did not when it was originally written – but combines features of epigram, elegy and epic.[52] Callimachus populates his narrative(s) with several recurring characters that gave a distinctive and unHomeric shape to the Hellenic past – Minos, Heracles, Danaus and his daughters, the Argonauts; female divinities (the Muses, the Graces, Athena, Artemis, Hera and Demeter) who shift the narrative emphasis from the dynamics of war to socially constructed categories of peace. A range of historical figures from Simonides, Phalaris the tyrant of Acragas, the Olympic victors Euthymus and Euthycles, to Berenice II (Ptolemy III's queen), Conon the royal astronomer, and Callimachus himself share space with characters hovering between the mythological and the fully fictional (e.g., Molorchus who hosts Heracles at the opening of book 3; the lovers Acontius and Cydippe in book 3; and a Roman named Gaius at the end of book 4).[53] The *Aetia* does not so much explain or even interrogate social constructs (particularly rituals) as reveal their cultural contingency, at times reinforcing the viability of a convention, at times underscoring its labile quality. Explanations ranging from the aesthetic to political are scarcely extricable one from the other and at the poem's center is the variety and mutability of human social arrangements.

Two examples will illustrate this: fr. 64 Harder takes the form of a funerary epigram in which the speaker, the fifth-century Cean poet Simonides complains that his tomb in Acragas has been desecrated and implies that there will be divine retaliation for the deed.

καὶ γ]ὰρ ἐμόν κοτε σῆμα, τό μοι πρὸ πόληος ἔχ[ευ]αν
Ζῆν'] Ἀκραγαντῖνοι Ξείνι[ο]ν ἁζόμενοι,
5 ...κ]ατ' οὖν ἤρειψεν ἀνὴρ κακός, εἴ τιν' ἀκούει[ς
Φοίνικ]α πτόλιος σχέτλιον ἡγεμόνα·
πύργῳ] δ' ἐγκατέλεξεν ἐμὴν λίθον οὐδὲ τὸ γράμμα
ἠδέσθη τὸ λέγον τόν [με Λεωπρέπεος
κεῖσθαι Κήϊον ἄνδρα τὸν ἱερόν, ὅς τὰ περισσά
10 .....] μνήμην πρῶτος ὅς ἐφρασάμην,
οὐδ' ὑμέας, Πολύδευκες, ὑπέτρεσεν, οἵ με μελάθρου
μέλλοντος πίπτειν ἐκτὸς ἔθεσθέ κοτε
δαιτυμόνων ἄπο μοῦνον, ὅτε Κραννώνιος αἰαῖ
ὤλισθεν μεγάλους οἶκος ἐπὶ Σκοπάδας.

For once my grave, which the people of Acragas, in reverence for Zeus who honors strangers, built outside the town, an evil man tore down. .if you have heard of a certain Phoenix, the town's merciless leader. He built my tombstone into the tower of the city walls and showed no regard for the inscription which said that I, the son of Leoprepes, was lying here, the holy man from Ceos, who first devised the extra [letters] ... and the art of remembering. He did not tremble at your example, Polydeuces, who, when the roof beam was about to collapse, once set me outside, the only one from among the guests, when – alas! – the Crannonian house fell on the mighty sons of Scopas.

On the surface the poet's *cri de coeur* would seem to be an indictment of the desecration of his tomb, but it also exposes the limits of human memory and its failings. Despite the fact that Simonides invented a technique for retaining facts, the preservation of his own memory depends on inscriptions on stone, which in turn require continuing existence and suitable placement to be efficacious. While the poet deplores Phoenix's actions, it was no doubt undertaken as part of the city's needs for safety; the verb Callimachus uses (ἐγκατέλεξεν) occurs earlier in Thucydides to describe Themistocles' rapid fortification of Athens that sometimes appropriated grave stelae (1.93.2). Finally, Simonides recalls an incident in his own poetic past in which the Dioscuri (Castor and Polydeuces) avenged an insult ostensibly to the poet. The Scopadae had refused to pay Simonides for an epinician because he devoted too much of his poetic text to praising the Dioscuri. Later when the Scopadae were hosting a banquet, one of the Dioscuri summoned Simonides from the hall immediately before it collapsed and killed those within.[54] But the anecdote might as easily be construed as the Dioscuri avenging the insult to themselves, thus calling into question the poet's expectation of privileged status.

Fr. 178 Harder, in which Callimachus describes a banquet that he attended in Alexandria, exposes similar lines of tension.[55]

Ἰκαρίου καὶ παιδὸς ἄγων ἐτέτειον ἁγιστύν,
Ἀτθίσιν οἰκτίστη, σὸν φάος, Ἠριγόνη,

```
5   ἐς δαίτην ἐκάλεσσεν ὁμηθέας, ἐν δέ νυ τοῖσι
    ξεῖνον ὃς Α[ἰ]γύπτῳ καινὸς ἀνεστρέφετο
    μεμβλωκὼς ἴδιόν τι κατὰ χρέος· ἦν δὲ γενέθλην
    Ἴκιος, ᾧ ξυνὴν εἶχον ἐγὼ κλισίην
    οὐκ ἐπιτάξ, ἀλλ' αἶνος Ὁμηρικός, αἰὲν ὁμοῖον
10  ὡς θεός, οὐ ψευδής, ἐς τὸν ὁμοῖον ἄγει.
    καὶ γὰρ ὁ Θρηϊκίην μὲν ἀπέστυγε χανδὸν ἄμυστιν
    ζωροποτεῖν, ὀλίγῳ δ' ἥδετο κισσυβίῳ.
    τῷ μὲν ἐγὼ τάδ' ἔλεξα περιστείχοντος ἀλείσου
    τὸ τρίτον, εὖτ' ἐδάην οὔνομα καὶ γενεήν·
15  'ἦ μάλ' ἔπος τόδ' ἀληθές, ὅ τ' οὐ μόνον ὕδατος αἶσαν,
    ἀλλ' ἔτι καὶ λέσχης οἶνος ἔχειν ἐθέλει.'
```

While celebrating the yearly festival of Icarius' child – your day, Erigone, most pitiable to Attic women – he invited congenial friends to the feast, and now among them a stranger who had recently taken up residence in Egypt, where he had come on some personal business. He was by birth an Ician, and with him I shared a couch – not by pre-arrangement: rather the Homeric proverb is not false, that the god always leads like to like. For he too hated to drink unmixed wine with his mouth wide open in large Thracian gulps, but enjoyed the small cup. As the beaker was going around for a third time, I said these things to him, after I had learned his name and birth: 'The saying is very true that wine needs to have a share not just of water, but also of conversation.'

The Athenian (Pollis), now resident in Egypt, has invited friends to celebrate an Attic festival of Dionysus, called the Aiora or 'Swing Festival'.[56] At once this incident portrays the cultural diversity of Alexandria as an Athenian, Cyrenean, and Ician immigrant all attending the same party; it provides a vignette of an ex-pat's nostalgia, since the Attic festival could only have been a private reminiscence not a state-sponsored event; and as such it calls into question the role of the cults of old Athens in this non-Attic place. The displacement of Pollis and his desire for familiar rituals sets out the circumstances of the Alexandrian immigrant in microcosm. They were far from their native cities and Alexandrian festivals were celebrations of the Ptolemaic state, not the familiar gods of the homeland. The oddity of Pollis' party is underscored by the calculated evocation of Plato's *Symposium*: as the guests recline, Callimachus turns to his couch mate, a man from the island of Icus, and dismisses deep drinking in favour of conversation.[57] But in the *Symposium* Agathon is celebrating his tragic victory with fellow Athenian citizens at an annual civic festival (the Lenaia); what Pollis celebrates has no civic status and the diverse ethnicities of his guests would suggest that they were unfamiliar with Attic rites.[58] Thus the local irrelevance of Pollis' celebration of Dionysus contrasts implicitly with the cultural embeddedness of Plato's gathering.

The Athenian Aiora commemorated Dionysus' gift of wine to the Athenians. According to the legend, Dionysus first revealed its power to Icarius, who shared its potency with friends. When they become intoxicated, imagining themselves to have been poisoned, they killed Icarius and buried his body secretly. His daughter Erigone, accompanied by her dog, Maera, searched for Icarius and, when she discovered his body, hanged herself on a nearby tree. Subsequently, the gods translate Erigone, Icarius, and her dog into constellations.[59] For denizens of Ptolemaic Egypt the Greek story would have borne an uncanny resemblance to an Egyptian rite celebrated as part of the festival of Isis, namely, the mourning for Osiris.[60] After his death at the hands of his brother Seth, his wife Isis searched for him accompanied by the jackal-headed divinity Anubis. Isis and Anubis subsequently became constellations. Does Callimachus' choice of a ritual with such narrative parallels destabilize the categories of Greek and non-Greek? Or does it imply some kinship between the Attic rite and local Egyptian behaviours? Or is this a reflection upon historical circumstance, in that the Ptolemies encouraged Greek migrants like Pollis at the same time that they publicly supported Egyptian cults?

In the novelty of these generic experiments Posidippus and Callimachus both anticipate features of *The Wire*, an American television series that ran from 2002 to 2008, to become the darling of literary critics.[61] Situated in the eastern port city of Baltimore, individual episodes of the series were focalized through the local government, the illegal drug trade, the port, the school system and the media. A recurring set of characters notionally linked the episodes, but the real focus was on the shifting perspectives and colliding hierarchies as experienced by those who control, connive at, or are victims of the system(s). *The Wire* is generically Protean, and its salient features are prefigured in these Hellenistic formal experiments. At its (or their) core are the affordances that result from generic experimentation: as Levine writes about *The Wire*: 'by shifting its focus from the power of individuals or elite groups to the intricate "political ecology" of a whole world of contending forms, *The Wire* allows us to see networks as linking other forms, but also derailing them and being derailed by them.'[62]

Conclusion

The Hellenistic monarchies were social experiments that differed from the traditional Greek city-state. The power of the throne, especially in Alexandria, encouraged literary enterprise by building a library (no doubt, for its own self-aggrandizement) and by motivating poets to migrate to the city. As a result of the library archaic and classical poetic genres took on the form that modern scholars have inherited. Within this new environment poets were, as I have argued, not anxious imitators of past literary glories but early adapters to their new political space. Within that space we can see them composing within the confines of inherited genres, should they prove useful (epic, hymn, iambic), reconfiguring genres to meet contemporary circumstances (paean and epinician, now written in elegiac metres), inventing entirely new genres (pastoral), and experimenting to overcome the narrative limitations of the familiar forms of elegy and epigram (Posidippus, Callimachus' *Aetia*). Whether composing within or outside of inherited genres theirs is a new poetics that uses the artifice and expectations of genre not so much to imitate the past but to explore the distinctive 'political ecology' in which they found themselves, with its competing ethnicities, social and religious practices, cultural baggage of old Greece, relationships to power, and (inevitably) the role(s) of the poet as artificers of memory.

Notes

1. 1981: 59–60.
2. Explicitly articulated in Dougherty and Kurke 1993 (though Jameson 1982: 26–7 would locate forms of historicism also as unaware of their own biases).
3. 2015: 4–5.
4. 2015: 6–12.
5. 2015: 132.
6. E.g., the original editors assigned POxy 2291 to Sappho; it was reassigned to Alcaeus because the apparent mention of 'dildo-receivers' (line 5: ολισβ[ο]δοκοισ) was deemed more suitable to his poetry (Alcaeus fr. 303A.5 Voigt). Ian Rutherford (2001: 237–8) argues that Bacchylides 23 is really a paean of Pindar, and see below, n. 21.
7. 1953: 8.
8. See, e.g., the exchange at Theocritus, *Id.* 15. 87–95, Posidippus, *epp.* 87–8 A-B, and the remarks of Fantuzzi and Hunter 2004: 372–7.
9. *Laws*, 700a8-e1, with omissions.
10. See, e.g, Csapo 2004, especially 245–8.
11. Plato explicitly connects degeneracy in musical practice with that of the polity (e.g., *Laws* 701). In Aristophanes' *Frogs* Dionysus brings Aeschylus back to the polis rather than Euripides because the former has supposedly given the better moral advice to the state (on the latter see now Halliwell 2011: 123–9).
12. 2000: 26. I do not mean to underestimate the importance of these philosophers' observations, but to urge scepticism in citing their opinions as evidence of contextualized generic practices.
13. *Eidolon*, 22 Dec. 2017. While not a traditional venue, Frampton's comments are valuable because they echo standard Hellenistic criticism (e.g., Peter Bing's *Well Read Muse*, whom she quotes) and are likely to have a much broader readership than peer-reviewed books and articles in the field.
14. E.g., the Ptolemaia, the Basileia, the Eleusinia, and the Arsinoeia were all celebrated in early Alexandria. The first three had poetic competitions (see Fraser 1972: 197–205).
15. Sistakou 2016: 25–30.
16. Cameron 1995: 60–103.
17. The scholiast on the now fragmentary ending of Theocritus, *Id.* 24 claims at line 171 that the poet asked for Heracles' help in granting him victory in the contest. Prima facie this suggests some sort of competition. See Cameron 1995: 54 and n. 197.
18. Barchiesi (2001: 151) describes this as bias against 'those authors [who] work for patrons, especially autocrats, not for audiences of fellow-citizens and patriots'.
19. See, e.g., Gelzer 1993: 130–1 discussing the Hellenistic as a period of literary decline. These views now associated with Droysen have their origins earlier, in the eighteenth century (Briant 2012: 3, 327–8).

20. Kroll 1924: 202–3 and see Barchiesi 2001: 146–9 on the dangers of the biological model that underpins Kroll's *Kreuzung* and the consequences for reception.
21. POxy 2368; and see Fearn 2007: 209 n.128, with the further discussion on Bacchylides 17 (pp. 210–11), and Rutherford 2001: 237–8.
22. For further examples of authorial indeterminacy see Rutherford 2001: 90–108.
23. The codex did not appear before the second century AD; therefore, all poetry possessed by the library will have been written in roll form, lengths of which varied from a few feet for a single poem up to 1,000–1,500 lines for grouped poems. The limitation of roll length is one reason why, e.g., Pindar's epinicia were grouped by Panhellenic event – it allowed for four rolls of about 1,000 lines each.
24. §§9–11. Now assigned to the second century BC, the text purports to be addressed to Philocrates and gives an account of the translation of the Septuagint into Greek under the auspices of Ptolemy II.
25. See Jacob 2013: 75 (in the same volume as Ryholt, n. 20, but with no acknowledgement of his arguments).
26. 2013: 23. The library of the Serapeum, which survived the destruction of the original Alexandrian library, is an example of such an Egyptian temple library.
27. *In Hippocratis epidemiorum* III 17A.600–8 Kuhn.
28. *Ep.* 37 Austin-Bastianini.
29. Hdt 1.23–4.
30. See above, n. 19.
31. This has been most thoroughly articulated by Gregory Nagy in numerous publications.
32. Thalmann 2011, especially chapters 4 and 7.
33. Pindar, *Pythian* 4, 5, 9 (for the kings of Cyrene) and Hdt. 4.179; see *Arg.* 4.1550–90, 1731–53).
34. See Malkin 1994: 169–81 and Calame 1990: 292–7.
35. See Mori 2008: 67–74 and Fantuzzi and Hunter 2004: 129–31.
36. *Arg.* 1.1012–78; 2.95–144.
37. Posidippus' new roll of epigrams includes a section on the reading and misreading of omens that might have served the same minatory function.
38. *HZeus* 85–90.
39. *HApollo* 2, 9–11, 105–12.
40. In Hellenistic courts defeating Gauls took on the same ideological contour that defeating Persians had had for Classical Greece (see Pausanias' long description of the Gaulish attack on Delphi, 10.19-5-23).
41. See, e.g., *HArtemis* 29–31 and *HDelos* 259.
42. He also preferred his son by Berenice (Ptolemy II) to Arsinoe I's in the succession.
43. *HZeus* 42–5.
44. *HApollo* 35–64.
45. For a detailed discussion of the Ptolemaic dimensions of Callimachus' hymns, see Stephens 2015: 14–22; 51; 108; 162.
46. Gifford 1999: 1–2.
47. Gifford 1999: 15.
48. For a fuller discussion of this dynamic see Stephens 2018: 57–84.

49. Barchiesi 2000: 171–3.
50. The initial debates about single author versus anthology have largely subsided, probably because of the convincing essays in *The New Posidippus* (2005).
51. Porter 2010b: 483–7.
52. Although Ovid imitated it in part, particularly with his interlocked tales of the *Metamorphoses* and the *Fasti*, it remains generically unique.
53. Fragments are easily accessible in Greek and English at the Dickinson Classical Commentaries *Aetia* website: http://dcc.dickinson.edu/callimachus-aetia.
54. The anecdote is alluded to in Theoc. *Id.* 16.36–45 and told by Cicero, *de Orat.* 2.86, and see Harder's commentary on the fragment (2012: 2.514–29).
55. The name of the host, according to Athenaeus 11.477C, was Pollis. We are entitled to be sceptical about it – Denis Feeney has pointed out the pun – Pollis/polis. But see Cameron 1995: 134 for a different view.
56. This has been identified with the third day of the Anthesteria. It is not clear from the fragment if they are meant to celebrate the whole festival or only this day.
57. Fr. 178.11–16 and Plato, *Sym.* 176a-e.
58. The two named are Cyrenean Callimachus and Ician Theogenes.
59. Eratosthenes of Cyrene wrote a hexameter poem on the subject (*Erigone*); see Apollodorus 3.14.7; Hyginus, *de astr.* 24, *fab.* 130.
60. We have documentary evidence that the Iseia was celebrated in early Alexandria, and a standard part of the rite was the lamentation of Isis for her missing husband Osiris (Perpillou-Thomas 1993: 94–8).
61. See Levine 2015: 166–7 for a sample of the critical responses.
62. Levine 2015: 149.

PART II
PROSE (AND SOME VERSE)

CHAPTER 5
THE POLITICS OF INFORMED FORM: PLATO AND WALTER BENJAMIN
Andrew Benjamin

Form is presentation.[1] And yet, presentation is not mere expression.[2] Presentation is informed form. While there are fundamentally different accounts of this configuration of form, all of which need to be understood, first, as differing accounts of the informing of form, and then secondly in terms of how the means of presentation are themselves conceived, the essential point is that there cannot be simple presentation. Moreover, any systematic account of presentation, which has to be understood as form's presence, needs to include within it the external registration of that presentation. Again, there cannot be pure receptivity; as though presentation simply occurs and is received as such. (Even if it were assumed, even if pure givenness were allowed, it would have been produced and thus marked by an already present form of impurity, namely the mark of that production.) That there can be the history of criticism, and thus that there has always been a recognition of the necessity for judgement (with a corresponding necessity to adduce criteria of judgement) means that when that history and the ensuing recognition are taken together, they underscore the presence of a complex reciprocity of relations defining both presentation and reception. Any one specific conception of presentation and thus equally any one specific process through which form is informed has an important effect on how that the reception of that presentation is then understood. Equally, differing positions within reception engender and attempt to sustain their own ways of understanding processes of presentation. Reciprocity, while having neither a singular designation nor an already fixed *modus operandi*, is central. Presentation and its reception, equally, reception and its own conception of presentation (thus also expression) create their own settings. This is neither to naturalize nor to historicize the reciprocity of presentation and reception. Another opening occurs. What is identified is the locus of criticism when thought philosophically. This thinking is philosophical since what is at stake is not the simple content of presentation and types of reception, but what grounds them and thus makes each one possible (a possibility with a sense of the historical that is to be differentiated from the equation of history with the chronology).

Thinking criticism philosophically creates the conditions for an investigation of the politics of form. Politics within such a formulation concerns the implicit and explicit ways that the interplay of presentation and reception are always situated. Moreover, it can never be just a politics of form as though form were a stable, already completed and determined entity. Indeed, it can be added that were form to be attributed such a quality then interpretation would be unnecessary. There is, however, a more significant consequence, namely, that the promulgation of the singular and thus already determined – form as an already given singularity – would result in the impossibility of separating interpretation and description. The suspension of the attribution to an object of an already determined quality means that any one particular is always incomplete. There is a further implication. Namely, that any particular remains open to further configurations of its work, hence any work is defined from the start in terms of a *yet-to-be-determined* quality, entails that here is only ever a politics of forming because what matters is the work's work.³ The latter, form present as forming, comprises the processes of effectuation and their reception. And yet this is a complex position. An example will make this point clearer.

Integral to Walter Benjamin's engagement with both the *Frühromantics* and Goethe, is the conception of the art work as 'criticizable'.⁴ 'Criticizability' (*Kritisierbarkeit*) becomes the term in connection with which the conceptions of presentation and modes of reception are then to be understood (understanding as criticism). At the end of Benjamin's analysis, he is able to show that neither German Romanticism, though more exactly Friedrich Schlegel and Novalis, nor Goethe, are able to develop a conception of the work of art as 'criticizable'. This is the case even though it is the demand central to Romanticism. For Benjamin, the term 'criticizable' pertains to what he describes as 'the media of forms'.⁵ In other words, it invokes a conception of form as that which is informed. The informing of form is not just a relation between the ideational and the particular. More exactly, it is a relation between between universal and particular. Equally, the informing of form is bound up with the release of meanings/interpretations. Within the language of both the *Frühromantics* and the argumentative procedures of his, Benjamin's, Dissertation on Romanticism, that release is located within and as part of the thinking of the Absolute. In that specific context form exists within the realm of the idea. However, the idea, in moving beyond its equation with beauty means that the ideational involves the complex of ideas whose conflict is the continual creation and recreation of history (again where the latter is thought philosophically). In other words, the idea loses its place within the purely 'eternal' and is incorporated within the work of history. Benjamin's writings on the *Frühromantics* are, after all, an attempt to contribute to 'the history of the concept of criticism'.⁶

Benjamin's concern therefore is the concept of criticism both as it arises within that setting and how that setting provides a particular configuration of the history of the problem of criticism. There are aspects of Benjamin's approach that are not immediately central. Nonetheless, what endures is the general supposition that 'the objects of a presentation concerned with the history of a problem are in various ways intertwined with those of the history of philosophy'.⁷ The argument has to be therefore that the conflicts that mark and define the history of philosophy continue to show themselves within the presuppositions of criticism where the latter is understood as a locus of the conceptual which is interarticulated from the start with the always already present ideational content whose work is the overdetermined relationship between matter and idea, i.e. the work's work. Overdetermination occurs because there cannot be a one-to-one correspondence between matter and idea. Ideational content cannot have a single presence. More significantly, the relation between the ideational and material presentation is the locus of contestation and argumentation. Within this setting the insistence of the Absolute as that which either has to be thought or has always already been thought unpins the interplay between criticism and philosophy.

While Benjamin's work on criticism, though more specifically the identification of 'criticizability' as criticism's condition of possibility, and thus his concern with the presentation of form are central to this engagement with the politics of form, the initial point of orientation for this project is Plato's analysis of poetry and painting as modes of presentation as they occur in the context of the *Republic*. Specifically, the argumentation as it develops in Book X. The importance of Plato for these concerns is twofold. The first is that in *Republic* Book X it is clear that form as expression – presentation as mimesis, mimesis as the process of presentation – is from the start inextricably bound up with political considerations. Hence, form as presentation cannot be separated from the political. Even though what is meant by the latter in such circumstances endures as an important question, the interweaving of form and the political means that the politics of form within Book X creates a setting that still has an important effect on contemporary encounters precisely because what arises within it is the always present connection between presentation and judgement. (Indeed, integral to the argument to be developed here is the claim that the relation between presentation and judgement circumscribes the domain in which a politics of form is to be thought.) The second reason for the importance of Plato lies in Benjamin's claim in *The Concept of Criticism in German Romanticism* that Goethe's conception of the work of art positions art as ultimately uncriticizable. For Benjamin, the refusal of the demand for criticizability occurs because of the reiterated presence in Goethe's conception of the work of art of a form of Platonism. Platonism, or at least a certain version thereof, continues to maintain a pervasive influence within the 'the history of the concept of criticism'.

It should always be remembered that Plato begins *Republic* Book X by positioning the engagement with poetry within the context of poetry's relation to the ordering of a state (*polis*). That relation is the connection to the political (the location of the *polis* – its stated presence –in a text called ΠΟΛΙΤΕΙΑ). In other words, the argument does not pertain to poetry as a form of mimetic presentation as though the latter were an end in itself. Rather, there is the necessity that a presentation should be taken up in terms as much of its reception's conditions of possibility, as it is the setting as well as the medium of its generation. As noted above, the link to the *polis* is there at the beginning. Book X opens thus:

> 'And truly,' I said, 'many other considerations assure me that we were entirely right in our organization of the state (ᾠκίζομεν τὴν πόλιν), and especially, I think, in the matter of poetry.'[8]
>
> 595A

While there are direct and contextual understandings of what is meant by the *polis* in the context of the Platonic dialogues, it can still be suggested that the term implies the necessary inscription of presentation within a domain of judgement that is not delimited strictly by individual concerns. In sum, that domain is the *polis*, in which poetry figures as a mode of presentation calling on judgement. To the extent that it is the interconnection of these elements that defines the specificity of any one of them, it can then be argued that the relationship between poetry and the political is far from arbitrary let alone forced. Indeed, it is that relationship, both its necessity and its ineliminability, that allows for the recognition of judgment's indispensability as the basis of a politics of form. There is an important addition here, namely, to posit the separation of poetry and the political is, in fact, to have forced them apart (a forcing apart which would of course have taken place in the name of another politics; hence the refusal of the political as itself naming the political).

An engagement with Plato cannot function as either a *defence* or a *critique* of any one position that might be attributed to him, when either term is used generally. It is rather that what Plato is trying to take up both in the *Republic* and other dialogues, though most particularly in the *Ion*, has a twofold quality. In the first instance, it pertains to an account of any one work's inception, which means the work's coming to presence as poetry. And therefore the coming to presence of a work as a particular. It is thus that a politics of form is always a politics of forming. What matters therefore is how poetry, as a form of presentation, as a process of invention, is understood. In the second, given that account, and within the terms set by it, what occurs is the work's reception. Developing an understanding of the latter is neither a straightforwardly historical nor sociological investigation. Rather, the question of engagement is philosophical for the precise reason that Walter Benjamin has already identified. Namely, that an engagement with a particular work is already an engagement with the particular's relation to the universal and thus – explicitly or implicitly – with the presence of both the universal and the particular. (The nature of that presence is, of course, inherently variable.) This underscores the point noted above, namely, that the issue of direct relevance for Plato is not presentation but judgement (the response to presentation). Again, what underpins the differing ways these positions unfold is that there cannot be pure particularity; the latter is the banal and unfulfillable dream of empiricism. As has been indicated, empiricism entails description not judgement. What will emerge in the *Ion*, with the move to the stated centrality of the hermeneutic, and thus with the reconfiguration of presentation, is the actual need for judgement. The move to the hermeneutic is not being adduced. On the contrary, it arises as much in response to the presence of a specific vocabulary in the text of the *Ion*, as it does in response to a genuine philosophical concern proper to Platonism itself, namely the inability of *techné* to account for the nature of work. *Techné* on its own cannot account for either the work of mimesis and or the presence of a work as a mimetic presentation. In sum, *techné* is limited to the work's actual production, it cannot account for the qualities of the work produced and thus their presence as an object of judgement.

There are a number of interrelated elements within the argumentation of Book X that are central here. Book X opens with a specific problem; namely, that a given presentation might be taken as furnishing, within and as the act of presentation, that in terms of which the presentation's judgement could be secured. This is, of course, an impossibility. Moreover, if it were taken to be the case that a simple presentation could be taken, albeit erroneously as an end-in-itself, then for Socrates, then there would need to be a specific response; a response which would undo such a possibility. For Socrates what would be needed is an 'antidote' (φάρμακον) and thus a way of undoing the immediate force of such an eventuality. While the term 'antidote' (φάρμακον) has an important history in terms of its current reception, it is nonetheless vital to underscore that what is invoked by its use here is a particular form of knowledge and thus the limitation of knowledge claims. The 'antidote' would help to secure knowing what it is that a presentation actually is. That would have been achieved by the 'antidote' having undone other possibilities.[9] Within that framework poets are included under the heading of 'all other imitators' (ἅπαντας τοὺς μιμητικούς, 595B) Knowledge functions as an 'antidote' to the extent that the true nature of the process of imitation is understood and thus the presentation can be construed as that which can be judged and thus as that which calls upon judgement. The 'antidote' therefore is intended to secure the presentation within the realm of 'criticizability'. This is the key point. Mimesis as a modality of presentation therefore has to be interpreted or understood in such a way that what appears not be conflated with what is. The move is from immediacy to mediacy. Once this position is opened up then what has to be addressed is the question of how the relationship between particular and universal is to be thought. It should always be remembered that the relationship between universal and particular, as a thinking of the Absolute, has already been given a number of important configurations within the *Republic* (and clearly elsewhere in Plato's *corpus*). The most exacting in Book X however occurs at 596A. The claim is that the 'form' or 'idea' is a type of singularity that stands opposed to a multiplicity and yet that multiplicity is comprised of particulars that have the same 'name' (ὄνομα). Hence, it is possible that there be both an 'idea' and a number of non-identical singularities, which in having the same name demand, again, that the relationship universal/singular be thought. (Its effective presence necessitates that it be thought and not simply assumed.) While the identity of a particular always needs consideration, what endures is a task that has two determining elements. The first is understanding the particular as the presentation of a specific and always already determined relation to the universal (idea/form). The second, within Plato, is the possibility of thinking the universal (form/idea) in its separation from the totality of particulars.

Consistent with the move from form to forming, thinking the relationship between universal and particular – noting in advance the generality implicit in such a project – is best approached in terms of the process of making; making as the coming to presence. (The indirect consequence is that both the necessity and the limit of *techné* are established thereby.) To return to the detail of Book X: the 'craftsman' has an eye or sight directed 'towards the idea' (πρὸς τὴν ἰδέαν, 596B). This comprises an element that is fundamental to processes of creation. The position has a certain generality. Note for example the relationship between the eye and the 'paradigm' that occurs in the *Timaeus*:

> But when the artificer (ὁ δημιουργός) of any object, in forming its shape and quality, keeps his gaze fixed on that which is uniform, using a model of this kind (παραδείγματι), that object, executed in this way, must of necessity be beautiful.[10]

The important point, in the context of the *Republic*, is that while the directed presence of the eyes occasions the production of the particular, that which enables the process to occur, namely that to which the craftsman's eye is turned, is not itself made. There is a process of creation that assumes the 'unmade'. The 'idea' was not made. (The claim is explicit: οὐ τὸ εἶδος ποιεῖ, 597A.) Understanding creation as a movement and thus as a process, and equally in order to understand the quality of the particular and thus what might be described as the particularity of the particular, it is essential to note that the way Plato's account of making occurs in Book X is via the distancing of an importantly different sense of production; a conception characterized by both reflection and immediacy, namely production as a form of mirroring.[11]

The mirror is used in order to clarify how a specific version of production is to be understood. The mirror is a mode of production. The mirror produces – or exactly reproduces – what is. With a mirror, there will be, for example, the 'swift production of the sun' (ταχὺ ... ἥλιον ποιήσεις, 596E). The mirror allows, from within a strict set of conditions, for production. Within this framework the mirror produces 'the appearance' thereby opening up as a possibility the conflation of what appears with what is. Moreover, though this is not a claim made directly by Plato, mirroring is a form of immediacy. The mirror presents immediately. And yet, the immediacy of the presentation, for Plato, stands opposed to the presentation of 'the being and truth' of what is. As suggested, immediacy has a number of defining qualities. Firstly, presentation is immediate in the sense that it occurs in the now of its happening; i.e. what occurs does so immediately. Secondly, immediacy is that which occurs both 'now' and without mediation. Immediacy, in this latter sense would be pure presence; to which it should be added that this purity is merely putative. And finally, though the position while announced will continue to be explored in greater detail, immediacy obviates the need for judgement.

In the celebrated discussion of the cabinet maker in Book X both the differing positions within production and the differing modalities of presentation occur. The passage in question is the following;

> 'What of the cabinet-maker? Were you not just now saying that he does not make the idea or form which we say is the real couch, the couch in itself, but only some particular couch?' 'Yes, I was.' 'Then if he does not make that which really is, he could not be said to make real being but something that resembles real being but is not that. If anyone should say that being in the complete sense belongs to the work of the cabinet-maker or to that of any other handicraftsman, he would run the risk of saying that which was not true (κινδυνεύει οὐκ ἂν ἀληθῆ λέγειν).'
>
> 597A

The distinctions at work in this formulation, while well-known are, nonetheless, still worth identifying. The form/idea (τὸ εἶδος) is 'the real couch'. The differentiation is not between the real and the false but between the real and the particular. The particular brings with it the problem of the possibility of its conflation with the universal and thus were that conflation not to have occurred, then what emerges is the question of how its relation to the universal is to be thought. The cabinet-maker – indeed any maker – operates on the level of particularity. The language is precise. The distinction is between ὅ ἔστι κλίνη and κλίνην τινά. Responding to Plato necessitates understanding how this distinction is set up, sustained and as importantly, the way its presence delimits a specific conception of the philosophical task. It should be clear that the problem concerns the status of the particular. The question to be addressed has specificity; it pertains to how the particular is to be thought. The presence of the particular as a given is no longer central. Givenness is the particular within the structure of empiricism. What matters now is the question of how the particularity of the particular is to be thought. Once this question orientates thought, and in the end the question of the particular becomes the one structuring the question of criticism, and furthermore, once it is conceded that the particular cannot be understood as either pure particularity, i.e. either particularity outside any relation to the universal (or idea), or as that which is 'real' – i.e. that which has the quality, in this instance, of ὅ ἔστι κλίνη, then what emerges is judgement's necessity. The reason for the necessity is clear. Judgment occurs because the particular – the particular's always specific identity – cannot yield an account of itself in terms of its own immediate presentation. Hence, judgement is the response to the question of the particularity of the particular once particularity is no longer take as an end-in-itself. This becomes the way a politics of form, at least philosophically, takes place. From another perspective, the politics of form cannot be separated from what has to be thought as the exigency of judgement; an exigency that brings both place (here the *polis*) and the conceptual into relation because judgement is bound up with the subject understood as a collectivity and not in terms of individual and individualizing acts (even though it is a subject that acts). Judgements, even knowledge claims that are in fact judgements, are situated within a form of commonality that combine communication and community (*polis*). An exigency that brings both place (here the *polis*) and the conceptual into relation.

The form/idea of the couch differs firstly from the one made by the craftsman and then secondly from the one present in the painting of the already made couch. The latter has been produced. Such couches have been made and can therefore be destroyed (unmade). They have a specific ontological status and are of necessity of finite duration. The idea of the couch, like the 'paradigm', is both ontologically and temporally distinct. Its mode of being – its ontologico-temporal quality – in the language of the *Cratylus* must be 'always the same as itself' (ἀεί ἐστιν οἷόν ἐστιν) (439D). (The adverb ἀεί identifies a temporality that cannot be delimited by a temporal scheme incorporating finite duration.) As the argumentation of Book X unfolds both the distinction and the nature of the form/idea and thus the unmade are given a quality and a location by the formulation ἡ ἐν τῇ φύσει (*Republic* 597B). The latter needs to be understood within the ontologico-temporal framework of the 'always' (ἀεί). Once other permutations of this formulation are brought to bear on this interpretation of φύσις, it then becomes clear that what occurs ἐν τῇ φύσει is marked by the necessity of singularity, production is linked to the particular, however the couch in question rather than being equated with particularity 'is itself the couch' (ὅ ἔστιν κλίνη). Two further instances of this mode of thought will clarify what is at stake.

In the *Phaedo*, in the discussion of opposites (τὸ ἐναντίον), on the level of things – the pragmatic things of the world – opposites can be, and are, generated in terms of each other.[12] However, when it is a question of the idea of the opposite – 'the opposite itself' (αὐτὸ τὸ ἐναντίον) – such a state of affairs is not possible. This impossibility has a double register. Plato adds that the impossibility of this occurring is as true 'in us' (ἐν ἡμῖν) as it is ἐν τῇ φύσει. Taken together they comprise a complex formulation. The latter is not the external world. Since clearly the locus of deeds, acts and things – πράγματα in general – and thus the place in which there is a reciprocity of opposites is in fact the world.[13] In the first instance, the impossibility in question pertains to 'us' insofar as it pertains to a specific possibility for thought. Within thought, as thought's project, it is possible to think the idea/form as a self-referring singularity; i.e. the idea itself. (In the context of Plato this is the thinking of the Absolute.) In other words, there is a necessity of direction in which what has to be thought is the idea/form in itself, and thus the object of thought is its presence as a self-referring singularity. This is, of course, the continual opening within the dialogues taken more generally. It is both the movement and the direction implicit in Socratic questioning.[14] It structures, for example, the way Socrates replies to Hippias in the *Hippias Major* concerning the distinction between 'a beautiful thing' and 'beauty'.[15] The latter is addressed as a response to the question 'what the beautiful is' (ὅ τι ἐστὶ τὸ καλόν) (287D). Hippias denies that there is a distinction between 'a beautiful thing' and 'beauty'. Socrates insists that there is one. Questioning should then lead inexorably in the direction in which the distinction can be thought, and thus to the position in which it has become possible to think 'beauty itself'. (Socratic questioning has a method, its own way of proceeding.) Hence Socrates attempts to make it clear to Hippias what is at stake in the question he has just been asked:

> He asked you not what is beautiful (οὐ τί ἐστι καλόν) but what the beautiful is (ἀλλ᾽ ὅτι ἐστὶ τὸ καλόν).

The answer to the first part of the question would be the particular. However, it is an answer that cannot address the particular other than as a mere appearance. As such it cannot account for its particularity. Within the framework of the distinction advanced within the *Hippias Major*, given that the first part of the question elicits a response to the demand to identify beautiful things, this must be held apart from the demand that beauty itself be thought. Given that there is a demand on thought that is itself determined by the specific nature of thought's object, there has to be a description of that state of affairs. It can be conjectured therefore that what φύσις designates in the context of the *Phaedo* is the being proper to 'the opposite itself' (αὐτὸ τὸ ἐναντίον), and of course, by extension, this is equally the case of other formulations in which what is stake is a self-referring singularity that is of necessity positioned outside a temporal scheme in which things come to be and then pass away; i.e. the temporality of finite duration. Hence, the use of the same formulation in the *Republic* should be interpreted in a similar way. It should be noted, in addition, that the formulation ἐν τῇ φύσει can be understood as the realm in which what is – *is* as designating being *in simpliciter* – is present as itself. It is this realm that can be thought; and thus, if the direction of Socratic questioning is followed, has to be thought.

If there is a way of summing up, albeit provisionally, what is at work here it would be to argue that what stands against the possibility of a mirroring, once the latter is conceived as a mode of production, a mode defined by the twofold sense of immediacy noted above, then it is not just the distinction between the particular and the universal but both the nature of that distinction and thus the ensuing recognition that the only way of addressing the particularity of the particular is by addressing its already present relation to the universal (here the idea/form). And again, this is a thinking of the Absolute's effective presence. The further point is that the impossibility of mirroring is linked to the necessity for judgement – and that judgement's own conditions of possibility are found in the universal/particular relation. Though, as will be seen, Benjamin's implicit response to Plato, one that centres on the figures of Schlegel and Goethe, is that the universal, *pace* Plato, cannot be taken as an object in and for itself. This becomes Goethe's mistake. While for Plato the form/idea can be thought (indeed it has to be thought), for Benjamin, Goethe positions 'primal images' (*Urbilden*) outside thought. Hence for Benjamin 'Goethe thought by renouncing thought'.[16] Plato, on the other hand, allows for complex forms of separation in which while the universal (form/idea) can be thought as an entity in its own right – indeed that is the demand, hence there is a thinking of the Absolute – understanding the particularity of the particular necessitates that it be thought as always already in relation to the universal (idea/form). In order to underscore the way such a set-up necessitates the centrality of judgement, what has to be argued next is that the structure of thought within which the universal/particular relation that can be found in the *Republic* unfolds, is also at work in the *Ion*. The significance of the *Ion* is that it is the dialogue in which Plato's own project as a type of hermeneutics is presented.[17]

While the entirety of the *Ion* warrants detailed investigation, there are two moments within it that are central to these current concerns. They pertain to the emergence of the hermeneutic as that which stands against a simple reiteration and repetition of words as though all that were of interest and importance were the words' own immediate presentation; a presentation in which words would take on the quality of simple immediacy. The initial formulation of the distancing of immediacy occurs with the emergence within the dialogue of a distinction between a rhapsode and a 'good rhapsode' (ἀγαθὸς ῥαψῳδός). Leaving aside any sense of irony that may accompany such a distinction, what actually matters here is what qualifies a rhapsode to be thought of as 'good'. In regard to this point the text is clear: 'a man can never become a good rhapsode without attending to what the poet says' (530C). The object of attention or concern is complex. The rhapsode's consideration moves away from 'words' (ἔπη) – again it is the word taken as an end in itself, the identification of mere appearing and being – and towards a knowledge of 'thought' (διάνοια). This is, of course, a fundamental reconfiguration of the quality of words. The dialogue then continues with the description of the task of this type of rhapsode:

> For the rhapsode ought to make himself an interpreter of the poet's thought to his audience (τὸν γὰρ ῥαψῳδὸν ἑρμηνέα δεῖ τοῦ ποιητοῦ τῆς διανοίας γίγνεσθαι τοῖς ἀκούουσι).
>
> 530C

Attending to what is said therefore, does not entail, or more exactly should not entail, a simple repetition of words. (Even though such a possibility will always be there. Hence genuine distinctions can be drawn between rhapsodes.) Mere repetition would be the equivalent of the process of mirroring: the reduction of words to empiricism's words. Or rather, it would be to understand the task of the rhapsode as having to mirror and thus to have provided an immediate repetition. Presentation would then be simple immediacy. (Once again, this would be no more than an invocation of a misunderstanding of the nature of words themselves. As such it would be no more than the posited possibility of pure immediacy). The argument has to be however that the 'good rhapsode', who, while in some clear sense is still repeating the words, nonetheless stands against immediacy. Following the use of the term ἑρμηνέα to qualify 'rhapsode', it is evident, on one level, that the 'good rhapsode' is now the one incorporated into the hermeneutic project; hence rhapsode as *hermeneus*. This specific designation attains greater clarification once attention is paid to the movement of interpretation, i.e. the release of meaning.

The movement is implicated in a complex of relations. There is both the rhapsode's relation to the poet and the poet's relation to the gods. The presence of the gods is not simply highlighted, at a slightly later stage in the dialogue, it is incorporated into the structure of the hermeneutic:

> the poets are merely the interpreters of the gods (ἑρμηνῆς εἰσιν τῶν θεῶν) according as each is possessed by one of the heavenly powers.
>
> 534E

While it goes without saying that 'the gods' have their specificity and a similar claim can be made for the Muses, the 'paradigm' and then finally, the 'form/idea', it can also be argued that all three play a similar role within an overall structure of thought. In regard to the passage noted above, central to its formulation, is a force; a force that enacts a specific understanding of production. Force is exerted and a type of connection is established. There is a giving and a taking over. The point of inception is the Muse. As Plato writes 'the Muse inspires' (ἡ Μοῦσα ἐνθέους) and 'inspired persons' inspire. There is a network of relations established by 'inspiration'. Inspiration is enthusiasm. It is to be occupied or possessed by the Gods. Ficino in his translation and commentary on both the *Ion* and *Phaedrus* understood this point exactly. Hence, in his commentary on the *Ion* he writes that 'it is not by human art (*arte humana*), but by divine infusion that poets produce (*proferunt*) poetry.'[18] For Plato in the *Symposium* this point is formulated by

Diotima when she argues that 'love' (ἔρως) is not directed towards 'the beautiful'. Rather, it is of the production (specifically, the engendering (γέννησις), or giving birth (τόκος) to the beautiful (206E).[19] This is, of course, also the point made in the *Ion* in the claim that the works of the 'good poet' have a particular form of inception. However, they are 'not from art (technique)' (οὐκ ἐκ τέχνης). *Arte humana is* τέχνη. Not only is *techné* absent from the production of poetry, again, if Ficino's lead is followed, it is equally absent in the realm of judgement. Ficino writes of Ion that, in his engagement with Homer, 'he does not judge by art (*non arte iudicat*)'. And thus, as Ficino goes on to note, 'what remains then is divine inspiration'. As a result, the question to be addressed is straightforward: What is the connection between the distancing of *techné* and the presence in 534E of ἑρμηνέα?[20] Importance here has to be attributed to the emergence of this question. (The question rather than the answer is central.) Indeed, the conjecture has to be that it is the very possibility of this question – the question that uncouples *techné* and the hermeneutic – that marks the divide in which both the hermeneutic project and the necessity for judgement attains actuality. Moreover, it is the separation of *techné* and the hermeneutic that reinforces the impossibility of equating description with genuine acts of judgement.

The rhapsode is the 'interpreter' of the poet's thought. The poet is the 'interpreter' of the gods. The poet becomes possessed; thus, the poet is en-thused. Rather than the immediacy that characterizes mirroring, the immediacy of the literal mirror, which is there as a possibility in the *Republic*, or the reduction of words to pure presence in the *Ion* (which would be the project of the failed rhapsode, a failure despite any bravura performance), there is the figure of the hermeneutic. The hermeneutic understood as initially having been delimited by the context of the *Ion* and then linked to the reiteration of ἑρμηνέα, has a twofold designation. It marks a relation between different entities; Gods and poets, muses and poets, poets and rhapsodes. It is therefore a relation defined by forms of difference.[21] Secondly, the hermeneutic as a carrying over, as interpretation, as the release of meaning, and where the role and task of the interpreter is a carrying over between that which is different – e.g. gods and poets – brings a doubled object into play. Poets are occupied – Ficino translates *katokoche* as '*occupatio*' – which means that the Muses work through them. Acts of creation are not intentional. They are, to use Kant's formulation in regard to works of genius, 'entirely opposed to the spirit of imitation (*Nachahmungsgeiste*)'.[22] 'Imitation' (*Nachahmung*) for Kant is an instance of a more general logic of mirroring. For Kant, the impossibility of mirroring, when it comes to the work of genius – hence the slightly tenuous but nonetheless fundamental distinction between *Nachmachung* and *Nachahmung* – is that which yields the demand for judgement. For Plato, the work by the poet or painter, cannot be understood either in terms of mirroring or the posited immediacy of words, were that object to be understood, to deploy the terminology of *Republic* 596E, beyond the hold of 'appearance' (φαινόμενα) and in terms defined by both 'reality (ὄντα) and truth (ἀλήθεια)'. Another conception of a work has to arise. Work is marked by an already present doubling.

In the first instance that doubling accounts ontologically for the nature of the object itself. And then, in the second, positions the object as interpretable – present as an actual object of judgement – precisely because it is the site of an already present form of irreducibility, e.g. the already present relation between thought and word. As suggested above, it is the presence of this form of relationality that characterizes the advent of the hermeneutic. Equally, it defines, in Plato's sense of the terms, the 'being' and 'truth' of the work. Furthermore, what is also occasioned by the distinction between words and thought, and thus the attribution to words of an ideational content, though by extension this in the end incorporates painting, theatre and music as instances of mimetic presentation, is that when they are taken together they comprise both the possibility and the necessity of a conception of judgement that is no longer delimited by the technical.[23] And this is the case even though the technical remains indispensable to production. Subjects act. ('Criticizability' has emerged.) Judgement depends upon both the critique of immediacy – and this, it might be argued, is the project of *Republic* Book X – and thus the necessity to reposition the object of interpretation, the locus of meaning's release, as the instantiated presence of the twofold quality identified earlier. The Platonic construal of this doubling encounters an inevitable limit. While the doubling continues to suggest both the necessity of the hermeneutic, which is the interpretation of the universal within the particular (and thus the particular as already related to the universal (form/idea)), it is also the case that there is the possibility of thinking the universal (form/idea) as itself. Were the universal to be thought as that which can exist *qua* object of thought without a necessary relation to a particular, then the necessity of the hermeneutic project is called into question. This occurs since thinking – understood as the pure thinking of being – would have distanced the necessity for judgement. (If there is a limit to the Platonic conception of the hermeneutic it occurs at the point at which the reason for its necessity works to undo its actual necessity.[24])

Prior to returning to Book X, it needs to be noted that there is a sense of judgement that is not linked directly to the hermeneutic. Rather, a form of judgement arises because of the presence of the 'stating' of that which is 'contradictory' (ἐναντία λέγειν).[25] In such a context the 'judgement' (γνώμη) emerges because of the need for an eventual 'correction' (ἐπανόρθωμα) of what had been said. This is, of course, what occurs during the discussion of a poem by Simonides that takes place in the *Protagoras* (340A-B). Despite the possibility, if not the necessity, of reconciling contradictions such a move must be seen as anticipatory, in the sense that it clears the way towards asking questions pertaining to the universal/particular relation (or the possibility of thinking the self-referring universal as an end-in-itself). Indeed, this is clear from the flow of argumentation in the passage to which reference was made above. The resolution of the 'contradiction' allows the question of the identity of the self-referring universal to be posed as a genuine question. Hence Socrates, having distanced the threat of contradiction, is then able to ask: 'do you consider becoming or being to be the same or different?' (340B) Answering this question takes place within the framework of the form of judgment that is bound up with the overcoming of the presence of a contradiction as an impediment to thought. In a sense 'judgements' of this precise nature open the way to the hermeneutic.

Central to the engagement with poetry and painting as instances of mimetic presentation is the possibility of a measured response. Setting the measure would be the knowledge of the quality of the presentation. The latter is the knowledge of its 'being' and its 'truth' *qua* presentation. There is a sense in which the content of the presentation is to a certain extent still a peripheral concern. It is thus that what then occurs, more or less at the end of the engagement with poetry in Book X, is the formulation of a position in which a genuine defence of poetry becomes possible. What is important about the formulation of this passage is the re-emergence of the language of the political. The passage in question is the following:

> And we would allow her advocates who are not poets but lovers of poetry (μὴ ποιητικοί, φιλοποιηταί) to plead her cause in discourse without metre (ἄνευ μέτρου λόγον), and show that she is not only delightful but beneficial to government and the life of man (ὠφελίμη πρὸς πολιτείας καὶ τὸν βίον τὸ ἀνθρώπινον).
>
> 607D

The defence of poetry has to concede its aesthetic dimension – the use of the term ἡδύς is clear – however the aesthetic, as the feeling of pleasure, has an important limit. Poetry has to have a 'beneficial' use (ὠφελίμη). The sense of benefit is not abstract. On the contrary, it is delimited in relation both to the polity and to 'human life'. If poetry is not linked to pleasure, or at least not limited to pleasure, then how is this delimitation to be understood? What poetry demands are specific modes of thought. Understanding the 'being' and the 'truth' of that which appears opens in two interrelated directions. The first, as has emerged, is the necessity of the interplay of the hermeneutic and judgement. Their presence results from a reconfiguration of the object. The second, and this is by far the more contentious, is that the demand that poetry makes on thought, a demand that is linked to the presence of the idea/form has had a transformation. If that demand is allowed to register it gives rise to the question of how to think the presence of the unconditioned within the *polis*. This is not just a complex question; it transforms the relationship between idea and the actual. The idea (the unconditioned) as that which has to be thought, and thus as creating the need for thought and judgement as necessary tasks within the *polis*. While Plato's 'paradigm' or 'idea/form' are not within the *polis*, it remains the case that what is opened up is the need to think the relationship between the unconditioned and the conditioned as a quality of the *polis* and thus, in that precise sense, within it. This is, in the end of course, the inevitable tension within Platonism. In sum, therefore, the always already present relation between poetry and the *polis* which are present here as a set of demands works to delimit any thinking of the politics of form. This is how a Platonic politics of form would need to be understood. Moreover the setting, taken as a totality, opens up the possibility of an engagement with Walter Benjamin's *The Concept of Criticism in German Romanticism* as well as the letter he wrote to Florens Christian Rang concerning criticism.

While Benjamin's work on the conceptions of both art and criticism within the writings of the *Frühromantics* and Goethe is sustained, and while what can be uncovered as problematic within their writings was identified in the continuity of the detail, Benjamin's own project nonetheless reaches a self-announced limit. What endures as a locus of investigation is the relation between 'the idea and the ideal of art', and yet Benjamin concedes that his own investigation cannot 'pass beyond the threshold of the problem'.[26] If there is a way ahead then 'only systematic thought can resolve it'. The argument here is that 'systematic thought' can be given a specific determination, one that while gesturing back to Plato inscribes a central part of Benjamin's project within the history of idealism. 'Systematic thought' involves having to think the presence of the unconditioned within the *polis*. A determination which can be reformulated as having to think the complex connection between judgement, that in terms of which judgement is itself possible, and place. As a result, the structure of the politics of form – and it is essential to be precise since what is at stake is a structure – that arises with Plato, will be engaged, overcome and continued within Benjamin's work. This occurs within the details of Benjamin's *Dissertation*, the letter to Rang and in the openings occasioned by both texts.

Benjamin's encounter with the *Frühromantics* and Goethe is delimited by a specific conception of the object and the responses that such a conception envisages. It is orientated as much by the presence of 'criticizability' as that which defines the art work, as it is the necessity to think the art work within a setting delineated by the identification of the task of thinking the Absolute. They are not the same. And yet, the legacy of Romanticism is that they have to be thought together. In other words, not only is the Absolute – equally the universal/particular relation – that which determines thought within the confines of Romantic and Post-Romantic philosophy, the locus of thought has become the work of art. Indeed, the move from Fichte to the *Frühromantics* can be understood, as Benjamin suggests, as the move from a definition of the philosophical in terms of consciousness to one defined by art. As a result, art becomes 'the Absolute medium of reflection'.[27] This is the situation of thought. Within it, for Goethe, what characterized the work of art was a specific modality of relation to the Absolute (for Goethe these are the *Urbilden*). Taken generally, particularity was defined in terms of a radical separation from the *Urbilden*. Hence the question of relation, within such a setting, has then to be staged in terms of that separation. There were continual moments of differentiation. Differentiation defined the particularity of the particular. Goethe, in his essay on the *Laocoön* group, writes of ancient art as 'self-contained' (*selbst-ständig*) and thus as 'complete in itself (*es geschlossen ist*). The radical divide emerges when Goethe's insistence on closure is juxtaposed with *Athenäums-Fragmente* 116. The passage from 116 that figures in Benjamin's *Dissertation* that is central here is the following:

> The Romantic poetry is still becoming; indeed, that is its true essence, that it is always only becoming, it can never be completed. *Die romantische Dichtart ist noch im Werden; ja das ist ihr eigentliches Wesen, daß sie ewig nur werden, nie vollendet sein kann.*[28]

While Goethe writes that 'a work of art' is 'complete in itself' (*ist sich vollendete*) for Schlegel as is clear from the above, 'it can never be completed (*nie vollendet sein kann*). There is a lot that can be argued in relation to other possibilities that might arise as a result of the distinction between the complete and the incomplete.[29] These designations can be seen as marking a clear distinction between Classicism and the work of the *Frühromantics*. Benjamin works as much with that separation as he does the possible affinities.

Benjamin formulates Goethe's position in ways that establish a clear set of connections with what has already been discovered about Plato.

> Art itself does not create its archetypes; they rest, prior to all created work, in that sphere of art where art is not creation but nature. To grasp the idea of nature and thereby to make it serviceable for the idea of art (for pure content) was in the end Goethe's mission in his investigation or *ur*-phenomenon.[30]

Even though the particularity of works existing in their separation from the *Urbilden* can be 'complete' and 'self-standing' – 'creation' as the equivalent to *techné* – the exact specificity of any one object is itself always 'contingent'.[31] Moreover, for Benjamin, the presence of this contingency is nothing other than the failure to think the Absolute, once that thinking is set within the transferral of thinking from the centrality of consciousness as the medium of reflection to art. If there is an important departure from the problem of contingency taken as the problem that arises in the move from consciousness to art, and contextually it arises in the German Romantics' response to Fichte that can be located in the writings of Schlegel and Novalis, then, for Benjamin, it occurs with Romanticism. And yet, despite the clear advance within Romanticism in this regard, what still endures, for Benjamin, as the limitation of the *Frühromantics* is their manner of engagement with the Absolute.

The difference between the *Frühromantics* and Goethe can be encapsulated in the figure of the torso. For Goethe, in Benjamin's formulation, the figure of the torso provided a way of thinking, perhaps even of imagining, the necessity of separation; a separation in which particularity emerged as simply contingent. For Romanticism, on the other hand, the torso is not an apposite figure. Separation, which is a relation of non-relation, must cede its place to a relation of interconnection. Hence Benjamin writes that for the *Frühromantics* the

> work of art cannot be a torso; it must be a mobile transitory moment in the living transcendental form. By limiting itself in its own form, it makes itself transitory in a contingent figure, but in that fleeting figure it makes itself eternal through criticism.[32]

Schlegel's attempt to overcome contingency is given a precise formulation by Benjamin. He writes that what Schlegel sought to undertake was *Die Aufhebung der Zufälligkeit*.[33] And yet this 'overcoming' of contingency fails. (The possible connection to Hegel in which the 'overcoming' would have become a 'sublation' needs to be noted insofar as this overcoming is precisely *not* Hegel's sublation.). Contingency returns because the price of its having been overcome is the eternality of the work and thus its dissolution into the Absolute. Benjamin's argument here is that this dissolution of the particularity of the particular into the Absolute means, not only that the particularity of the art work remains unthought, more exactly, it remains unthinkable.

Benjamin continued to return to the topic of criticism. And thus, continued his deliberations on the politics of form. In his letter to Florens Christian Rang written on 9 December 1923, a letter whose ostensible concerns circle around the question of criticism, he describes 'the task of interpretation' as the 'gathering or assembling of creaturely life in the Idea' (*das creatürliche Leben in der Idee zu versammeln*).[34] Moreover, 'life' and 'creatures' are also both involved when he clarifies what is meant by Goethe's conception of individual works of art as 'contingent'. The example Benjamin used was, as already noted, the 'torso'. The torso exemplifies a fractured or broken relation to the ideal. It announces the relation of non-relation; namely, here, the contingent particular given with its radical separation from the Absolute. To use Benjamin's term, it would be a relation that would only then be possible through 'resemblance' (*Gleichen*). The ideal would remain always distanced. As part of his consideration of this position he clarifies what he takes Romantic criticism to involve. He notes that

> They conceived these investigations as analogous to morphological studies, which were designed to elicit the relations of the creature to life (*die Beziehungen der Wesen auf das Leben zu erforschen.*)[35]

Romantic criticism can be differentiated from what Benjamin describes as 'the propositions of normative poetics'.[36] Such a poetics had only one interest which, if the analogy with 'anatomical studies' is maintained, is delimited by a concern with the individual rather than a more general concern with individual's relation to life. While Benjamin uses two different formulations – *das creatürliche Leben* and *der Wesen* – they both refer to how the creature's relation to life is to be understood. Now, given that in both what is central is a type of connection between the particular and the universal where the latter is present in the letter to Rang and in the *Dissertation* as either the Idea or the Absolute, what has to be pursued are the differing way in which relationality is thought within them. The supposition here is that the letter to Rang provides the most perspicacious way in.

In more general terms what continues is the issue of how to think the universal/particular relation. A number of moments within the letter are of paramount importance, furnishing vital components for an engagement with that concern. Benjamin notes the presence of a form of interconnection that holds between art works. In a demanding formulation, he writes: 'The essential relation between art works remains intense' (*Die Wesentliche Verbindung unter Kunstwerken bleiben intensiv.*) Benjamin's language is precise. It is not merely a question of a relation but of an 'essential relation' (*Wesentliche Verbindung*). Furthermore, there is the question of what does it mean for that relation to remain 'intense'? This is the opening to another analogy. Benjamin writes, as though in response to that question, that in this respect, works of art are similar to philosophical systems, in that the so-called history of philosophy is either an uninteresting history of dogma or even of philosophers, or the history of problems.[37]

There is the return of a recognition of history in terms of problems. This can be read as a recapitulation of the opening of the *Dissertation*. What is stake however is the refusal of any conception of historical time as conventionally understood. (Hence the polemical claim made in the letter that 'there is no such thing as art history'.) Transformed with it, of course, is how the object is itself conceived i.e. here the object is the particular object of criticism or interpretation. What Benjamin is moving towards is a position that accounts for what can be described as the becoming-historical of the object. In other words, the creation of the historical event. Thus, there is the always potential entry into history that undoes the proposition of the always already historical. Indeed, the corollary is that, as he suggests in regard to the 'work of art', 'its essence is to be without history (*seinem Wesentlichen nach geschichtlos*)'.[38] While difficult, his position is clear. The work of art's 'essential quality', its being present as 'historical-less' (*geschichtlos*), is the very precondition of its becoming historical. Works of art are located outside the simple movement of time. (That simple movement is the equation of historical time with chronology.[39]) For Benjamin 'they are models of nature that await neither the day, as the movement from night to day, nor the 'judgement day' (*Gereichtag*) as the end of days. The 'historical-less' nature of art work demands the project of criticism. Benjamin writes:

> criticism (where it is identical with interpretation and the opposite of all current methods of art appreciation) is the presentation of an idea (*Darstellung einer Idee*). Ideas' intensive infinitude characterises them as monads. Allow me to define it: criticism is the mortification of works. Not that consciousness is enhanced in them (Romantic!) but that knowledge (*des Wissens*) takes up residence in them.[40]

Criticism therefore is the release of meaning in the form of knowledge. That it is 'knowledge' is of fundamental importance.

The language of monads comes, as Benjamin continues to note, from the writings of Leibniz. Benjamin's own relation to Leibniz is itself an important area of research in its own right.[41] Within Leibniz's writings on the infinite, the creature is also apparent. In his *Réponse à la lettre de M. Foucher* concerning questions of both movement and the dynamic Leibniz notes the following in relation to division and thus the infinite:

> I believe that that there is no part of matter which is not, I do not say divisible, but actually divided (*actuellement divisée*), and as a result, the smallest particle ought to be considered as a world full of an infinity of different creatures (*un monde plein d'une infinité de creatures differentes*).[42]

An 'infinity of different creatures' is much like the world in which the infinite has actuality, or even in the language of *La monadologie* of a present' which 'est gros de l'avenir'. In both cases what is set up is a world (a present) that is incomplete because it contains both the possibility and the eventual form of the future within it.[43] Not only is the future a quality of the present, the nature of the present – here as time, world and work of art – is reworked in the process. Integral to that process is the creation of a setting in which actuality, the world and the work of art are, at any (and every) moment, incomplete. Benjamin's use of the terms 'intensive', perhaps in drawing on the detail of these sources, allows for what has already been identified as gathering the 'creaturely life into the Idea'. Rather than connecting creatures 'to life' (*auf das Leben*) the infinity of difference is there to be released. Creatures abound. Criticism is an enlivening: a paradoxically triumphant mortification. It shows states of incompletion. Knowledge is linked to that presentation; presence as the presentation of a potentiality. This creates the setting in which it becomes possible to return to Benjamin's claim noted earlier that the 'essential relation between art works remains intense' (*Die Wesentliche Verbindung unter Kunstwerken bleiben intensiv*).

The qualification of the 'relation' as 'essential' means that it is present as pure relationality. In other words, a relation without determination, in the precise sense that it is always to be determined. It is a relation therefore that is always there *in potentia*. Once this description is taken as having generality, such that it addresses the ontology of the art work, then what this entails is that art works have the quality of intensive infinites. Again, what this designation of the art work involves needs to be made precise. The presence of this quality means that any fixed and determined instances – interpretive claims – are the actualizations, the release, of the pure potentiality for meaning. While this position, in the end, provides an account, as Benjamin's work unfolds, of how the 'dialectical image' functions, what it set up here is the demanding problem of how the positions that appear in the letter to Rang, once connected to the project of the *Dissertation*, can be marshalled for the development of a more nuanced account of the politics of form. Again, an answer has to start with the impossibility of thinking particularity that arose in the context of the engagement with the *Frühromantics* and Goethe. The question to be addressed concerns the retained possibility not just of thinking particularity but more significantly of developing another understanding of what particularity entails. The answer to this reformulation of the question of particularity hinges on two elements at work within Benjamin's claim (i.e. the claim that the 'essential relation between art works remains intense', *Die Wesentliche Verbindung unter Kunstwerken bleiben intensiv*) that need to be developed.

As a beginning, it is clear that the use of the term 'essential' positions that relation in terms of that which is *yet-to-be-determined*. It is pure because it awaits determination. This first element informs the next, that the relation 'remaining intensive' (*bleiben intensiv*) positions art works within the continuity of their *coming-into-relation*. Particularity is therefore the after-effect of a specific *coming-into-relation*. The precondition for this possibility is that the essential quality of relationality involves that which is *always-to-be-determined*. Here the Absolute can begin to be rethought as having to include the continuity of potentiality and then the particular as a specific actualization; an actualization that is of necessity incomplete. Particularity is retained within incompletion as a specific determination of the release of meaning. To the extent that the two elements noted above are accepted, it is then not difficult to see that the claim made in *On the Concept of History* that the 'historical materialist' should 'blast a specific era out of the homogenous course of history' is not only compatible with the critique of the *Frühromantics* it also indicates what becomes possible as a result of that critique.[44] A possibility, moreover, that depends upon it. If Benjamin's interpretation is correct, then the dissolution of the particular in the Absolute not only precludes this possibility, it also undoes a mode of relationality – a mode that is brought about – between the past and the present that Benjamin identifies (also in *On the Concept of History*) as a 'constellation'. The 'constellation' is not just another mode of relationality it is the counter-measure to that dissolution. It is one which the present, as an 'era', 'has formed with a definite earlier one'.[45] The 'constellation' as it appears here is not just a reiteration of the intensive relation between art works, it results from both the nature of the relation and thus the conception of the object – object as monad – within such a relation. Within that relation – and it can be a relation across times if time is understood simply chronologically – art works become historical as a result of that relation. The precondition for this possibility is a reconfiguration of the connection between the particular and the Absolute. The reconfiguration has a determinate form.

The reconfiguration of the Absolute within this context is not a simple repositioning of the unconditioned. The position is subtler. It can be described as the complexification of the Absolute. To recapitulate there are number of decisive elements here. Firstly, the Platonic conception of the universal/particular relation – as a thinking of the Absolute – involved a determination of the particular by the universal in which the universal can be thought as an *end-in-itself*. Secondly, Goethe's reiteration of that setting maintains the universal (now the *Urbild*) as an unthinkable *end-on-itself*, and with it a conception of the art work as complete in itself. A completion thought in terms of a radical separation in which the particular's connection to the *Urbild* occurs in terms of a type of semblance. Thirdly, the counter position in Schlegel and Novalis can be understood as necessitating the dissipation of particulars into the universal such that particularity becomes unthinkable, in the precise sense that the particularity of the particular is absorbed. Finally, the response that is implicit in what can be described as Benjamin's continual reformulation of the universal/particular relation does not involve abandoning the project of thinking the Absolute (universal), but, as was indicated, its reconfiguration.[46] A position that is already clear in his claim that criticism is the 'presentation of an idea' (*Darstellung einer Idee*). As there is an original relation then there has to be the assumption, to recall the formulation noted at the outset, that form, which here would be the 'presentation', is always already informed.

What has been described as a reconfiguration of the universal/particular relation has two interrelated elements. The first part is an implicit premise; namely that that the particular's relation to the universal is there to be uncovered and determined in every instance. In regard to the work of art this is a formal description of the movement of criticism. However, it is a movement that is accompanied by another, one that presupposes that the particular is incomplete – hence the push away from Goethe (and of course Winckelmann and the generalizable project of Classicism) towards the legacy of Romanticism – in the precise sense that the object eschews any possible reduction to an already determined and thus complete singularity. The movement in question is the *coming-into-relation*, another modality of forming, that not only defines the connection between art works, it also assumes the particular's potential for a reconfiguration as a result of its having the potential for a *coming-into-relation*. This is of course another formulation of what Benjamin means by a 'constellation'. Moreover, as constellations continue to reposition and thus re-imagine the 'same' image, hence the move from the single image to the 'dialectical image', the latter can then be incorporated into what has already been identified as the becoming-historical of the object. As a result of uncovering this complex of relations not only is particularity reworked, this is equally true for what counts as the informing of form.[47] It is essential to note that what is at stake here is a judgement and not simply an experience. 'Judgement' is not Benjamin's term. The claim is simply that the experience of the dialectical image has the form of a judgment. Benjamin is clear in *On the Concept of History* that 'the image is perceived by historical materialism.'[48] Hence it is an informed perception. Moreover, it locates perception within a politics of form. The claim made in the same Thesis that the 'past can be seized only as an image that flashes up at the moment of its recognisability (*Erkennbarkeit*), and is never seen again' announces the move to judgement. Recognizability (*Erkennbarkeit*), is a mode of knowing. The politics of form is still bound to judgement, and judgement must continue to be linked to what Plato identified as 'government and the life of man' (*Republic* 607D). However it is not just that both government and human life have a different quality, a changed situation: more emphatically, the critique of the *Frühromantics* and of Goethe demands the interarticulation of those differences within another thinking of the philosophical project whose point of orientation is that critique. While that which is at work within a contemporary politics of form will always have its own specific conditions and delimitations the interplay of the conditioned and the unconditioned in Plato and the way it informs the necessity of the link between judgement and knowledge in Benjamin should continue to play a defining role.

Notes

1. This paper forms part of larger project funded by the Australian Research Council (ARC DP160103644) entitled *Place, Commonality and the Human. Towards a New Philosophical Anthropology*. I want to thank Phiroze Vasunia for his comments on an earlier version.
2. The separation of presentation and expression is an important theme within contemporary philosophy. Note, for example, that such an approach is central to the way Heidegger begins to address the poetical in his '... Poetically Man Dwells ...' (Heidegger 2000). He argues that once viewed merely as a form of 'expression' (*Ausdruck*) 'language can sink (*herabsinken*) into a mere medium of the printed word'. The structure of expression does not create the setting in which the particularity of language works.
3. I have tried to develop the idea of the work of art as at work – hence the work's work – in the opening chapters of A. Benjamin 2015.
4. References to Walter Benjamin are his *Selected Works* (W. Benjamin 1996–2003) (henceforth SW) followed by the *Gesammelte Schriften* (1980) (henceforth GS).
5. SW.I.177/GS. I.1.107.

6. Beatrice Hanssen's work on Benjamin overall, and in particular her writings on his *Dissertation*, demand close attention. See amongst others, Hanssen 1995. The collection we edited together still contains most of the important studies on the topic in English (see Hanssen and Benjamin, eds 2003, and in addition Richer 2016).
7. SW.I.177/GS. I.1.107
8. All references to the *Republic* are to the Loeb edition (Plato 1930–35).
9. The reference here is, of course, to Jacques Derrida's analysis of the *pharmakon* (Derrida 1972). While in no way diminishing the importance of that study, it is nonetheless still clear that in the context of *Republic* 538E that the term *pharmakon*, presented as an 'antidote', plays a particular argumentative role.
10. References to the *Timaeus* are to the Loeb edition (Plato 1929).
11. Halliwell 2002: 133–47.
12. References to the *Phaedo* are to the Loeb edition (Plato 1914).
13. Further evidence for the viability of such an interpretation can be found in Burnet's treatment of this formulation in his commentary on the *Phaedo* (see Plato 1963: 102).
14. For another way of maintaining this difference see the important distinction drawn by Dodds in his commentary on the *Gorgias* between what he calls *ti*-questions versus *poion*-questions (Plato 1991).
15. References to the *Hippias Major* (*Greater Hippias*) are to the Loeb edn (Plato 1926).
16. SW I.181/ GS. I.1.114.
17. References to the *Ion* are to the Loeb edn (Plato 1925a: 401–48).
18. This text can be found in Ficino 2008.
19. References to the *Symposium* are to the Loeb edn (Plato 1925b).
20. There is, of course a real question here of the relation between Hermes and what has already been identified as the presence of ερμηνέα. The distinction with all the attendant problems is identified by Plato in the *Cratylus*. See 407E-408B
21. This point is also argued – though to different ends – by Jean-Luc Nancy (1982).
22. Kant 2009: §47. For a more detailed interpretation of Kant on genius see Benjamin (2019).
23. While the argument leads in another direction Silke-Maria Weineck (1998) also finds an implicit theory of criticism (judgement) in the argumentation of the *Ion*. For another discussion of the difficulties of securing a definition of inspiration or enthusiasm that holds it apart from madness see Farness 1985: 167–8. It should also be noted that there would be an important link between enthusiasm, genius and melancholia. As that history unfold the link to Plato and Ficino becomes more complex. See in this regard Daval 2009.
24. I have tried to show that there is a different though related set of problems that attend the conception of hermeneutics in Philo. While Philo demonstrates the impossibility of maintaining both the literal and thus the immediate as the locus of interpretation and hence the move to allegory arises as a result, the movement of allegoresis is in the end stayed - a staying the argumentative basis for which is Philo's Platonism – because of what becomes a literalization of the allegorical. See Benjamin 2016.
25. See also *Gorgias* 483A
26. SW.I.183/ GS. I.1.117.
27. SW.I.137/ GS. I.1.44.
28. Athenäums-Fragmente 116 in Schlegel 1988: 115.

29. Goethe 2008.
30. SW.I. 180/GS.I. 112.
31. For a discussion of this sense of contingency see Ferris 2003: 186. Ferris' work is still the most sustained scholarly account of Benjamin's relation to Goethe.
32. SW. I. 182/ GS. I.1.117.
33. Howard Caygill in his exemplary discussion of the *Dissertation* draws attention to this formulation (Caygill 1998: 46–9). The prompt behind Benjamin's use of the term *Aufhebung* remains open to further speculation.
34. Benjamin 1994: 225; Benjamin (1996): 393.
35. SW.I. 200/GS. I.1.115.
36. SW.I. 200/GS. I.1.115
37. C. 224/B. 393.
38. C. 224/B. 393.
39. I have engaged with that possibility is a sustained way on a number of occasions. See, for example, Benjamin 2013: 222–43.
40. C. 224/B. 393.
41. The work that is central to this project has been undertaken, thus far, by Paula L. Schwebel. Her articles are central to the development of a radically new and important development within studies on Walter Benjamin. See, *inter alia*, Schwebel 2012, 2014 and 2017.
42. Leibniz 1985: 1.416.
43. Leibniz 1985: 6.610 *(La Monadologie)*.
44. SW.4. 396/GS. I.2.702.
45. SW.4. 396/GS. I.2.702
46. Goethe 2008: 72.
47. There is yet to be an adequate sustained account of Benjamin's work on the image written in English. The clear point of departure for the development of such an account would be, of course, the work of Sigrid Weigel. The most recent formulation of her position can be found in Weigel 2015. See in addition Dubow 2007.
48. SW.4. 390/GS.I.2.695.

CHAPTER 6
PLATO'S *SEVENTH LETTER* OR HOW TO FASHION A SUBJECT OF RESISTANCE[1]
Paul Allen Miller

When we think of Plato's politics, we generally think more about philosopher-kings than figures of resistance. In part this comes from conventional liberal readings of the *Republic*, certainly from the time of Popper forward (1945), but in part it comes from the *Seventh Letter* itself, which makes what seems to be a clear statement in favour of philosophers ruling:

> And finally I understood that all cities now are governed badly: for matters concerning the existing laws are almost incurable without some wondrous means and some good luck. It was necessary to say, while praising proper (*orthē*) philosophy, that it is from this alone that it is possible to envisage both just public matters and all the things concerning private individuals. And so the nations of men will not cease from evils, until the tribe of those who properly and truly philosophize (*philosophountōn orthōs ge kai alēthōs*) comes into positions of political leadership (*arkhas . . . tas politikas*) or the tribe of those exercising power in the cities would, through some divine fate, actually come to philosophize (*ontōs philosophēsēi*).
>
> 326a4–b4[2]

This passage is typically read in light of *Republic* 5 (473d) that argues philosophers must become kings or king-philosophers if there is to be surcease from the evils that afflict us (Souilhé 1960: 30n1). The assumption is then made that the *Seventh Letter* advocates for a kind of philosophical monarchy, not to say dictatorship: a rule by those who know or have been taught the truth. As Popper and others writing in the wake of European fascism and Stalinist totalitarianism have argued, such a rule would not only be necessarily illiberal but could also be positively oppressive.

I want to contend that such an interpretation is a mistake. My argument will have three major sections. In section one, I will argue that what is known as the philosophical digression in the *Seventh Letter* is primarily concerned with the formation of the philosophical subject. This subject, as depicted by Plato, is not someone who has received a prescribed doctrine or even a person to whom a knowing subject has transmitted a defined set of information. Rather, the philosophical subject is someone who has undergone rigorous, interpersonal, dialogic training, and through that training he or she has developed the ability to be critical of received ideas, to question the given nature of their own perceptions, and to interrogate being itself. Philosophy has a separate status from other disciplines and cannot be defined either as a set of truths or as a content the pre-exists the moment of its articulation. 'What is spoken here is not the same as in other sciences (*mathēmata*), but as a result of a great amount of time being spent together (*sunousia*) concerning this very matter (*pragma*) and of living together, suddenly just as a light is kindled from a fire that has *blazed up*, that very thing having been born in the soul then nourishes itself" (341c4-d2, emphasis mine). Philosophy is a process, a mode of inquiry, a way of being. Philosophers are not those who know the truth but those who seek it in a rigorous fashion. They are literally 'lovers of wisdom'.

In the second section I then will draw the necessary conclusions about what this would mean if we accept the Platonic contention that only philosophers should rule or at least only rulers who have been trained in philosophy. What this 'rule' would entail, I argue, is something very different from what is generally understood as a philosopher-king, that is, someone who is in possession of the truth and who would then impose that truth on others by means of persuasion perhaps in the first instance but always by command in the last. After all, how can one be king if one does not rule? Instead, we would argue that the philosophical rule is a paradox: it would always be a regime of power yet to come, a form of government perpetually in process and perpetually open to contestation, since the philosopher is by definition one who is always in pursuit, rather than in possession, of the truth. We will conclude this section by expanding the object of our focus from the *Seventh Letter* and its particular understanding of a certain form of philosophical instruction to other dialogues including the *Republic* and the *Symposium*. There I will contend that, far from advocating for an idiosyncratic or unPlatonic understanding of the philosophical subject, the *Seventh Letter* elaborates a model of philosophical instruction that is in fact cognate with the corpus as a whole. It is in this section that we will briefly address the perennial question of the authenticity of the letter.

Finally, in our third section, we will contend that this model of the formation of the philosophically trained political subject is particularly apt for the struggles of our own day, that Plato far from elaborating an elitist politics of conformity and subordination to authority, instead elaborates a model of principled resistance, of an unyielding a search to find and speak the truth to and for power (*parrhēsia*). It is this model that attracted the attention of Michel Foucault in the last years of his life, when he commented extensively on the *Seventh Letter* in his lectures at the Collège de France. In short, we will argue that the *Seventh Letter*'s portrait of the formation of the philosophical subject is what Foucault would term a 'spiritual practice' aimed at the creation of a subject of resistance and hence far removed from Popper's vision of the Stalinist sage.

The excursus or digression at the heart of the *Seventh Letter* has long been the subject of controversy. In many ways, it is the philosophical core of the letter, but at the same time, it has seemed alien to its professed aims (Souilhé 1960: xlviii-lv; Hamilton 1973: 136–7; Harward 2014: 213–14). The *Seventh Letter*, which is by far the longest of the Platonic *Epistles*, presents itself as a missive offering political advice to the friends and family of Dion of Syracuse, shortly after his assassination. Dion was killed in the aftermath of leading a successful effort to overthrow his uncle, Dionysius the Younger, the tyrant of Syracuse. Plato had come to know Dion during his first visit to Syracuse when he visited the court of Dionysius the Elder. He was impressed by the philosophical earnestness of the young man, and he found in Dion an eager student. When Dionysius the Younger succeeded to the throne, Plato returned at the invitation of Dion with the intent of initiating the youthful ruler into philosophy and finally realizing his vision of philosophical rule. The attempt was unsuccessful and Dion himself had to leave Sicily for the Greek mainland to which Plato soon returned as well. Plato would go back to Sicily a third time, again at the insistence of Dion and those around him. He was determined to see once and for all whether Dionysius possessed the philosophical proclivities that Dion and others attributed to him, and he was hopeful that he could find a resolution to the dispute between the two kinsmen. When this third voyage ended in failure, Dion led an expedition from Greece to Sicily that overthrew the tyrant, but, in the subsequent political unrest, Dion fell victim to the machinations of one of the allies who had accompanied him from Greece. It is in this context that Plato seeks to offer his advice in response to a request from Dion's allies and kinsmen.

The letter begins with a brief introduction (323d10–324b8), followed by an autobiographical section in which Plato recounts how he came to believe that only those who practise philosophy should rule in the wake of the depredations of the Thirty and the subsequent execution of Socrates by the restored democracy (324b9–326b4). There follow the stories of his first (364b5–328c3) and second voyages to Sicily (328c4–330b8). He then offers his basic advice to the friends and family of Dion (330b9–331d6). These are largely generalities, but several points are worth noting in passing. Plato compares the role of the leader of the state to that of a doctor,[3] who must choose the right remedy based not on what might immediately be the most popular, but on what is appropriate for a given constitution, thus implicitly acknowledging that a plurality of constitutions is possible and perhaps even desirable. He then argues that the courageous counsellor is not the one who seeks to advise those in power how to accomplish their own ends, but rather those of the city, even under the threat of death. Nonetheless, while the willingness to be potentially the object of violence is inherent in the role of the honest counsellor, the willingness to use force to get others to accept your political and ethical views is explicitly rejected, even in the case of those over whom you have great authority such as your own sons. The friends and family of Dion are urged not to pursue their ends through violence but through persuasion and the example of an ethical life.

The linkage between mode of life and the political subject is made more explicit in the next section (331d7–334c3), where Plato recounts how he counselled Dionysius the Younger that he should live each day as master of himself and of his desires. If he did, he would acquire faithful friends and allies both within Syracuse and across Sicily, and this would secure his rule and the harmony of the island. Such behaviour, however, would mean abstaining from the rich banquets and sexual indulgences that were typical of the Syracusan court. Nonetheless, in this way, Dionysius might achieve the stability and hegemony in Sicily that had eluded his father. But the young tyrant did not heed Plato's counsel and disastrous results ensued.

Plato, then, draws the appropriate conclusions for the friends and family of Dion to whom he is offering counsel (334c4–337e3). He argues that enslaving others benefits neither the enslaver nor the enslaved, and that only souls possessed of small and unfree manners (*smikra kai aneleuthra ēthē*), that is, those knowing nothing of the good and the just, will strive to carry off plunder taken from others. Political tyranny is thus shown, in brief, to be a function of the malformation or poor training of the soul. At the same time, Plato argues that the desire to experience what is finest for oneself and the city is necessarily the desire to experience what is wholly correct and fine. Hence enlightened self-interest should lead one to prefer the good and the just. The basic argument here is that, in the last analysis, there is a convergence between the political, the aesthetic and the ethical subject. This advice, Plato indicates, has particular salience in Sicily, since it is known for the opulence of its feasting, the license of its mores, and the illiberality and violence of its politics. The tyrant, as in the *Republic* (Book 9, 571a–578c), is the one who has no limits to his desires.

Plato then continues with his narrative, recounting the events of his second voyage to Sicily and beginning to tell those of the third (337e3–341a7). Dionysius's court, we find out, was filled with people recounting bits and pieces of philosophical hearsay, and Plato concedes that the young tyrant was 'not altogether unsuited for learning and eager for praise' (338c5–d8). These facts were used by Dion to convince Plato that on his third voyage he should try once again to counsel Dionysius, since 'it was not at all remarkable that a young man who had heard philosophical discussions would be seized with a desire for the best life' (339e5). And so it was that Plato determined that he should make a test (*elegkhos*) of Dionysius on his return to determine 'whether in actuality he had been lit aflame by philosophy as by a fire' (340b1–2). As Harward's commentary notes (2014: 211), this image of enlightenment as a flame will be central to the philosophical digression, and the narrative portions of the epistle in fact become more and more directly related to the content of the so-called digression as we approach the core of the letter itself. At the same time, the distinction between genuine philosophical knowledge and desire, as opposed to mere philosophical hearsay, becomes a recurring theme (cf. *parakousmata* 338d3, 340b6). An opposition is thus established between the mere repetition of philosophemes, the treatment of philosophy as a repeatable knowledge and a form of information, and the practice of philosophy as an experience, one which, in its essence, is strictly unrepeatable. Philosophy is not a profession (Foucault 2008: 318). It is not a skill set. It is a form of life that is to be practised every day (340d1–6).

When Plato arrives in Syracuse, however, he discovers that Dionysius has a written a book, a kind of précis or resume of philosophy. As Plato makes clear nothing could be more misguided. Dionysius, it seems, had taken the bits and pieces of things he had heard from others (341b3), transcribed them, and presented them as his own. He represented himself as a learned man but not as someone given to the hard work of philosophy, of living the life of the philosopher. Plato says he knows nothing of the matters on which the young tyrant writes, but he knows others who have written such books, and 'who they are, they do not know themselves' (*hoitines de, oud' autoi hautous*, 341b6). Such people are not philosophers. They lack the self-knowledge that Plato has

Socrates in the *Apology* (21b–22d) and the *Phaedrus* (229c–230a) posit as the prerequisite to real philosophical insight.

Such self-knowledge changes the way one lives one's life. This knowledge and its effect is the matter of philosophy (*pragma* 340b8; Harward 2014: 211). This is its purchase on the real (Foucault 2008: 210–20). The mere repetition of what you have heard on philosophical topics no more makes you a philosopher than the rote memorization of the periodic table makes you a chemist or the ability to scan verse makes you a poet. Philosophy is something you do, not something you know. Thus, when Plato disclaims having ever written anything on 'these matters', he is not announcing a secret doctrine that is only delivered orally (Szlezák 1999; Foucault 2008: 228), nor attacking writing per se (Foucault 2008: 234–5 contra Derrida 1972; cf. Miller 2007: 183–201). Rather, as every reader of the dialogues knows from their own experience, Platonic writing offers numerous challenges to the reader. The typical dialogue is far from presenting in summary form a series of philosophical truths to be accepted or a set of propositions that forms a system. The dialogues often include myths, end in aporia or confusion, or are of such complexity in their artistic framing that they cannot simply be accepted as *ex cathedra* pronouncements. Rather readers are required to engage with the dialogues, pose questions to them, moving backward and forwards across these texts, coming to their own provisional conclusions (Gurd 2012: 33–4). The dialogues, as such, differ fundamentally both from the oral repetition of rote sets of philosophical 'truths' and from written compilations that purport to transmit philosophy as a form of information. Rather the engagement with the Platonic text resembles nothing so much as what Plato defines in this passage as the nature of true philosophical instruction:

> For [philosophy] is in no way a discourse (*rhēton*) that is like other forms of knowledge. But it is from spending a great deal of time together concerning the matter itself and from living with it (*suzēn*) that all of a sudden a light is kindled, just as when a fire leaps forth, which once this flame has been born in the soul then it nourishes itself.
>
> 341c6–d2

Philosophy is not a knowledge to be learned or a skill to be honed. It is not a set of truths to be repeated, a faith to be professed or an object to be exchanged (Nightingale 1995: 48). It is a practice, a form of life. It is the love of wisdom, its consistent and determined pursuit, not its possession or repetition.

At this point, the narrative of Plato's three voyages to Syracuse pauses, as does his recounting of the advice he would offer to Dion's relatives and friends, and we begin what is known as the philosophical digression (342a7–345c4). And while these next few Stepahnos pages do interrupt the narrative flow of the letter, and while they do not offer any specific political advice to those around Dion, this passage is anything but unmotivated within the structure of the letter as a whole, and indeed it forms the epistle's philosophical core. Hence, I would argue, it offers the letter's most coherent vision of both the philosophical subject and the politics of its formation. If philosophers are to rule, then the nature of what constitutes philosophy must be central to our understanding, as indeed must the form of its instruction.

I want now to read closely several passages from the 'digression', before in the next section turning to draw the political consequences thereof. In this passage, Plato seeks to define the three elements that make up knowledge or *epistēmē*. That knowledge takes up a specific attitude in relation to being. The subject of philosophy, we learn, is formed not through the transmission of knowledge, but through the deliberate and critical manipulation of these three elements to produce ever new relations between knowledge and the being it purports to know, creating a kind of intellectual friction before, eventually, producing the spark of enlightenment.

Knowledge as normally understood for Plato is a repeatable structure. It is dependent upon a framework that seeks to align language (*onoma*), argument (*logos*), image and perception (*eidolon*), the totality of which is called *epistēmē*,[4] often translated 'knowledge'. But for Plato in the *Seventh Letter*, philosophy's concern is not so much with these three elements and their correct alignment to produce repeatable knowledge, as with the contingency of those structures in relation to what makes them possible, which he calls being (*on*) and the known (*gnōston*) (342 a-b). Thus, every identifiable phenomenon has a name (*onoma*). Plato uses the example of a circle. We can then make propositions (*logoi*) about that phenomenon. For example, 'circles are round'. Lastly, we can check those propositions against the images we either receive or make of circles (*eidōla*), whether through culture or personal experience, and when we perceive an alignment between these three – yes, the name circle is applied to things that are round – we then have *epistēmē*.

Now certain forms of empirical research would stop there. Philosophy however, at least on Plato's understanding, is only beginning. Rather than being primarily concerned with the proper correlation between names and things, or between propositions and perceptions (*pace* Heidegger 1982, 1988), philosophy demands a continuous running up and down of the relations between these categories and of their hierarchies of correlation: a continuous rubbing of them against one another to find the slippages and friction points between them (343e). In the same manner, Socrates in the *elegkhos* continuously seeks agreement with his interlocutor about a given proposition and then tests that proposition against a variety of cases, generalizations, and counterexamples, often leaving his interlocutors not in the possession of firm knowledge, from which they can deduce positive prescriptions concerning the nature of things or the organization of social life, but in a state of perplexity or *aporia*, as the solid links between names, arguments, and perception become frayed, and a moment of what belies any contingent epistemic reality becomes visible (Hadot 1995 : 55–7, 103; Nehamas 1998 : 82–5; Blondell 2002 : 100, 124; compare *Sophist* 230a-d).

To return to our example, then, the reality of the circle qua circle (as opposed to that of any particular circular object), which seemed to inhere in both the name itself and the propositions in which it appeared and to be confirmed by personal perception and the social imaginary, when adequately examined and tested, begins to float free of these empirical constraints and instead comes to constitute the ideal object of geometry, an object that possesses specific and universal mathematical qualities that exist apart from any of it empirical instantiations. For those empirical instantiations are always possessed of a certain contingency, a certain element of that which is opposed to the thing itself in its intrinsic being. There indeed is no drawing or rendition of the circle that does not contain an element, however, small it may be of the straight (*eutheos*, 343a5–9). No ball is ever perfectly round. A factual part of our existence, the empirical circle, that was a function of our perception and our use of language and reason is now revealed to have its being *as* a circle apart from those elements of factual knowledge in the circle *qua* circle. And hence what is known (*gnōston*) is shown to transcend knowledge as repeatable information (*epistēmē*) and to consist in the experience of both the initial recognition of the correspondence of the first three elements and then, through their progressive manipulation, in the recognition that the reality to which they gesture ultimately exceeds their grasp. If this is true for an object as simple and intuitive as a circle, it is all the more the case with more abstract concepts like the good, the just, and the true, which structure our norms of political existence.

The aim of philosophical life, then, is not the production of repeatable empirical knowledge but the revelation of its limitations, the demonstration of the ways in which it always falls short of being. Philosophy does not seek to confirm the reality of our perceptions or their correspondence to the pre-existing names and categories that make up our daily existence but rather it precipitates the deconstruction of their preconceived unity, and does so as the predicate to the production of new knowledge, new understandings, new truths possessed of a more adequate, or at least different, relation to being itself. There is, however, no self-sufficient metalanguage that can be recorded in a book or repeated by others to guarantee the truth:

> Indeed, the argument (*logos*) itself concerning argument (*peri logou*),[5] if it consists of nouns (*onomatōn*) and verbs (*rhēmatōn*), is in no way sufficiently grounded in its solidity. There are a thousand arguments concerning each of these four elements that they lack clarity. But the greatest is what we said before: that concerning these two things, being and quality, the soul seeks to know not what sort of thing something is but what it is. Yet each of the four elements offers to the soul, through argument and experience, not what is sought, rather each thing that is said and demonstrated presents itself as being easily refuted by the senses and so fills a man with practically every perplexity and confusion. Consequently, on the one hand, we are not accustomed to seek the truth through onerous training, and on the other, the first image that comes to us suffices, and using them we do not become laughingstocks to one another, even though we are being questioned by those who are able to toss about the four elements and to refute them.
>
> 343b4–d2

Indeed, Plato argues that in many circumstances, the person who is glibly able to manipulate the first four elements can make the person with knowledge of the fifth, that is, the person who understands how the knowledge of the empirical world always falls short of being adequate to itself, appear foolish whether in speech, in writing, or in the give and take of question and answer (343d5). The problem, then, is less that of speech versus writing, than that of the repeatable and the unrepeatable, of knowledge as data as opposed to knowledge as discovery.

The philosopher, who does not accept the givenness of our experiential world, will often appear foolish or even ignorant to those more adept at navigating the world of commonsense. Like the philosophers who return to the cave in the *Republic*, their insight may seem blindness. But the philosopher has a specific way of interrogating the terms that purport to name the world, the sensory images that embody it, and the arguments that link them together. Rather than seeing these relations as stable and self-identical, in which case fundamentally new knowledge would be impossible, since language and perception would be united in a way that would be completely adequate to the world, instead the philosopher 'passing through of all these things, moving up and down in relation to each thing, at length gives birth to knowledge of the ordered system of the world to a well constituted soul' (343e1–3). The philosopher does not pass on information but rather leads a constant inquiry into the relation between knowledge, naming, argument, and perception in relation to being, moving from the givenness of our world to its failure adequately to account for itself, a process that engenders a new process of naming and argument in relation to the images of the world we receive and a new set of knowledges, in a continuing process that leads not to a final set of adequate propositions, but to a moment of insight based on difference, founded on a critical attitude taken up in relation to being and its understanding in the world.

Plato explains, philosophy is an interactive process that normally takes place between a teacher and a student, although there is no reason why that teacher must be present in human form. The question is far more one of attitude and of a sustained dialogic interplay than that of oral versus written, present versus absent, or even human versus nonhuman/divine. Dionysius's book is nothing but the recording of bits of philosophical discourse heard or overheard and then repeated. In contrast, it is precisely through the deliberate and applied manipulation of the first three elements, and particularly of the slippages and resistances between them, that insight is sparked:

> It is necessary to learn these things, the true and the false, from the whole of being with all the work (*tribēs*) and time I spoke of at the beginning. But by rubbing (*tribomena*) each of these things against one another with exertion – names and arguments, observations and perceptions – by testing them in good faith and by using questions and answers without rancor or envy, reflection and intellect *shine forth*, extending to the limits of human potential.
>
> 344b, emphasis mine

The recollection here of the earlier image of the spark of understanding blazing forth is not to be missed. Philosophy is like being near a fire that ignites the soul (Foucault 2008: 229). It is in the first instance a desire, but it is also a practice and a way of life that, far from founding an authoritarian state, has at its core the interrogation of the accepted names and arguments for things in order to produce new knowledge, new relations to being, and hence a necessary resistance to claims of authority that are rooted in pretensions to epistemic and political absolutism. If philosophy cannot be learned and transmitted as a given set of observations, as what Plato terms *mathēmata*, then the philosopher himself can never be a lawgiver per se, can never be the person who transmits a set of unchanging norms that seek to govern others (Foucault 2008: 229–34).

What, then, would it mean for philosophers to rule? In the first place, it would not be an agnostic infinite deferral of action. As the example of Dion and those around him indicates, a philosophical politics cannot be just another form of quietism or mere contemplation. It must speak to power. Moments of decision come, actions must be taken. But these actions are never per se philosophical. They are not, nor can they be, justified in themselves apart from the context of their occurrence. Just as philosophical statements uttered out of context and reproduced in a book do not possess the spark of enlightenment, so there is no rote set of political nostrums, whether recorded in the *Republic* or elsewhere, that if only they were followed would produce philosophical rule.

Plato in his letters lays down four predicates to philosophical rule. First, one must a have a group of trusted, like-minded friends (325d1). To rule alone is a fantasy that can only survive based on tyranny and fear. Second, those who would lead must be given over to the sober, self-correcting, infinite pursuit of the truth outlined in the philosophical digression. This precludes the possession of a totalitarian truth that will be enforced on others and instead manifests itself most profoundly in an infinite willingness to question oneself and others. This questioning does not mean that the philosopher will simply dither and refuse to make a commitment when the moment comes for decisive action. Socrates did not abandon his post, whether in war or as a philosophical gadfly (*Apology* 28d10–31c3). But it also means refusing to do what one knows to be either evil or merely expedient because one's friends or the member's of one's party support it, or because it falls under a certain rubric. Thus, as Plato reminds us at the beginning of the *Seventh Letter*, Socrates knew many of those who participated in the rule of the Thirty, a number of whom were Plato's kinsmen, and a case can even be made that Socrates initially supported their rule – he had certainly voiced a number critiques of Athenian democracy, if the dialogues are to be believed – nonetheless, when Socrates was asked to participate in what amounted to an extrajudicial killing, he refused at the peril of his own life (324d2–325a4 cf *Apology* 32c). Third, then, the philosopher must be committed to living a life that, rather than given over to the immediate pursuit of his every desire, is committed to the kind of rigorous inquiry outlined in the philosophical digression, a form of life that makes the individual thoughtful (*phronimos*), self-controlled (*sōphōn*), and possessed of virtue (*aretē*, 326 b9–c6). This is a form of life based on self-knowledge and self-reflection. Finally, and here I am drawing on the *Fifth Letter*, although this is consonant with what has come before, there are a plurality of possible constitutions and the best advice any counselor can give is for that constitution to speak in its own voice:

> Each constitution has its own voice, just like certain animals, there is one for democracy, another for oligarchy, and another for monarchy; very many would say they know these constitutions. But for the most part they eschew their recognition, except for a few. Whichever constitution would speak in its own voice to gods and men and would deliver deeds in accord with that voice always prospers and preserves itself, and imitating another it is corrupted.
>
> *321d4–e2*[6]

Thus, far from the image of philosopher as dictator, or even the philosopher as benevolent monarch, there is a strong sense that philosophical rule is almost an oxymoron, at least a paradox. It is dependent on the willing assent of others, it avoids all claims of absolute knowledge and the absolutization of one's own desires over those of others, and it recognizes a plurality of possible constitutions.

If we return to the actual passage in the *Seventh Letter* concerned with philosophical governance and read it closely, another sense can be construed than that of monarchical rule, in the sense of one person or a group of people coercing others to live in a certain way. What Plato says is that after his disillusion with the rule of the Thirty, and after Socrates' execution at the hands of the restored democracy, when he realized he did not have the political support in the form friends and allies necessary to make change in Athens and when he had surveyed the other cities of Greece and saw that they were governed little better, he 'was forced to say, while praising proper philosophy, that it is only from philosophy that it becomes possible to envisage (*katidein*) both just things in the realm of politics and in private life' (326a6–8). Thus on the one hand the philosopher is the political subject par excellence, but on the other he has that status not from possessing a set of prescribed truths, but from a capacity to 'envision, behold, regard' just things (*LSJ*). One might even say 'to imagine'. Owing to this capacity, Plato then concludes:

> And so the tribes of men will not cease from evils before either the tribe that philosophizes correctly (*orthōs*) and truly (*alēthōs*) comes into positions of political leadership (*arkhas … tas politikas*) or that of those who exercise power (*dunasteuontōn*) in cities would actually (*ontōs*) philosophize.
>
> *326a8–b4*

There is in fact nothing in this passage about philosophers 'ruling'. Rather what is envisaged is one of two things. Either those who truly philosophize, as outlined in the philosophical digression, would take office (that is, assume a position of leadership) whether in a democracy or under some other form of constitution, or those who currently exercise power would actually undertake the set of activities that qualify as the love of wisdom. Political leaders thus envisioned would not simply have those who spout philosophical discourses and tropes in their presence, nor would they themselves merely be able to repeat those discourses and tropes or even to inscribe them within the confines of a book, but they must *be* philosophers. That is to say, they must live with the matter (*pragma*) of philosophy, and they must in this living together with its concerns continuously run up and down the various possible correlations between language, argument, and perception to interrogate the foundations of knowledge and its changing relation to being. In this way, it becomes possible to think beyond the given, in this way it becomes possible to imagine new ways of living both in the *polis* and as an individual, in this way it becomes possible to know who you are and pursue the just as someone who is thoughtful, moderate and possessed of virtue. This is not the rule of professional philosophers, but the possibility of those who would imagine new and more complete visions of the just and the good to come into positions of leadership in our communities or the possibility to educate and fundamentally change those who exercise power within them (ask yourself how many of our current political leaders would qualify). As the cases of Dionysius and Dion both demonstrate, neither of these possibilities is easy or assured, but that is not to say we should not act to further this possibility.

Now the informed interlocutor might well say at this point, 'that is a very nice picture you paint, and a possible reading of the *Seventh Letter*, but is it Plato?' And while I will refrain just a bit longer from engaging the arguments surrounding the authenticity of Plato's letters, I want to begin by contending there is nothing I have argued here that is not consonant with the wider sweep of Plato's corpus. We need go no further than the *Symposium*, where Eros, as mediator between gods and men, in his role as a *daimōn*, is said to be always the desire for what we do not have. Eros is, in fact, in the last analysis, a figure for philosophy, he is even described in terms that directly recall Socrates himself, and philosophy, we are reminded in the dialogue, is not the possession of wisdom but its desire. Only the gods are wise, but humans, who by definition die and therefore desire, can only *desire* wisdom, can only *love* wisdom, can only be *philos* toward *sophia*. Consequently, the philosopher cannot be the source of wisdom, transferred from one person to another in the form of information, but can only be he who stimulates its desire in others and through that desire leads them to the good.

By the same token, it might be objected that, even if the *Seventh Letter* and the *Fifth* allow us to imagine a variety of possible constitutions and forms of philosophical leadership that would be very different from any kind of autocratic rule, the *Republic* is much less equivocal: both making clear its support for monarchy over democracy and the need for philosophical rulers possessed of the kind of absolute knowledge we see portrayed in the analogy of the divided line. There are a number of responses that can be made here from the perspective of reading the letters. On the most banal level, the letters purport to give practical political advice. They are not creating a utopian Kallipolis to be ruled by a specially selected and educated elite, which Socrates in the *Republic* admits is not a practical blueprint but 'a pattern laid up in heaven' (9.592a). The letters are (or purport to be) giving advice to friends and comrades about what they should do in specific situations, which are sometimes fraught with personal peril and not merely theoretical.

At the same time, as I have argued elsewhere at some length and will summarize briefly here, the absolute knowledge that the philosopher king is sometimes said to possess is in fact anything but absolute (2015). Upon closer inspection, it turns out to be a series of semblances: a series of waking visions, analogies and artful fictions, that while they too may approach being do not directly apprehend it in an immediate sense. As Socrates says when he introduces the comparison of the 'good' to the sun, an image that will govern much of the central discussion of the *Republic* up to and including Book 7's Myth of the Cave:

> It would also be very satisfying for me [to explain the good], my friend, I said, but I fear that I will not be able; and being eager but behaving shamelessly I will become a laughing stock. But, my fine gentlemen, let us leave aside what is the good itself for the moment. To arrive at the way things seem to me now (*tou ge dokountos emoi*) appears (*phainetai*) beyond our present attempt. But I wish to say what appears (*phainetai*) to be both the offspring of the good (*ekgonos te tou agathou*) and most similar to that (*homoiotatos ekeinōi*).
>
> Republic 6.506d5–e2

The language in this passage is intensely figurative, using conceits, metaphors and similes rather than literal denotation, and is replete with the language of semblance (*dokeo, phainomai, homoios*). The Good is not described. It is certainly not indicated or demonstrated. Rather the impression it makes on a given individual is evoked in a way that at once points beyond the figure used to convey that impression and calls constant attention to the gap between the figure and that which it seeks to represent.

When Glaucon responds that Socrates should go ahead with his description of the child of the Good so that he can then lay out the *narrative* of the father (*tou patros... tēn diēgēsin*, 506e3–4), Socrates replies that he would like to be able to produce this narrative and for Adeimantos and Glaucon to be able to receive it, but he cannot, and they should be careful lest he unwittingly deceive them by passing on an argument that is spurious concerning this child. This extended metadiscourse underlines that Socrates' tale is not to be accepted at face value. The brothers must be wary, lest in narrating through a similitude the impression of how the Good seems to him now, Socrates should pass off a bastard for a legitimate child.

Now it will be objected that the simile of the divided line *does* posit access to a world beyond appearances, however arduous the path, and it is the cognition of this world that stands at the most exalted reaches of dialectic and is what distinguishes *noēsis* from mere *dianoia*. Thus at 510b8, Socrates describes the highest form of cognition as moving from assumptions or hypotheses to first principles 'without likenesses (*eikonōn*)' and using the 'forms themselves'. At 510e3–511a2, Socrates says that thought uses likenesses (*eikosin*) when seeking to know/see (*idein*) those very things that one would not know/see (*idoi*) otherwise than through *dianoia*, whereas at 511c1 he says that *noēsis* makes no use of sense perception (*aisthētōi*). And, it is for this reason that all the conventional readings of this passage, see the line as divided between *doxa* (the realm of likenesses and objects in the world) and that of *epistēmē*, the realm of *dianoia*, which uses likenesses and hence still functions in the world of semblance, and of *noēsis*, which dispenses with appearance altogether and deals with the forms themselves (Jowett and Campbell 1894,

309, 313; Adam 1963, vol. 2, 65, 156; Diès 1965, lxvi; Chambry 1967, 143; Denyer 2007, 305). If this is the case, then we are presented here with a very different concept of knowledge than that found in the philosophical digression.

Nonetheless, I would contend that the conventional reading offers an incomplete understanding of the simile. There are a number of reasons for advocating a more critical interpretation of the text.[7] In many ways, the issue, however, can be boiled down to what is the ontological status of the *eikōn* and what does it mean to know/see. Plato introduces the divided line to illustrate the fact that there are two forms of knowledge, perception and thought (509d4). Thus while Plato consistently speaks of the higher reaches of thought as working without *eikones* and speaks of *eikones* as mere images such as reflections seen in pools or shadows (both of which reappear in the cave), these *eikones* are in every case visual diagrams. They are images used as models from which deductions can be made and reliable conclusions reached, such as drawings of squares or triangles that are employed to solve problems in geometry and thus are like the *eidōla* of the *Seventh Letter* (cf. 509d10–510a5; 510d5–511a2).

These, however, are not the only kinds of *eikones* deployed by Socrates in the *Republic*. Whether we are speaking of the likeness of the 'sun', or the myth of the 'cave', these are all referred to as *eikones* in the text, but they are clearly not diagrams from which deductions are to be made. Rather they open new ways of thinking, which allow their own premises to be questioned. Indeed, if we read carefully the final description of the noetic in the passage under review, we quickly see that rather than qualifying it as the exclusion of the world semblance (*doxa*) and of likeness (*eikōn*), it both asserts the impossibility of escaping that world, even as it posits a different use and different relationship to the doxic. What follows is a very literal translation, which strives to make apparent the complex semantic and imagistic play in Plato's Greek that often gets lost in more standard renderings[8]:

> This then is the *eidos* of the intelligible of which I was speaking with the soul compelled to use the assumptions it has put under itself (*hupothesesi*)[9] concerning the pursuit of this *eidos*, not going to the first principle (*archēn*), since it is not able to step out from (*ekbainein*) and above its assumptions, but using as likenesses (*eikōsi*) the things from which likenesses are made (*apeiskatheisin*) below and those things which in relation to those others have been judged manifest in accordance with their appearance (*enargesi dedoxasmenois*) and are honoured.
>
> 511a4–9

The noetic, then, is not a realm of pure intellection. Even at the top of the divided line, the soul's intellection is dependent on the hypotheses that it has placed under itself as assumptions. The noetic does not escape representation (*eikosi*). It does not escape inscription. But its relation to representation is different. Rather than taking its assumptions as axioms to be used in the manner of a geometric proof, the noetic soul uses those assumptions themselves as likenesses. These mental images are opined/ judged/ believed in (*doxazō*) on the basis of the way they seem to be clear/visible (*enargēs*) in relation to the more common category of images, that is to say, on the way they appear. These likenesses are not used to create self-identical chains of deduction but to explore their own premises and that which lies beyond them, to be critical, to think differently. In this way the philosopher is not trapped in a self-referential dream, but is he who has a vision that points beyond itself by refusing to leave its own assumptions unquestioned (*Republic* 533b–c3). The philosopher, is the thinker who always uses the realm of semblance as way to go beyond the seeming self-evidence of his own knowledge. Thus at the end of the Myth of the Cave, we are told that the true philosopher, who has been freed from the shackles of the cave and drug into the light of the sun, and becomes accustomed to the light, even he, scarcely is able to see (*horasthai*) the idea (*idea*) of the Good. He does not intuit it, he does not know it, he literally almost, with difficulty (*mogis*), catches a glimpse of fire of the sun (*Republic* 7.517b7–c4), like the spark of enlightenment kindled through the process outlined in the *Seventh Letter*.

Frank (2018) offers a even more radical critique of the view that the *Republic* calls for philosopher kings, who are possessed of absolute knowledge of the good, to rule. While Frank and I do not agree on every passage or the accent to place on every concept at play in the *Republic*,[10] we wind up in a very similar place.[11] To wit, everything depends on what it is understood by the work of philosophy. If by philosophy we understand information, that is a content that can be transferred directly from master to student, whether orally or in writing, then the reign of philosopher kings, who have received this information and will now codify it as law and impose it upon the ruled, will differ little from that of the tyrant, whether it be the abstract tyrant of *Republic* 9 or the actual tyrants of Syracuse detailed in the *Seventh Letter*. Yes, the tyrant may pursue his own limitless desires, and the philosopher king, if we grant the currency of the conventional reading of the *Republic*, may be filled with the more impersonal desire that his strict curriculum has inculcated within him, but from the perspective of the ruled the effect may be little different in terms of the ruler's ability to be receptive to their desires or to enter into a sincere dialogue as opposed to the dictation of absolutes. Yet as the *Seventh Letter* makes clear, no matter how much philosophy Dionysius and the members of his court have heard, no matter the number or type of philosophemes they repeat, and no matter how accurately those philosophemes may be recorded in the tyrant's book, this is not the work of philosophy. Philosophy is a practice of inquiry, a continuous conversation in which the elements of knowledge are rubbed one against the other to produce a spark of enlightenment, a momentary illumination that leads not to a final codification, but to an expanded and renewed conversation, whether that conversation takes place between individuals, between those individuals and a text, or within the individuals themselves. In actuality, for those of us who are readers of the dialogues it is inevitably all three.

This on my understanding is the essence of Frank's argument. The *Republic* is not a blueprint for a master constitution that Plato advocates is to be imposed on the recalcitrant cities of the Greek world by a class of enlightened guardians, nor is it a straightforward description of the nature of philosophy and its ideal city, however utopian such a project may be. It is a profound meditation on the nature of justice in the city and the soul, a discussion between flawed and partial characters that is meant to be read and reread. Indeed, the practice of reading as an iterative and dialogic process is central to Frank's understanding of what the *Republic* is (2018: 1–33).[12] The 'soul is summoned to reflection' as Socrates notes, 'when it receives different and even contradictory indices, whether from perception, instruction, or its own internal cogitation, and this reflection is what leads to the desire we call philosophy, the love of wisdom' (*philo-sophia*; Frank 2018: 43, 74). The practice of dialogic reading is a continuous summons to reflection as we experience both perplexity and moments of insight in our encounters with these complex and variegated texts. Philosophy on this view, as Socrates says, is a series of 'free and beautiful discussions whose sole aim is to seek the truth' (Frank 2018: 135, citing *Republic* 6, 499a). This is not however what the philosopher kings of Glaucon and Adeimantus's ideal city are pictured as engaging in. As Frank observes:

> Most telling, perhaps is that the philosopher kings never actually speak. When, for example, the philosopher kings order the desires of the 'ordinary majority' (431c–d), they are not depicted as doing so by discursive methods ... If the 'serious truth' of the *Republic* is to be found in the free and beautiful discussions of philosophy, then that truth, it seems ... is not to be associated with the philosopher-kings.
>
> *Frank 2018: 136–7*

It is surely no accident, then, that at several points throughout the *Republic* Socrates disclaims ownership of the ideal city (*kallipolis*), noting that this is the city desired by the brothers, and the justice found therein is the justice appropriate to such a constitution. There is then nothing in Frank's reading or my own of the *Republic* that necessarily contradicts the vision of philosophy found in the *Seventh Letter*.

Nor are our positions necessarily outliers. While certainly the conventional reading of the *Republic* has existed for centuries, a counter tradition has also been present, which I will outline in summary form below. This counter tradition is not just of recent vintage, but has been part of Platonic thought from the first generations of the Academy and of the skepticism that has been associated with that name. Thus, as noted at the beginning of this section, it has long been recognized that in the *Symposium* the philosopher is not the possessor of wisdom but its lover, one who pursues wisdom through a set of rigorous practices, which bear upon lifestyle, dialogue, and education (Brown 1994: 169–70; Hunter 2004: 86–7). Knowledge, on this view, is not a prefabricated object that can be exchanged, but something arrived at through a practice of dialogue and free discussion that prepares students to approach knowledge on their own terms (Festugière 1950: 42–3, 19; Hadot 1995: 104–6). Plato, as Hampton acknowledges, 'never makes a direct claim to absolute knowledge' (1994: 236). Rather, *philosophia* is the pursuit 'not the attainment of knowledge' (Saxonhouse 1994: 82).

That pursuit is a form of self-fashioning. Philosophy is the creation of a certain type of subject, produced through a sustained dialogic engagement with others and the self (Koyré 1962: 20). That dialogue in Socratic practice takes place in the form of the *elegkhos*, a systematic set of questions and answers designed to test the limits of the interlocutor's knowledge, as showcased in dialogues such as the *Apology* or the *Ion* and featured in Socrates' questioning of Agathon in the *Symposium*. The purpose of the *elegkhos* is not to found an unassailable epistemological position nor to produce knowledge that can be possessed and transmitted but to convince the interlocutor of their soul's internal incoherence and of the consequent necessity to care for themselves as a propaideutic to caring for others (Hadot 1995: 55, 102–5; Nehamas 1998: 75; Blondell 2002: 124). The goal of dialectical interchange is not to 'teach' in the conventional sense, to fill the student with knowledge, but to provoke the interlocutor into an active understanding and to break the hold of the immediate upon the soul (Brown 1994: 166–7; Blondell 2002: 100). It is less concerned with conformity and obedience than with transcending the limitations of the self as a knowing, erotic, social and political being (Gadamer 1991: 4–5).

From this perspective, the forms, serve less as a means to make the given conform to the objects of absolute knowledge than to make possible the transcendence of the immediate on both the personal and the political level. The Platonic texts present less a rigid dichotomy between two worlds – the temporal and eternal, the fallen and the perfected – than the possibility of imagining a more just, a more rational and a more beautiful world, of going beyond the given within the world. The forms are what make objects recognizable *qua* objects – the table *qua* table, the city *qua* city, justice *qua* justice – and hence make possible such questions as: is this object what it should be, is there a better table, a better city, a more perfect justice to come (Zuckert 1996: 73; Gadamer 1988: 260; 1065: 92; compare *Parmenides* 132b-d; 135b-c; *Sophist* 250c)?

Thus while there has been since the nineteenth century a question about whether Plato's letters are authentic (Edelstein 1966), the first thing we need to recognize is that there is nothing in the *Seventh Letter* that is at such variance with positions found elsewhere in the Platonic corpus as to make us think this text is not part of that larger body. Moreover, on a philosophical level, it really does not matter whether the text was written by Plato himself, since it contains nothing substantive that should be excluded. Even those who doubt its provenance have by and large seen the *Seventh Letter* as emanating from within the Academy and as having been written only shortly after Plato's death. At the same time, it is important to recognize that none of the ancient authorities doubt the authenticity of the letters, and Cicero and Plutarch both testify to their existence and utility. It is only once we arrive in the nineteenth century and the age of philological skepticism that doubts arose and there were sustained attempts to prove the letters forgeries. While this re-examination has cast the provenance of some of the less important letters into doubt, few today question the value of the *Seventh Letter* as a guide to Platonic thought (Festugière 1950: 61; Souilhé 1960: xxi, l-lviii; Morrow 1962: 1–16; Hamilton 1973: 105–6; Foucault 2008: 193; Harward 2014: 59–96).

In 1983 Foucault gave his annual series of lectures at the Collège de France on the topic *Le Gouvernement de soi et des autres*. Continuing the work began in the previous year's *L'Herméneutique du sujet* (2001), he explores the formation of the philosophical subject of antiquity as a truth-teller in relation both to itself and to others. The formation of this truth-telling subject, whom Foucault labels the 'parrhesiast', from the Greek word for 'frank speech', *parrhēsia* (literally, 'all-telling'), has political and ethical consequences that were as pertinent in the France of 1983 as they are today. Foucault turns to antiquity to undertake a series of commentaries on ancient texts in order trace the genealogy of the philosophical subject as one who speaks truth to power (Gros 2008: 348–9, 357). The philosophical subject does so not by making pronouncements on specific policies, nor as a professional philosopher giving lessons in a university setting, but by confronting power with the real of philosophy, with its labor, its experience (Foucault 2008: 210–11, 318; Gros 2008: 358–61). Foucault thus defines the central concern of the course as:

> I want to try to see how truth-telling, the obligation and the possibility of truth-telling in the procedures of government are able to show how the individual constitutes itself in relation to itself and in relation to others. Truth-telling in the procedures of government and the constitution of an individual as a subject for himself and for others: it's a little bit of this that I would like to talk to you about this year.
>
> *2008: 42*

In doing so, Foucault is pursuing his project of establishing what he terms 'the ontology of the present': that is, the being of our present moment, the way in which reality is defined and exists for us, not in the form of a transcendental deduction, but as a thousand barely audible voices that inform, contradict and determine one another and exist in a recursive relationship between present and past that in turn constitutes the future as a determined set of possibilities (2008: 22). From such a perspective, his reading of Plato's *Seventh Letter* is hardly antiquarian.

Parrhēsia is not just the fact of making a true statement. It is the self-conscious act of speaking the truth. It represents a decision and, consequently, a way of being as a subject (Foucault 2008: 62, 64). It is not something that just happens, and it also involves a certain risk. Whether it is Socrates before the Athenian people, Plato before Dionysius the Younger, Seneca before Nero, Emma Goldman before the American bar, or Solzhenitzen before the Soviet state, the parrhesiast puts themselves at risk to speak their truth. 'Parrhesiasts are those who, at the limit, accept to die in order to have spoken the truth. Or more precisely, parrhesiasts are those who undertake to speak the truth at a price that has not been determined, which could include even their own death' (Foucault 2008: 56). For Foucault, the philosopher in antiquity, insofar as he leads a philosophical life, insofar as he dedicates himself to finding and speaking the truth and not simply to repeating philosophical truisms or repeating certain philosophemes, is the parrhesiast par excellence. And this too is his political function:

> Philosophical discourse in its truth, inside the game it necessarily plays with politics in order find there its truth, does not have to project what a political action ought to be. He does speak truth about the political action, he does not speak truth

for the political action, he speaks truth in relation to political action, in relation to the exercise of politics, in relation to the political personage.

Foucault 2008: 265

As Plato and Dion were to Dionysius, the philosopher is to be a 'truth speaker' in the Nietzshean mode: a person who undertakes to speak the truth as a self-conscious act in relation to the exercise of power, an act that must always call that power into question, and that must always freely risk the life of the speaker. The parrhesiast speaks not to advance a particular political position, which would instrumentalize and subordinate truth to power, but he or she speaks the truth as a risk to both life and power (Foucault 2008: 51–4, 64).

Thus, in his very detailed reading of the *Seventh Letter*, which has throughout this essay inspired my own, Foucault argues that Plato defines the role of the philosopher as one who must expose to the tyrant the *pragma* of philosophy: the labor of interrogation and self-transformation that constitutes philosophy's relation to the real (2008: 220). That labor in turn is defined most clearly in the philosophical digression and the five elements of knowledge we discussed above. What Foucault want to draw our attention to more than the five elements is the labor (*tribē*) that goes into rubbing them against one another, the productive friction of insistent inquiry that leads to the spark of enlightenment (2008: 230–2). And it is precisely that *tribē* that Dionysius refuses in favour of writing his book, in favor of a philosophical performance that does not transform either his life or his rule, but serves instead as at best a harmless ornament or at worst a malicious mystification (2008: 227). It is, however, the philosopher's role to put the tyrant to the test (*elegkhos*) and to expose his lack of seriousness. In doing so he speaks the truth to power, not to advance a certain prefabricated political agenda or to enact specific policy proposals, though undoubtedly he has views on all these matters, but to confront power with alternative truths.

> For Plato, and in a general fashion it seems to me for all of Western philosophy, the true wager has never been to tell politicians what to do. Their wager has always been, before the politicians, before political practice, before politics, to exist as a philosophic discourse and philosophic truth-telling.
>
> *Foucault 2008: 266–7*

The philosopher as parrhesiast is not the possessor of absolute knowledge but the subject of resistance precisely insofar as he is a philosopher.

At the beginning of the *Seventh Letter*, Plato narrates his disillusionment with Athenian politics, whether in the form of the reactionary oligarchy of the Thirty or the restored radical democracy. His conclusion is that under current circumstances he would withdraw from Athenian politics to focus on philosophy until such time as either philosophers come into positions of leadership within the *polis* or those who lead the *polis* become philosophers. In the past, this pronouncement has been read as an endorsement of political rule by an all-knowing class of mandarins. This essay has argued that such a reading fundamentally misunderstands what Plato means by philosophy in the *Seventh Letter* and in the wider corpus.

Philosophy for Plato is not a body of knowledge. It is not a set of repeatable observations that gain in truth value the more frequently they are shown to correspond to an external reality. *Philosophia* is a mode of being, a form of life. The dialogue form on a certain level exemplifies that mode. It is not an accident that Plato never wrote a treatise and never within the dialogues speaks in his own name. The philosophical digression imagines a set of continuing interactions between two interlocutors who through their determined application 'rub off' the smooth surface of our accepted truths and expose the rough edges of our object world and our experience. The subjects formed from such an ongoing set of interactions between language, argument, perception and bodies of knowledge will neither be compliant before constituted structures of power, accepting their given and unchangeable nature, nor all-knowing rulers, who possessed of a stable truth would force others to conform. Philosophical rule under such circumstances would be at best a paradox, for it would be rule by the subjects of resistance, by the antithesis of arrogant, unanswerable power. *Vive la résistance!*

Notes

1. A shorter and modified version of this chapter appears in Chinese translation under the title, 澳門理工學報（人文社會科學版） in the *Journal of Macao Polytechnic Institute* (Social Science and Humanities).
2. All translations are my own unless otherwise stated.
3. Compare *Gorgias* (475d7, 521a2–5, 521e2–4).
4. Plato is not always consistent in his use of these terms. As Brisson and Pradeau (2007) observe, elsewhere *epistēmē* has a meaning much closer to what Plato here terms *gnōsis*.
5. Some translate 'definitions'. This certainly makes the argument clearer but loses the self-reflexive perspective of *logos* being brought to bear on *logos*, that is to say of the attempt to formulate a metalanguage. See Souilhé (1960), Hamilton (1973) and Harward (2014) among others.
6. Compare Foucault (2003: 195–6).
7. Some of these are of a rather technical nature and concern questions such as whether the line is divided into equal (*isa*) or unequal (*anisa*) segments and, if unequal, which portion should be larger. Disputes about these issues go back to the ancient scholia, Plutarch, and Proclus. Without taking a position on the technical issues per se, these disputes demonstrate that the divided line is anything but a transparent illustration of a clear and stable truth, that the interpretive issues are not a product of either latter day ignorance of the ancient context or postmodern skepticism, and that the simile itself was meant to be received critically and provoke debate. See Adam 1963 and Chambry 1967 for their notes on 509d6; Slings' apparatus criticus (2003) and Denyer's excellent discussion (2007: 292–4).
8. See for example, Shorey (1935), with his numerous notes: 'This then is the class that I described as intelligible, it is true, but with reservation that the soul is compelled to employ assumptions in the investigations of it, not preceding to a first principle because of its inability

to rise above its assumptions, and second that it uses as images or likenesses the very objects that are themselves copied or adumbrated by the class below them, and that in comparison with these latter are esteemed as clear and held in honour.' Or more recently, Reeve (2004): 'This then is the kind of thing that I said was intelligible. The soul is forced to use hypotheses in the investigation of it, not traveling up to a first principle, since it cannot escape or get above its hypotheses, but using as images the very things of which images were made by the things below, and which by comparison to their images, were thought to be clear and to be honored as such.' Both do a creditable job, but the Greek resists smooth translation.

9. Compare 511b4, where the hypotheses are not simply assumptions, but are that which you place (*tithêmi*) under (*hupo*) yourself, that you then step off of as you approach being.
10. And indeed, as she makes clear, as good readers we should not.
11. I should note that for many years I have had benefit of her conversation on these topics.
12. Compare my argument (Miller 1994) on the importance of rereading for constituting the interiority of what I term there 'lyric subjectivity'.

CHAPTER 7
BODY POLITICS IN ARISTOTLE'S *POETICS* AND *RHETORIC*
Nancy Worman

In book 3 of the *Rhetoric*, when discussing analogical metaphors, Aristotle remarks that an old man should not wear a red cloak if he wants to persuade an audience (1405a13–14). I have been engaging with this image for a long time; it has become for me something like what Shirley Barlow once called an 'obsessive object'.[1] While she was talking about Ion's broom in Euripides' play, and thus about a dramatic object, I am interested in Aristotle's cloak for reasons that may not look at first glance to be very related to the handling of a prop. But cloak and broom turn out to share a curious affinity when one analyzes the effects that Aristotle's philosophical priorities have on theatrical and oratorical settings.

On the surface, at least, the *Poetics* and *Rhetoric* appear largely to ignore both the particularities of their topics in the contemporary moment and the details of the democratic practices and venues.[2] Both treatises, in their different ways and to greater and lesser extents, distance the arts from their contemporary settings, in order to establish their 'proper' parameters as distinct from their malformations on the ground – that is, in Athens and environs in the mid-fourth century. That these texts promote a quasi-philosophical model at the expense of one more fully engaged with poetic and rhetorical practices is perhaps not so contentious. I am interested here in how this affects the representation of the genres in question in relation to embodied perception, since the philosophical model entails, in the case of the *Poetics*, a near-complete foreclosure of the context of performance and, in the case of the *Rhetoric*, an emphasis on hearing over seeing, as if the orator would ideally communicate with his audience as a disembodied voice poured directly into his listeners' ears. Both treatises denigrate audiences as shallow and corrupt in tastes and relegate embodied practices and objects (e.g., a red cloak) for the most part to metaphors and referential gestures that indicate them as falling 'outside of the subject', as Aristotle puts it in the *Rhetoric* (ἔξω τοῦ πράγματος, 1354a15 and *passim*).[3] Key elements in this strategic downplaying are style, emotion and delivery – that is to say, those central to embodied performance.

In pointing to such gestures I mean among other things to counter Edith Hall's influential claim that there is no polis in the *Poetics*, by which she means primarily Athenian ritual and civic practices, since this is not strictly the case, as I shall show.[4] I want also to highlight how these dismissive gestures and figurative embodiments nevertheless shape a kind of shadow inhabitation that unsettles Aristotle's philosophical formalism and prompts questions about the ethical and aesthetic values subtending his approach. The Athenian context is not so much absent as muted and disdained, such that a sharp contrast emerges between tragedy as embodied enactment and spectacle, and the treatise's uneasy treatment of that embodiment and the transference of its aesthetic and affective weight elsewhere – namely, to metaphors of viewing and bodily form.

In the case of the *Rhetoric*, Aristotle similarly disparages the venue and its contemporary practices and practitioners but without the more thorough isolating of the genre that marks his discussion of tragedy. He does belittle the attention paid by other writers of technical treatises (*technai*) to the speaker's self-presentation and to the audience, but he cannot dismiss either entirely.[5] The Assembly members, judges or spectators are particularly central, since they stand in a limiting, material relation to the *telos* of rhetoric – that at which every speech aims (*Rhet.* 1357b37–58a2).[6] While the general aim of oratory is persuasion, and the ends (*telē*) of each type of oratory are distinct, orators must calibrate the presentation of their characters and speeches to audiences.[7] The envisioned audiences of speeches are thus determinate of form to an extent that the audiences of tragedies cannot be, given that although the latter also sit in judgement they do so in a much more attenuated manner.

Despite the limiting relationship that audiences must have to the shape of speeches, when Aristotle discusses those aspects of oratory that come perilously close to addressing the Athenian setting – again, style, delivery, the emotions – he substitutes an abstracted perceiver, a 'hearer' (*akroatēs*) for what we would normally construe as an audience member in a fuller sense, but this one for the most part only has ears, as his chosen label indicates. He also almost entirely elides spectacle, including the details of the setting, aspects of delivery such as the orator's deportment, facial expression, clothing and so on, and the audience's engagement and reactions.[8] While this perceiver must, again, be more regularly attended to in a treatise focused on persuasion, he remains mostly disembodied and yet often denigrated for his love of spectacle and superficial effects. These two aspects of Aristotle's treatment sit oddly together, as the forlorn hearer is represented as most attuned to precisely what he lacks in the treatise – that is, visual and other sensory capacities and bodily presence.

In what follows I address such problems effectively from the outside in: from audiences to speakers' styles, delivery to figurative bodies, and finally bodies and emotions. First, however, I want to explain why I find it interesting or important to discuss embodiment in the first place, since it is so clearly tangential to Aristotle's scheme. The scornful references to actual practices and audiences, together with the figurative sleight of hand – 'Look! Over here! A red cloak!' – raise what for me are urgent questions about his philosophical conceits and their implicit politics.

Bodies between tragedy and oratory

While many theorists of tragedy, ancient and modern, share a sense that an unnerving combination of shame and attraction attaches to the experience of viewing tragic sights and experiencing their impact in language, Aristotle instead emphasizes the craft of reproducing (*mimêsis*), which gives pleasure even when it is of corpses or disgusting animals (ch. 4, *Po.* 1448b10–12).⁹ The *Poetics* represents this reproducing as itself a thing of great value, if well executed. In this view the spectacle of debased bodies would give a straightforward, enlightening pleasure, but for Aristotle this is also secondary, since he does not consider visual effects, or tragic spectacle more generally, to be very central to the dramatic idiom. Not only does he claim for tragedy a power independent of its enactment; he also considers the 'shuddering and pity' (φρίττειν καὶ ἐλεεῖν) that good tragedies arouse affects that the plot alone should be able to generate.¹⁰

The *Rhetoric* is a much more porous text in this regard. Because persuasion, whether in the courts or Assembly, is essentially transactional, the audience – and indeed, warts-and-all people more generally – must be included in the calculation of successful techniques, including visual effects. This reality clearly impedes Aristotle's impulse to abstract and systematize in relation to generic form and necessitates what are essentially human taxonomies, including of harms and benefits, virtues and vices, emotions and statuses, and so on.¹¹ And yet oratory also offers a different way around the messy contingencies of lived experience, in that it only involves one actor, no spectacle to speak of, and an audience that can be rendered only nominally present. It is thus much less tendentious to reduce its affective surround essentially to linguistic exchange (i.e., speaking and hearing) while also populating the edges of the argument with human inhabitations in their many characteristics and attitudes.

It may be helpful to recall here that actual dramatic and oratorical performances were ideology in action and something more, civic practices that developed in concert with, became central to, and yet also often exceeded or countered the values and practices of the radical democracy.¹² The philosophical reflections on these practices, in contrast, were written as the democracy was unravelling; and they aimed at the control and correction of the citizen body and bodies. But if Plato and Aristotle both appear focused on behavioural modelling in this more local sense, they simultaneously operate with a broader sense of the political, one that looks beyond any actual polis and its interests and yet engages with poetry and persuasion primarily in relation to the education of citizens more generally conceived.¹³ In this respect they have more in common with writers of tragedy, who raise questions about the ethics of human experience and the place of humans in the cosmos, than they do with writers (e.g., historians, orators) focused more narrowly on democratic practices.

Indeed, Aristotle finds that tragedy lends itself much more readily to abstraction; as he characterizes it in the *Poetics*, it is quite philosophical in its contemplation of universals (τὰ καθόλου, 9, 1451b5–10). Similarly, he deems the art of oratory, *rhetorikē*, the 'antistrophe' (ἀντίστροφος) of dialectic and aims to demonstrate its philosophical parallelisms. My provisional hunch is that Aristotle treats *poiētikē* as more potentially philosophical than *rhetorikē* and that the *Poetics* is, accordingly, a more fully 'philosophized' treatise, while rhetoric and the *Rhetoric* both reveal themselves to be less vulnerable to such pressures. From this prospect, then, the *Poetics* serves as the 'philosophical' other to the *Rhetoric*.

Plato and Aristotle share this philosophical, aesthetically attuned sense of the political not only with tragedy itself but also with some of its most noteworthy modern post-Marxist theorists, such as Raymond Williams and Jacques Rancière. What they do not share is precisely the theoretical link that undergirds my critique: namely, the intersection of aesthetics and politics at the points where ideological formulations manifest themselves in embodiment and lived practices.[14] When, for instance, Rancière characterizes Aristotle as 'redefining the politicity' of tragedy, he means that Aristotle is resetting the genre's conceptual parameters not only in relation to its narrower political profile (e.g., its nature as a democratic institution, its staging of democratic vs authoritarian values and practices), but also in relation to its ideology more generally. For Rancière this ideological containment centers on the politics of aesthetics in the sense of controlling or correcting what gets seen and felt as real and valuable (what he calls 'the distribution of the sensible', *le partage du sensible*) in particular venues at specific historical moments.[15] From his perspective, then, Aristotle's treatise attempts to cordon off tragedy in its 'proper' form from precisely those live sensations and inhabited experiences so central to tragic enactment in the civic setting.

The move that Rancière characterizes as a redefinition of tragedy's political character in this broader sense is also one that Williams would have recognized as a containment and formalization of 'feeling and thinking that is indeed social and material', as he puts it in his study *Marxism and Literature*.[16] From this angle Aristotle's urge towards formalism verges on travesty, as it purposely removes from consideration what he (Williams) takes to be most germane to apprehending what he calls 'structures of feeling', a phrase that he uses to capture 'meanings and values as they are actively lived and felt'.[17] These shape cultural production – the historical, material and affective conditions in which art emerges in and through its practices. Williams regards formalizing moves as guided by 'an abstracting, unilinear universalism', which by idealizing art isolates it from historical and social contingencies.[18]

I circle back to these thinkers below; at this point I call attention to them as a frame for appreciating the fact that while tragedy confronts the body in pain as an aesthetic object in its particular context – that is, in direct relation to sense and sensation – Aristotle conceives of plot as an embodied form that ought to be 'good for seeing' (*eusunoptos*) and yet independent of its viewing in the dramatic scene.[19] The perfection of this plot-as-body dovetails in alarming ways with his pervasive disdain for tragic enactment before a 'weak' and 'corrupt' audience. That is, his emphasis on unity and perfection as the 'bodily' characteristics of tragic form resonates ideologically in contrast to embodied dramatic practices in the civic setting with their diversely enacted plottings, actors and audiences. Recognizing Aristotle's elitist reaction to the contingencies of art in practice should thus foster both awareness of the developments of the form within a particular period (i.e., its emergent materialities) and the wider politics at play in Aristotle's putatively apolitical treatise (e.g., his denigration of these very materialities).[20] While ancient and modern theorists share a concern with this broader sense of the political, they part ways most distinctly around what gets valued: embodied, material contexts (i.e., a generalized historicity) for the post-Marxists versus abstracted, elevating forms (i.e., a deracinated aesthetics) for Plato and Aristotle.

A pressing question throughout my discussion is whether we can make the same political critique of Aristotle's treatment of rhetoric, and if not, what this means for my charge that his brand of philosophy may make for bad politics. Here again I do not mean the casual manner in which he mentions punishing slaves or using the testimony of torture victims (just for instance), although both are in keeping with the reprehensible myopia and subsequent distortions of a 'universalist' philosophizing. Rather, the question is to what extent the *Rhetoric* fosters a parallel redefinition of oratory's 'politicity' and pursues a similar plan of abstracting up and away from lived practices.

In what follows I consider such questions from four angles: audiences, style, plotting or argument, and emotions.

Disappointing audiences

In the *Rhetoric* and in the *Politics* as well, also likely conceived and presented during the time that tragedy was becoming widely disseminated and Athenian politicians were making patriotic claims upon it, Aristotle discusses artistic practices such as drama and music in relation to oratory in the former and civic education in the latter. Unlike those of his contemporaries who were busy celebrating Athenian civic practices, he is quick to point out the vulgar character of style and delivery (to which I return below) and the corruption of the crowd, or at least of some segments of it.

In book 3 of the *Rhetoric* this leads him to disparage poetic contests and styles as guides for oratorical performances, as performance itself is the province of dramatic poetry. Aristotle notes with asperity that both actors and those adept at delivery win more favor, because the hearer has corrupt tastes (διὰ τὴν τοῦ ἀκροατοῦ μοχθηρίαν, 1404a5-8, cf. διὰ τὴν μοχθηρίαν τῶν πολιτῶν, 1403b31-35). This hearer is distracted by outward appearances, such that to those most ignorant the simple (or 'silly', εὐήθη) expressions of poets appear greatest on the strength of their styles (1404a9-28). Because of such weaknesses, it would be best if one could avoid stirring the hearer's emotions altogether (1404a3-4). We can compare a caution right at the outset of the *Rhetoric* that one ought not 'warp' (διαστρέφειν) citizen audiences by leading them to anger and the like (1354a24-5). Elsewhere Aristotle (following Aristophanes and Plato) links this aesthetic distortion to concerns about musical education, in which 'twisting' (i.e., new, overly modulated) melodies have ill effects on civic character. The *Politics*, for instance, warns about the dangers of training in music (*mousikê*): exposure to the wrong sorts can make the young citizen effeminate and vulgar (φορτικός), his soul 'twisted' (cf. παρεστραμμέναι) like the melodies of decadent strains (1342a20-3, cf. 1339a-b,).[21]

Here crowd-pleasing musical performers and vulgar spectators come together in a degrading symbiosis, in which the spectators affect the quality of the music and themselves shape the styles of the players – even, Aristotle says, in their bodies (καὶ τὰ σώματα, 1341b18).[22] This occurs because the unrefined citizens expect such contortions,

149

a situation to be tolerated in the lower classes but not emulated in the education of the elite. For Aristophanes such effects are bound up with manliness and an appropriately robust attitude toward a decadent intellectualism; for Plato they also concern the well-being of the soul.[23] In the *Poetics* as well as the *Rhetoric* and *Politics*, Aristotle seems to consider both, repeatedly expressing concerns about the impact of popular tastes for sensationalist contortions (musical and gestural) on both poets and audience members.

Despite the overtly abstracting tendencies of Aristotle's philosophical inclinations, then, the Athenian setting constantly intrudes upon his treatises, including the *Poetics*. In the case of the discussion of tragedy the details of this setting are not overtly labelled as specific to Athens, and yet that text is clearly situated in reaction to the perceived disarray that attends its democratic practices. In fact this type of top-down denigration of the tastes of the Athenian masses (whom the influential commentator Gerald Else once wryly termed 'the groundlings') is more prominent in the *Poetics* than scholars have tended to notice. Consider Aristotle's mockery of spectators who like bad plots and of the poets who pander to them (1453a33–5, ch. 9). These are 'episodic' plots in which actions follow randomly on one another; Aristotle argues that they come about because of actors (ὑποκριτάς), as well as the impact of the competitive festival occasion (cf. ἀγωνίσματα), which often compels poets to strain the plot beyond its capacity and distort the sequence of events (παρὰ τὴν δύναμιν παρατείνοντες τὸν μῦθον πολλάκις διαστρέφειν ἀναγκάζονται τὸ ἐφεξῆς) (1451b35–52a1). A bit later we see one result of this: the preference for 'double plots' (i.e., those with different ends for good and bad characters), which he attributes to the 'weakness' of the spectators (τὴν τῶν θεάτρων ἀσθένειαν), since the poets follow their lead and pander to their wishes (1453a31–5).

Or consider Aristotle's pondering whether the dramatic form as a whole must be 'vulgar' (φορτική), since performers think that they ought to engage in elaborate bodily movements to grab the audience's attention (cf. πολλὴν κίνησιν κινοῦνται) (1461b27–30). Thankfully, this low pandering can be blamed once again on the performers rather than the poetic form; just as some flute players may be overly 'kinetic' and some dancing may be crude, so do some actors indulge themselves and the audience by their exaggerrated imitations of, for instance, low-brow female characters. Luckily (if that's the word for it), even if music and spectacle engender pleasures 'most vividly' (αἱ ἡδοναὶ . . . ἐνεργέστατα), the power of good tragic plotting comes through in the reading alone, such that in the best of circumstances one could dispense with performance altogether (1462a12–18).

So here we have at least some indications of ways in which the historically contingent, embodied, material settings of these civic festivals and speeches shaped and were shaped by structures of feeling, precisely the kind of artistic practice in emergence that leads Williams to reject formalist accounts of cultural production. The dynamics by which actors or speakers and audience together draw out emergent styles through somatic engagement – styles that are, by the way, in keeping with changes charted by writers from Aristophanes on – is precisely what formalist accounts such as Aristotle's would be necessarily pitched against. An emphasis on form in itself implies that there is a perfect one, an isolatable still point independent of the material, experiential process that gave it shape, place and moment. And yet there those bodies and materialities are, crowding in, impinging on plot and argument.

Distancing effects

Both the *Poetics* and the *Rhetoric* associate mimesis directly with poetic expression in performance: 'The poets, as is natural, thus began to set things in motion in the beginning; for words are mimetic, and the voice is the most mimetic of our faculties' (*Rhet.* 1404a21–2, cf. *Poet.* 1447a10–15).[24] Thus how one imitates (i.e., the style in which one forges a mimesis) should also be relatively unproblematic, especially if it is poetic in kind. This turns out not to be the case, however. Although style (*lexis*) in the *Poetics* is treated as one essential component among many, the *Rhetoric* sets forth why style might itself be a cause for concern to anyone aiming to address a topic in an unvarnished manner.[25] In Book 3 it is intimately bound up with delivery (*hupokrisis*), and both are concerned with the creation of effects – with, say, appearing to be like someone whom the audience might trust. Even the study of style and delivery is a latecomer and the topic appears 'vulgar' (καὶ δοκεῖ φορτικὸν εἶναι) (*Rhet.* 1403b31–1404a1).[26] Style may be necessary but it is also concerned with appearances and aimed at the hearer (ἀλλ᾽ ἅπαντα φαντασία ταῦτ᾽ ἐστὶ καὶ πρὸς τὸν ἀκροατήν, 1404a15); and 'poetic' modes, the type used by such elaborate stylists as Gorgias, are laughable and outmoded (γελοῖον μιμεῖσθαι τούτους οἳ αὐτοὶ οὐκέτι χρῶνται ἐκείνῳ τῷ τρόπῳ, 1404a24–8, 35–9).

Aristotle thus treats style as essentially ornamental in nature, an add-on that is all performance effect (cf. φαντασία) aimed at the audience but powerful and necessary (*Rhet.* 1404a5–12). Style, and secondarily delivery, shows its special powers from far off, as it were; in large public forums for poetry and oratory, those who make the most striking, artistic use of stylistic elements win prizes and sway their audiences (*Rhet.* 1403b31–1404a1, 1404a16–19).[27] Effective style is also 'foreign' (ξένην), since people and things from far away inspire wonder, and this wonder gives pleasure (*Rhet.* 1404b8–11):

> For just as humans experience in relation to strangers versus
> fellow citizens, so too do they experience in relation to style. Thus
> it is necessary to make the discourse strange; for styles from
> far off are wondrous, and the wondrous is pleasant.[28]

As with viewing the 'body' of the plot in the *Poetics*, which I analyse in the next section, this elevation of distanced aesthetic pleasure, which amounts to a curious brand of exoticism, replaces actual citizen experiences with an abstraction – in this case style. While the analogy teases with its suggestion of live sensations as if one were spectating in an arena, what the argument actually focuses on is characterizing style in this general sense.

If we now consider what comes next in the treatise, my favorite cloak may look a bit different from how it did at the outset of this discussion. Aristotle proffers the cloak as a metaphor for appropriate analogizing (i.e., a metaphor for metaphor): 'But it is necessary to consider, as a red cloak is fitting for a young man, what is for an old one, for the same clothing does not suit both' (ἀλλὰ δεῖ σκοπεῖν, ὡς νέῳ φοινικίς, οὕτω γέροντι τί, οὐ γὰρ ἡ αὐτὴ πρέπει ἐσθής (1405a13–14).[29] The passage as a whole suggests that metaphor, while exciting and thus desirable, must be carefully shaped in order to escape detection. It may seem all the more striking, then, that in the course of an analytical discussion about style we are suddenly talking about a young man's outerwear. And charmed by the turn to clothing, we may feel the urge to take this analogy further, so that, encouraged by the representation of metaphorical style as foreign, we recognize metaphor itself as its special fabric. And once we start thinking about clothes, well, we are in dangerous territory within Aristotle's own scheme, as elsewhere he regards as trivial such surface effects (cf. again the comment about *phantasia*, cited above). But figurative usage encourages such enchantments, which is also to say that even if the cloak may seem to be offered as a neutral object indicating a concept, it comes freighted with ideological implications. While in the case of Euripides and his broom such associations may be more explicit, since the poet is especially attentive in his deployment of what Donna Haraway refers to as 'material-semiotic' nodes, this is a more important point to make about Aristotle, in whose treatises bodies and objects usually purport to serve this impartial function.[30]

Viewing perfect bodies

The *Rhetoric* aims explicitly at forging a systematic analysis centred on argument, namely the rhetorical syllogism (*enthumeme*). The *enthumeme* ought to serve as the core of the speech, in that it is fully focused on and operates within the bounds of the subject at hand, as opposed to the speaker's character or the audience's emotions. We could thus consider the *enthumeme* a form parallel to plot in tragedy, given that, among other things, it orders relationships among elements (e.g., premise, middle term and conclusion) as plot does with beginning, middle and end of the drama. But the *Rhetoric* does not situate this abstraction as the *telos* of rhetoric, as the *Poetics* does for plot; and while it does at the outset deem enthymeme the 'body' of the proof (σῆμα τῆς πίστεως, 1354a14–15), this is not a pivotal image in the treatise and so does not register as subordinating actual bodies on the ground to the 'body' of the argument.

In this section I want to take a fuller look at the 'body' of the plot, since it is the one figurative body or object among many to which Aristotle fully attends. His stringent formalism turns on a distinctive configuration offered at a central point in the *Poetics*, just after the discussion in chapter 6 in which he sets forth the necessary parts of tragedy, with plot as the crucial element. Here, in chapter 7, he foregrounds a very different kind of embodiment, introducing it as an analogy for assessing the proper scope of a tragic plot. This is the image of the creaturely body 'good for viewing' (εὐσύνοπτον, ch. 7, *Poet.* 1450b32–51a5; cf. ch. 23 as well). The properly scaled and thus aesthetically pleasing tragic plot should resemble a beautiful creature (καλὸν ζῷον, 1450b34, 38), being neither a mite nor a leviathan and thus easy to take in and assess as properly integrated and whole (μιᾶς τε εἶναι καὶ ταύτης ὅλης, *Poet.* 1451a32).[31] Like proportionate bodies that afford contemplation, when plots are to scale they achieve coherent recall (εὐμνημόνευτον).

The analogical metaphor, despite its invocation of embodiment and the experience of spectators, does little to offset the abstract vision of unity and proportion that anchors how Aristotle reconceives the tragic aesthetic. In fact, true to his disappointment in actual audiences and his emphasis on ordering principles inherent to the art, he dismisses the setting of the civic practice of tragedy as having any relevance in determining the appropriate scale and proportions of the plot. As he puts it, 'The limit of the [plot] length that relates to the contests and the affective experience [αἴσθησιν] is not intrinsic to the art [τῆς τέχνης]'; instead, it emerges from the nature of the action central to the plot (ὁ δὲ κατ᾽ αὐτὴν τὴν φύσιν τοῦ πράγματος ὅρος) (*Poet.* 14551a6–10).[32] It is this unified, proportional, naturally generated plotting that ought, as Aristotle says in a later chapter, to arouse the pity and fear in the audience, rather than spectacle (1452b28–30) – that is, rather than the viewing of actual bodies and their traumas. The latter is the purview of the second-rate poet, who aims at sensationalism (τὸ τερατῶδες) rather than the fear that is the appropriate pleasure (ἡδονὴν ... τὴν οἰκείαν) of tragedy (1453b8–11).

In chapter 6 Aristotle identifies plot as 'the beginning and as it were the soul' (ἀρχὴ μέν οὖν καὶ οἷον ψυχὴ) of tragedy (1450a38). Poulheria Kyriakou has highlighted that elsewhere he treats the soul as the beginning of every living being; she suggests that the statement ought to be taken together with that about viewing the creature plot in chapter 7, as a means of understanding *muthos* as a living, organic entity.[33] While this may sound somewhat fanciful, especially since Aristotle's use of οἷον could signal that ψυχή is a metaphor, it encourages awareness of his transfer of the vibrancy of embodied life and aesthetic experience from actual enactment to abstract form.[34] It is worth noting in this regard that for Aristotle dramatic mimesis is of an action (*praxis*) rather than a character, which ought to serve to activate and animate his notion of plot further.

So it seems that this spirited, moving, apportioned form is the primary body on display in the *Poetics*, the one that if balanced, complete and scaled in a manner intrinsic to the action, alone ought to give rise to aesthetic and affective experiences in the audience members – any audiences anywhere, whether reading or viewing the drama. Aristotle's figurative analogies effectively displace the vibrancy and situatedness of tragic embodiment onto a form much more serene, not to mention inhuman, a well-proportioned creature that exists out of time and is beautiful in a quite different way. This is why he argues that the dramatic contests and audience experiences are not part of the tragic art strictly defined and thus ought not to determine scale. When taken together with his warnings discussed earlier about the distortions that result from such impingements, it also furthers a sense of an implicit hierarchy of aesthetic (and political) valuations.[35] The live context of dramatic contests – of actors and audiences in the historical moment with its particular materialities (e.g., the water clock) and emergent inclinations (e.g., increasingly gymnastic deportments) – has a deleterious effect on the plot's body. Playing to the feeble crowd leads to its stretching and twisting, so that it becomes contorted and loses its natural balance and perfection. Poor plot! Were it not for actual people and their limitations and debased pleasures, it would be free to settle into its innate parameters.[36]

Aristotle's assertions thus set the frame for viewing tragic mimesis and the plot in particular from this distance, as an object of the imagination, a nonhuman but organic entity, generated by its own natural proportional relations and by human capacities for perceiving these. While by now this aesthetic claim should be obvious, it also champions values with ideological underpinnings that may be less so. These are essentially the Platonic ones of wholeness, completion, balance and unity, which Aristotle presents as alone manifestly natural and right, rather than the contingent, limited and 'twisted' parameters that the performance setting and its players (including poets, actors, judges and audience members) impose.[37]

Aristotle's treatise distills this multi-level experience into a single, 'natural' form, one notably unencumbered by the twists and turns of so much tragic plotting, as well as apparently uninflected by ideological particulars such as class and citizen status or gender.[38] This universalizing perspective allows him to say flatly, as if stating a fact, that while a woman and a slave may be good (χρηστή), even though the one is inferior and the other 'wholly base' (τὸ δὲ ὅλως φαῦλον), it is not fitting that the female character be depicted as either courageous or fearsomely intelligent (ἀνδρείαν ἢ δεινήν) (1454a20–4). It may seem low on my part to take pot shots at Aristotle, blinded as he is by the prejudices of his time and cultural milieu, but it is largely due to his own formalism and scientific 'objectivity' that few scholars of the *Poetics* have shown interest in this type of biased gesture. And by biased, I don't just mean denigrating of women and slaves, since who didn't indulge in such sport in the classical period? I also mean more broadly, in relation to tragedy's 'politicity', in Rancière's sense – that is, in relation to what aspects of lived experience are emphasized and valued.[39]

Missing emotions

Aristotle's *Poetics* initially presents the spectatorship of corpses (or near corpses) within tragic representation as a learning experience, and a pleasant one at that. But what kind of audience member would take away from the end of the *Oedipus* (for instance) an enjoyment whose keenest edge is a shallow type of art appreciation ('Ah, nicely done!')? If tragedies are in fact so resonant with the shock of the body's devolution, why is this sense of what Edmund Burke called 'delightful horror' so much in the background of Aristotle's treatise?[40] And how are we to understand the ideological motivations of this downplaying of the powers of tragic spectacle in all of its situated particularities? Perhaps we could consider the discussions of pity and fear, as well as catharsis, as nods in this direction, although if so they would be notably restrained and understated ones. For instance, despite the incredibly abundant scholarship on *catharsis* in the *Poetics*, Aristotle mentions it only once and then very briefly. Some scholars have even wondered whether it could be an interpolation on the strength of its mention in book 8 of the *Politics*, where he pledges to discuss it more fully in his treatment of poetry.⁴¹ As for pity and fear, Aristotle scarcely acknowledges either as reactions to viewing tragic bodies, instead focusing attention on how plots (and thus actions) achieve such dynamics.

That said, since he still finds it necessary to countenance, if in a very limited fashion, the mimesis of suffering and the pleasurable pain that it generates in audiences as intrinsic to tragedy, he has somehow to acknowledge affective experience and thus the performance setting. In chapter 12, as if in passing, he introduces *pathos*, which he defines rather singularly as a 'destructive or painful act' (πρᾶξις φθαρτικὴ ἢ ὀδυνηρά) – that is, as if it encompassed something intermediate between the representation of suffering and its affective impact. He considers this *pathos* a third part of the plot, together with reversal and recognition, and he highlights once again the viewing of corpses as well as those in pain and wounded (οἵ τε ἐν τῷ φανερῷ θάνατοι καὶ αἱ περιωδυνίαι καὶ τρώσεις) (1452b10–13).

This would appear to conflict in striking ways with Aristotle's emphasis on the perfect and beautiful body of the plot as the only one that should achieve emotional transport. But if we take this moment together with the acknowledgment late in the treatise (chapter 26) that viewing tragic enactment offers the most vivid pleasures, it is possible to trace the spectral outline of what Aristotle is working so hard to suppress: the 'sweet violence', to borrow Terry Eagleton's phrase, of confronting (again) Oedipus' scarred carapace at the play's end. That is: the chorus recoiling en masse on stage in the Theater of Dionysus and the audience enthralled by the embodied, material experience, at a specific historical and political moment.⁴² This is precisely the affective hinge of *pathos* at which Aristotle nods and that Sophocles places centre stage. For the philosopher this *pathos* at best affords the audience, as the chorus exclaims, 'so much to learn and see!' (πολλὰ πυθέσθαι, πολλὰ δ' ἀθρῆσαι, *OT* 1305); at its worst it plays to the corrupt desires of that same audience for sensationalist thrills and horror. Perhaps it is the debasing potentialities of just this sort of moment that drives Aristotle to replace the body in pain and its affective stimulations with the beautiful proportions of the plot.

I think that it is here, at the conjunction between bodies and 'bodies' (i.e., between experiencing tragedy and its formal components), that we can discern the outlines of an ideological perspective quite distinct from that intimated by tragedy's emphasis on the body in pain. By 'ideological' I mean, again, not so much a narrowly historical but rather a more broadly aesthetic and political perspective. Experiencing the *pathos* of tragic embodiment is precisely what Aristotle cannot address adequately. If he is to preserve his thesis that the poetic form is independent of its enactment, an essentially political move that his aesthetics necessitates, then he must set aside the affective experience in context, not only that expressed by actors within the dramatic frame but also how this enactment resonates with audiences. This is what gets felt, registered, recognized and evaluated; it is what Williams would identify as structures of feeling and Rancière as the distribution of the sensible, within the material setting and historical moment.

In this regard as in others, things appear to play out a bit differently in the *Rhetoric*, at least in a limited sense. As I mentioned in the section on audiences, Aristotle does worry initially about 'warping' citizen judges by playing on their feelings, but he also acknowledges the need to attend to emotions in persuasive contexts. Thus in book 2, when discussing the eliciting of pity he emphasizes the persuasive capacity of both visualizing language and visual effects that occur as if in close proximity between speaker and audience (8.14–16, 1386a29–b7). He notes the effectiveness of calling forth visual elements of the objects of pity such as 'gestures, voices, clothing, and generally delivery' (σχήμασι καὶ φωναῖς καὶ ἐσθῆσι καὶ ὅλως ὑποκρίσει), all of which render these objects as if literally before the eyes (πρὸ ὀμμάτων) (1386a29–34). He also promotes the use of actual objects for similar effect, what he terms visual 'signs' (τὰ σημεῖα, 1386a36), displays of things such as clothing related to the victim, which by a material metonymy similar to props in tragedy render the suffering literally before the eyes (ἐν ὀφθαλμοῖς φαινομένου τοῦ πάθους, 1386b7).[43]

Since in book 3 of the *Rhetoric* Aristotle emphasizes the capacity of good (i.e., recognizable but not too familiar) metaphors to bring things vividly 'before the eyes' (πρὸ ὀμμάτων, *Rhet.* 1410b33–5, 1411a24–35, 1411b22–5, etc.),[44] it is striking that he also uses the phrase in this passage in book 2, for descriptions of objects such as clothing as well as actual viewing, as of props onstage. I don't, however, want to exaggerate the impact of this sudden (and quite brief) turn to enactment; bodies and things in the *Rhetoric* as in the *Poetics* are much more likely to be figurative and to enliven discussion of an abstract form, as we saw in the case of style. And yet this passage in book 2 contrasts quite a bit with the treatment of pity in the *Poetics*, where Aristotle argues that its eliciting in the audience along with fear occurs in the best dramas only in relation to the plotting (14, 1453b1–6). If, on the other hand, dramatists seek to arouse audiences by the spectacle (διὰ τῆς ὄψεως) – that is, by precisely such things as gestures, props and costumes – this will result in sensationalizing (cf. again τὸ τερατῶδες), which is not germane to tragedy (1453b7–10).

Aristotle's purposeful distancing from and transferral of bodies and their materialities to the figurative realm should, then, be taken together with his disparaging of the actual Athenian performance setting, with its varieties of types and inclinations, its motley players and audience members. If, in anticipation (and some pre-correction) of modern theorizing about affect and material settings, Williams and Rancière highlight the embodied, emergent sensations involved in communal, interactive aesthetic experience, then Aristotle's emphasis on the unity and purity of form represents not only philosophical abstraction but also the institutionalizing, hierarchical values of an essentially dictatorial perspective. His notion of proper form determined by a right-thinking elite drives him to cordon off the body of knowledge that he terms *poiêtikê*, as well as the body of the plot, from its setting and occasion. This is why he cannot address *pathos* in any fuller fashion – precisely because it is lodged between actor and chorus and actors and audience, in the inhabited, dynamic contingencies of experiencing tragic enactment.

This is not quite so true of the *Rhetoric*, where (as I have tried to show) the audience is much more closely implicated in the form. And yet Aristotle does his utmost to focus attention on the argument – the 'body' of the proof (as with plot for drama), which is itself the core of the speech – and to disparage style and delivery, as well as those in the audience at which they are aimed. These 'hearers' may be warped by emotional appeals and easily distracted by spectacle, but they are all Aristotle has if he is to adhere to democratic modes of practising rhetoric. Democracy thus puts a limit on the extent to which the philosopher can extract form from setting.

The political tenor of Aristotle's aesthetics that I emphasize here indicates his hostility to contemporary contingencies that he himself clearly regards as democratic (i.e., the corrupt tastes of the citizen audiences, the pandering of actors). My assessment urges attention to the active, material embodiment of the arts in their practices that hover like so many spectres on the edges of Aristotle's treatises, as well as to Aristotle's reactions to their particularities. The indications in the *Poetics* and *Rhetoric* of these reactions suggest that they shaped his arguments in very central ways; and theorizing tragic enactment and oratorical performance with our post-Marxists illuminates – at least in flashes – the lived experience that Aristotle himself makes some effort to foreclose.

Notes

1. Barlow 1971: 48.
2. As Johanna Hanink has pointed out, the *Poetics* came into being during a period marked by the ascendancy of actors, an aspect of this context particularly disparaged by Aristotle (Hanink 2014). Another element in this cultural environment, which Hanink also emphasizes, is tragedy's early canonization during this period, which aimed at consolidating it as a uniquely Athenian art form. As she points out (191–2), Aristotle also participated in this effort by constructing lists of dithyrambic and dramatic contest rankings, thus offsetting his ahistorical theorizing with some record keeping. See also Easterling 1993; Csapo 2010; Csapo et al. 2014.
3. On metaphor in Aristotle, see most infamously and provocatively Derrida [1972] 1982; also McCall 1969; Ricoeur 1978; Moran 1989, 1996; Newman 2001, 2002; Leidl 2003; Worman 2015: ch. 1.
4. Hall 1996. That said, I would also question the impression that other scholars have put forward, of Aristotle's analysis as clearly latter day, universalizing, or even 'Macedonian'. Such readings emphasize that he was writing a good century after the first flourishing of the tragic festivals and, as some argue, at a distance from their original setting, so that his treatise evidences an outsider preservationist's sense of the form as general and summary (cf. e.g., DuBois 2004; also Hanink 2014).
5. In the case of the speaker, he acknowledges that one must represent oneself as 'some sort' (*poios tis*), but enters into little detail beyond generally beneficent characteristics (see esp. the beginning of book 2).
6. Cf. Cope *ad loc.*
7. As Aristotle himself puts it, 'Since all people welcome speeches composed for their own characters and like them, it is not unclear how those giving speeches will appear to be certain sorts – both themselves and their speeches' (ὥστ' ἐπεὶ ἀποδέχονται πάντας τοὺς τῷ σφετέρῳ ἤθη λεγομένους τοὺς λόγους καὶ τοὺς ὁμοίους, οὐκ ἄδηλον πῶς χρώμενοι τοῖς λόγοις τοιοῦντοι φαινοῦνται οἱ αὐτοὶ καὶ οἱ λόγοι, 1390a25–7).

8. Versus plot for tragedy (*Poet.* 1450a22–3: τὰ πράγματα καὶ ὁ μῦθος τέλος τῆς τραγῳδίας). See *Rhet.* 1358b2–3 (1.3.2): ὥστε τὸ τέλος πρὸς τοῦτόν ἐστιν, λέγω δὲ τὸν ἀκροατήν. See Porter 2010b on voice in the *Rhetoric*; also Graff 2001 on the 'written style'.

9. Cf. Socrates' example of Leontius in book 4 of the *Republic*, who struggles with his desire to look at actual corpses he encounters, in the process chastising his own eyes: 'Oh you evil-spirited things, fill yourselves full of the beautiful sight' (ὦ κακοδαίμονες, ἐμπλήσθητε τοῦ καλοῦ θεάματος, 440a4). While Socrates is theorizing about appetite (*epithumia*), Aristotle seems narrowly concerned with representation.

10. Cf. *Poet.* 1450b18–20: 'The power of tragedy exists independent of performance and actors, and anyway the costumer's art is more effective than the poets' for the creation of spectacle' (ἡ γὰρ τῆς τραγῳδίας δύναμις καὶ ἄνευ ἀγῶνος καὶ ὑποκριτῶν ἔστιν, ἔτι δὲ κυριωτέρα περὶ τὴν ἀπεργασίαν τῶν ὄψεων ἡ τοῦ σκευοποιοῦ τέχνη τῆς τῶν ποιητῶν ἐστιν); and 1453b1–7, on which see further below.

11. Again, Aristotle also compensates by relegating embodiment and visual signs largely to his own analogies, including (as mentioned) in the discussion of metaphor.

12. Modern literary theorists such as Terry Eagleton have argued for resisting a common scholarly inclination to pit tragedy and its analysis against each other as, effectively, creative disorder versus stultifying order (Eagleton 2003: 20–1). On the democratic context, see most influentially Goldhill 2000 on the 'democratic' character of tragedy, and the correctives of Rhodes 2003.

13. See Loraux 2002; Pucci 2015.

14. Williams 1966, 1977; Rancière [2002] 2004. These theorists are not alone in emphasizing the relations between ideologies and practices, of course, but they are among the most influential for classicists in recent years.

15. Rancière 2000: 17–18.

16. Williams 1977: 19, 131–5.

17. Williams 1977: 132; cf. 38–9, 180–1 and Williams 1966: 18–19.

18. Williams 1977: 19.

19. On the complexities of semiotic reference in drama, see Ubersfeld 1977; Serpieri 1978; Elam1980; Issacharoff 1989.

20. See Bourdieu 1996 [*Rules of Art*] on art and elite judgment; and Wright 2009 on the ancient context.

21. Cf. the *Rhetoric* (1403b): artful (i.e., too poetic) oratorical styles may skew the soul of the hearer (e.g., παραλογίζεται τε γὰρ ψυχή, 1408a20), indulging his already corrupt instincts and leading him further astray (cf. φορτικώτητα, 1395b1–2; τοῦ ἀκροατοῦ μοχθηρίαν, 1404a8). See also Worman 2008: 101–2, 284–93.

22. See Green 2002; Valakas 2002.

23. E.g., *Clouds* 964–83; *Republic*, etc. In the *Poetics* Aristotle also highlights the impact of poetry on the soul, but unlike Plato (or Aristophanes, for that matter), it is once again plot that is most bound up with this elusive entity. Not only is plot the 'soul' of tragedy; it also contains parts (μέρη) that are most 'soul-leading' (τὰ μέγιστα οἷς ψυχαγωγεῖ) (i.e., recognition and reversal) (*Poet.* 1450a33–4). As Victoria Wohl has pointed out, *psychogogia* is ideology in action, whereby the aesthetic and affective form of the drama shapes audience experience and understanding, drawing attention to some things while adumbrating others (Wohl 2015: 134–7).

24. ἤρξαντο μὲν οὖν κινῆσαι τὸ πρῶτον, ὥσπερ πέφυκεν, οἱ ποιηταί· τὰ γὰρ ὀνόματα μιμήματα ἐστίν, ὑπῆρξεν δὲ καὶ ἡ φωνὴ πάντων μιμητικώτατον τῶν μορίων ἡμῖν.

25. As are lyric expression (*melopoiia*) and spectacle (*opsis*), since Aristotle regards plot (*muthos*), thought (*dianoia*), and character (*ethos*) as much more central to the discussion of what constitutes good dramatic writing. Style is merely listed as the fourth element and glossed as 'expression through word choice' for both speeches and poetic interludes (τέταρτον δὲ τῶν μὲν λόγων ἡ λέξις· λέγω δέ, ὥσπερ πρότερον εἴρηται, λέξιν εἶναι τὴν διὰ τῆς ὀνομασίας ἑρμηνείαν, ὃ καὶ ἐπὶ τῶν ἐμμέτρων καὶ ἐπὶ τῶν λόγων ἔχει τὴν αὐτὴν δύναμιν) (*Poet.* 1450b13–20); (cf. Halliwell 1987: 57).

26. Again, see further in Worman 2003: 287–93.

27. Cf. the evocative cadence of Roland Barthes, 'Style is a distance, a difference' (1971: 6). See further in Worman 2015: 49–52; cf. Worman 2002.

28. ὥσπερ γὰρ πρὸς τοὺς ξένους οἱ ἄνθρωποι καὶ πρὸς τοὺς πολίτας, τὸ αὐτὸ πάσχουσιν καὶ πρὸς τὴν λέξιν· διὸ δεῖ ποιεῖν ξένην τὴν διάλεκτον· θαυμασταὶ γὰρ τῶν ἀπόντων εἰσίν, ἡδὺ δὲ τὸ θαυμαστόν ἐστιν.

29. E.g., Isoc. 5.25–7; cf. Pl. *Gorg.* 465b4–5. Later theorists also make use of the analogy (e.g., Cic. *Orat.* 78–9; DH *Dem.* 18.35–41, *Isoc.* 12.22, 13.4–7, 15.15; Anaxim. *Ars rhet.* proem 2.2).

30. Haraway 1988: 584–9, 595–6; she means precisely those material bits that protrude, as it were, functioning as indicators of the edges of what we can see, ideologically speaking.

31. Cf. Pl. *Phdr.* 264c1–5. In his plot-as-body analogy Aristotle is largely following Plato, although he identifies plot instead of *logos* as the *eusynoptic* creature (cf. also in the *Republic*). It may be important that, as with Plato, the bodies invoked are animal, or at least creaturely in some general sense, so that the body natural and perfect for the viewing is precisely not commensurate with those human ones onstage and in the audience. Further, the emphasis on this proportionality as natural and inherent increases the sense that there is some gain to be had from the object of contemplation being both not human and offered to the human eye. It may be useful to recall here that 'shapes of the most disgusting beasts' (θηρίων τε μορφὰς τῶν ἀτιμοτάτων) are with corpses Aristotle's two examples of representations that give pleasure to viewers.

32. Cf. Aristotle's argument in *Politics* 8 that lowly crowds elicit from professional performers debased styles that even effect their bodily movements (*Pol.* 1341b18); see further below.

33. Kyriakou 1993, citing *De Anima* 412a27–14b26. See also Lucas ad 1449a15.; and contrast Else 1938: 189.

34. Note that the sentence could read as 'therefore plot is the beginning as soul is [for a living creature]' – and thus more the vivifying force of tragedy (with thanks to Iakovos Vasiliou for pointing this out). In chapter 6 we learn that plot is not only the beginning but also the end (τέλος, 1450a22) of tragedy, in the sense of its aim, and not to be confused with the creature plot's proportionally related beginning, middle and end in chapter 7. The earlier terms indicate a more general sense of the plot as having a propulsion that is natural to it (cf. 1451a9–10), developing like a living organism, while the later focuses on this propulsive body ('body') in its parts.

35. As Alex Purves has emphasized in a discussion of Iliadic plotting, in this it is like the ideal city of the *Politics*, which has the right expanse and number of citizens (1326b, 1327a), as well as like a well-rounded (i.e., periodic) sentence and a good assembly speech in the *Rhetoric* (1414a) (Purves 2010: 25–30); cf. Porter 2010b: 96–101.

36. Not that Aristotle really thinks that the perfect plot exists independent of its plotter; as Kyriakou points out, there are indications in the *Poetics* that these live in the minds of poets, who by their own natures incline toward one genre or another (1449a3–4) and follow Homer – whether he did this by skill or nature (ἤτοι διὰ τέχνην ἢ διὰ φύσιν) – in discovering appropriate plots (1451a24). See Kyriakou 1993: 351–6, arguing against Halliwell 1986.

37. As Wohl puts it, 'Aristotle's aesthetic of unity naturalizes tragic form' (2015: 134).

38. See Wohl 2015 here too, on the politics of Euripides' plotting.
39. Hall 1996 has noted that when discussing particular plots and characters Aristotle avoids references to Athenian mytho-historical figures; he also rarely mentions female characters.
40. Burke [1767] 1958: 73.
41. As he may well have done in the lost second book of the *Poetics*; see Else 1938: 198. Cf. Ford 1995 on *Politics* 1341b. See also Lear [1988] 1999.
42. E.g., the first years of the Peloponnesian War; and possibly during Macedonian ascendancy almost a century later.
43. Cope (*ad loc.*) compares Orestes' display of the cloak in the *Choephoroi* that his mother used to entrap and murder his father.
44. Cf. *Rhet.* 1412a11–13, regarding the capacity to see likeness in things 'very far apart' (τὸ ὅμοιον καὶ ἐν πολὺ διέχουσι θεωρεῖν εὐστόχου).

CHAPTER 8
ARISTOTLE'S LOST WORKS FOR THE PUBLIC AND THE POLITICS OF ACADEMIC FORM
Edith Hall

> Nothing is easier than to write so that no one can understand; just as, contrarily, nothing is more difficult than to express deep things in such a way that everyone must necessarily grasp them.
>
> Schopenhauer[1]

Introduction: obscurity and obscurantism

On 23 February 2017, the then White House chief strategist Stephen K. Bannon announced to the Conservative Political Action Conference that Donald Trump's administration was intent upon 'deconstruction of the administrative state'.[2] Being a bookish person, Bannon knew that the word 'deconstruction' is associated by the public, even if they have not heard of Jacques Derrida, with their stereotype of the smug left-liberal intellectual snob. Bannon thus co-opted for the Alt-Right the term most emblematic of what Trump's supporters see as the 'irrelevant' privileged liberal intelligentsia, who spout metalinguistic jargon while moving seamlessly between elite universities, the hated media and the Washington political class.

Bannon, of course, is an arch-obscurantist himself. What Nietzsche called 'the black art of obscurantism',[3] as practised by ruling classes terrified of transparency, today obfuscates the workings of capitalism. The bank-created Special Purpose Vehicles which produced the 2008 financial crisis were instruments for obscuring the real financial situation by *hiding* debts.[4] Neoliberal financial institutions exploit confusion and jargon to get rich by mystification. But obscurantism as a charge is usually laid against the very intellectuals Bannon and his political allies have targeted as the enemies of 'ordinary' working people. Anti-intellectualism is a marker of the new Right; it 'abounds in order to mystify the world and in particular to support the project of neoliberal globalisation'.[5] This species of anti-intellectualism 'disparages theory because it secretly fears that theorists will uncover the truth about the big picture'.[6]

In a penetrating article, Ineke Sluiter explores the rich debate about obscurity within the ancient exegetical tradition. Commentators distinguished between unintentional and intentional obscurity, both of which can be either good or bad. Unintentional obscurity is defensible either when it is the result of words and concepts changing their meanings over time, or when the subject-matter is inherently opaque. Intentional obscurity is deemed culpable if it is designed to impede refutation; both ancient and medieval scholars symbolised it as a cuttlefish discharging ink.[7] Intentional obscurity may be commended by ancient commentators, however, if it is deliberately chosen by an author (1) to avoid obscenity or blasphemy, (2) to produce an impressive 'sublime' effect, (3) to stimulate the reader into an effortful grappling with the text, or (4) to exclude outsiders or the uninitiated.[8] Intentional obscurity can have political applications, as well, either by protecting the safety of the author, or by leaving the meaning open to reinterpretation by readers, as the Aristotelian *Constitution of Athens* (9.2) says that Solon intentionally passed obscurely worded legislation so that citizens could have some autonomy in interpreting it.[9]

On these ancient criteria, assuming that no academic today would want deliberately to exclude anyone else from a field of knowledge,[10] the only relevant justifiable category of *intentional* obscurity would be the one that stimulated readers to an interpretive effort. But the situation has changed. Given the hyper-specialization of academic research, much obscurity is the result of something neither completely unintentional nor actively premeditated: the tacit avoidance of extra effort. Controversial American pragmatic philosophy professor Terrance MacMullan argues in *The Daily Show and Philosophy*,

> Most intellectuals simply don't bother to try to engage the public ... The isolation of intellectuals became more extreme when they started emulating European theorists ... I suspect ... that this isolation is largely self-imposed, since it's much easier and more comfortable to speak to someone who shares your assumptions and uses your terms than someone who might challenge your assumptions in unexpected ways or ask you to explain what you mean.[11]

If we write obscurely and make no effort to communicate our findings beyond academia, our error may be one of what Aristotle labelled omission rather than commission (*NE* 3.1113b2).

Alternatively, we may invoke the defensive arguments, unknown to ancient commentators, of the same twentieth-century Continental thinkers mistrusted by MacMullan. Theodor Adorno defended obscurity as a weapon against the pollution of societal analysis by positivist discourse; he believed this discourse naturalised the market and hierarchies.[12] Herbert Marcuse responded to the criticism that theory was remote from the 'ordinary' language of the 'commonsensical-person-in-the-street' by proposing that everyday speech perpetuated mindsets that prevent people from seeing beneath the societal surface to the invisible structures perpetuating the status quo.[13] Jacques Derrida wanted to liberate language from its oppressive and colonial past in order to escape from herd mentality and write the world in new ways.[14] Gilles Deleuze and Felix Guattari think the problem is caused by our criteria of taste and class: we are hostile to the conflation of ideas we prefer to keep separate, such as popularity and intellectualism.[15] I take all these points, but tend to agree with Aristotle, who would have found such thinkers' attitudes to the views of 'the many' patronising and overly dismissive. He respected the 'wisdom of the crowd', believed in a democratic 'hive mind', and recommended launching any enquiry from *endoxa*, commonly held beliefs, even though these were to be subjected to the most vigorous examination and repudiation where necessary.[16]

Both old and new arguments are being used to wage the current Obscurantism Wars. It has never been more necessary for academics to reflect on the nature of their public communications. Some disciplines have been more proactive than others. Historians and philosophers of science have been discussing their writing forms since the early 1970s.[17] Sociologists have held whole conferences on how they write. One concludes that instead of writing 'as if we are member of a secret society whose manuscripts are intelligible only to fellow followers of social science esoterica', we need to be 'writers who struggle to find ways to join artful, clever, subtle and tasteful prose on the one hand, to life-like representations of real people and their lived experience on the other'.[18] The UK Academy of Medical Sciences now advocates the appending of 'lay summaries' to *all* publications of biomedical and health research results and supplies advice on how to write them accessibly.[19]

It is time for classicists to become similarly self-conscious, listen to Falstaff begging his grandiose-mouthed crony Pistol to deliver his news 'like a man of this world',[20] and think about the forms in which to communicate exciting, creative research publicly. In an incisive article, Siobhain Lyons suggests we use Aristotle's idea of the mean to mediate between healthy inventiveness and alienating obscurity.[21] Staying with Aristotle, my article proposes that we might find help in his lost addresses to the general public, his 'exoteric' dialogues, which differed from his surviving works. This is how Ammonius of Alexandria put it around AD 500, in his commentary on Aristotle's *Categories* (6.25–7.4). In his works for his students,

> Aristotle is, as regards the thought, terse, compressed, and full of questions, and as regards the language quite ordinary, owing to his search for precise truth and clearness, he sometimes even invents words if necessary. In the dialogues, which he has written for the many, he aims at a certain fullness, a careful choice of diction and metaphor, and modifies the style of his diction to suit the speakers, and in short does everything that can beautify his style.

Routinely circulating our ideas in two published forms, a 'plain' academic one aiming above all at succinctness and precision, and fearless about introducing unfamiliar new terms, and the other at pleasurable readability, might be a constructive policy.

In an ideal society, research conducted at universities would be made systematically available to the public, enabling more people to join conversations about society, culture and science in informed and instrumental ways. The road to such a utopian dialogue between professional and lay intellectuals is littered with obstacles, some of which would require wholesale reform of the economic infrastructure of academia – it would entail controlling the dissemination of research by commercial publishers and the inflated cost of journal subscriptions, for example. But an obstacle easier to remove is public obliviousness to much scholarly discourse produced within academia and shared almost exclusively between academics.

Historically, although the 'objective' prose treatise has long been dominant, intellectual work was presented in diverse genres. Philosophers have been particularly adventurous, expounding their ideas in verse (Empedocles, Lucretius), dialogues (Plato, Augustine, Berkeley, Hume), introspective meditations (Augustine, Descartes), Exegetical Commentary (Neoplatonists, Maimonides, the Arabic philosopher Averroes/Ibn Rushd) and aphoristic prose (Heraclitus, Marcus Aurelius, Wittgenstein). Others have used the manual (Machiavelli), sermon (Joseph Butler), biography (the ancient *Life of Aesop*), autobiography (Augustine's *Confessions*), disputation (Aquinas), prayer (Parmenides, Anselm), compilation (Sextus Empiricus' *Outlines of Pyrrhonism*), polemic (Nietzsche's *The Birth of Tragedy*) and compendium (Bernard Mandeville's *The Fable of the Bees*). Rousseau published philosophy in the form of fiction, soliloquies and even an opera, *The Village Soothsayer*.[22]

Since the rise of the modern university and professionalization of academia in the nineteenth century, however, even in philosophy there has been a notable drift towards 'homogeneity'.[23] The form taken by academic works has become largely identical. It is similar to the surviving works of Aristotle. These needed, as Cicero wrote, application of great mental effort,[24] and were as dry as Petrarch complained when he read Aristotle on virtue. Petrarch conceded Aristotle's acumen, but it effected no moral change in him: 'Unchanged is the mind as it was, the desire is unchanged, unchanged am I.' Aristotle, according to Petrarch, succeeded in teaching what virtue is, but failed to win over one's heart because he lacked the diction needed to instil desire for the good and resentment of the bad he enjoyed in Cicero and Seneca.[25]

Like Aristotle, we write prose texts in an 'objective' third person in which the first-person voice of the scholar and an assumed collective readership denoted by the first-person plural, if it sounds cool and measured, may be used sparingly. Such treatises today generally take the form of essays or articles of between 5,000 and 12,000 words or books of upwards of 40,000. They systematically name and agree with, modify or repudiate other specialists in the field, as Aristotle often does with previous thinkers.[26] Such exchanges require complicated notes and bibliographies like the annotated reading-lists Aristotle sometimes supplies.

In most fields, moreover, there are canonical reference works alluded to via unexplained abbreviations. Our writing uses topic-specific terminology and vocabulary, the understanding of some of which is shared by other specialists in the same field across time: two experts in ancient philosophy, whether in the eighteenth or the twenty-first century, would for example not need to clarify what 'peripatetic' thought meant as a category. A lay person who wanted to explore ancient philosophy would need to learn this term, too. But many other types of academic language and vocabulary have less obvious meanings and shorter shelf lives. It is not at all clear that the self-educator needs to add examples of ephemeral jargon to their vocabulary. Derrida's term 'arche-writing', for example, was on many academic lips in the 1980s, including those of classicists, but is rarely to be encountered today.

The example of Aristotle

In the history of Western scholarship, ancient treatises on every kind of subject-matter have exerted an incalculable influence on the form taken by scholarly discourse. The prose treatise of which our academic articles and books are direct descendants became the dominant form by the fifth century BC, although continuing to have rivals throughout antiquity. Brought to a high artistic level already in the historiography of Herodotus and Thucydides and the works of most of the sophists, the prose treatise had already won the argument by the time of Aristotle, whose own *extant* works used nothing else. And Aristotle matters because of his transdisciplinary status.[27] He founded logic and branches of natural science including zoology and meteorology, and authored the earliest surviving or foundational treatises in physics, philosophy of mind, sense-perception, rhetoric, poetics and both ethics and metaphysics as fields of enquiry distinct from politics.

Aristotle's acknowledged intellectual supremacy by the early fourteenth century, long before the invention of printing, was the reason why Dante put him first in the list of ancient intellectuals he saw residing in Limbo (Plato, Socrates, Democritus, Diogenes, Anaxagoras, Thales, Empedocles, Heraclitus, Zeno, Dioscorides, Orpheus, Cicero, Linus, Seneca, Euclid, Ptolemy, Hippocrates and Galen); this 'philosophical family' is joined by just two medieval figures, both Aristotelians – the Persian polymath Avicenna (Abu Ali Sina) and Averroes (Ibn Rushd). The latter, as Dante reminds us, 'wrote the vast commentary' on Aristotle. Aristotle sits supreme amongst them; 'they all gaze at him, all honour him' (*Inferno* 4.131–3).

His role as leader and unifier of all academic disciplines is similarly underscored in the painting 'Aristotle with a Bust of Homer', now in the Metropolitan Museum of Art. Rembrandt painted it in 1653. Besides the standing philosopher and the bust, Rembrandt included a medallion suspended from the heavy gold chain. Aristotle's gaze suggests his distinctive term for intellectual contemplation and activity – *theoria*; the chain probably represents the interrelationship of all the arts and sciences. The chain which connects the knowledge of particulars in *all* fields is the chain of philosophy.[28]

In *Metaphysics*, Aristotle repeatedly uses sculpture to illustrate what he means by his four causes. But the painting's conjunction of Homer with a golden chain would prompt any classically educated seventeenth-century viewer to think of the chain with which Zeus in the *Iliad* boasts he could drag earth, sea and all the other gods to Olympus, and bind them there to dangle (8.18–27). Zeus's golden chain was adopted by the Neoplatonists as an emblem of the mind of God or of divine order in the universe. In the sixteenth and seventeenth centuries it became a familiar image of philosophy, dialectic and reason as well as cosmology. But in 1650, three years before Rembrandt painted the picture, renowned classicist and fellow Dutchman Vossius suggested the new interpretation which seems to underlie Rembrandt's conception: enquiry into all fields of knowledge is united by philosophy like the links in an unbreakable chain.[29]

The unrivalled place occupied by Aristotle in the transdisciplinary history of learned discourse means that the form of his treatises has had an exceptional impact on the forms of written discourse academics still use today. Few of us would consider expressing our ideas in poetry or dramatic dialogue form; if we did we would find it harder to find academic positions or secure tenure. Austere, humourless prose, multiple references to other scholars, and technical vocabulary incomprehensible to laypeople – the characteristics which have long been ascribed to Aristotle's treatises[30] – are the norm rather than the exception. In contemporary academic research, 'the results of its production also have been professionalized and rationalized, and, for that, diversity or nonconformity is a liability, not an advantage.'[31]

The Internet has brought new possibilities for extending the fruits of research and intellectual debate to a far wider audience (blogposts, online lectures, podcasts and websites). But such public-facing communication forms as these have not as yet counted towards increasing a scholar's employability in the way that an article published in an esteemed hard-copy peer-reviewed journal or a Harvard University Press monograph would count. The same can be said for writing in 'popular' magazines and periodicals or broadcasting on television or radio. Some academics have been engaged in this kind of work for decades, but have even so attracted opprobrium for 'dumbing down' their subject or 'popularizing' it in ways that more inward-looking scholars regard as vulgar or superficial.

But surely academics actually have a *duty* to the rest of society to share the fruits of even arduous thinking and recondite investigations with everyone else, especially (although not exclusively) where their own educations, salaries or research grants have been partially funded by the public? If so, then they are also under an obligation to maximize the accessibility of their public communications. Ideally, these would be inspiring and pleasurable to read as well.

Aristotle had a bifurcated approach to scholarship. One the one hand, he engaged in advanced seminars and discussion with his Lyceum students/colleagues on specialist topics, seeking to push forward the horizons of understanding and create new terminology where necessary for new concepts. On the other, he wrote treatises for general circulation, in simpler language, adorned with the arresting images and comparisons he recommends to any communicator in his *Rhetoric*. Several were in dialogue form.[32]

These works, known in antiquity as Aristotle's 'exoteric' or 'outward-facing' works, were designed, I believe, for the people he often mentions as all 'the others' (in addition to philosophers) who, he is convinced, can grasp complicated intellectual ideas, even if perhaps not quite so well as professional thinkers: a famous example occurs in his *Poetics* 1448b, where he asserts that learning about things gives great pleasure not only to philosophers but to 'the others' as well (ἀλλὰ καὶ τοῖς ἄλλοις).

Aristotle's exoteric works

Aristotle is therefore both the founding father of the conventional form usually adopted by academics when disseminating their research and the first scholar of whom we know purposefully to produce a less esoteric type of work with a lay readership in mind. But the exoteric works disappeared at some point in the early Middle Ages. When he died in 322 BC at Euboean Chalcis, he left Theophrastus his entire library, doubtless including all the papyrus texts of both types of book, which he had either written himself or dictated to colleagues or slaves. They were presumably kept at the Lyceum until Theophrastus died in around 287 BC. But then Aristotle's works began a terrifying odyssey involving disappearance, damage, partial 'rescue' by Sulla, paraphrase, transformation through commentary by later philosophers with agendas and complete disappearance.

The fullest account of the textual history of Aristotle's *oeuvre* occurs in Strabo (13.1.54). Theophrastus left his own and Aristotle's works to their student Coriscus. Coriscus' son Neleus took it away to his hometown in Scepsis (Kurşuntepe), and bequeathed it to his heirs, 'ordinary people' (ἰδιώταις ἀνθρώποις). When they heard how zealously the Attalid kings to whom their city was subject were searching for books to equip the Pergamum library, they hid the Peripatetic works in a trench. Much later, when the books had been damaged by moisture and moths, their descendants sold them to Apellicon of Teos, a wealthy book-collector living in Athens in the early first century BC:

> But Apellicon was a bibliophile rather than a philosopher; and therefore, seeking a restoration of the parts that had been eaten through, he made new copies of the text, filling up the gaps incorrectly, and published the books full of errors. The result was that the earlier school of Peripatetics who came after Theophrastus had no books at all, with the exception of only a few, mostly exoteric works (οὐκ ἔχουσιν ὅλως τὰ βιβλία πλὴν ὀλίγων, καὶ μάλιστα τῶν ἐξωτερικῶν). They were therefore able to philosophise about nothing in a practical way, but only to recite propositions (μηδὲν ἔχειν φιλοσοφεῖν πραγματικῶς, ἀλλὰ θέσεις ληκυθίζειν), whereas the later school, from the time the books in question appeared, though better able to philosophise and Aristotelise, were forced to call most of their statements probabilities, because of the large number of errors (ἄμεινον μὲν ἐκείνων φιλοσοφεῖν καὶ ἀριστοτελίζειν, ἀναγκάζεσθαι μέντοι τὰ πολλὰ εἰκότα λέγειν διὰ τὸ πλῆθος τῶν ἁμαρτιῶν).

Apellicon's first recension of Aristotle was a disaster. It destabilized forever the trustworthiness of the transmitted texts.

The information Strabo supplies about the exoteric works, however, is important. They remained available to the Peripatetics of the third and second centuries BC, so they must have existed in more copies than the papyrus rolls which were taken to Scepsis. In content, they contained 'theses' which could be read out (the precise connotation of the verb *lēkuthizein* is obscure): the noun *thesis* can mean many things in Greek philosophical prose – hypothesis, thesis, assumed position, proposition, position requiring proof, general question or determination. But the Peripatetics' recital of these theses, whatever they were, is contrasted to the 'doing of philosophy practically' – that is, inductive or deductive reasoning from premises or evidence to reach new conclusions. They contained information or ideas but, at least according to Strabo, did not form the basis of new enquiries.

Apellicon's library, Strabo continues, was taken to Rome by Sulla when he took Athens in 84 BC during the Mithradatic Wars. The learned Pontic Greek grammarian Tyrannion succeeded in getting access to the collection, but so did 'certain booksellers who used bad copyists and would not collate the texts' (καὶ βιβλιοπῶλαί τινες γραφεῦσι φαύλοις χρώμενοι καὶ οὐκ ἀντιβάλλοντες). This is why that the small proportion of Aristotle's treatises which were transmitted subsequent to these hair-raising first few centuries, whether in Greek, Latin and/or Arabic, are in prose of uneven texture ranging from compressed 'lecture notes' and expanded spreadsheets[33] to polished prose which may have been performed in public since it avoids hiatus, such as the later books of the *Politics*.[34]

One of the few explicit references in Aristotle's own works to his exoteric treatises, occurs in the *Poetics*, although here he does not use the term *exoteric* (1454b): 'Keep, then, a careful eye on these rules and also on the *aisthēseis*, which are necessarily bound up with the poet's craft; for they offer many opportunities of going wrong. But this subject has been adequately discussed in the published treatises (ἐν τοῖς ἐκδεδομένοις λόγοις).' In the context, *aesthesis* probably signifies the last two of the six constituents of tragedy, which he has told us in 1450a-b, are, in order of importance, plot, characterization, thought, diction, song-making and spectacle. Aristotle seems to mean that he has written about the errors that a playwright can make with the musical and visual dimensions of tragedy in a book that has already been published (a standard meaning of ἐκδίδωμι in the passive voice; see Isocrates 5.11). Could it be that these dimensions of tragedy are the most noticeable ones, which the general public found easiest to discuss?

The other pertinent Aristotelian references, however, use the term *exoteric*. In the *Eudemian Ethics* (1.1217b20–25) he addresses the Platonic concept of the 'form' (ἰδέα) of the good and of forms in general:

> If we are to speak about it concisely, we say that in the first place to assert the existence of a form not only of the good but of anything else is a mere idle abstraction, but this has been considered in various ways in both the exoteric discourses (καὶ ἐν τοῖς ἐξωτερικοῖς λόγοις) and in those about philosophy (κατὰ φιλοσοφίαν).

Both exoteric treatises and treatises 'about philosophy' have already demonstrated that the concept of the forms is not useful. The distinction here implies that Aristotle regards the exoteric works as not philosophical in the strict sense. Nevertheless, people other than philosophers have been offered access to a discussion of the forms and why the concept is pointless (see further below, p. 175).

The distinction between different kinds of goods – those external to the self and those internal to the soul – was also made publicly available. Later in the *Eudemian Ethics*, we learn that 'all goods are either external or within the consciousness, and of these two kinds the latter are preferable, as we class them even [or 'and'] in the extraneous discourses (καθάπερ διαιρούμεθα καὶ ἐν τοῖς ἐξωτερικοῖς λόγοις, 2.1218b34). Much depends on the meaning of *kai* here. Is Aristotle implying that this classification is so elementary that 'even' the public can grasp it, or nudging his students to remember the comparison of internal and external goods which are 'also' discussed in the treatises that have been made widely available?

Two passages of the *Nicomachean Ethics* also refer to previously existing discussions in the exoteric works. First, Aristotle reminds us that when it comes to the soul, 'some things are said about it, adequately enough, even [or 'also'] in the exoteric works too (καὶ ἐν τοῖς ἐξωτερικοῖς λόγοις ἀρκούντως ἔνια), and we must use these, for example, that one part of the soul is irrational, another part rational' (1.1102a26–8). This instance has caused problems because the division of the soul into rational and irrational parts is not Aristotle's own view in *On the Soul*. But the problem disappears when it is accepted that the division does form the basis of the current discussion in the *Nicomachean Ethics*. The implication is this: in order for a Lyceum student to understand a lecture delivered by Aristotle, Aristotle regards a knowledge of other, exoteric (i.e. previously published or circulated works) as a prerequisite. This is certainly the implication of the other reference to exoteric works in the *Nicomachean Ethics* (6.1140a1–3), where Aristotle distinguishes between making objects (*poiesis*) and doing things (*praxis*), 'a distinction we may adopt also/even from the extraneous discourses' (πιστεύομεν δὲ περὶ αὐτῶν καὶ τοῖς ἐξωτερικοῖς λόγοις).

Finally, Aristotle says there has been an exploration in the exoteric treatises of 'the principles concerning household management and the control of slaves, that man is by nature a political animal; and so even when men have no need of assistance from each other they none the less desire to live together' (*Politics* 3.1278b30). Now, this material is covered in detail in book I of the *Politics*. Had the first part of the *Politics* (which is some of Aristotle's most polished and lucid prose) already been made available 'exoterically'? This is not necessarily the correct inference. It is equally possible that Aristotle had published a simplified and accessible version of the argument in *Politics* I, fundamental to his entire system, about the household as the basis of the human community.

Aristotle, therefore, refers to exoteric treatises which addressed several branches of philosophy: aesthetics (the mistakes tragedians could make), ontology (the uselessness of the concept of the forms), philosophy of mind (the superiority of internal over external goods, the structure of the soul), ethics (the distinction between poiesis and praxis), and politics (the partnerships in the household as the primary building-blocks of the city-state which human animals gather together to construct). But most of the references concern propositions – perhaps *theses* – fundamental to his entire intellectual system, which could apparently be articulated in a way that could be understood by everyone. He seems to have assumed that his advanced students – those fledgling *philosophoi* who could grapple with the complexity of his treatises *kata philosophian* – would be familiar with these exoteric works. Perhaps it was through reading them that they had conceived their passion for philosophical enquiry and enrolled at the Lyceum in the first place.

Other evidence for Aristotle's exoteric works, often addressing their form, appears in ancient authors. The exoteric works even had short prefaces to entice the reader into opening the papyrus roll (Cic. *Att.* 4.16.2). Eschewing preambles, they plunged straight into the central argument (Basil, *Ep.* 135). They were a treat to read, even by 'the multitude', since they were 'full of light and translucent; their usefulness is not unmixed with enjoyment and pleasure; Aphrodite and the Graces blossom on them' (Themistius. *Or.* 319 c). They were often or customarily in dialogue form. In a letter to Quintus (33.5.1), Cicero says that Sallustius had read a draft of Cicero's work on the best state and citizen. Sallustius responded by suggesting that the discussion of these topics would be lent greater authority if Cicero spoke in his own persona. Sallustius then suggested that Aristotle could furnish a model for Cicero, because he 'presented himself as speaker, in the things he wrote about the state and the leading man' (*Aristotelem deinque, quae de re publica et praestanti viro scribat, ipsum loqui*). Since Aristotle appears as a speaker in no extant treatises, it was likely in exoteric works that he had presented an alternative, dialogue rendition of some of the political arguments which occur in both his *Politics* and his *Rhetoric*. As Plato knew well, argumentation is easier to follow when presented in the form of a playscript. It thus makes suitable introductory reading for a lay thinker.

Plutarch discusses the distinction between Aristotle's popular and advanced treatises, in his *Life of Alexander* (7.3–5): 'Alexander seems not only to have received [Aristotle's] ethical and political instruction but also to have had access to those secret and more profound doctrines which [philosophical] men privately label "acroamatic" and "epoptic" and do not extend to the masses'. 'Acroamatic' implies that Aristotle communicated some doctrines only orally, and 'epoptic' is a term usually connected with initiation rituals. But, apparently, these 'oral' communications were published after Alexander had left Greece, when Aristotle returned to Athens from Macedon and opened his Lyceum. Plutarch tells that Alexander became angry when he learned of their publication, and wrote to Aristotle asking how he could outclass other men if the works that he had studied 'shall become the common property of everyone' (πάντων ἔσονται κοινοί). Alexander was aware that the social elite needed to maintain the exclusivity of academic knowledge if the hierarchy between themselves and the rest of humanity were not to be eroded. Aristotle's reply as reported by Plutarch is humorous: the book in question seems to have been the *Metaphysics*: 'For the metaphysical treatises are unusable for tuition or study, since they were written as a memorandum for those who had already trained in their contents' (ἀληθῶς γὰρ ἡ μετὰ τὰ φυσικὰ πραγματεία πρὸς διδασκαλίαν καὶ μάθησιν οὐδὲν ἔχουσα χρήσιμον ὑπόδειγμα τοῖς πεπαιδευμένοις ἀπ' ἀρχῆς γέγραπται). Plutarch knows that Aristotle's metaphysical ideas had a reputation for being more challenging to the reader than those on ethics and politics.

Another light on the popular understanding of Aristotle's works is shed by a passage in Lucian's dialogue *Vitarum Auctio* (26–7). Zeus and Hermes organise an auction of personifications of philosophical schools, including Pythagoreanism, Cynicism, Platonism, Epicureanism and Stoicism. The final 'lot' for sale is Peripatetic Philosophy. Hermes, the auctioneer, recommends this school as 'the most intelligent and comprehensive', and also 'temperate, equitable and applicable in life' – the last three qualities using distinctively Aristotelian vocabulary. Even better, he is 'double' (διπλοῦς):

He has one appearance from the outside, and another from the inside. So, if you purchase him, remember that one of him is called exoteric and the other esoteric.

Lucian knows that his own readership can buy either exoteric or esoteric treatises by Aristotle, and may have coined the latter word here to provide a contrast with 'exoteric' in a context where Plutarch had have used 'acroamatic'.

This 'double' philosophical school emerges as the most attractive from Lucian's treatise. In the next interchange, Hermes offers a competent enough paraphrase of Aristotle's distinction between different kinds of good in his *Nicomachean Ethics*: there are three types, 'in the soul, in the body and external ones' (ἐν ψυχῇ, ἐν σώματι, ἐν τοῖς ἐκτός). The dealer's response is revealing: Peripatetic thought 'thinks appropriately for humans' or 'in a way that a human can understand' (ἀνθρώπινα φρονεῖ) It can offer all kinds of information that is 'useful' as well as 'awesome'; here Lucian shows an amusing grasp of Aristotelian natural science, especially the colourful zoology of *History of Animals*: Hermes assures the book dealer that this school of philosophy will elucidate the lifespan of the mosquito, how deep sunlight can penetrate the sea, the nature of the oyster's soul, reproduction, birth, embryology, 'and how the human being can laugh, but the ass does not laugh nor do carpentry nor shipping'.

One lost exoteric work in dialogue form, probably entitled *Nerinthus* was written to honour the type of individual whom Aristotle seems to have envisaged as the reader of such public-facing works. A Corinthian farmer read Plato's *Gorgias* and 'forthwith gave up his farm and his vines, put his soul under Plato's guidance, and made it a seed-bed and a planting ground for Plato's philosophy' (Themistius, *Or.* 295 c-d). In *On Pleasure* Aristotle derided epideictic speakers who looked silly when describing Black Sea marvels they had never personally seen to crowds including business people 'who have just returned from the Phasis or the Borysthenes' (Athenaeus, *Deipn.* 6d). The association of Aristotle's dialogues for the public with the 'ordinary working man' also appears in an anecdote concerning his most famous exoteric work, indeed one of the most renowned philosophical treatises in antiquity, the *Protrepticus*, or *Encouragement to Philosophy*. The tale is preserved by Stobaeus (*Flor.* 4.32.21) via the Hellenistic Cynic philosopher Teles of Megara and Zeno, the founder of Stoicism.

Zeno's teacher, Crates of Thebes, 'as he sat in a shoemaker's workshop, read aloud the *Protrepticus*, which Aristotle had written to Themison king of Cyprus, saying that no one had greater advantages for becoming a philosopher; he had great wealth, so that he could afford to spend money on philosophy, and had reputation as well. 'As he read, the shoemaker listened while he went on with his stitching, and Crates said: "I think, Philiscus, that I shall inscribe a *Protrepticus* to you; for I see you have more advantages for the study of philosophy than were his for whom Aristotle wrote."' The dialogue was suitable for carrying around and reading while undertaking everyday errands, and comprehensible to a cobbler.

By pointing out that a humble craftsman like Philiscus may be better equipped to philosophise than King Themison, the anecdote also stresses the familiar Aristotelian theme that intrinsic goods are more valuable than external goods such as wealth and its trappings, the topic of another fragment:

> Happiness depends not on having many possessions but on the condition of the soul. For one would say that it is not the body which is decked with splendid clothing that is happy, but that which is healthy and in good condition, even if it has none of these things; and in the same way, if the soul has been disciplined, such a soul and such a man are to be called happy, not a man splendidly decked with outer things but himself worthless. It is not the horse which has a golden bit and costly harness, but is itself a poor creature, that we think worth anything; what we praise is the horse that is in good condition. Besides, when worthless men get abundant possessions, they come to value these more than the good of the soul; which is the basest of all conditions.[35]

To illustrate how external appearances are a poor guide to true goods, which are intrinsic to the soul, Aristotle used the myth of Lynceus, gifted with the superpower of X-ray vision. 'Strength, size, beauty are a laugh and nothing more, and beauty seems to be beauty only because we see nothing accurately. If one could have seen as clearly as they say Lynceus did, who saw through walls and trees, would one ever have thought any man endurable to look at, when one saw of what poor materials he is made?'[36] This passage comes from Iamblichus, who paraphrased and excerpted extensively from Aristotle's *Protrepticus* in his own *Encouragement to Philosophy* (early fourth century AD). Some passages are occasionally held to be direct quotations from Aristotle, such as this rousing pronouncement that philosophical enquiry is desirable for its own sake rather than because it confers a monetary advantage:

> For as we travel to Olympia for the sake of the spectacle itself, even if nothing were to follow from it (for the spectacle itself is worth more than much wealth), and as we view the Dionysia not in order to gain anything from the actors (indeed we spend money on them), and as there are many other spectacles we should prefer to much wealth, so too the contemplation of the universe is to be honoured above all the things that are thought useful. For surely it cannot be right that we should take great pains to go to see men imitating women and slaves, or fighting and running, just for the sake of the spectacle, and not think it right to view without payment the nature and reality of things.
>
> Iamblichus, Protr. 52. 16-54.5 Pistelli

Some modern scholars have used Iamblichus in an attempt to reconstruct Aristotle's inspiring exhortation wholesale.[37] They have supplemented Iamblichus with other ancient commentators on Aristotle and the fragments of Cicero's lost *Hortensius*, a dialogue which was modelled on the *Protrepticus* (*Hist. Aug.* 2.97.20-2),[38] in which the figure of Cicero proposed to interlocutors that philosophy was a better leisure pursuit than fine art, literature or rhetoric. This implies that the main speaker in Aristotle's *Protrepticus* was Aristotle himself.

In my view a precise reconstruction of the *Protrepticus* is, sadly, too ambitious, but certain other themes were so renowned that several authorities mention them. Aristotle used the riddling, tricksy argument that even to refute the existence or usefulness of philosophy required using philosophical argumentation (Alexander of Aphrodisias' commentary on Aristotle's *Topics*, composed around AD 200, 149.9–17):

> Suppose someone said we ought not to pursue philosophy. Then, since even to inquire whether we ought to philosophize or not is (as Aristotle himself said in the *Protrepticus*) to philosophize, and since to pursue philosophical insight is also to philosophize, by showing that each of these two things is natural to man we shall on all counts refute the proposition proposed.

There are other surprises in the fragments of the *Protrepticus*. Aristotle cracked a joke for which there is no parallel in his surviving work: he said that Anacyndaraxes (the father of Sardanapalus) was 'even sillier than the name of his father would suggest' (Iamblichus, *Protrept.* 56. 13–59 Pistelli). He used catchy nicknames, such as 'old children' to describe unphilosophical grown men who, like unweaned infants, can't tell truth from falsehood or indeed draw any distinctions between any things whatsoever (Chalcidius, *In Tim.* 208–9, ed. Wrobel).

The Macedonian anthologist Stobaeus in the fifth century AD quotes an excerpt from Aristotle's *On Good Birth* which indicates that in it the figure of Aristotle reported, at a later date, a dialogue in which he had participated (Stob. 4.29 A 24). His interlocutor had said, 'With regard to good birth, I for my part am quite at a loss to say whom one should call well-born.' The reported dialogue continues, with Aristotle the narrator quoting Aristotle:

> 'Your difficulty', I said, 'is quite natural; for both among the many and even more among the wise there is division of opinion and obscurity of statement, particularly about the significance of good birth. What I mean is this: Is it a precious and good thing, or, as Lycophron the sophist wrote, something altogether trivial? Comparing it with other goods, he says the attractiveness of good birth is obscure, and its dignity a matter of words; i.e. that the preference for it is a matter of opinion, and in truth there is no difference between the low-born and the well-born.'

Stobaeus continues (4.29.A 25), showing that Aristotle referred to the ideas about good birth propounded by Socrates, Simonides, and Theognis, the last of whom he quoted directly. The easy style, with its allusions to the ideas of famous thinkers and poets, flows like the most accessible Platonic dialogue.

A sad loss amongst Aristotle's dialogues is his *On Philosophy*, which complemented his *Protrepticus* with a picture of how philosophy first developed. The fragments are lively and colourful: he discussed the provenance of the Delphic injunction 'know thyself', and decided that it was the Pythia herself rather than any male sage who had first invented it (Clem. *Strom.* 1.14.60.3). He discussed Zoroastrianism, its metaphysical dualism and high antiquity, claiming that Zoroaster lived six thousand years before the death of Plato (Pliny, *N.H.* 30.3). He appealed to the non-expert philosopher by discussing the importance of proverbs and sayings as concise expressions of primordial beliefs (Synesius, *Encomium of Calvitius* 22.85 c.0).

Aristotle's influential *Eudemus, or On the Soul* was also a dialogue. It was written to memorialise his friend Eudemus of Cyprus, to whom the *Eudemian Ethics* was dedicated. Eudemus was an alumnus of Plato's Academy who died fighting in Syracuse in about 354 BC (Cicero, *de Div.* 1.25.3; Plut. *Life of Dion* 22.3). One long fragment, which Plutarch says he is quoting verbatim (αὐτὰς τὰς τοῦ φιλοσόφου λέξεις παραθέσθαι), is preserved in Plutarch's consolatory letter to Apollonius (*Mor.* 115b-e). It features a passage in Aristotle's own voice in which he converses with a high-status listener:

> 'This is why, O mightiest and most blessed of men, we not only consider the dead to be blessed and happy, but also believe that it is impious to say anything untrue or slanderous about them because they are already better than us and our superiors. And this is such a primal and ancient belief of ours that nobody know when or by whom it was first stated, but it has been maintained as a conviction for all time. Additionally, reflect on the saying which is on everyone's lips and has been circulated in common parlance for many years.'
>
> 'Which one?' he said. And the other one [Aristotle] replied,
>
> 'That not to be born is the best of all, and to be dead is better than to be alive.'

At this point the figure of Aristotle introduces a fable, which requires him to bring the satyr Silenus to life in the dialogue by the use of *oratio recta*:

> 'So, for example, they say that Silenus, after the hunt when Midas captured him, when Midas kept putting questions to him, asking what is the best and most desirable of things for all people, at first refused to define it and kept an unbroken silence. But when eventually by using every stratagem Midas with difficulty coerced him into responding, Silenus, under pressure, said this: "Short-lived progeny of a spirit of travail and a harsh fate, why are you forcing me to say what it is better for you not to know? The least painful life is the one spent in ignorance of one's private sorrows. For humans it is completely impossible to have what is the best of all things, or even to have a share in its nature, so it is best for all men and all women not to be born. But the next best thing, and the best of those that are achievable by humans, but still only second best, is to die as soon as possible after being born." It is clear therefore that Silenus made this pronouncement in the belief that existence in death is superior to the time spent alive.'[39]

The use of the fable and the impersonation of the mythical satyr, unlike anything in Aristotle's surviving treatises, are reminiscent of Plato's liveliest narratives. The sonorous diction used by the sagacious satyr reminds us that Ammonius admired the way Aristotle's exoteric works modified 'the style of his diction to suit the speakers' (see above, p. 163). The reference to the Sicilian mimes of Sophron and Xenarchus alongside the Socratic dialogues in Aristotle's *Poetics* (1447b1) alerts us to his interest in the history of the form. In his own popular dialogue *On Poets* he expanded the discussion to include discussion of Plato's form and style (Diog. Laert. 3.37(25¦) and of other dialogists preceding Plato: Athenaeus, *Deipn.* 10.505 b-c quotes him: 'Are we then to deny that the so-called mimes of Sophron, which aren't even in metre, are stories and imitations, or the dialogues of Alexamenos of Teos, written before the Socratic dialogues?'

Moreover, in ventriloquizing the wise Silenus, Aristotle plays into the association of the figure of the philosopher, especially Socrates, with the satyr.[40] The appeal to well-known sayings is consistent with Aristotle's respect for *endoxa*, or popularly held beliefs, in his extant treatises. It is intriguing that Aristotle does not say that he believes in life after death, which would run counter to his prevailing view as expressed in his surviving works. But we know that he was aware that this idea was challenging for general audiences, indeed it was literally 'unfriendly' (*aphilon*) for people to believe that the friendship bonds which held together Greek society were completely dissolved by death (*NE* 1.1101a22–4).[41]

Nor does he here use dialectical argument to arrive at the conclusion: Aristotle quotes a mythical figure, and concludes that he believed in the superiority of the existence enjoyed by the dead. This method is consistent with the ancient commentators' opinion that Aristotle freely used unexamined arguments from probability in his exoteric works.[42] But his most fundamental philosophical positions, especially his rejection of Plato's ideal world of eternal forms, were promulgated vigorously in the popular treatises. As Proclus put it, 'there was nothing in Plato that Aristotle rejected so firmly as the theory of Ideas', in his writings not only on logic but on ethics, physics and metaphysics, 'and in his dialogues, where he asseverates most clearly that he cannot agree with this doctrine, even if he lays himself open to the charge of opposing it from love of polemic'.[43]

Conclusion

I do not believe that most academics are premeditated obscurantists whose goal is to exclude those not initiated into their esoteric discourse. Nor do I believe they deliberately want to alienate those whose capacity to read their scholarly publications is restricted by their price-tags or by intolerance of arcane articles and monographs bristling with metalanguage, bibliographical references and footnotes. I agree with Lyons that there are long-term political, social and economic reasons why the academic industry has forgotten its primordial obligation to extend knowledge to others outside its own circle.[44] But we can help to defuse the hostility against academic obscurantists that anti-intellectual populists whip up by ensuring that our ideas circulate in digestible form in the public sphere. This exercise could offer the additional benefit of practice in writing even specialised prose for our peers more clearly as well.

Aristotle's example can help us with both tasks. He would never have advocated deliberate obscurity in scholarly discourse any more than in popular treatises. He objects to it in some detail in *Rhetoric* III.⁴⁵ But when he needed to express advanced ideas with maximum precision for his erudite colleagues, he did adopt terse and neologistic language and dense dialectical reasoning. And he also spent a considerable amount of time advocating the practice of philosophy by everyone and explaining his central ideas in shorter works designed to circulate widely. In these he made efforts to make philosophising attractive by the use of dialogue form involving colourful characterisation of the interlocutors as well as ornaments such as allusion to myth and fable, humour, vivid images and the avoidance of concentrated syllogistic or inductive method. This form won him high praise: Cicero spoke of the oratorical 'river of gold' which Aristotle poured forth (*flumen orationis aureum fundens Aristoteles, Lucullus* 38 par. 119), which implies that the dialogues worked splendidly in live delivery.

I am not proposing merely that we adopt dialogue form in our written work. Sir George Stock was inspired by the example of Aristotle's exoteric works when he wrote *Lectures in the Lyceum: Or, Aristotle's Ethics for English Readers* (1897). He introduced interlocutors into some chapters – Theophrastus, Nicomachus and Eudemus. But they are used so ineffectively that the book remains dry and unattractive. Much the same, sadly, can be said of Jonathan Barnes' attempt at dialogue form in *Coffee with Aristotle* (2008). But I *am* proposing that as a community we should discuss our relationship with the public more seriously. The digital age and Youtube have brought fine new media for communication, although the short book or pamphlet in accessible prose, preferably opening with a version of the argument in an even shorter preface, seems to me offer as much scope as it did when Crates read out Aristotle's *Protrepticus* to that cobbler. It is important, too, that the *Protrepticus* breathed confidence into its readers, arguing that intellectual labour could make everyone good citizens and was far from difficult (Iambl. *Protr.* b.37. 3–41). Most inspiring of all, Aristotle's motive in writing in two different forms was philanthropic: he did it, according to Elias, an Alexandrian commentator in the sixth century AD, simply because 'he wished to benefit *all* mankind' (*in Cat.* 114. 15).⁴⁶

Notes

1. Schopenhauer 1965 [1891]: 608: 'Und doch ist nicht leichter, als so schrieben, das kein Mensch es versteht, wie hingegen nicht schwerer, als bedeutende Gedanken so auszudrücken, dass jeder sie verstehen muss.'
2. See e.g. https://www.washingtonpost.com/politics/top-wh-strategist-vows-a-daily-fight-for-deconstruction-of-the-administrative-state/2017/02/23/03f6b8da-f9ea-11e6-bf01-d47f8cf9b643_story.html accessed 21 May 2012. Thanks to Sara Monoson for pointing this out to me. See further http://edithorial.blogspot.co.uk/2017/02/.
3. Nietzsche 1879: 27.
4. See Tandon 2009.
5. Agger 2008: 424.

6. Agger 2008: 424.
7. Atticus fr. 7, drawn from Eusebius, *Preparation for the Gospel* 15.9.13; Schmitt 1965.
8. A charge laid, by e.g. Card 1991: xix, against many writers today, who, he claims, 'have based their entire careers on the premise that anything that the general public can understand without mediation is worthless drivel'.
9. Sluiter 2016. I am very grateful to Professor Sluiter for discussing obscurity and obscurantism with me.
10. Lee 1912 and Kogan 1969 are rather more sceptical than I am here about some academics' conscious motives.
11. MacMullan 2007: 61. See also Billig 1995; Schechner 1995; Dutton 1999; Elster 2011.
12. Adorno 1973 [1964].
13. Marcuse 1964.
14. Derrida 1996.
15. Deleuze and Guattari 1994: 108.
16. See Hall 2018: 54–5.
17. Stern 1970; Hacking 1992; Crombie 1994; Ritchie 2012.
18. Kroll-Smith 2008: 396.
19. https://acmedsci.ac.uk/more/news/10-tips-for-writing-a-lay-summary accessed 21 May 2012. Thanks to Richard Poynder for pointing this out to me.
20. *Henry IV Part 2*, Act 5, Scene 3.
21. Lyons 2014: 33–5.
22. Lavery and Groarke 2010: 13, 31–5.
23. Lang 2010: 220.
24. Quoted by Nonius Marcellus, *De compendiosa doctrina* 394.26–8 ed. Lindsay (1903).
25. *De sui ipsius et multorum ignorantia* (1367) p. 266 ed. Fenzi (1999).
26. For the references to other authors in the *Rhetoric*, *Poetics* and *Nicomachean Ethics* see Hinman (1935).
27. See in general Taub 2017.
28. Carroll 1984: 48; Hall 2017.
29. Vossius 1696: 38, 229.
30. Cicero is the primary ancient defender of Aristotle's style, describing it as the most 'sinewy' or 'vigorous' (*nervosus*) of philosophical prose, in contrast to the 'richness' of Plato and the 'sweetness' of Theophrastus (*Brutus* 31.121). When writing to his brother Quintus, Cicero's praise for the charm of Aristotle's language as well as his erudition, prolific productivity and originality, is copious (10.1.83). On the other hand, he acknowledges the difficulty, even obscurity, of some of Aristotle's writing (*Topica* 1.2).
31. Lang 2010: 221.
32. Ross 1952: viii.
33. Missiakoulis 2008.
34. Blass 1892: 140; Dirlmeier 1984: 1–4; Schütrumpf 1989.
35. *POxy* 666 = Stob. 3.3.25.
36. Iamblichus, *Protrepticus* 47.5–21 ed. Pistelli (1888); see also Boethius, *Consol.* 3.8.

37. See Düring 1961; Chroust 1964; and especially the project led by Douglas S. Hutchinson and Monte Ransome Johnson at the University of Toronto, http://www.protrepticus.info/.
38. Bernays 1863; see Moraux 1975.
39. On the 'better never to have been born' trope, which Aristotle's Silenus shares with the author of *Ecclesiastes* 4.1–2 and the chorus of Sophocles' *OC* 1224–35, see Hall 2010: 10–11.
40. See Tanner 2017.
41. See Hall 2018c: ch. 10.
42. See above p. 167–8 and e.g. Elias *In Cat.* 114. 25.
43. Proclus in Philoponus, *De aeternitate mundi contra Proclum* 31.17 ed. Rabe (1899).
44. Lyons 2014: 34.
45. See Consigny 1987. Aristotle has however been accused of 'obscurantism' of a kind resembling that associated with the contemporary political right by MacIntyre 1996: 83, a charge from which he is defended by van Alstyne 1998.
46. This article has been much improved by the comments of my editor, Phiroze Vasunia, and of Paul Cartledge. I am very grateful to both of them. When I delivered the paper at the original conference in 2016, comments from Carol Atack and Tim Whitmarsh proved particularly useful, as did those of Sara Monoson when I delivered a slightly different version at Northwestern University, Illinois in January 2017.

CHAPTER 9
POLITICS AND FORM IN XENOPHON
Rosie Harman

Xenophon's works are full of unexpected shifts in structure and peculiarities in tone: his narratives and arguments sometimes seem to change direction mid-flow, pointing the reader in opposite directions at once. In this chapter, I will suggest that these oddities of Xenophon's style, which are such a distinctive feature of his writing but have proved a puzzle to scholars, can be explained in terms of the political effect of his works. For Xenophon, problems of form reveal and instantiate the political problems of his time. I argue that the disjunctive feel of Xenophon's writing, rather than being a problem to be explained away, must be addressed as fundamental to his works' historical significance.

A notorious example is the ending of the *Cyropaedia*.[1] Here, after almost 8 books presenting an apparent praise of the achievements of Cyrus the Great and his Persians, the final chapter suddenly changes tack to argue that contemporary Persia is the most corrupt, decadent and immoral of states (*Cyr.* 8.8). A similar shift famously takes place in chapter 14 of the *Lakedaimonion Politeia*: whereas the other chapters seem to praise the mythical Spartan lawgiver Lycurgus' organization of Spartan institutions (and the text is usually read as a eulogy of Spartan society),[2] the penultimate chapter transforms into a savage critique of contemporary Sparta. Although these shifts can of course be understood as shifts in content, as the texts move from one argument about the nature of Persia or Sparta to another, as we shall see in due course, they can also usefully be understood in terms of form: one mode of writing, with its own rhetorical mechanisms, ways of addressing and drawing in the reader, and in-built expectations for interpretation, gives way to another. Such a perspective offers a new way of approaching problems in Xenophon's writing.

These awkward passages have been approached in a number of ways, which all aim to smooth over the disturbing resonances produced by these sudden shifts in direction. They have been regarded as later interpolations;[3] the 1914 Loeb translation of the *Cyropaedia* by Walter Miller interposes a note within the body of the text between chapters 8.7 and 8.8 commenting that although it has been deemed necessary to include the coming chapter as it is found in all manuscript versions, 'the reader is recommended to close the book at this point and read no further'.[4] Another approach has been to regard these chapters as later additions made by Xenophon when his admiration for Persia and Sparta was dashed by historical events.[5]

Of those who see the problematic chapters as original, the majority attempt to wipe out all sense of contradiction either by arguing that Xenophon's focus on contemporary degeneration gives added weight to his praise of the past achievements of Cyrus the

Great and Lycurgus by showing the catastrophe that ensued when their models of rule were no longer applied,[6] or (in the case of the *Lak. Pol.*) by seeing Xenophon as offering a careful, dispassionate analysis of Sparta's positive and negative characteristics.[7] Alternatively, these texts have been read as wholly condemnatory, either (in the case of the *Lak. Pol.*) by reading the apparent praise of Sparta in the earlier portion of the work as a heavily veiled ironic pastiche through privileging the rather strange leaps and contradictions in its argument,[8] or (in the case of the *Cyropaedia*) by linking the final chapter to the disturbing aspects of the representation of Cyrus as a ruler which occur throughout the text;[9] these aspects of the texts are further discussed below. These different interpretations have led to huge variations in the dating of the texts, based on assumptions about Xenophon's biography which have been used, rather reductively, to speculate on his attitude towards Sparta and Persia at different times.[10]

Readings which claim a logical continuity between *Cyr.* 8.8, *Lak. Pol.* 14 and the rest of their respective texts do not do justice to the very real sense of shock which these chapters generate in the reader. Although these chapters do refer to a present when the Spartans no longer follow the laws of Lycurgus and the Persians are no longer like the Persians of Cyrus' time, the earlier portions of these texts do not appear to deal only with a lost past. On the contrary, in reading the *Lak. Pol.* one gets the impression that one is being presented with the nature of Spartan society very much as it is in the present:[11] the text describes what the reader would see and experience on an imagined visit to Sparta (*Lak. Pol.* 3.5, 9.1, 13.5), and advises the reader to look at the Spartans if they wish to test out the truth of the text's assertions (*Lak. Pol.* 1.10, 2.14), for example. Similarly, the *Cyropaedia* repeatedly links Cyrus' time with the now, noting, as it describes Persian customs, that they are still practised today.[12] The swift shift in argument at *Lak. Pol.* 14 and *Cyr.* 8.8, as the texts suddenly impose a distinction between past and present which the reader had not been aware of up till this point, disorients the reader.

Readings which deny a contradiction between these chapters and the earlier portions of their texts aim to explain away those texts' complexities; as we shall see, these complexities must be understood as intrinsic to the functioning of these texts. I will argue that the disjunctions in Xenophon's writing, which produce such an unsettling reading experience, enact and instantiate the political problems which the texts address.[13] I suggest that it will be useful to approach these questions through an examination of the concept of genre.

Xenophon is unusual for his period in that he wrote works across a number of genres, including historiography, rhetorical set pieces and Socratic dialogue. He also produced works which are difficult to classify in terms of pre-existing prose genres. The *Anabasis* is in some ways akin to history writing in its account of real events, but its focus on the narrow experiences of an individual and his men on a journey has also led to it being compared to the *Odyssey*.[14] The framing of the narrative via the experiences of the character 'Xenophon', presented in the third person, have also led scholars to attempt to categorize the text using the terminology of autobiography.[15]

Similarly, the *Cyropaedia* has been described as historiography, political philosophy, biography, or as an early version of the novel – centuries before the novel's inception.[16] In these texts Xenophon has been described as producing experimental prose which sits between classifiable forms, or even as initiating previously unknown genres.[17]

I would like to examine a couple of examples of occasions where Xenophon seems to switch from one form of writing to another mid-text. The examples that I will focus on come from texts we can broadly describe as narrative historiography – the *Hellenica* and *Anabasis* (and we will go on briefly to compare these examples with the examples from the *Cyropaedia* and *Lak. Pol.* mentioned above). In the *Hellenica* my example will involve a shift from narration of events to dialogue; in the *Anabasis* the shift I am interested in is from narration of events to the language of praise; and we have already noted the shifts in the *Cyropaedia* and *Lak. Pol.* from praise to blame.[18] I would like to approach these shifts in focus, organization and tone as shifts in 'genre'.[19] By using the term 'genre' in this context I am not attempting to suggest that we should be interested in labelling different sections of Xenophon's writing within any given text under different genre appellations. To attempt to do so would beg the question of how to approach Xenophon's writing as such: since we have no clear way of classifying the *Cyropaedia* (for example) as a whole, attempting to come up with subsidiary classifications for the majority of the work on the one hand and the final chapter on the other is not a meaningful exercise. Rather, what I am suggesting is that the concept of genre as an analytical category provides a useful heuristic tool with which to approach Xenophon's disjunctive style and cut-up structure.

In the light of Adorno's examination of form as a crystallization of social relations,[20] Conte has posited a reading of genre as the instantiation of an ideological model for understanding the world, whereby within any particular genre, particular ways of thinking about the way the world works are inscribed, encoded and imposed on the reader[21] – or, in the language of Jauss, a particular horizon of expectation is offered to the reader, which both reflects and constructs historical experience.[22] Bakhtin's examination of the co-existence and interaction of different such generic models is helpful in the case of Xenophon. Bakhtin posits the modern novel as a dialogic form, where different generic voices come into conflict and affect each other, producing a hybridized or 'double-voiced' text. He argues that this produces a unique political experience, whereby the text clashes together different ideological modes and conceptions which impinge and reflect on each other.[23] As we shall see, this concept of dialogism is helpful for a reading of Xenophon.

To a certain extent, we could see Bakhtin's dialogism as a characteristic of early Greek historiography per se. In the fifth and early fourth centuries BC, prior to Aristotelian literary criticism, there is not yet a fixed genre of history writing – and indeed prose writing as such is still very much a new and experimental form.[24] Xenophon's combination of – for example – impersonal narration of events with dialogue is nothing new. In Herodotus and Thucydides we see repeated movements between narration and direct speech, whether presented as set piece speeches or as dialogue.[25] Indeed, as Boedeker has shown, from the earliest inception of historiography Herodotus' text is defined through and against prior forms of writing in prose and verse.[26] Herodotus' distinctive contribution, his articulation and questioning of modes of authority and categories of truth value, is performed through a negotiation between different genres, each encoding their own expectations.[27] I will suggest that Xenophon's historical narration not only participates in a similar dynamic, but produces a particularly marked awareness of genre as a problem.[28]

I will begin with an example from the *Hellenica*, in order to indicate some of the political effects of Xenophon's disjunctions in focus, tone and structure.[29] In a second step, we will move on to an example from the *Anabasis*, where the stakes are slightly different – where Xenophon's writing seems to inscribe awareness of the constructed nature of the text as a text and to allow the nature of its contract with the reader to become open to speculation, producing in the reader a critical cognizance of the political effects of form. A third section will place the production of formal awareness in the context of some other examples from fourth-century BC prose writing, examining the evocation of readerly critical attentiveness to the effects of praise discourse in both Xenophon and his contemporaries. In a final step, we will use the insights gained in these discussions to return to the problem of the *Cyropaedia*'s ending in conjunction with the analogous problem of the *Lak. Pol.*'s chapter 14, offering a reading of Xenophon's disjunctive style in terms of both the ideological contradictions of Xenophon's time and the textual construction of critical reading practices.

Hellenica 4.1.1–4.1.15

At the opening of *Hellenica* book 4, Xenophon presents a dialogue between Agesilaus, King of Sparta, Spithridates, a Persian who has revolted from the Persian King (3.4.10), and Otys, King of the Paphlagonians, regarding the prospect of Otys marrying Spithridates' daughter. Agesilaus first questions Spithridates as to whether he would be willing to give his daughter to Otys; next Agesilaus holds a dialogue with Otys in which he leads Otys to consider marrying Spithridates' daughter.

What is particularly striking about the sequence is the detail with which Xenophon presents this narrative moment. Rather than simply summarizing the arrangement of the marriage in a couple of lines, we are treated to direct speech between the participants, much of it presented via question-and-answer exchanges along the lines of Socratic dialogue:[30]

> [Agesilaus] began a conversation with Otys by asking, 'Tell me, Otys, what kind of family does Spithridates comes from?' Otys replied that he was not inferior to any of the Persians. 'You have seen how handsome his son is?' 'Yes, indeed. In fact, I dined with him last evening.' 'And yet they say that Spithridates' daughter is even more attractive than his son.' 'Yes, by Zeus,' said Otys, 'she is beautiful indeed.'
>
> 4.1.6[31]

The narrative slows right down, presenting a (largely) mimetic blow-by-blow account of the verbal interaction through which the marriage got arranged. The sequence stands in striking contrast to the surrounding context, which presents a dense, impersonally narrated account of fast-moving events. Book 3 ends with an account of the fighting between the Thebans and Spartans at Haliartus in Boeotia (3.5.17–25): the movement of troops (3.5.17), the fighting outside the walls (3.5.18–19), the death of Lysander (3.5.19), the Theban pursuit of Lysander's troops (3.5.19) and their self-defence (3.5.20), the departure of the Phocians (3.5.21), the arrival of Pausanias (3.5.21), the arrival of the Athenians in support of Thebes (3.5.22), Pausanias' request for the return of bodies under truce (3.5.23), the Spartan withdrawal (3.5.24), and Pausanias' prosecution, abscondment and death (3.5.25). Major incidents, such as the death of Lysander or the dishonour, exile and death of Pausanias, are treated in a couple of swiftly narrated lines. It is all the more remarkable, therefore, when the text continues with a shift not only from events in Greece to events in Asia, but to an intricately presented dialogue on the arrangement of a marriage.

In terms of the wider narrative context, the arrangement of the marriage does not seem to have that great a significance.[32] Its aim is presumably to shore up the newly agreed alliance between the Spartans, Spithridates and the Paphlagonians,[33] but this alliance in fact falls apart within a few short chapters: Agesilaus' subordinate Herippidas refuses to share booty with Spithridates and the Paphlagonians after their joint capture of Pharnabazus' camp, and Spithridates and the Paphlagonians respond by packing up in the night and going over to Ariaeus (4.1.26–7). We are told that their desertion 'caused Agesilaus more grief than anything else that happened in this campaign' (4.1.28). This statement marks how the arrangements so carefully set up in fact came to nothing; the comment draws our attention to the disparity between the space given to the account of the establishment of the marriage agreement and its lack of long-term historical impact.

Xenophon's use of the dialogue therefore could do with some explanation. As Gray has shown, a particular function of dialogue as a form is that unlike impersonal narration or even a set-piece speech, it most effectively communicates the processes of manipulation of one interlocutor by another.[34] We are shown step by step how Agesilaus leads Spithridates and Otys to fall in with his plans. Agesilaus' initial exchange with Spithridates reveals Spithridates' willingness to agree to the marriage but his assumption of Otys' unwillingness, on the grounds that Otys is a great king whereas he is an exile (4.1.4). Agesilaus' subsequent persuasion of Otys pre-empts this potential difficulty by insisting on the high birth and great power of Spithridates (4.1.7).[35] As Gray indicates, the result is a reversal of attitudes: Otys seems to have been led by Agesilaus to believe that, rather than being the loser in the arrangement, he would get the most out of the marriage deal, and it is now he who shows eagerness while doubting Spithridates' willingness (4.1.10–12).[36] Agesilaus then stages the need to persuade Spithridates, sending Herippidas out to speak to him, as though this were the first time the arrangement had been mentioned (4.1.11). The dialogue form, which shows Agesilaus' persuasive moves and Otys' responses, reveals Agesilaus' methods in asserting control over his interlocutor, and the clever way in which he is able to achieve his aims.[37]

We must ask about the political effect of this dialogue on the reader. One function of dialogue is to introduce a range of competing voices. Indeed, one reading of Platonic dialogue would see dialogue as an essentially democratic genre, by staging and involving the reader in the openness of debate. However, Platonic dialogue frequently privileges the controlling voice of Socrates, whose arguments trump or overshadow those of other speakers.[38] In this context, dialogue has a contrary political effect: it offers alternative positions to the reader, but only to close those alternative positions down. In the *Hellenica*'s scene of Agesilaus' marriage brokerage, the dialogue form works not only to demonstrate the controlling power of Agesilaus' voice at the expense of other voices, but to draw the reader in to this dynamic, so that the reader acquiesces to the powerful voice of Agesilaus just as his interlocutors do. As we are shown each step in Agesilaus' persuasive process, it is difficult not to be impressed and won over by him, just as the internal audience seems to be.[39] We are drawn in, identifying with Agesilaus as he takes control of his audience, and taking pleasure in witnessing his success. But in doing so, we are also acquiescing to the power of Agesilaus, who argues, for example, that Otys' alliance with him will be an alliance with the whole of Greece since Sparta is the leader of Greece (4.1.8).[40] What we are witnessing is, after all, an attempt to consolidate Sparta's military and economic self-interest in Asia Minor, as the aftermath of the dialogue, when Spithridates and the Paphlagonians are used for a military venture but not permitted to share the spoils, makes clear.

The scene shows a potentially disturbing political moment: a Spartan arranging an alliance with a Persian and a Paphlagonian.[41] In contrast to the language of Greek versus barbarian with which the venture of Agesilaus in Asia is earlier described,[42] in this scene we are shown that it is quite possible for Agesilaus to throw in with Persians (elsewhere the enemy; in the *Anabasis* Spithridates appears as a subordinate of Pharnabazus who fights against the 10,000 in Bithynia: *An.* 6.5.7) and Paphlagonians (depicted in the *Anabasis* as an extremely alien people)[43] when it suits his interests.[44] One effect of the use of the dialogue form, however, is effectively to obscure the potentially shocking political realities which this episode encodes. The dialogue, which takes us up close and personal with the various speakers, presents a jokey exchange with an erotic feel (note the comments on the attractiveness of the son, with whom Otys dined last night, and of the daughter); in the *Agesilaus,* Spithridates' son Megabates is presented as a beautiful centre of erotic interest for Agesilaus (*Ag.* 5.5). We could be in the erotic environment of the symposium, where elite males rub shoulders. The ideal reader (positioned as male and elite) might be led by the charming and witty tone of the exchange[45] to feel almost as if witnessing the interactions of peers. The dialogue both calls on the reader's acceptance of Spartan power mongering, and, by the comfortable ease of the interaction, smoothes over and obscures the reader's awareness that this is indeed what pleasurable identification with Agesilaus' charming, clever and controlling voice would imply.

However, as noted above, the introduction of the dialogue embodies a shift which is sudden and jarring. In the previous sequence we are in Boeotia, where Thebans, Athenians, Spartans and allied Greek communities square off. If in the marriage dialogue it is obvious with whom we are to identify – with the clever and seductive Spartan leader whose successful building of his power against the Persian King forms the central concern of this portion of the text – in this earlier narrative the interests of Sparta compete with the interests of other Greeks. As we read the dialogue, the easy seductiveness of Agesilaus' voice lulls us into identification and acceptance; yet as we read, the contrast with the preceding narrative impinges on our experience of the dialogue, undercutting our pleasure and making us aware of the political context of Agesilaus' actions. Equally, our experience of the dialogue and our immersion in our enjoyment of Agesilaus' success reflect back on our reading of the conflicts in Greece, calling on us to consider whether we might be able to read Spartan actions not as a narrative of competing hegemonies, where each side promotes only its own interests, but as a narrative of Greek endeavour.

Hellenica's book 3 seems to pose this problem more widely – as we shift backwards and forwards from events in Asia (Spartan action under the leadership of Thibron and Dercylidas, 3.1.1–3.2.20) to events in Greece (Sparta's conquest of Elis and problems in Sparta, 3.2.21–3.3.11), to events in Asia (Sparta's expedition under Agesilaus, 3.4.1–3.4.29) to events in Greece (the attempts of other Greek states to oppose Sparta, 3.5.1–3.5.25). The focus throughout is on Sparta, but whereas the sequences set in Asia make reference to the language of Greek–barbarian conflict,[46] in the sequences set in Greece, the Asian endeavour is set in the context of Sparta's imposition of hegemony on other Greeks. The campaign of Dercylidas is framed through the claim that in threatening to besiege Greek cities until they capitulate and accept Spartan governance and garrisons, the Spartan commander is providing 'freedom and autonomy' (3.1.16; 3.1.20–1).[47] In one sequence, Dercylidas takes over the cities of the Troad region which had previously been under the control of the Greek Meidias, who had himself taken them over following his assassination of his mother-in-law Mania (also Greek), who had won a concession from Pharnabazus to rule them in the place of her deceased husband, based on her continued supply of tribute to him. In a dialogue with Meidias after the capitulation of Gergis and Meidias's home city of Skepsis, Dercylidas questions Meidias on the extent of his property inherited from his father:

> 'Meidias, tell me, did your father leave you in charge of his house?' 'Yes, indeed,' Meidias replied. 'And how many properties were there? How many estates? How many pastures?'
>
> *3.1.25*

The rest of Dercylidas' exchange with Meidias and the other Skepsians present concerns who now owns the house of Mania in Gergis, which Meidias had taken for himself. The conclusion is reached that since Mania served Pharnabazus, now that Dercylidas is fighting Pharnabazus and in that context has captured her property, it must belong to him:

> When Meidias had finished making his list of his inheritance, Dercylidas said, 'Now tell me, to whom did Mania belong?' They all said that she belonged to Pharnabazus. 'Well then,' he continued, 'is it not the case that all of her property

also belonged to Pharnabazus?' 'Yes, indeed,' they replied. Dercylidas then said, 'Well, then, those possessions would now belong to us, since we now are in control of them and Pharnabazus is our enemy.'

3.1.26

Dercylidas proceeds to take over the house of Mania. We are subsequently presented with another dialogue exchange. Meidias asks where he will live now ('And what about me? Where am I to live, Dercylidas?', 3.1.28); Dercylidas replies that he will live 'In that very place where it is most just for you to live, Meidias – in your hometown of Skepsis and in your father's house' (3.1.28).

As with Agesilaus' dialogue with Spithridates and Otys, in this dialogue we witness Dercylidas' mastery of the interaction[48] and are invited to identify with him, taking pleasure in his pithy put-down of the upstart Meidias who has inappropriately grasped what does not belong to him. Of course, simultaneously, our awareness of the wider context might allow us to feel some discomfort. If it is just for Meidias to stay in his native city and his father's house, we might wonder if the same might arguably apply to Dercylidas and the Spartans: do they really have more right to these cities than Meidias did?[49] However, the use of dialogue in this sequence of the narrative discourages such disturbing suggestions, allowing us to imagine that we are there, listening in to the encounter, witnessing and appreciating Dercylidas' cleverness and poise, and enjoying his triumph over Meidias. The insertion of dialogue interacts with the wider surrounding narrative: whereas the surrounding context might allow a more critical perspective on Spartan power, the dialogue encourages a sympathetic and unquestioning attitude towards Spartan actions.[50]

In these shifts between the wider contextualising narrative and the dialogue, the reader experiences a shift in the horizons of expectation on offer. Each mode of presentation engages the reader in a different way and has its own political repercussions. By moving between them, the reader is forced to experience the narrative through a shifting political lens. Each mode impinges on the experience of the other, allowing each experience in turn to be questioned by an alternative experience. Through presenting different ways of telling the story, the reader is forced to question what that story means.[51] In the *Hellenica*, the reader is both immersed in an admiring identification with Spartan leaders and reminded of the threatening dangers of Spartan power.

Anabasis 1.9

Our second example comes from *Anabasis* book 1, where, after Cyrus the Younger's death at Cunaxa, we are presented with an account of his life, reviewing his childhood and youth, and his methods of leading men and of ruling his satrapy (1.9).[52] The chapter focuses on Cyrus' various virtues and frames its account of Cyrus through the language of praise:[53] Cyrus is 'the most kingly and the most worthy to rule of all the Persians who have been born since Cyrus the Great' (1.9.1).[54] As a boy, while being educated among the Persian elite, he was regarded as 'the best of them all in all respects' (1.9.2) and was 'the most modest of his fellows, and even more obedient to his elders than were his inferiors in rank' (1.9.5). He was conspicuous in performing the practices marking elite status, being 'the most devoted to horses and the most skilful in managing horses' (1.9.5), 'the most eager to learn and most eager in practising military accomplishments, alike the use of the bow and javelin' (1.9.5), and he was 'fondest of hunting, and more than that, fondest of incurring danger in his pursuit of wild animals' (1.9.6). The chapter also suggests that he was the most successful leader through his methods of managing rule over others. We are told that 'he counted it of the utmost importance, when he concluded a treaty or compact with anyone or made anyone any promise, under no circumstances to prove false to his word' (1.9.7). His firm maintenance of control is indicated:

> None could say that he permitted malefactors and wicked men to laugh at him; on the contrary, he was merciless in the last degree in punishing them, and one might often see along the roads people who had lost feet or hands or eyes; thus in Cyrus' province it became possible for either Greek or barbarian, provided he were guilty of no wrongdoing, to travel fearlessly wherever he wished, carrying with him whatever it was in his interest to have.
>
> 1.9.13

Cyrus' methods of winning loyalty too are explained:

> Whomsoever in his army he found willing to meet dangers, these men he would not only appoint as rulers of the territory he was subduing, but would honour thereafter with other gifts also. Thus the brave were seen to be most prosperous, while cowards were deemed fit to be their slaves. Consequently Cyrus had men in great abundance who were willing to meet danger wherever they thought that he would observe them.
>
> 1.9.14–15

The chapter invites the reader's admiration for and identification with Cyrus. The account of his elite virtues through his training as a youth in military skills, horsemanship and hunting allows the elite Greek reader to perceive Cyrus in terms of familiar, comfortable and appealing class values. Cyrus' Persianness is acknowledged. His education takes place at the King's court ('All the sons of the noblest Persians are educated at the King's court. There one may learn discretion and self-control in full measure, and nothing that is base can be either seen or heard': 1.9.3), and his military skills are Persian (the bow and javelin: 1.9.5). Yet these Persian aspects are assimilated and absorbed into a discourse of elite self-articulation which is still recognizable to a Greek.

The description of the absolute effects of his power in the account of the mutilated miscreants to be encountered on the roads is framed from the perspective of the wealthy traveller who would be pleased to be able to transport his possessions in safety, untroubled by the threat of robbery by the wayward poor ('thus in Cyrus' province it became possible for either Greek or barbarian, provided he were guilty of no wrongdoing, to travel

fearlessly wherever he wished, carrying with him whatever it was in his interest to have':
1.9.13). The lines of distinction are between the well-off traveller and the robber, not
between Greek and barbarian: the interests of the elite are imagined as shared across
ethnic/linguistic lines, assimilating the reader's interests to the interests of those who
maintain order in the Persian sphere.

Similarly, in chapter 1.9, the ability of Cyrus cleverly to control and win over followers
is presented as something which someone who might be interested in different practices
of ruling should admire:[55] in other words, the perspective seems to be that of a potential
ruler. We might compare the accounts of the qualities of leadership of Clearchus,
Proxenus and Menon presented after their murders (2.6), where we learn, for example,
that harshness and severity are effective in winning the troops' confidence in situations
of danger but cannot sustain soldiers' loyalty when the danger is removed (2.6.9–12),
whereas overly gentle treatment will win the respect of fellow officers, but not of the men
(2.6.19).[56] Chapter 1.9 orients its ideal reader to share the political interests of Cyrus as
ruler and to value Cyrus as a model to emulate.

However, we must note that the reader reaches chapter 1.9 after having experienced the
earlier portions of book 1, which presents a different sort of account of Cyrus' behaviour as
a ruler – a narrative of his leadership of the Greek mercenary force. We follow the Persian
prince as he builds his rebellion against the Persian King by collecting his mercenary army
and leading them to battle against the King's forces at Cunaxa. A central focus of the
narrative is on his methods of successfully controlling his Greek forces: how he manages
to get the Greeks to continue in his service after they come to realise their mission – to
attack the Persian King – and are reluctant to go on, for example. In the light of this, chapter
1.9 has a slightly curious and unstable feel:[57] we are offered a series of assertions informing
us how to respond to and understand Cyrus as a figure of power which position the Greek
reader in relation to him in a rather different way to the previous narrative account.

To some extent, the chapter's assertions seem to elucidate, recontextualize and build
on ways of relating to Cyrus which have already been on offer in the narrative and which
the reader might already, at least partially, have experienced. The licensing and
encouragement of a desire for identification with Cyrus – to see him as an appropriate
figure for the 10,000 Greeks to follow, whose success the reader can root for – in many
ways underpins the reader's experience of book 1: without this possibility, we would be
left with a slightly grubby narrative of mercenary Greeks selling themselves to a Persian
pretender promoting his own self-advancement.[58]

Nevertheless, the praise of how he gains enthusiastic loyalty from allies and followers
might to some extent also disconcert the reader. It focuses on his strategies of
manipulation – for example, his methods of conspicuously rewarding those who obey in
order to encourage further obedience: those who are most loyal are made wealthy, are
made rulers of territory or given gifts. This directly recalls Cyrus' relations with the
10,000 Greeks: 'For the generals and captains who came overseas to serve him for
the sake of money judged that loyal obedience to Cyrus was worth more to them than
their mere monthly pay. Again, so surely as a man performed with credit any service that
he assigned him, Cyrus never let his zeal go unrewarded' (1.9.17–18). While admiring

Cyrus' clever strategies of command, we also see how those strategies are brought to bear on the Greeks. We are reminded that the Greek mercenaries are motivated by both payment and promises of greater future rewards, and that Cyrus not only bribes, but also tricks and coerces them. The claim that he would never deceive his allies (1.9.7) seems to stand in direct contradiction to what we have seen of Cyrus in book 1, where he deliberately deceives the Greeks, concealing from them the true purpose of their journey and directly lying about it when challenged (1.4.20–1).[59]

The narrative at 1.1–8 periodically reminds us that the relationship between Cyrus and the Greek mercenaries is a relationship of power: as their commander, Cyrus is their paymaster but, as a Persian, is also potentially a threat. When the Greeks consider deserting from Cyrus, fear is expressed regarding what might befall them at Cyrus' hands. Clearchus warns, 'Remember that while this Cyrus is a valuable friend when he is your friend, he is a most dangerous foe when he is your enemy' (1.3.12); see also the fears expressed after the desertion of Xenias and Pasion (although we are subsequently told of the Greeks' pleasure when Cyrus decided to respond magnanimously, 1.4.8–9): 'After they had disappeared, a report went around that Cyrus was pursuing them with warships; and while some people prayed that they might be captured, because, as they said, they were cowards, yet others felt pity for them if they should be caught' (1.4.7). Although the 10,000 remain Cyrus' followers, at certain moments the bonds between them are revealed as fragile. In the light of this, the praise of Cyrus' punishment of opponents ('It was manifest also that whenever a man conferred any benefit upon Cyrus or did him harm, he always strove to outdo him', 1.9.11; see also the mention of Orontas, 1.9.29) might seem slightly jarring. Similarly, the description of his treatment of malefactors, which imaginatively places the reader in the position of the traveller witnessing for himself the gory after-effects of Cyrus' merciless punishments ('one might often see along the roads people who had lost feet or hands or eyes', 1.9.13), confronts the reader with the potential violence of Cyrus' regime, and might provoke alarm and distaste as much as reassurance.[60]

Although the possibility of identification with Cyrus is very much on offer in the earlier portions of book 1, such a position is also repeatedly undermined at those moments where Cyrus' exploitation of the Greeks for his own purposes becomes evident. The narrative at 1.1–8 offers a double awareness, as we are invited to identify simultaneously with Cyrus as impressive figure of elite power *and* with the Greeks whom he controls – even as the interests of each are shown, at moments, to diverge.[61] However, in contrast, at 1.9 all aspects of Cyrus' behaviour, including his manipulative characteristics, are presented via the language of praise. As we move from the narrative account of Cyrus' dealings with the 10,000 into the praise of his abilities as leader, the shift into praise – a shift of tone and register, as well as subject matter – encompasses a shift in the horizons of expectation on offer to the reader. This shift in the expectations placed on the reader's experience instantiates a shift in political self-consciousness: the text demands a move into absolute acceptance of Cyrus as model to emulate, and of political identification with him as an ideal of elite power. But, problematically, acquiescence to this political perspective would stand at variance to the earlier experience of political tension created in certain aspects of the representation of his dealings with the Greeks.

In the shift between the narrative and praise portions of Cyrus' representation, the political experience encoded by one formal mode impinges on and affects the reader's experience of the other mode. The shift into praise at 1.9 invites the reader to look back on the earlier narrative in a new light, repositioning themselves so as to accept and accommodate its praise. But the process works the other way around too: we cannot read 1.9 without the experience of its claims being affected by our prior experience of Cyrus at 1.1–8. The effect is similar to that of our example from the *Hellenica*, where the narrative account of events in Greece and the up-close engagement with Spartan leaders in dialogue offer contrasting political perspectives which engage the reader in different ways of understanding, relating to and positioning themselves against Spartan figures of power and their actions. However, the *Anabasis*'s shift into praise at 1.9 has a slightly more disconcerting effect. The reader is invited to engage politically with Cyrus in ways which are not just different, but, at least to a certain extent, contradictory. The language of praise at 1.9 can seem a little hard to swallow in the light of what has gone before.

Whereas the shifts between impersonal narrative and moments of dialogue in the *Hellenica*, discussed above, remind the reader of different possible political perspectives, and in clashing these perspectives together open up for the reader a critical political self-consciousness, in *Anabasis* 1.9 we also become aware of the mediating effects of the text as such. By forcing the reader to accept a new model of understanding, but one which in some ways feels difficult to accept in the light of the wider reading experience, the reader becomes conscious of the text as a literary construction. The impositions demanded by the formal regime of praise become perceptible to the reader.

Praise and readerly critical awareness

In the examples discussed so far, shifts in emphasis, focus and argument are accomplished through and entail shifts in the form of writing, producing shifts in the ideological awareness of the reader, and allowing a complex and nuanced engagement in Xenophon's representation of political figures and political action. In our second example there seems, further, to be opened up for the reader an understanding of the way that form imposes ideological expectations. While immersed in the exposition of praise in *Anabasis* 1.9, the reader is led to accept its arguments; but the contrast with the earlier narrative account allows some awareness of the constraints of the praise form.

In contemporary Greek literature, 'paradoxical' encomia praising subjects difficult to praise evoke the reader's awareness of the artificiality of praise as a form. Extant examples are Gorgias' *Encomium of Helen* and Isocrates' *Helen* and *Busiris*; we also have evidence of encomia to notorious courtesans or figures such as Clytemnestra and Paris, and to counterintuitive or incongruous subjects such as death, mice, bumblebees and salt.[62] By using the traditional language of praise to praise the unpraisable, such accounts expose 'the contingency of the value systems that regulate the orthodox use of praise', revealing 'the role that rhetoric plays in creating and dismantling "orthodox" beliefs and values'.[63]

Plato invites a similar critical reflection on the encomium genre in the *Symposium*. The various symposiasts offer speeches in praise of *eros*, only for Socrates to express disappointment that the praise speech as professed by them is concerned not with telling the truth, but with ascribing the greatest and most beautiful qualities to the speech's subject, whether or not it really possesses them.[64] Socrates reveals the way that praise discourse is constrained by its conventions. The reader, who so far may have been carried along by their enjoyment of the speeches, is challenged to rethink and question the nature and implications of their engagement in them. Socrates' criticism allows the reader to look back on the expectations encouraged by the speeches at a critical distance.

As Nightingale has shown, Plato's appropriation and importation into his dialogues of various rhetorical genres (such as the funeral oration in the *Menexenus*, or the encomium in the *Symposium* or *Lysis*) is used to throw into relief the new genre of philosophy. In the *Symposium*, the praise speeches offered by the other symposiasts are criticized and then trumped as Socrates goes on to offer his own account of *eros*, thereby setting out in contrast the possibility of a new form of philosophical discourse.[65] With reference to distinctions articulated by Bakhtin, Nightingale describes the relationship between different genres set up by Plato as suggestive of parody:[66] the appropriated genre, such as the encomium in the *Symposium*, is offered explicitly to be rejected, and to show up by contrast the superiority of Socratic philosophy.

This is not the sort of relationship between forms which we find in Xenophon. The reader is not led to reject one of the offered forms in preference for the other – to distance themselves, for example, from the view of the Spartans offered in Agesilaus' marriage-brokerage dialogue in favour of a view proposed by the *Hellenica*'s narrative of the conflicts in Greece (or the other way around). Both visions are offered as different but equally possible ways of perceiving and relating to Spartan power. In the *Anabasis*, the reader is not led to reject the praise of Cyrus at *Anab.* 1.9 in the light of the experience of the earlier narrative. Rather the Greek reader is asked to take it seriously, to perceive Cyrus as an admirable icon of elite power with whom they can identify, while also being made aware, through the sense of disjunction created through the text's discontinuities, that their identification with Cyrus' power can only ever be partial, and is undermined by awareness of the realities of the context in which his power is enacted. The reader is fully engaged in the horizons of expectation created by each of the juxtaposed formal modes, which each have their own authority, but also impact upon and question each other. As Nightingale notes, in a hybridized text which appropriates and imports the language of another genre, 'When the targeted genre is denied authority, parody may decrease the "dialogism" of the text. Non-parodic hybrids which grant the targeted genre full semantic autonomy, by contrast, have a greater degree of "dialogism"'[57]

A closer comparison to the use of praise discourse at *Anabasis* 1.9 might be the interrogation of the conventions of praise in Isocrates' *Panathenaicus*,[68] which presents a series of arguments about Greek history seeking to prove that Athens has always acted for the communal good of the Greeks whereas Sparta has acted out of self-interest; but in the final chapters the narrator changes tack, claiming to have become uneasy about his criticisms of Sparta (Isoc. *Panath.* 231–2). He reads the speech up to this point to his pupils, one of whom claims to perceive that the speech has been produced with a double meaning (Isoc. *Panath.* 239–40), so that its statements about Sparta (such as that Sparta conquered its neighbours in the Peloponnese) are just as capable of being read as praise as they are capable of being taken as criticism[69] – but, the primary narrator explicitly refuses either to authorise or reject the pupil's interpretation (Isoc. *Panath.* 265).[70] Isocrates' treatment of praise and blame should not be seen as parodic: the possibility of praising Athens and blaming Sparta is not overturned by the pupil's re-reading. Rather the speech allows its audience to perceive how the same historical events are equally capable of being transformed into either praise or blame – which renders the pupil's view just as easy to undercut as the initial speaker's argument. The text does not valorise or reject either one, but, through their juxtaposition, reveals how the conventional expectations of the rhetoric of praise or blame intervene in the processes of political response – even as the reader experiences their effects and is swayed by them. The result is a greater critical awareness about how political claims, and political self-positioning, work.

Xenophon expresses a similar set of concerns in the *Agesilaus*, which offers a rhetoric of praise of Agesilaus which is both highly emotive and affecting, and produces critical awareness of its conventions.[71] The text praises Agesilaus as a champion of Greek values: a lover of Greeks and hater of Persians (*Ages.* 7.4, 7.7) who defended Greeks in Asia and subdued Persians (*Ages.* 1.8, 1.34), lamented violence between Greeks (*Ages.* 7.4–6) and was a virtuous example of austere personal behaviour in contrast to the luxuriousness of the Persian King (*Ages.* 8.6–9.5); yet in many places its rhetoric has a contrived feel, as the text skates over Agesilaus' violent promotion of Spartan interests at the expense of other Greeks, or even finds ways to reconfigure these actions as signs of Panhellenic commitment.[72] In questioning how best to go about praising Agesilaus' organization of his troops for battle, the *Agesilaus* draws attention to the way that Agesilaus' actions are being fitted into the constraints of the praise form:

> I am not going to say that he had far fewer and far inferior forces but that he nevertheless accepted battle. If I were to say this, I think I would show Agesilaus as foolish and myself as stupid, if I praised him for rashly endangering the greatest interests. On the contrary, I admire him for this very reason – that he equipped himself with a force in no way smaller than that of the enemy.
>
> Ages. 2.7[73]

Unable to praise Agesilaus' bravery for entering battle with a much smaller force (like Leonidas), the narrator instead flips the expected argument on its head, and praises his powers of organization in equipping a good-sized army: we see that any action can be made to conform to the requirements of praise. Similarly, the text evinces repeated concern that the reader may not be convinced by its claims, offering strenuous proofs to win over the resistant reader whose scepticism is expected, and licensed ('In case anyone should think this statement incredible...', *Ages.* 3.2; 'What opinion some hold in regard to these matters I know well enough ... No doubt when these things are known to few, many have a right to be sceptical: but we all know this, that the greater a man's fame, the fiercer is the light that beats on all his actions', *Ages.* 5.6; 'If anyone doubts this . . .', *Ages.* 8.7).[74]

The text's comment on Agesilaus's forced restoration of exiles to Thebes, Corinth and Phleius indicates the ideological problems posed by the rhetorical contortions of praise discourse, where all actions must be praised: 'Possibly some may censure these actions on other grounds, but at least it is obvious that they were prompted by a spirit of true comradeship' (*Ages.* 2.21).[75] This is reminiscent of the claim at *Anabasis* 1.9 regarding Cyrus' treatment of Milesian exiles: 'All the cities of their own accord chose Cyrus rather than Tissaphernes, with the exception of Miletus; and the reason why the Milesians feared him was that he would not prove false to the exiles from their city' (*An.* 1.9.9). In each case, these commanders' violent interventions in the affairs of Greek states are transformed into items to praise.[76] The resistance of Miletus, rather than a sign that Cyrus was not really supported by all, becomes an indication of Cyrus' loyalty to his allies. Similarly, Agesilaus' depredations against other Greek cities become a sign of his care for his supporters. Whereas the contortions effected by the praise rhetoric of the *Anabasis* remain more implicit, the *Agesilaus* directly addresses the possibility that what is being praised might just as easily be open to criticism.

The *Agesilaus*' licensing of readerly critical distance should not be read as parodic: the text's repeated, insistent call on the reader to admire the achievements of Agesilaus and to perceive him as a champion of Greek values in his contests against Persia speak to the real purchase that such sentiments had on an elite Greek audience. It is quite possible, and ideologically desirable, for the reader to perceive Agesilaus in such a way: to see his military successes as signs of Greek success; to appropriate his actions in Asia as part of a reassuring narrative of Greek supremacy; to identify with Agesilaus as a symbol of Greek power. The text is motivated by and constructs such responses. Yet in enabling readerly awareness of the artificiality of its formal devices and in flagging the possibility that the reader might perceive and feel resistant to their constraints, the text simultaneously gives evidence of and produces an awareness that the story is not so simple: Agesilaus, the infamous Spartan power-monger, does not fit so easily into the categories on offer through the praise form. The problems of form reflect and instantiate the political difficulties posed by Spartan leadership to a Greek audience.[77]

Praise and blame: *Cyr.* 8.8 and *Lak. Pol.* 14

We opened this chapter by noting the problems posed to scholars by the apparent shifts from praise to blame at *Cyr.* 8.3 and *Lak. Pol.* 14. The preceding discussion of similar shifts in argument, tone and structure in Xenophon, and of the production of readerly critical awareness of praise rhetoric as a form in Xenophon's prose contemporaries and in Xenophon himself, allows us a new way of approaching this problem.

Both in the *Cyropaedia* and the *Lak. Pol.*, aspects of the achievements of Cyrus the Great and of Spartan society which are praised by the texts strike the reader as strange or disturbing. Cyrus manipulates and exploits his potential followers and allies, and after his successful conquest of his empire takes up strategies of rule (such as overwhelming his subjects with false displays of grandeur, fancy robes and make-up) which receive explicit criticism in the earlier stages of the text.[78] In the *Lak. Pol.* the Spartans' utter difference from other Greeks (manifested in such practices as wife-swapping, *Lak. Pol.* 1.7–8) figures their alien qualities, and many of the arguments about their customs (such as arguments justifying their training of boys in theft, *Lak. Pol.*, 2.6–9) seem logically strained.[79] While these texts ask the reader to take seriously and accept the praise of Cyrus the Great as most impressive leader and of Sparta as most impressive Greek state, such disturbing elements simultaneously make identifying with Persian power or with Spartan culture a slightly uncomfortable experience. As with Cyrus the Younger in the *Anabasis*, the *Cyropaedia*'s Cyrus the Great offers an appealing icon of Greek power to the elite Greek reader: a figure who can successfully conquer vast territories and rule over huge numbers of men; and the *Lak. Pol.*'s exposition on the success of Sparta offers the reader a reassuring image of Greek success. Yet as with Cyrus the Younger, Cyrus the Great is a Persian whose assertion of power led to the subjugation of Greeks; and far from representing wider Greek interests, Spartan success came at a cost to other Greeks. The texts create a horizon of expectation within which Cyrus' establishment of imperial rule and Spartan exceptionalism are to be admired and identified with as models for Greek success, while also enabling awareness that such an identification might not fully be possible.

When we reach the end of the *Cyropaedia* at *Cyr.* 8.8 or the penultimate chapter of the *Lak. Pol.* at *Lak. Pol.* 14, we are faced with a shift from the language of praise to the language of blame, as the contemporary degeneracy of Persia and Sparta are placed before our eyes.[80] A different way of thinking about each is offered. Rather than icons of Greek virtue and success as leaders of the Greek world, Spartans are here those who use their power to advance their interests at the expense of other Greeks:

> And there was a time when they took care always to be worthy of leadership. But now they prefer to busy themselves with how to acquire leadership rather than how to be worthy of it. This was why in the old days the Greeks used to go to Lacedaemon and ask them to take the lead against wrong-doers. But now many exhort one another to prevent them from regaining their ascendancy.
>
> *Lak. Pol. 14.5–6*[81]

Similarly, in the *Cyropaedia* the focus on the present day reminds the reader forcibly of the threat still posed in the current time by the empire established by Cyrus the Great.

These blaming chapters, coming at (or near) the end of their texts, impact upon the reader's experience of the texts up to this point. By imposing a new expectation for response which rejects Persian and Spartan power as a foreign and hostile force, the experience of those moments in the earlier portion of the texts where the reader may have felt alienated from Persian imperial exploitation or Spartan cultural difference is recalled and reinforced. Yet the dominance of the repeated appeals to praise across the majority of the texts and the comforting pleasures of identification with the powerful which they allow also impact upon the reader's experience of the rhetoric of blame at *Cyr.* 8.8 and *Lak. Pol.* 14, preventing the reader from fully accepting a world-view in which Spartan leadership and Persian imperial might are simply the enemy, and have no ideological appeal. As we move between different arguments and formal registers, the shift in the models of ideological expectation that they encode open up for the reader a critical awareness of the difficulties posed by Spartan and Persian power.

The contradiction between horizons of expectation as we move from praise to blame also draws attention to the ideological effects of form. We are made aware that these texts do not offer a transparent window onto reality, but that the perceptions of the world which they offer are a construction, and are subject to manipulation, contestation and argument. This creates a dialectical relationship between reader and text. Rather than passively accepting the image of the world which the text imposes,[82] the reader is involved in an active, questioning engagement. The reading process becomes an arena for reflection on the construction of ideological meaning.

Conclusion

In this discussion we have seen how Xenophon's works contain shifts in focus, argument, tone and structure which carry different expectations for interpretation, offering a disjunctive, dialogical reading experience which reflects and instantiates the ideological contradictions inherent in his subject matter. In those moments in which such shifts impose particularly striking contradictions, Xenophon's writing also enables the reader to become attentive to the ways in which texts impose ideological meaning; as we have seen, in doing so Xenophon is participating in a wider literary discourse apparent in his fourth-century BC prose contemporaries. The reader is made aware not only of the ideological contradictions of their world, but of how ideological meaning is constructed by texts. The effect is the creation of an active, critically engaged reader. Far from imposing a unified and dominant image of the world to which the reader is expected passively to assent, Xenophon's writing reveals the plurality of expectations of the world which might be possible, places those expectations in tension with each other and reveals the processes through which the text itself creates those expectations.

Notes

1. See Tamiolaki 2017: 192–3 on the 'enigma' of the *Cyropaedia*'s epilogue.
2. Ollier 1934: xiii; Tigerstedt 1965: 162–9; Hodkinson 1994: 190–5; Rebenich 1998: 18; Lipka 2002: 31–2. See Humble 2004: 215 n.3 for further bibliography.
3. On both texts: Hirsch 1985: 91–7. On *Cyr.*: Bizos 1971: xxvi-xxxvi.
4. Miller 1914: 439.
5. On *Cyr.*: Eichler 1880; Georges 1994: 234. On *Lak. Pol.*: Delebecque 1957: 194–5; Luccioni 1947: 171. In the case of the *Lak. Pol.* a problem for this interpretation has been the position

of chap. 14 as the penultimate, not final chapter; this has led to the suggestion that chap. 14 was not originally in its current position, but was transposed with chap. 15 by later editors: Breitenbach 1967: 1751–2.

6. On *Lak. Pol.*: Gray 2007: 217–21. On *Cyr.*: Due 1989: 16–22; Gray 2011: 246–63. Gruen 2011: 58–65 also rejects contradiction between *Cyr.* 8.8 and the earlier text, reading *Cyr.* 8.8 as parodying contemporary stereotypes of Persia.

7. Humble 2004.

8. Strauss 1939; followed by Proietti 1987 and Higgins 1977. See Dorion 2010]: 286–8 on *Lak. Pol.* 14 and *Cyr.* 8.8 in the light of Strauss.

9. Too 1998: 286–8; Pangle 1994: 149–50; Nadon 2001: 139–46; Carlier 2010 [1978]; 362–6.

10. The *Lak. Pol.* has been dated to the 390s by those who see it as enthusiastic propaganda for Sparta written in thanks for Sparta's protection of Xenophon while in exile, with chapter 14 a later addition (e.g. Ollier 1934: xxiii–xxix), but to the 360s by those who believe that it betrays Xenophon's disillusionment with Sparta and could therefore only have been written after Agesilaus' death; on this model, chapter 14 is an original part of the work (e.g. Cartledge 1987: 57). On the assumption that it is a later addition, chapter 14 has been variously dated based on different suggestions as to which event could have disillusioned Xenophon about Sparta, such as Phoebidas' seizure of the Cadmea in 382 or Sphodrias' attack on the Piraeus in 378. See Ollier 1934: xxiii–xxix. MacDowell 1986: 12 dates Xenophon's disillusionment to his first visit to Sparta in the 390s. See Humble 2004: 219–220 for an overview of the different arguments about how to date both chapter 14 and the *Lak. Pol.* as a whole. A similar approach has been taken to the *Cyropaedia*: one reading places the rest of the text before, and the final chapter after, the betrayal of the leaders of the Satraps' Revolt in 362 (Georges 1994: 234).

11. Gray 2011: 256: 'Xenophon asserts that readers all know that the Spartans are in the present tense most obedient to the laws (8.1), which contradicts his description of the disobedience of their harmosts in the epilogue.'

12. See the use of the phrase *eti kai nun*; see Due 2002 on the *Cyropaedia*'s narratorial interventions.

13. Cf. Wohl 2015: 1–5 on Euripides.

14. Gauthier 1985; Lossau 1990; Bradley 2001; Purves 2010.

15. Momigliano 1993: 57.

16. On the genre of the *Cyropaedia*, see Reichel 1995; Tamiolaki 2017: 180–9; Gera 1993: 1–13. For the generic complexity of the *Lak. Pol.*, see Humble 2014.

17. Contrast Nicolai 2014, who suggests that the modern difficulty with genre categorization in Xenophon is based on a failure to understand the contemporary inseparability of historical and sophistic writing.

18. See Gray 2011: 75 on the rhetoric of blame in *Cyr.* 8.8 and *Lak. Pol.* 14.

19. Tamiolaki 2017: 181: 'the blending of genres does not concern only the *Cyropaedia*, but constitutes a distinctive feature of the whole Xenophontic corpus: the *Hellenica* and the *Anabasis* accommodate elements of encomiastic literature and Socratic-type conversations'. Cf. Tuplin 1997: 67, who describes the *Cyropaedia* as operating within a 'crosscut of four "ordinary" genres: historiography, encomium, Socratic dialectic, and technical pamphlet'.

20. Adorno 1997: 6.

21. Conte 1994: 112: 'Every genre is a model of reality which mediates the empirical world.'

22. Jauss 1982: 41: 'The horizon of expectations of literature distinguishes itself before the horizon of expectations of historical lived praxis in that it not only preserves actual

experiences, but also anticipates unrealized possibility, broadens the limited space of social behaviour for new desires, claims, and goals, and thereby opens paths of future experience … [The new form of art] can make possible a new perception of things by preforming the content of a new experience first brought to light in the form of literature.' On genre, see Jauss 1982: 23: 'A corresponding process of the continuous establishing and altering of horizons also determines the relationship of the individual text to the succession of texts that forms the genre. The new text evokes for the reader (listener) the horizon of expectations and rules familiar from earlier texts, which are then varied, corrected, altered, or even just reproduced.'

23. Bakhtin 1981. See 324–5 on different forms of 'double-voiced discourse', including 'the discourse of a whole incorporated genre': 'A potential dialogue is embedded in them, one as yet unfolded, a concentrated dialogue of two voices, two world views, two languages.'

24. Pelling 1999; Marincola 1999; Goldhill 2002.

25. See Gray 1981: 333 on elements of dialogue in Herodotus; see Boyarin 2012 on dialogue form at Thucydides 5.84–116 (the Melian Dialogue).

26. Boedeker 2000.

27. Boedeker 2000: 114–15. Cf. Pelling 1999: 334–5: 'So the reader, inevitably trying to define what sort of text this is, finds false leads and distractions: there are initial intimations, but redefinition is swiftly needed … It is clear, too, that this is not just a casual game with the reader, not a playing with discourse for discourse's sake or to strike an original clever pose. This is about meaning, how one can make sense of events.'

28. Cf. Nicolai 2014: 82: 'Such experimentation with literary genres allows [Xenophon] to use the codes and communicative strategies appropriate to these pre-existing genres without the new work losing its own identity.'

29. On the complexities of form in the *Hellenica*, see Marincola 1999: 310–11; Marincola 2017: 105–7 (see esp. 107 for comments on the use of dialogue); Dillery 1995: 9–11, 17–27.

30. See Gera 1993: 26–131 and Humble 2018 on Socratic dialogue in Xenophon's non-Socratic writing.

31. Translations from Xen. *Hell.* are taken from Marincola 2009, with my own adaptations.

32. Gray 1981: 323.

33. As Gray 1989: 49 notes, the details of the political alliance are not Xenophon's focus; instead he focuses on the betrothal.

34. Gray 1981: 324. Cf. Boyarin 2012: 54: 'dialogue allows one party to control and manage the discourse in such wise as to assure his own "victory"'. Cf. also Demont 2014 on dialogue in the *Cyropaedia* as producing readerly engagement with Cyrus as controller of the interaction.

35. Gray 1981: 322.

36. Gray 1989: 51; Gray 1981: 323.

37. Gray 1981: 324.

38. See the debate between Euben 1996 and Barber 1996: whereas Euben reads Plato as offering, through its multivocal and dialectical structure, an instantiation of democratic practice, in contrast, Barber argues that unlike the dialectics of tragedy, Plato's Socrates 'looks past the muddled *agon* towards a domain of immovable truth; to reach that domain, he may embark on the road of discourse, but this hardly gives him a talent for the genuine polyphony that is the *sine qua non* of democratic politics' (Barber 1996: 364). On the controlling power of Socrates' voice cf. Boyarin 2012: 61–4; Barrett 1987: 59–62.

39. Cf. Hau 2016: 231: 'Agesilaus uses his likeable personality and social skills to make friends and benefit Sparta at one stroke.'

40. Krentz 1995: 184. Cf. Gish 2009: 341: 'Agesilaus does not hesitate to speak openly of Sparta as the sole super-power and hegemonic leader of all the Greeks in Hellas and Asia Minor.'
41. See Vlassopoulos 2017: 363 on the *Hellenica*'s marriage-brokerage dialogue as an example of the 'complex political-military triangulations between Greeks, Persians and other non-Greeks'.
42. See *Hell.* 3.4.16–19, the description of Agesilaus' camp at Ephesus, where the spectacle of exercising and garlanded Greeks is contrasted with the white, flabby bodies of barbarian prisoners; see Dillery 1995: 113 on Agesilaus' Ephesus camp as an 'emblem of panhellenism'.
43. See the depiction of Paphlagonian incomprehension of Greek cultural practices (*An.* 6.1.1–13).
44. See Dillery 1995: 23–4, 107–19 on the problematic representation of Agesilaus in the context of Panhellenist thought.
45. See Gray 1989: 12 on 'charm' in Xenophon's depiction of conversation between protagonists.
46. Dillery 1995: 102–3. See the language describing the Ionian cities' request for Spartan assistance in opposition to the rule of Tissaphernes: they send ambassadors 'asking that the Lacedaemonians, since they were leaders of all Hellas, should undertake to protect them also, the Greeks in Asia, in order that their land might not be laid waste and that they themselves might be free' (*Hell.* 3.1.3). At Cebren the city is handed over to Dercylidas by Greeks in the city who 'preferred to be on the side of the Greeks rather than of the barbarian' (3.1.18); after gaining control of Skepsis Dercylidas exhorts the citizens 'to order their public life as Greeks and freemen should' (*Hell.* 3.1.21): Dillery 1995: 105.
47. Dillery 1995: 102–6.
48. Cf. Gray 1981: 330 on the demonstration of Dercylidas' control of his army and imposition of discipline.
49. Cf. the language of 'justice': Derkylidas claims that it is most just (δικαιότατον, 3.1.28) for Meidias to live in his native city and his father's house; Derkylidas earlier promises Meidias that he will get his just deserts (καὶ ὁ Δερκυλίδας μέντοι ἔλεγεν ὡς τῶν δικαίων οὐδενὸς ἀτυχήσοι, 3.1.22). See Gray 1981: 329; Marincola 2017: 114–15.
50. It is important to note that not all moments of dialogue involving Spartan leaders lead to a privileging of the leader's voice. For example, in the dialogue between Agesilaus and Leotychidas regarding which of them has the right to the Spartan kingship after the death of Agis (*Hell.* 3.3.1–4), the relative position of the interlocutors seems much more equal: each has a claim to the throne, and makes equally convincing arguments. Although Agesilaus is eventually chosen as king, the representation of the dispute over the succession suggests a subtle questioning of Agesilaus' position: cf. Laforse 2013: 33.
51. Cf. Conte 1994: 121 (on the confrontation between bucolic and elegy in Virgil's tenth *Eclogue*): 'It is only because the same *carmina* can be intoned in both the elegiac register and the bucolic one ... that we can become aware of the "formative" function each register possesses.'
52. On form and its ideological implications in Xen. *An.*, see Bradley 2001; Purves 2010.
53. Cf. Gray 2011: 75 on the 'obituaries' of Cyrus and of the Greek generals (Xen. *An.* 2.6): 'The style of Xenophon's obituaries is most of all in keeping with the tradition of praise and blame in rhetoric.' See also Gray 2011: 73–4 on the persuasive rhetorical devices in Xen. *An.* 1.9.
54. Translations from Xen. *An.* are taken from Brownson 1998.
55. Buzzetti 2014: 67.
56. Buzzetti 2014: 104–8.

57. Cf. Braun 2004: 107.
58. Cf. Rood 2004: 309–12; Azoulay 2004a.
59. Hirsch 1985: 23–4; Flower 2012: 191; Braun 2004: 110.
60. Higgins 1977: 83; Flower 2012: 189; Braun 2004: 113.
61. See Harman 2013: 90.
62. See Nightingale 1995: 100–1. Courtesans: Athenaeus 13 592c; Clytemnestra: Quintilian, *Inst.* 2.17.4; Paris: Aristotle, *Rhet.* 1401b20–3; death: Cicero, *Tusc.* 1.48.116; mice: Aristotle, *Rhet.* 1401a13–15, 1401b15–16; bumblebees: Isocrates, *Helen* 12; salt: Isocrates, *Helen* 12, Plato, *Symp.* 177b.
63. Nightingale 1995: 102.
64. Following Agathon's speech, Socrates ironically responds: 'In my foolishness, I thought you should tell the truth about whatever you praise, that this should be your basis ... But now it appears that this is not what it is to praise anything whatever; rather it is to apply to the object the grandest and the most beautiful qualities, whether he actually has them or not' (Plato, *Symp.* 198d-e). Nightingale 1995: 112.
65. Nightingale 1995: 93–132; Nightingale 1993.
66. Nightingale 1995: 6–8. See Nightingale 1995: 7, f.n. 19 on Bakhtin's terminology. On parodic dialogism within a hybridized text: Bakhtin 1981: 363–4.
67. See Nightingale 1995: 7.
68. See Nicolai 2014 on Isocrates' explicit discussion of his use of a combination of elements from different genres, and on the similarity to Xenophon.
69. See Isoc. *Panath.* 253–4 for the pupil's suggestion that Sparta's conquest of Peloponnesian neighbours might be read as exhalting Sparta; contrast Isoc. *Panath.* 45–7, where the same actions are criticized.
70. Livingstone 1998: 276.
71. See Noël 2014 and Humble (2020) on the *Agesilaus*' relation to contemporary praise genres. See Dillery 2017: 202 and Pontier 2010 on the *Agesilaus* as a text which presents multiple 'retellings' of the story of Agesilaus' life.
72. Laforse 2013; Harman 2012. The text's peculiarities have led it to being read as an apology for Agesilaus: Hirsch 1985: 51; Hamilton 1994: 212.
73. Translations from Xen. *Ages.* are taken from Marchant 1925, with adaptations.
74. Contrast Bundy 1986: 40 (with Xen. *Ages.* referenced at n.14) on 'the use of real or imaginary objections as foil' in both choral and prose rhetorical contexts, and their functioning as a 'frequent means of amplification in enkomia of all kinds'. Cf. Dillery 2017: 204; Pelling 2017: 254. Although the *Agesilaus*'s rhetorical suggestions of doubt do indeed allow the more forceful restatement of praise, I suggest that they simultaneously open up for the reader an awareness of the potential contentiousness of the praise.
75. Cf. Dillery 2017: 204 on the criticism of Agesilaus at Xen. *Ages.* 2.21 as a 'puncturing of the encomiastic fabric' of the text through its acknowledgement of competing views of Agesilaus.
76. See Braun 2004: 110–12 on Cyrus' actions.
77. See Harman 2012 for further discussion.
78. Tatum 1989; Too 1998; Azoulay 2004b; Gray 2011: 263–90.
79. Strauss 1939; Proietti 1987; Higgins 1977.

80. Gray 2011: 255 (on Xen. *Cyr.* 8.8): 'It is partly the rhetorical nature of the epilogue that causes dissonances between the main text and the epilogue.'
81. Translation taken from Jackson 2006.
82. See Conte 1994: 116: 'Genre, modelling the world upon its own language, invites us to believe that nothing exists outside the image that it knows how to give of the world.'

PART III
WORD AND IMAGE

CHAPTER 10
THE POLITICS OF FORM IN EIGHTEENTH-CENTURY VISIONS OF ANCIENT GREECE
Daniel Orrells

The previous chapters in this volume have emphasized the importance of thinking about form, in order to gain a deeper understanding of the politics of ancient Greek culture, which has often been sublimated by modern thinkers into the realms of the spiritual, the abstract and the intellectual. Indeed, it might be said that the form of ancient Greek culture has been characterized in modernity by its formlessness. Johann Joachim Winckelmann's descriptions of the white(ned) marble of classical sculpture have profoundly influenced subsequent historians, philosophers, artists and architects in their vision of ancient Greece. The austere simplicity of Greek forms, which were supposedly colourless contours, apparently transparent like the purest waves in an ocean, conducted the viewer of ancient Greek art to contemplate higher, more philosophical truths. As one critic has memorably put it, Winckelmann celebrated 'the beauty of the invisible'.[1] The formlessness of ancient Greek form was a product of Winckelmann's Lutheran bias for the spiritual word over the material image. Winckelmann saw Greek sculpture through Protestant Christianity and it had a profound impact on European intellectual life in the decades around the year 1800. In his 1764 *History of the Art of Antiquity*, Winckelmann sought to establish a narrative that proceeds from Egyptian beginnings, via Etruscan developments, to Greek flowering and to Roman decline. He used contemporary schemes of Enlightenment historiography to construct a history of the 'origin, growth, change, and fall of art, together with the various styles of peoples, periods, and artists'.[2] Winckelmann thereby became a key figure in the history of the institutionalization and professionalization of classical studies – *Altertumswissenschaft* – as a university discipline.[3] He and many of his followers sought to extricate ancient Greek culture from its emergence out of the eastern Mediterranean and distinguish it from its Near Eastern and Egyptian neighbours. If Winckelmann saw ancient Greece through Protestant eyes, then Georg Wilhelm Friedrich Hegel would influentially argue that ancient Greek culture was a station on the way to a mature Protestant modernity. Hegel contrasted 'Oriental' symbolic art, on the one hand, with classical Greek art on the other, which managed to balance perfectly the sensuous and the spiritual, so that Greek art became the highest expression of the freedom of spirit so far. This construction of the formlessness of Greek form emerged, then, out of a history of anti-Catholic and Orientalist politics across the eighteenth and nineteenth centuries in Enlightenment and post-Enlightenment intellectual history.[4]

If we turn to the first edition of Winckelmann's *History*, we can see how much space and significance the word takes over the image, reflecting Winckelmann's arguments about the formless and spiritual nature of Greek art. That original edition of Winckelmann's *History* was jejunely decorated with a mere twenty-four engravings – vignettes and cul-de-lampes – which adorn the beginnings and ends of chapters, offering his readers very little visualization of Greek beauty. Indeed, there is nothing to be seen of Winckelmann's favourite classical Greek sculptures such as the Apollo Belvedere and the Hercules Torso, to which he devotes, in contrast, many words of carefully written ekphrasis. Instead, the images in the book top and tail his chapters on the different periods of the history of ancient art, and are mostly examples of artists who imitated earlier styles or anticipated later developments. In the text, Winckelmann places these ancient objects into separate historical periods, thereby offering a demonstration of his skill as an antiquarian scholar. The images seem designed to visualize the different 'national' styles of ancient artistic traditions.

But if we take a closer look at this book, we will see that Winckelmann envisions the complications in distinguishing ancient Greek art from its Mediterranean neighbours. The vignette which heads the Preface to the *History* is an image of a Roman relief probably in commemoration of Augustus' victory in Actium (see Fig. 10.1). Apollo appears with long hair in the costume of a citharode, accompanied by Artemis and Leto; he is making a libation with Nike/Victory in front of a wall of a holy precinct, in which rising above the partition can be seen a temple with Corinthian columns.[5] Winckelmann, on the other hand, saw 'four draped female deities in a procession', correctly recognizing Artemis (or 'Diana' as he calls her) and Victory. What interested Winckelmann was the contrast between the deities' archaic-looking costumes and the architecture in the background: 'At first glance, the work could seem to be in an Etruscan style, but the architecture of the temple challenges this. It thus seems that this work is a product of a later Greek master who wanted to imitate the style of the more ancient period'.[6] Despite the archaic, Etruscan look of the clothing of the goddesses, Winckelmann realized that the Corinthian columns would have appeared only later (at the end of the fifth century BC). The relief provided Winckelmann with a way of imaging the deterioration of ancient art after its highpoint in the classical Greek period. 'The decline of art', Winckelmann wrote on the relief, 'must inevitably have become noticeable when comparisons were drawn with the works of the highest and most beautiful period, and it is likely that a few artists sought to return to the grand manner of their predecessors.' He continued: 'In this way, it may have happened that, just as things in the world often move in a circle and return to where they started, artists strove to imitate the earlier style, which with its only slightly curved contours approximated Egyptian work.... I believe that what we have here is one of the distinguishing features or characteristics of the Egyptian style.'[7] The relief, as Winckelmann saw it, is an example of a later piece trying to imitate style of earlier periods. In correctly registering the archaizing nature of the relief, Winckelmann demonstrates his antiquarian abilities to differentiate between ancient artistic traditions.

At the same time, however, Winckelmann also presents in front of his reader's eyes how ancient art was a complicated series of imitation and impersonation. Indeed, an image of the work of a Greek artist under imperial Rome might also be seen to visualize

Vorrede.

Die Geschichte der Kunst des Alterthums, welche ich zu schreiben unternommen habe, ist keine bloße Erzählung der Zeitfolge und der Veränderungen in derselben, sondern ich nehme das Wort Geschichte in der weiteren Bedeutung, welche dasselbe in der Griechischen Sprache hat, und meine Absicht ist, einen Versuch eines Lehrgebäudes zu liefern. Dieses habe ich in dem Ersten Theile, in der Abhandlung von der Kunst der alten Völker, von jedem insbesondere, vornehmlich aber in Absicht der Griechischen Kunst, auszuführen gesuchet. Der Zweyte Theil enthält die Geschichte der Kunst im engeren Verstande, das

Figure 10.1 Winckelmann, *Geschichte*, Preface.

Winckelmann's own position when he was writing his *History* in the 1750s and 60s, as he imagined himself a Hellene toiling under the patronage of powerful masters in Rome. Winckelmann's relief certainly visualized an important contemporary issue for his eighteenth-century readers, when painters and sculptors were turning back to the ancient world for artistic inspiration in an attempt to revivify the artistic tradition of the ancient Greeks. Underpinned by an intense interest specifically in ancient Greek material and visual culture, what art historians now call 'neoclassicism' was evolving precisely in the 1750s and 60s.[8] Winckelmann's vignette powerfully envisions a later Greek's attempt to look back to an earlier, better period of Greek art – an attempt which at the same time, nevertheless, takes place in a complicated, cluttered cultural environment. Just as Winckelmann sought to distinguish the Greek artistic form from its Egyptian and Etruscan predecessors and its Roman successors, so his relief at the beginning of his text also visualized how the work of the Greek artist was part of a larger Mediterranean history. The image showcases, for Winckelmann, the work of a Greek artist living in the Roman Empire using an archaizing, Egyptianizing style which blurs Etruscan and Greek forms. The relief, then, visualizes the complexities of situating ancient Greek culture in relation to the rest of the Mediterranean for the eighteenth-century viewer. Even if Winckelmann uses this image to put his antiquarian skills on display, so he also ends up showing how ancient Greek art looked back to the achievements of the Etruscans and the Egyptians just as it was also made possible by the patronage of Rome.

The image, which opens Winckelmann's *History* and this chapter, vividly introduces the issues to be explored here. The construction of the formlessness of the ancient Greek form in the eighteenth century occurred in a specific political context. This chapter examines the origins of this process of turning Greek art into a formless, immaterial pre-Protestant spirit, which distinguished it from its 'Oriental' predecessors and its consumption in Italy: how was ancient Greek art viewed and visualized in the mid-eighteenth century, when Winckelmann was constructing his invisible vision of Greece? What were the intellectual contests in visualizing the form of ancient Greece in relation to its Mediterranean context? What did it mean in the eighteenth century to see what ancient Greece looked like on the eve of the institutionalization of classical studies? On the one hand, Winckelmann asked his readers to imagine him praying in the Lycian groves to the Apollo Belvedere or comparing the colourless contours of the Hercules Torso to the waves in the sea. At the conclusion of his *History*, he compared the history of ancient art to the outline of a hero projected onto the sails of a boat receding ever further from the shore.[9] On the other hand, however, his vignette at the beginning of his Preface displays the product of a Greek sculptor working under the Roman Empire and displaying the marked influence of Etruscan and Egyptian cultures.

This new interest in specifying Greek material culture in distinction to other Mediterranean artefacts and objects developed at a time when very few Greek artefacts made their way into the collections of western European connoisseurs, meaning that the pieces of Greek sculpture that did make their way westwards were viewed within Italian, French and British – that is, western European – contexts of collecting culture. With his *Recueil d'Antiquités égyptiennes, étrusques, grecques, romaines et gauloises* (1752–67), the famous French antiquarian collector and connoisseur, the Comte de Caylus, sought to provide a repository of engravings of ancient objects which rendered these artefacts 'common to all those people who cultivate letters ... and in being reunited from the different niches of the cabinets of the curious, they then form in a certain manner a body of light [*lumière*], all of whose parts mutually enlighten one another' (1: iii). But only the palaces of princes, Caylus points out, have really been able to amass a collection of ancient Greek pieces: other collectors hardly have a hope of gathering together a substantial collection of Greek antiquities, especially as the Italians have been extremely strict on exporting Greek pieces. Winckelmann addressed the same theme, when he prefaced his famous ekphrasis of the Apollo Belvedere by saying that Nero had plundered the statue: another Italian prince and his Greek sculptures ... Furthermore, the viewing of ancient Greek art in situ seemed a distant possibility to many at a time when Athens remained under Ottoman rule. Caylus had managed to travel to Greece and the Levant, but this was unusual among eighteenth-century antiquarians.[10] Even if Winckelmann sought to disentangle ancient Greek culture from the rest of the Mediterranean, Greek art could only be seen in the eighteenth century in an 'Oriental' context or within western European collections.

This chapter begins by turning to the Comte de Caylus' *Recueil*, which was a major antiquarian publication of the middle of the eighteenth century. As we shall see, Caylus was fascinated by the ruins of ancient Egypt and the undeciphered hieroglyphs. The paucity of Greek sculpture on the western European antiquities market in the mid-eighteenth century meant that it could become fetishized for its fragmentary scarcity. Indeed, the exotic mysteriousness of ancient Egypt framed Caylus' view and visualization of the fragments of ancient Greek culture, which he managed to get his hands on. The rarity of Greek artefacts created both an economic demand and an antiquarian curiosity for seeking out ancient Greek culture. This chapter moves on to examine the publications of those individuals who managed to travel to the Ottoman province. As we shall see, the Scot James 'Athenian' Stuart and the Frenchman Julien-David Le Roy produced markedly different and competing visions of classical Greek architecture. While the canvas of British and French national rivalries acted as an important background in Stuart's and Le Roy's contrasting receptions of Greek architecture, the competition to 'liberate' Greece from the Ottomans was key to exploring the possibilities of visualizing Greek architectural forms in the eighteenth century.

If the relationship between Greece and the East was fundamental to the conceptualization of ancient Greek form in the mid eighteenth century by antiquarians from a western European perspective, then these issues converge in one of the most lavish and technologically advanced publications produced in the 1700s. The chapter closes with Pierre-François Hugues, the self-styled 'Baron d'Hancarville', who as a French antiquarian had befriended the British Envoy Extraordinary in Naples Sir William Hamilton, who had agreed to allow d'Hancarville to produce a catalogue of Hamilton's ancient vase collection. D'Hancarville's publication reflects the impact of the mid-century fascination with the hieroglyph. Caylus was writing at the end of a long history of glamourizing ancient Egypt: since the Renaissance and into the early-modern period, antiquarians and philosophers argued that the hieroglyphs contained arcane wisdom. The idea that Egyptian hieroglyphs were beautiful visual images which might also be texts containing learned wisdom was very seductive in the mid-eighteenth century. Indeed, it made a profound impression on d'Hancarville who argued that the paintings on Hamilton's vases could actually be read as texts containing the history of ancient art.

This 'hieroglyphization' of ancient Greek art – seeing image as text containing profound truths – also helped d'Hancarville see Hamilton's vases as extremely ancient. To the French antiquarian, these vases looked very old indeed and were products of the earliest period of painting down to the period between Etruscan decline and the rise of Greek art. D'Hancarville thereby pushed the history of the Greek artistic tradition back in time. At the same time, however, the images on the vases also reminded d'Hancarville of life in contemporary Naples, where modern Catholic culture could be seen to be a survival of ancient paganism. D'Hancarville's sumptuous publication brings together all the issues visualized in Winckelmann's vignette, where we saw a later Greek artist working in Rome, who looked back to earlier periods as he Etruscanized and Egyptianized his relief sculpture: Hamilton's vases paintings are produced by Greek artists living on the Italian mainland and made artworks which remind d'Hancarville of modern Neapolitan life, and yet they are also objects of oldest antiquity, alongside ancient Egypt, to be seen as images which act as texts divulging the truth about the history of ancient art. D'Hancarville's account, then, represented the culmination of the eighteenth-century visualization of Greek artistic form, which emerged against a background of Orientalizing and Catholic-Italian tropes.

D'Hancarville's envisioning of ancient Greek art stood in contrast to that of Winckelmann, who, on the other hand, endowed ancient Greece with unique environmental and cultural conditions which separated it from the rest of the Mediterranean. Winckelmann's description of the Greek climate and political life provided the lynchpins in an argument about the exemplarity of ancient Greek art, which would be so foundational to debates about the relationship between Greece and the rest of antiquity from the late eighteenth, through the nineteenth and into the twentieth centuries. But even if Winckelmann's text sought to emphasize the exceptionality of the Greeks, his vignette heading his Preface positions Greek art as following a heritage of Egyptian and Etruscan traditions within a system of Roman patronage. The eighteenth-century visual debates about Greek form in relation to the rest of the Mediterranean were programmatic to a subsequent long history of political debates about the relationship between ancient Greece, Egypt and the Near East, which since the *Black Athena* controversy in the 1990s have become recognised as foundational to the reification of classical studies as a discipline which cordoned itself off from Egyptology and Assyriology in the nineteenth century.[11]

In exploring the politics of the eighteenth-century debates about the form of Greek culture, this chapter excavates the historical background to today's discussions about the politics of form in Greek studies. As James Porter has recently argued, 'the problem of materiality, which has a gamut of associations that are specific – and let's face it: *peculiar* – to the disciplines of Classics, standing as they uniquely do in relation to the material past of Greco-Roman antiquity and athwart the contemporary, modern (or postmodern) present'. Even as *Altertumswissenschaft* emerged out of the so-called 'material turn' of antiquarianism in the eighteenth century, modernity's relationship to the politics, ethics and erotics of ancient forms has been continually antagonistic, awkward, troubled and unsettled. 'Classics is as much a matter of matter as it is fundamentally a repression of this fact.' This chapter provides a historical canvas to the 'queasy relation' identified by Porter between Classics and the materiality of form, which is energising Greek studies and has produced the collection of essays in this volume.[12]

Caylus' Egypt and the lure of the Greek fragment

Anne-Claude-Philippe de Thubières, de Grimoard, de Pestels, de Lévis, Comte de Caylus, was a leading antiquarian in the European republic of letters. As a teenager, he had distinguished himself on the battlefield, receiving the praise of Louis XIV. By 1714, in his early twenties, however, he had given up on a military career and travelled to Italy. The tour was to be definitive for the young man, who went on to visit Constantinople, Greece, Germany and England. Settling down in Paris, he inserted himself into the centre of the arts and antiquities market, populated by artists, patrons, collectors and connoisseurs.[13] Caylus' travels, which were much more extensive than many of his contemporaries, ensured that he had a more generous perspective on Mediterranean culture in comparison to other antiquarians, like Winckelmann, who were beginning to insist on the superiority of Greek art. The *Recueil*, he writes, maps out 'the history of the Arts' (1: ix). His historical narrative envisioned a diffusion of culture and good taste and design across the ancient Mediterranean. 'The source and cradle of [Etruscan] art' seems to have been founded upon the 'reciprocal trade between the Egyptians and the Etruscans. The period cannot be fixed, but it goes back to a very distant past' (1: 78). And while some ancient Greeks, from 'a vanity full of ingratitude' (1: 117) chose to forget what they owed their predecessors, others, such as Pausanias, have recorded, Caylus argues, commonalities between Egyptian and Greek art. The ancient Egyptians held a fascination over Caylus, who looked back to a longer tradition of 'Egyptomania'. Athanasius Kircher had argued that hieroglyphs contained esoteric wisdom and prefigured Christian theological doctrine. Before that, the translation of Iamblichus' *The Mysteries of the Egyptians* by Marsilio Ficino had encouraged various other Renaissance scholars to see Egyptian wisdom along with that of Zoroaster, Orpheus and Pythagoras, as containing a combination of Platonist and Christian thought-systems. The hidden truths of the Egyptian hieroglyphs captured the imagination of other intellectuals, such as Giordano Bruno, who saw the invention of hieroglyphs as an *ars memoriae* and ancient Egypt more generally as a museum, or memory theatre, of history.[14]

The frontispieces in several of the volumes of the *Recueil* feature various Egyptian motifs. In that of volume 3, antiquity is represented in Egyptian form, prodigious in size and covered by an immense veil, tired out by Time, who bustles around in an effort to hide and obscure antiquity (see Fig. 10.2). A group of putti lifts parts of this veil in order to uncover the object of their curiosity. The image dramatizes a competition between the efforts of the antiquarian and the ravages of time.[15] In the frontispiece to volume 4, a somewhat more complex image of the passing of time is presented (see Fig. 10.3). The different epochs, all treated in the same manner, have a scythe, a beard and are weighed down by old age. They are placed on different planes and are depicted as distancing

The Politics of Form in Greek Literature

Figure 10.2 Caylus, *Recueil*, volume 3, frontispiece.

themselves from the immediate plane in the image. The Graeco-Roman past is symbolized in the foreground by the excavation of a classical torso, while Egyptian antiquity is represented in the background by a pyramid and pyramidal structures both natural and manmade. As Caylus explains in his notes, 'this allegory depicts study and the work of antiquaries who must apply themselves to distinguishing the centuries. The

Figure 10.3 Caylus, *Recueil*, volume 4, frontispiece.

one figure of time can represent them in similar circumstances' (4: xiii). Like Winckelmann, as we saw, Caylus viewed the most important task of the antiquarian as the differentiation of ancient 'national' styles or 'goûts' of each 'nation' (1: vii). While the various ancient epochs of art might look the same (the figure of Time used repeatedly), their differences need to be discerned.

And yet the fingers of one figure of Time breach the right side of the frame, hinting that Caylus' attempts at encapsulating and containing antiquity within a historical narrative framework might not be so secure. The piercing of the image points to a tantalising possibility outside of the frame in a long-ago Egyptian past. Whereas in one frontispiece Caylus visualized the history of ancient art as a revelation of Egypt, here he revels in the inaccessibility of the relics of Egyptian antiquity. In the frontispiece to volume 5, Caylus presents us with a large ruinous pyramid with six tiny figures in the foreground (see Fig. 10.4). The caption ('RUDERIBUS PRETIOSA SUIS', 'valuable rubble') comments

Figure 10.4 Caylus, *Recueil*, volume 5, frontispiece.

upon the image. Whilst his *Recueil* sought to organise the scattered remains of the ancient world into a narrative, there is also an aesthetic pleasure to be gained from looking at a ruin. This is an artistic image which makes a plea for taking pleasure in the fragments of ancient relics. The pyramid is a summit to be climbed – a mountain of learning to be surmounted – and yet it is precarious. No one in the picture is even trying it: the stones might slip away from the climber's grasp. Just as the image figures the possibility of connoisseurship as a summit to be ascended, so it also looks perilous and foreboding. At the peak, there is nothing, merely a blank space. The juxtaposition of the Latin words for 'rubble' and 'precious' appears to be a reworking of a line by Martial (*Epigram* 6.15), about an ant imprisoned in amber and ironically made precious in death. The image, then, becomes a wry observation about the contrast between undervalued living objects and the massive value antiquarians attach to dead, inanimate ones At the same time, it alerts Caylus' readers to the importance of textuality for viewing antiquity: Caylus' manipulation of Martial's poem controls and frames the interpretation of the image.

The fascination about the lost origins of art is also thematized in the title-page image in volume 5 (see Fig. 10.5). It is an image of a statue of the Nile, after a statue preserved

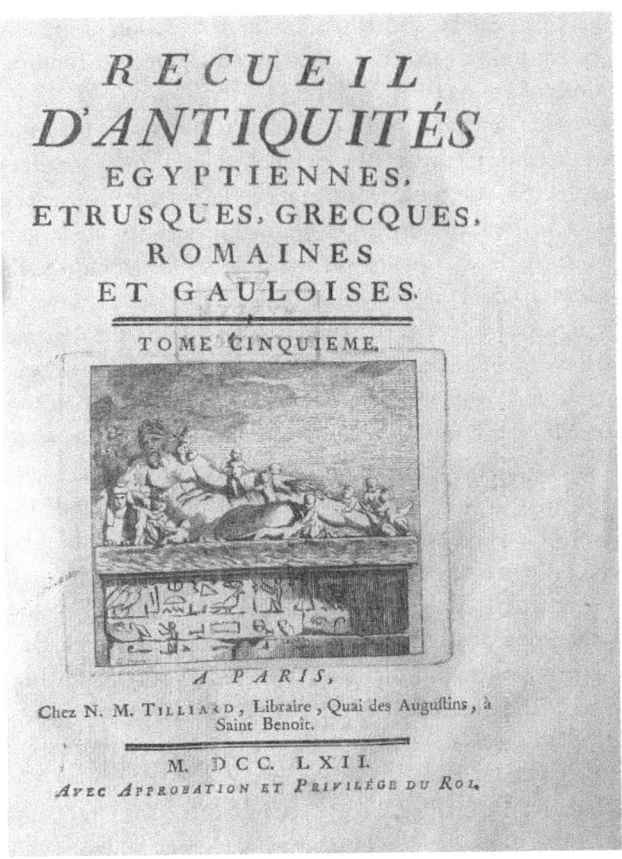

Figure 10.5 Caylus, *Recueil*, volume 5, title page.

in Rome, according to Caylus' explication. The head is hidden in clouds. The composition, Caylus explains, does not just remind us of the ancients' ignorance of the source of this river, but it also bears allusion to the obscurity which reigns over the origin and the establishment of the Egyptians themselves. And, as Caylus, explains, he has added imaginary hieroglyphs on the pedestal, in order to leave no doubt to the spirit of the piece. While Egyptian hieroglyphs were figured by early-modern scholars up to and including Caylus as a source of arcane wisdom, here Caylus presents his reader with a highly self-conscious image of the indecipherability of Egyptian antiquity. Yet again, then, the use of text is key to Caylus' image-making. In his frontispiece, he had appropriated language from Martial, to convey his message to his reader about the thrilling mysteriousness of ancient art. In the image on the title page opposite that frontispiece, Caylus fabricates a set of hieroglyphs to impress a similar meaning. This theme of the unfathomability of antiquity literally framed the experience of reading the *Recueil* for Caylus' audience, presented as it repeatedly was on the frontispieces and title pages.[16] But these images also focalize the significance of the relationship between the ancient object and the modern viewer in that Caylus uses text as a way of labelling and controlling the meaning of his images. But if he relies on an ancient epigram in his frontispiece, in his title page he underlines, by the concoction of made-up hieroglyphs, that these images are modern constructions by an eighteenth-century viewer, just as much as illustrations of antiquarian artefacts.

This is also the mode in which images of ancient Greek art are presented in the *Recueil* which often emphasize the pleasures of viewing the tantalisingly small remains of Greek art. In one plate (plate 53, volume 1), for instance, Caylus offers up a series of fragments which 'alone can nourish the taste, foster emulation and stimulate genius in modern artists' (1: 141) (see Fig. 10.6). Caylus was training his readers to see the detail: that is when the brilliance of Greek art becomes visible. On a fragment of a painting from Herculaneum, he writes 'it will be easy to find there the spirit, the slightness of touch and the skill of the artist' (1: 152). In another plate (plate 46.1, volume 1), we can see, Caylus suggests, a fragment of a statue of Venus. But artists should not look too closely, Caylus advises, as the air has over time 'injured' the surface of the marble: instead they should stand back and admire it (see Fig. 10.7). Caylus encourages the viewer to enjoy the object's hazy fragmentariness. And just as Caylus' use of text signified the unfathomable ruins of the history of ancient art, so again through the presence of text in the image is the intangibility of the ancient Greek body beautiful repeatedly figured in Caylus' illustrations. The vignette to the chapter on Greek art in the first volume represents a grave monument, supposedly found in Athens, of an athlete who had competed in the lampadephoria, a relay race on foot using a torch which was passed between the runners. Caylus' explication of the image (1: 117 – see Fig. 10.8) conjures up a world of Greek athleticism. And yet, this is a grave monument, which mourns the passing of that world. In the vignette to the chapter on Greek art in the second volume, Calyus shows his readers the pedestal of a lost statue (2: 105 – see Fig. 10.9). The Greek says: 'The town [of Sparta] has erected this monument in honour of Menippus Eudaimonides who brought back the prize'. As Caylus writes in his explication, 'This teaches us that the Spartans also

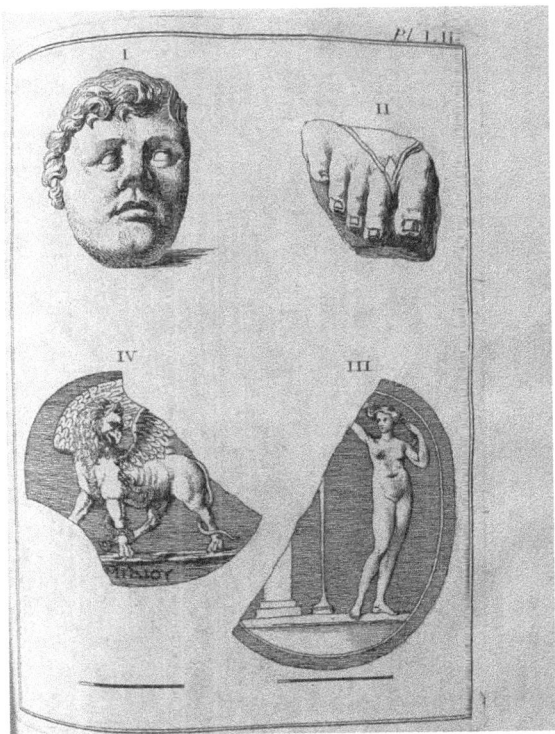

Figure 10.6 Caylus, *Recueil*, volume 1, plate 53.

Figure 10.7 Caylus, *Recueil*, volume 1, plate 46.1.

Figure 10.8 Caylus, *Recueil*, volume 1, Greek art chapter vignette.

erected statues to their citizens, winners in the Games'. This time, the engraver has inserted the outline of two feet, where he imagines the statue might have stood. The image marks the absence of the Greek body beautiful – merely a footprint, a trace of the past remains. Although the *Recueil* was supposed to visualize the remains of ancient art, Caylus often ends up visualizing ancient written texts describing that material culture. Caylus' interest in the beautiful, barely visible, fragmentary line, reaches its logical conclusion in another plate (plate 56.4, volume 1: 154 – see Fig. 10.10), when he reproduces what he thinks could be the incomplete signature of either Athenodorus or

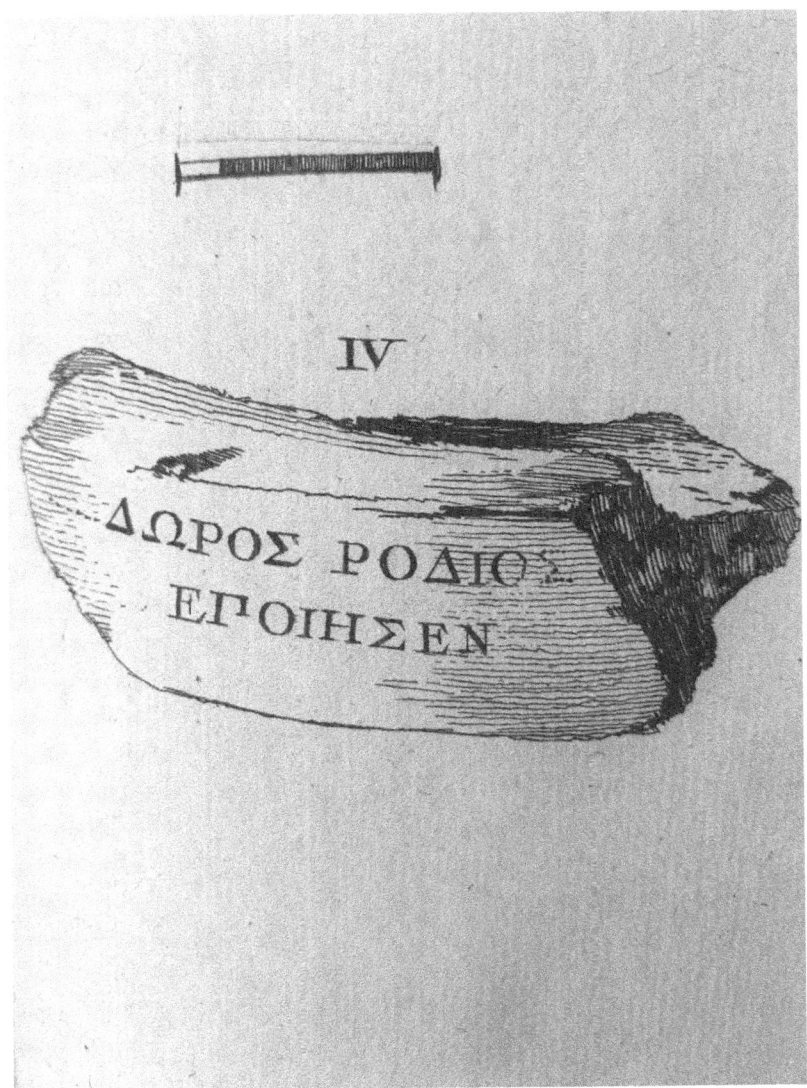

Figure 10.9 Caylus, *Recueil*, volume 2, Greek art chapter vignette.

Polydorus, the sculptors who, along with Agesander, had, according to Pliny (*Natural History* 37.5), produced Laocoon and his sons: '... dorus of Rhodes made this'. Rather than illustrating any Greek sculpture, Caylus becomes the connoisseur who is more excited by the identification of the Greek artist's signature. Caylus' aestheticization of the signature reflects the cultural and economic context in which the *Recueil* appeared, when antiquities were circulating in a growing European art market. The signature became an important guarantor in disputes over artistic attribution and monetary value. The signature provided value: it underwrote beauty.[17] At the same time, the fascination with fragmentary

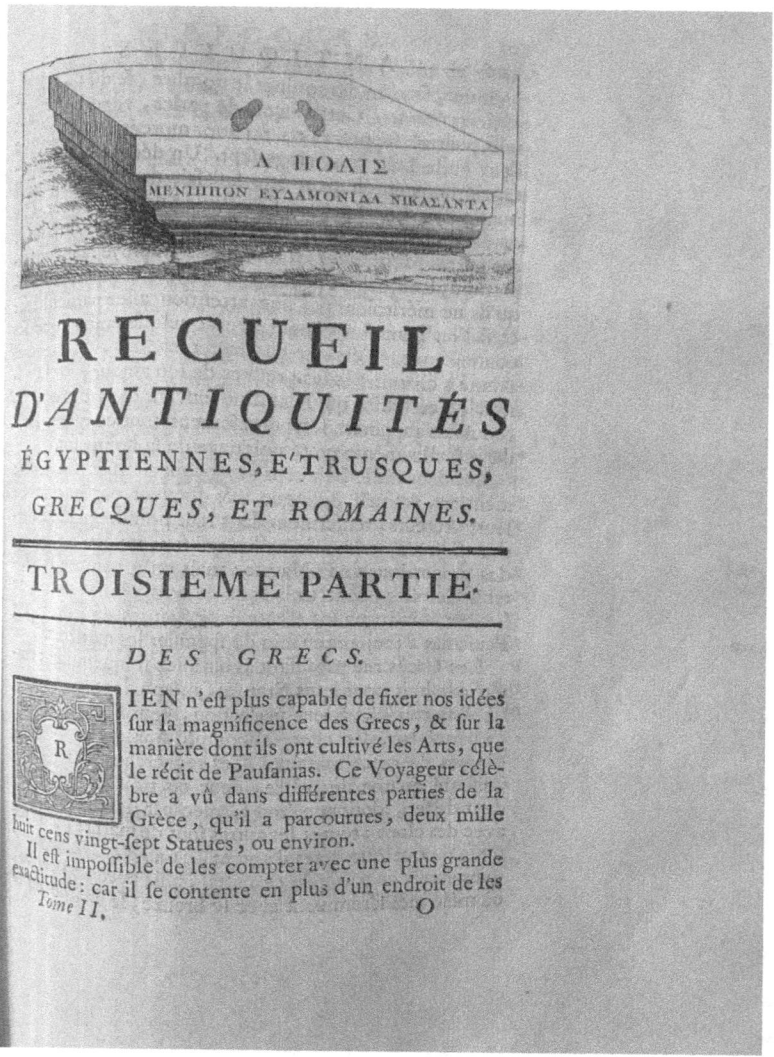

Figure 10.10 Caylus, *Recueil*, volume 1, plate 56.4.

texts also reflects Caylus' captivation by the Egyptian hieroglyph. The image-as-text, the possibility that the image could divulge a textual narrative, had become a powerful idea in eighteenth-century antiquarianism. And yet, the text was also a signifier of the disappearance of the body of art, of the loss of the past, of the illegibility of antiquity. Like many of his eighteenth-century contemporaries, Caylus' Egypt, and therefore his view of antiquity, oscillated between enlightenment and esotericism.[18] Caylus visually dramatized the complex relationship between ancient object and modern viewer, an issue which also emerges in mid-eighteenth-century visualizations of classical Athenian architecture, as we shall now see.

Stuart and Le Roy in Ottoman Athens

In the years Caylus was publishing his *Recueil* – between 1752 and 1764, with a posthumous volume appearing in 1767 – Winckelmann was busy formulating his ideas about the history of ancient art, including the relationship between Greece's predecessors and successors in the artistic tradition. Greek art was seen, by Winckelmann, as both a timeless model for the modern arts as well as a historically specific, that is, inimitable cultural production.[19] This tension, between seeing Greece as a paradigm for modern artistic practice and as an unrepeatable and forever-past moment in time, was also a question about the relationship between Greece and the Orient: how exceptional was ancient Greece to be? It was an issue which was extravagantly visualized in the publications by James 'Athenian' Stuart and Julien-David Le Roy about ancient Athenian architecture, which came out between 1758 and 1770. If eighteenth-century Orientalism underpinned the efforts of antiquarians – if Greece began to require differentiating from Egyptian predecessors and Roman successors – the Orientalizing politics of the form of ancient Greece was abundantly on display in the productions of Le Roy and Stuart.

As we have just seen with Caylus, the otherness of contemporary Greece shaped eighteenth-century characterizations of ancient Greek art as seductively fragmentary and inaccessible. But Greece had not been completely inaccessible to western European travellers in the early-modern period, when a steady stream of diplomats, merchants and visitors – including Caylus – had managed to see the eastern Mediterranean and record what they saw both in travelogues and in images between the late seventeenth and first half of the eighteenth centuries.[20] James Stuart and Nicolas Revett's 1762 *The Antiquities of Athens* marked a significant moment in the history of the visual documentation of ancient Greek culture, and has been viewed until the twentieth century as providing accurate illustrations of Athenian edifices, structures and design.[21] Finally, it appeared, Greece could be seen.

Stuart was the son of a Scottish sailor, whose death left the family in poverty. A very good artist, Stuart was apprenticed as a child to a fan painter. At around the age of 30, he travelled to Italy, where, supporting himself as a painter and cicerone, he developed his knowledge of art and architecture. Some ten years later, he managed to travel to Greece with his friend Revett, where together they measured and recorded antiquities. After returning to London in 1755, Stuart started working on *The Antiquities of* Athens, with a view to improving architects' and artists' understanding of Greek design and form. The organization of the plates in *The Antiquities of Athens* emphasized the idea that ancient Greek architecture was being disinterred for the reader to view. After the preface, Stuart and Revett greet their reader with a general view of Athens (see Fig. 10.11). The archway (deemed to be the front of a reservoir which supplied Athens with its water) acts as a gate, welcoming the visitor-reader into the *Antiquities of Athens*. The distance of the city from the reader is reflected in the organization of the image, with Athens faintly perceptible in the background in contrast to the much darker, more detailed foreground, which has been populated by Turkish figures. Indeed the archer framed by the columns competes with Athens as the subject of the image. As Stuart and Revett note in the

Figure 10.11 Stuart/Revett, *Antiquities of Athens*, General View of Athens.

description of the engraving, 'The figures represent Hassan Agâ, the *Vaiwode* [local governor] of Athens, accompanied by the principal Turks of the City and by their Servants. He delighted in Archery, and desired to be thus represented in this View; his greatest random shot was 1753 English feet' (1762: x).[22] His arrow looks as if it is aimed at Athens, drawing Stuart's readers' eyes over in that direction, but also reminding them of the 'Burden, which an avaricious or cruel Governor may attempt to lay on' the local Athenians, 'oppressed as they are at present' (x). The picturesque scene establishes a sense of the historical otherness of Athens in relationship to eighteenth-century modernity: Ottoman rule stands between the ancient city and Stuart's and Revett's readership. The image, then, bespeaks the historical specificity of the scene and acts as an 'attestation of presence' of Stuart and Revett on the road to Athens.[23]

This visual organization is replicated in each picturesque scene which welcomes the reader at the beginning of the five chapters in the book, as each chapter focuses on a single monument. The first chapter opens with a street scene 'of a Doric portico in Athens', in the words of the title of the chapter (see Fig. 10.12). As with the general view of Athens, the contrast between the darker foreground and lighter background can also be seen here. In the description of the image, Stuart and Revett explain the identities of all the figures depicted: a Greek servant, the French consul sat down, flanked by a Turk and a Greek, 'for the Sake of exhibiting the different Habits of this Country' and 'a

Figure 10.12 Stuart/Revett, *Antiquities of Athens*, Doric Portico.

common Turk and an ordinary serving Maid' (3) at the fountain which the consul had rebuilt to the 'esteem' of the local Turks (3). The shadow-casting structure to the right is the church of 'St Saviour's, now deserted and in a ruinous condition' and the minaret of the Turkish mosque is just visible between the columns of the classical structure. Stuart's exhibition of the different layers of culture is represented by his layering of history in the image, which is structurally arranged as a series of frames so that the portico is embedded into the centre of the engraving, surrounded by subsequent cultures on all sides. The ancient monument is made deliberately hard to see. Indeed, Stuart and Revett concede that the picturesque mode of visualization was intended to half-reveal and half-conceal, when in the description of the engraving they admit altering the truth of what they had actually seen, turning the position of the fountain slightly, 'so as to give the Reader a View of this Kind of Turkish Fabrick' (3). As with the engraving of the general view of Athens, Turkish modernity jostles for attention with Hellenic antiquity as the subject of the image. When the reader turns over the page, however, they are met with a long series of detailed architectural drawings framed by numerical measurements. While Stuart and Revett did little actual excavation themselves on their visit to Athens, the organisation of their plates conveys the sense that the ancient monuments have been disinterred from their historical contexts and turned into timeless, ahistorical designs, to be adopted and adapted by contemporary architects. In the 'Proposal' to *The Antiquities of Athens*, Stuart and Revett had wanted to demonstrate the Athenian edifice as 'conforming to Vitruvius', even if Stuart had, on at least one occasion, to amend the original building in his plan of it, to make it fit with the Roman text.[24] Seeing Greek architecture for Stuart and Revett, then, meant exhuming it from its historical specificity and visualizing it as conforming to unchanging, eternal mathematical metrologies. The visual structure of *The Antiquities of Athens* responded to the fact that Greece was under Ottoman rule and not nearly so accessible as Italy and that its monuments were literally hemmed in and built on, by subsequent edifices: they could not so easily be transported and inserted into the western European antiquities market or become acquired by a public museum and be utilized as material for neoclassical art and design. Stuart and Revett's publication sought to bypass these difficulties in viewing and visualizing ancient Greece by taking five Athenian monuments out of their historical as well as their geographical contexts. As Jason M. Kelly has shown, 'by portraying the ruined classical landscape against its modern inhabitants, the archaeological topographies functioned to compress the universal historical narrative into single, static images' which contrasted the timeless exemplarity of ancient Greek culture with modern 'Oriental' decay and decline. 'The Antiquities of Athens ... may have highlighted the importance of empiricism, but an underlying metanarrative about aesthetic ideals and ethnohistorical processes was ever present'.[25]

The organization of *The Antiquities of Athens* was in stark contrast to that in Julien-David Le Roy's *Les ruines des plus beaux monumens de la Grèce*, which had first appeared in 1758.[26] Le Roy's publication had been supported by Caylus and the latter's art circle, and was viewed as a project of national prestige. Taking advantage of good diplomatic relations between France and the Ottoman Empire, Le Roy spent three months in Athens and then went onto Constantinople (as opposed to the three years spent by Stuart and Revett). He employed the best engravers and architects to produce the illustrations. Stuart and Revett used the picturesque mode in order to represent the ruined condition of ancient Greek architecture, hidden under so many strata of history that they were willing to reposition a Turkish edifice to make the latter more visible. At the same time, they were highly critical of Le Roy's picturesque views which, they showed, were inaccurate and took liberties to provide a beautiful effect for the viewer. The difference, however, between the English and the French publications was that the latter had not provided architectural drawings which liberated the Greek monument from its historical specificity alongside the picturesque views. Instead, Le Roy's *Les ruines* was organised as a travelogue, as the Frenchman described his voyage from Rome to Athens and then his historical tour around the ancient monuments of the city, which were punctuated by picturesque views of what could be seen there. This was then followed by a historical account of the architectural orders and architectural design, furnished with technical illustrations. The monuments, which had been picturesquely depicted, were not directly accompanied by diagrammatic visualisations. In 1770 Le Roy came to publish a second, enlarged edition of *Les ruines*, he did not alter his picturesque engravings in light of the criticisms of Stuart and Revett. He responded to Stuart's critiques (2004: 207 and 208 n.3; 1770: 1: v-vi) by explicitly contrasting his views of the ancient buildings in Athens with the Scotsman's 'slavishly' accurate measurements.[27] While Le Roy did contend that he took fuller and more precise measurements on the ground, he wanted, unlike Stuart and Revett, as he claims, to 'make a livelier impression on the viewer and fill his mind with all the admiration that strikes when we see the monuments themselves' (2004: 207; 1770: 1: vi). Le Roy would continue in a footnote to critique Stuart's illustrations in that they do not follow

> a recognised principle among painters, sculptors and persons of taste that for an object in a picture to make a powerful impression on the beholder, it must not in any way be smothered by extraneous objects. Judge by this principle some of Mr Stuart's drawings and my own. The foreground of his view of the ruins in the bazaar offers only walls, unsightly roofs, and diminutive figures lost in a great, dark mass; only in the distance across and above all this, do we glimpse the tops of the columns of the building [see Fig. 10.13]. I took my view of this magnificent ruin from the foot of the building itself; I depicted its columns at full length; I showed the stress, which forms one side, roofed over in a highly picturesque manner. Finally, I conveyed an idea of the animated, present-day scene by showing the merchants who have their stalls there.
>
> *2004: 208, note 3; 1770: 1: vi, note b*

Stuart's view of the bazaar is indeed quite different from Le Roy's. As the Frenchman says, the foreground in *Antiquities of Athens* is shrouded in black darkness (the standard format for the picturesque scenes in this book, as we have seen), populated only by a

Figure 10.13 Stuart/Revett, *Antiquities of Athens*, bazaar.

handful of figures, whilst the Greek 'stoa or portico' (as Stuart titles his chapter on this structure (1762: 37)) is barely visible further back in the plate. Stuart says that his view is

> taken from a Window up one pair of stairs in the house of Nicolas Logotheti, the British Consul at Athens. This Front is encumbered with Houses, Magazines and Workshops, which are built against it, and obstruct the View of it in such a manner as to render its general disposition quite unintelligible to those who stand any where on the level of the Street: and they conceal a great part of it, even from the Spectator who is placed in the most favourable Situation. These Magazines and Work-Shops are occupied by Sope Makers; there is a considerable number of those Manufacturers here.
>
> *1762: 41–2*

Stuart goes on to explain that the figures at the front 'represent a Turkish *Aga* or Gentleman, receiving a Visiter' along with 'an Albanese Groom with his Masters Horses' at the bottom right (Stuart 1762: 41–2). As we now might expect, when Stuart's readers turn over the page after this obstructed view, they are greeted with a long series of detailed architectural drawings delineating various sections of the building. The first is the plan, which includes dotted lines to represent 'restorations' where parts of the original edifice Stuart and Revett found were 'destroyed, and in others [where] the difficulty of gaining admission into the Houses of Turks who have Families, was an obstacle to our enquiries' (1762: 42). Stuart, then, positions his reader as a British subject, from a window of the Consul's house and covers up and then unveils the antiquities of Athens which lie hidden under the chaos of the Ottoman present. His architectural drawings fill in and restore what can no longer be seen, extracting the monument from its present-day context.

Le Roy, on the other hand, offers his readership a different sort of vicarious experience of the traveller to Athens as his picturesque view of the bazaar positions his reader as a traveller at ground level at the heart of the scene with the ancient ruins looming, bathed in the rays of the sun (see Fig. 10.14). The plate, then, is a re-creation of a single moment in a traveller's journey through the city. Whereas Stuart and Revett move from the specificities of the Athenian present to ahistorical diagrams of Greek architectural beauty, Le Roy concludes his account of the bazaar with a description of how it felt on the day he visited: 'The magnificence of the ruin, the picturesque effect produced by the variety of houses that line it, and the greenery that covers them, enhanced by the masses of shadow and light that the Sun creates, render this street an enchanting sight in summer' (2004: 413; 1770: 2: 17). But Le Roy does not then try to abstract the truth of Greek architecture out of that historically specific experience. That experience was itself described as 'picturesque'. Le Roy's picturesque scene was also a visualization of his theory about how architecture was to be seen, a theory which he outlines in an essay in the 1770 edition. Le Roy attempts here to elucidate the nature of architectural principles which stand outside of historical and cultural difference. There are certain universal axioms that say that an 'edifice, whatever its nature, must be well built; a dwelling must be situated in a health place' and 'there are principles founded on the laws of mechanics' (2004: 367; 1770: 2: iii).

Visions of Ancient Greece

Figure 10.14 Le Roy, *Les ruines*, bazaar.

What should count as beautiful, however, might be seen as having been 'adopted either by all peoples on Earth or solely by the most enlightened nations, past and present' (2004: 367; 1770: 2: iii). Beauty, it seems, might be both universal and subjective. Interestingly, this is how Le Roy theorizes the way Greek architecture is seen by its viewer. On the one hand, then, 'the Greeks invented and brought to the highest pitch of perfection' a form of architecture, which 'is spreading [*se répand*] across the surface of the Earth' (2004: 281; 1770: 2: xvii). On the other hand, however, the timeless beauty of Greek architectural forms themselves can only be experienced subjectively within specific historical moments. Le Roy describes the act of viewing a peristyle, whose façade is made up of columns 'that stand some way clear of [a wall] to form a colonnade.' This façade

> will possess a real beauty . . . namely, the varied and striking views that its columns present to the spectator as they jut out from the back wall of the colonnade. This property of multiplying, without enfeebling, the sensations that we receive at the sight of a building is one more notable advantage that is more evident in colonnades than in any other species of decoration.
>
> *2004: 371; 1770: 2: vii*

The scene 'will come to life as the spectator moves, presenting him with a succession of highly varied views created by the infinity of possible combinations of the simple objects

225

that he perceives.' Such a scene 'will present a thousand different faces to the spectator' (2004: 371; 1770: 2: vii).

For Le Roy, then, there is no single, accurate, truthful perspective on beautiful architecture, which can be extracted from the historical moment, as for Stuart and Revett. Beautiful architecture can only be experienced in a series of infinite moments, comparable to a literary narrative:

> The architect's art, like the poet's, lies in multiplying these sensations by making them successive – rather than restricting them .... As Monsieur [Jean-François] Marmontel says in his *Poétique françoise*, a poem that offers the imagination a succession of varied images interests us more than a picture that shows us only a single moment taken from nature.
>
> *2004: 370; 1770: 2: vi*

Seeing beautiful architecture is comprised of a sequence of moments, like reading a text. 'The rich variety of this spectacle' can only happen, then, within time: 'Even after several hours, the spectator will not exhaust the prospects afforded by the colonnade of the Louvre; indeed, new ones will appear at every hour of the day. Every new position of the sun causes the shadows of the columns or of the soffit they support to fall on different parts of the wall' (2004: 372; 1770: 2: viii). Le Roy's history of architecture places ancient Greek architecture at the pinnacle of ancient and modern architectural achievement precisely because it affords a particular sort of voyeuristic pleasure in viewing partial, 'ruinous' perspectives, so that it might be said that he also debunks the stability of the Greek ideal, in that that ideal becomes multiplied, continuously altering and changing as it is being viewed by the viewer, as is captured in his picturesque views such as that of the bazaar. Le Roy's picturesque views emphasise the partiality of the perspective: the reader's position is not that of an omniscient viewer who has command over the entire scene; the plates are populated by other human and animal subjects, reflecting upon the multiple perspectives which these buildings afford; and the plates depict the buildings as ruins, accentuating the idea that these buildings cannot be seen as a whole. Viewing a building unfolds in time.

Le Roy's aesthetic reflected a pervasive interest in the picturesque in the mid eighteenth century, which celebrated variety and intricacy. The picturesque view became a visual expression of what the eighteenth-century traveller saw on their voyages. The picturesque celebrated the journey of the spectator, who could take pleasure in the ever-changing scenes of nature unfolding in front of them. As such, then, the picturesque provided the viewer with visual meditations on notions of temporality and historicity. Moreover, contemporary discussions about the pleasures of the promenade emphasised the notion that gardens and landscapes afforded a variety of visual experiences which could stimulate imagination and prompt focus on the spectator's positionality. Le Roy took pleasure in the radical possibility that there simply was no single authoritative mode of viewing and visualising classical Greek art and architecture.[28] And just as Winckelmann's vignette and Caylus' images explored the relationship between ancient artefact and eighteenth-century readership, so in the visual debate between Stuart and Le Roy, the nature of the relationship between classical Athenian architecture and the modern viewer was continuously on display. Their images of Hellenic antiquity articulated their differing conceptualizations of that relationship. Stuart's engravings sought to position his reader as the English viewer who could use his technical expertise to transform Athenian architecture into timeless forms. Le Roy, on the other hand, placed his French readers 'where the Turks hold their market', so that they can enjoy 'the magnificence of the ruin, the picturesque effect produced by the variety of the houses' (2004: 413; 1770: 2: 17). But as we shall now see, the historical relationship between ancient and modern as framed by contemporary eighteenth-century Orientalism was even more sumptuously imaged in d'Hancarville's catalogue of Sir William Hamilton's vases.

D'Hancarville's Greeks: both ancient and modern

Hamilton arrived in Naples in November 1764 to become Envoy Extraordinary to the court of the King of the Two Sicilies. He was captivated by the local landscape and what lay beneath its surface. He was fascinated by both volcanology and vase collecting. Soon after his arrival in post, he hired an itinerant scholar to produce a catalogue of his vases. Born to an impoverished cloth merchant in Nancy on 1 January 1729, d'Hancarville passed through life, assuming innumerable aliases and identities. Winckelmann aptly named him an 'Avanturier' and vacillated between admiration and suspicion for this questionable personality.[29] In one letter, he warns a friend to be wary of him: '[w]hen you show him your gems keep a very close look-out to see what he is doing with his hands'.[30] On the other hand, Winckelmann obviously respected d'Hancarville's intellectual abilities: he had him installed as librarian to Cardinal Albani.[31] A child prodigy, an army officer, a scholarly entertainer (or entertaining scholar) in the circles of many a *philosophe* as well as at royal courts, a conspirator in imperial plots across Europe and a pornographer – the canvas of d'Hancarville's life was nothing if not colourful. In the 1760s, he found himself resident at Naples, where he managed to convince Hamilton that he was the man who could publish an edition of the ambassador's collection. Over a period of ten years, between 1767 and 1776, costing Hamilton tens of thousands of pounds, four sumptuous elephantine folios appeared containing over five hundred plates of vase paintings in terracotta and black enhanced with other colours. D'Hancarville's publication, *Antiquités Étrusques, Grecques et Romaines, Tirées du Cabinet de M. Hamilton, Envoyé Extraordinaire de S.M. Britannique en cour de Naples*, competed with the great antiquarian books of the eighteenth century: it was the first ever colour-plate book on the history of art in a standard edition of several hundred copies.[32]

In the frontispiece to volume 4 of his *Antiquités*, Baron d'Hancarville presented a lavish image memorial of the Comte de Caylus (see Fig. 10.15). The visual references to the engravings we have already examined in Caylus' *Recueil* should be clear: the pyramid at the back of the image and the modern hieroglyphs decorating the image. Interestingly, the

Figure 10.15 Hamilton/D'Hancarville, *Antiquities*, volume 4, frontispiece.

image also looks back to those Greek inscriptions which were bereft of a body in Caylus' *Recueil*. A medallion with Caylus' profile is placed at the head of the image in the upper third of the pyramid in the background of the image, while a pedestal at the bottom left acts as a visual support for the text in the centre. The inscription commemorates the death of Caylus, 'the most deserving man'. While in Caylus' images the inscriptions emphasize the disappearance of the beautiful Greek body, here the text replaces the body, as the inscription occupies the position between Caylus' head in profile and the pedestal where the torso and limbs could have been. The replacement of the visualized body by the text is also explored in the frontispiece to volume 2, where d'Hancarville this time envisions his mourning of the loss of Winckelmann (see Fig. 10.16). An inscription again dominates the

Figure 10.16 Hamilton/D'Hancarville, *Antiquities*, volume 2, frontispiece.

centre of the image, lamenting over Winckelmann's death 'far from home' ('ORCO PEREGRINO').[33] The tomb in this frontispiece, then, is a cenotaph. The emptiness of the tomb is echoed by the unpopulated columbarium niches (originally used by ancient Romans for the safekeeping of cinerary urns) and the two missing paving stones at the bottom of the image. The engraving presents a sign bereft of a signified, the text without a body. In both frontispieces, d'Hancarville heralds the text as the work of art, the work of art as a text.

D'Hancarville's entombment of Winckelmann and Caylus also highlights his wish to bury their histories of art in favour of his own historical narrative. And his interest in the relationship between (modern) text and (ancient) image was central to his contest with his fellow antiquarians. While, in the four volumes of the *Antiquités*, d'Hancarville's theories about the history of art changed, he consistently argued that ancient objects and images depicted evidence about the origins of art. In the first two volumes, he proposed that art referenced its natural origins: statues look back to tree trunks, candelabra to stripped vines and vases to shells. In the latter two volumes, d'Hancarville avoids postulating an natural, founding moment for the history of representation and contends that early peoples set up 'signs' of commemoration for various different reasons whether it was out of a need to convey a message or to memorialise a specific event and that classical art records those original meanings. Whichever the precise narrative d'Hancarville offered, he argued that ancient art records its own origins, so that the ancient image or object might resemble a modern historiographical text composed of signs. Or as d'Hancarville put it himself, 'their history written by themselves [*leur histoire écrite par eux mêmes*] can be read [*se lit*] on these monuments' (*Antiquités* 4: 9). D'Hancarville's vision of the comparability of image and text is envisioned, for example, in a pair of vignettes in volume 2, whose inscriptions mirror each other: just like a picture, so poetry will be': 'similar to poetry may a picture be' (see Fig. 10.17). The first is, of course, a quotation from Horace (*Ars Poetica*), while the second is the opening line from Charles Alphonse Dufresnoy's 1668 poem *De Arte Graphica*, which was an important and highly influential aesthetic document arguing that painting should imitate poetry. The dictum *ut pictura poesis* would become a central maxim of art theory in the eighteenth century.[34] The hieroglyphic frieze framing the Horatian dictum reflects the eighteenth-century vision of ancient Egyptian hieroglyphs as comprising a combination image and text as picture-writing. The mirroring of Horace and Dufresnoy visualizes d'Hancarville's argument about the mirroring between ancient image and modern historiographical text.

While Caylus' visual experiments with hieroglyphs and pyramids were designed to connote the mystery of the origins of antiquity, d'Hancarville's appropriation of these Egyptianizing motifs, however, signalled the latter's intellectual position against Caylus, in that art actually recorded its own origins. D'Hancarville was also critical of Winckelmann's lionization of classical Greek art. The Frenchman in Naples argued that Hamilton's vases paintings were evidence of the earliest stages in the history of painting. In volume 3, for instance, d'Hancarville proposed that a vase painting was by a contemporary of Euchir, whose *floruit* was around 1200 BC and who was named by Pliny

Visions of Ancient Greece

Figure 10.17 Hamilton/D'Hancarville, *Antiquities*, volume 2, vignettes.

(*Natural History* 7.205) as the inventor of painting. The image, in d'Hancarville's eyes, depicts the allegorical figures of Song and Meditation (see Fig. 10.18). 'The drawing of the muses recalls that of children, on the one hand, but, on the other, 'the intention, the arrangement, the ideas it develops, show it is a man who is responsible and even one who is very ingenious in his work' (*Antiquités* 3: 202–3). The painting looks like it is done by a child and by a man: it looks primitive as well as mature. In contrast to Winckelmann, then, d'Hancarville celebrates the beauty of what he sees to be the earliest Greek paintings. Moreover, this very ancient work of art also looks very modern, as it records the efforts of an artist attempting to do something entirely new: it would have reminded d'Hancarville's readers of contemporary, eighteenth-century efforts in the 1760s and 70s to forge a new classical art based on the veneration of Greek rather than Roman art.

Hamilton's primitive Greek vases, however, were also seen by d'Hancarville within the context of Catholic Naples. In Winckelmann's *History*, the word took precedence over the image, reflecting Winckelmann's Lutheran textualization and spiritualization of Greek art. In d'Hancarville's *Antiquités*, however, the historiographical text has been transformed into lavish, sumptuous images. Naples was a feast for the antiquarian's eyes. In 1776, Sir William Hamilton would bring out *Campi Phlegraei: Observations on the volcanos of the two Sicilies*, furnished with coloured plates by Pietro Fabris of volcanic specimens, views of volcanic craters and their surroundings as well as panoramic views

231

Figure 10.18 Hamilton/D'Hancarville, *Antiquities*, volume 1, Song and Meditation.

which included classical ruins and sites known from classical texts. These images juxtaposed prehistoric geological time, ancient culture and the modern viewer.[35] It was not lost on Hamilton that Vesuvius had both destroyed and preserved ancient Pompeian life. The volcanic eruptions also provided a physical backdrop to the view of Naples as an eruption of a very old, feudal, Catholic past. The Bay of Naples offered the northern

European traveller and tourist the chance to step a very long way back in time and encounter a shadier, less civilized classicism quite unlike the glorious grandeurs of Rome.³⁶ The exciting anticipation of a strange world was stimulated by the appearance of numerous phallic artefacts from the sites of Pompeii and Herculaneum. William Hamilton himself reported on such finds and he famously uncovered evidence of what he perceived to be the survival of ancient phallic worship in the supposedly superstitious ceremonies of the southern Italian Catholic church.³⁷ Hamilton's Greek vases looked both primitive and modern, then, because of both the Orientalizing – more specifically Egyptianizing – motifs and themes in mid-eighteenth-century antiquarianism and the exoticizing excitement of Neapolitan culture.

D'Hancarville's interpretation of Hamilton's Greek vases did not, however, stand the test of time: classical archaeologists and ancient historians would date the artefacts much later and did not adopt his semiotic theories. Even if his 1764 *History* was quickly criticized for various errors in dating and judgement, Winckelmann's overall vision of Greece shaped the nineteenth-century visualization of Hellenic antiquity. As the professional study of classical Greece and Rome was cordoned off from Egyptology and Assyriology, the rise of the nation state and the development of discourses of racial difference would cement the boundaries between academic departments over the course of the nineteenth century.³⁸ Advances in excavation recording methods, archaeologists' attempts at *Quellenforschung* and then photography added new dimensions to the visualization of ancient Greece after 1800. D'Hancarville's vision of primitive Greek art would, nevertheless, have a very different reception history in the nineteenth century amongst a wide range of intellectuals attracted to a very different ancient Greece. He would go on to argue that the Greek god Dionysus, the Roman equivalent Bacchus and the Brahma of the Hindus were all versions of an original, prehistoric worship of the generative and reproductive force of nature.

D'Hancarville's vision of antiquity was one among a crowded arena of debates in the eighteenth and nineteenth centuries about the relationship between Greece and Egypt and the Near East, debates which Martin Bernal's trilogy *Black Athena: The Afroasiastic Roots of Classical Civilization* most recently reignited in the 1980s and 90s.³⁹ Bernal argued that the eighteenth century witnessed 'the triumph of Egypt'.⁴⁰ If Renaissance and early-modern scholars often saw timeless philosophical and scientific truths recorded in Egyptian hieroglyphs and monuments, then the eighteenth century, following the Quarrel of the Ancients and Moderns, repeatedly turned back to ancient Egypt as the historical locus for the origins of modern developments in science and philosophy. Eighteenth-century radical thinkers, freemasons and historians frequently looked back to the Egyptians as the source for the emergence of Greco-Roman civilization. Bernal contended that this fascination with Egypt transformed into a captivation by Greece at the end of the eighteenth century. Winckelmann, for Bernal, was 'the greatest champion of Greek youth and beauty in the mid-18th century', and therefore a pivotal figure in his cultural history.⁴¹ But already in the 1760s, Johann Gottfried Herder had questioned the claims made by Winckelmann in his *History* about the indigenousness of ancient Greek art: 'the chain between the peoples is clearly missing ... The link between Egyptians and

Greeks, Phoenicians and Greeks, Greeks and Parthians, Greeks and Etruscans is insufficiently sharply drawn.'[42] As we have explored in this chapter, Caylus visualized a 'diffusionist' narrative of his history of art, while d'Hancarville saw the Egyptian hieroglyph as foundational to reading ancient artistic 'texts'. Stuart, on the other hand, was eager to extricate Athenian architectural form from its Ottoman setting, whereas Le Roy saw it as an opportunity to envision his arguments about the historicity of ancient Greek architecture. Winckelmann's textual descriptions of the beautiful invisibility of Greek art emerged out of a context of debates about the relationship between the Greek, Egyptian, Etruscan and Roman forms. And yet, as we saw at the beginning of this chapter, the images which illustrate Winckelmann's *History* visualize a messier, more complicated image of the connections between ancient Greece and its neighbours. Bernal argued for a profound rupture between the Egyptomania of the eighteenth century and the philhellenism of the nineteenth. However, the eighteenth-century debates about the relationship between ancient Greece and the rest of the Mediterranean and Near East would continue through the nineteenth and twentieth centuries, as discussions about Phoenicia, Egypt and Nubia would continue to spark intense debate. Bernal's *Black Athena* was the latest chapter in a longer intellectual history.[43] By focussing on the tensions between the invisibility of Greek form in Winckelmann's text and the visibility of the complications of extricating Greece from its Mediterranean context in Winckelmann's images, we have been afforded an important perspective on eighteenth-century political debates about the form of ancient Greece. Winckelmann's textual compartmentalization of ancient artistic traditions, which sought to distinguish sharply between Egyptian, Etruscan, Greek and Roman cultures, helped to provide a rationale for the organization of university disciplines in the nineteenth century, which cordoned off the study of ancient Greece and Rome from Egyptology and Assyriology. But the eighteenth-century visualization of ancient Greece, including Winckelmann's own, told a very different story about Greece and its neighbours. The politics of the (in)visibility of Greek form in the eighteenth century would provide the frames of reference for subsequent nineteenth- and twentieth-century debates about that foundational theme in the history of classical scholarship: the relationship between Greece, Egypt and the Near East.

Notes

1. On the rhetoric of Winckelmann's descriptions of Greek sculpture, see Stafford 1980.
2. Winckelmann 2006a: 71. On Winckelmann within his Enlightenment context, see Décultot 2000.
3. On Winckelmann's influence within the university system and beyond, see Potts 1994; Marchand 1996; Sünderhauf 2004; and Harloe 2013.
4. On the Lutheran basis of modern philhellenist aesthetics, see Squire 2009; on Hegel's Orientalism, see Germana 2017a and 2017b; and on nineteenth-century German Orientalist scholarship more generally, see Marchand 2009.

5. See Zanker 1987: 70-2 and figure 50; Bol 1989-98: 1: 380-88 and plates 218-21, with further bibliography; Winckelmann 2006b: 365-6, nos. 846, 846a). On Winckelmann on this vignette, see also Osterkamp 1989.
6. Winckelmann 2006a: 239 and Winckelmann 2002: 466, 441.
7. Winckelmann 2006a: 239 and Winckelmann 2002: 466.
8. For accounts of eighteenth-century European neoclassical art, see Rosenblum 1967 and Städel Museum 2013.
9. See Winckelmann (2006a: 333-4; 323; and 351.
10. See discussion at Watkin 2006: 25.
11. On race, ethnicity, the history of classical scholarship and the *Black Athena* debate, see Orrells, Bhambra and Roynon 2011.
12. Porter 2003: 67, 65, 72.
13. On Caylus' life and work, see also Nisard 1877; Rocheblave 1889; Aghion 2002; Cronk and Peeters 2004; and Rees 2006.
14. For the Renaissance interest in Egyptian esoteric wisdom, see Walker 1972; Yates 2002 [1964]; Allen 1970 and Iversen 1993.
15. See also Griener 1998 on eighteenth-century antiquarian images of unveiling.
16. On eighteenth-century Egyptomania, see Humbert, Pantazzi and Ziegler 1994; Assmann 2014; and Graczyk 2015.
17. On the signature in Enlightenment culture, see Kamuf 1988 and on the economics of eighteenth-century art, see Craske 1997.
18. See Graczyk 2015.
19. See Potts 1994 and Potts 2006.
20. See Middleton 2004: 30-9) on the visualization of Greek architecture between the 1670s and the 1760s.
21. On Stuart, see the essays collected in Soros 2006.
22. Citations from Stuart's *Antiquities* will henceforth appear in the text.
23. Kaufman 1989: 65.
24. See Salmon 2007: 126.
25. Kelly 2009: 227, 226.
26. On Le Roy, see Middleton 2004; Armstrong 2011.
27. Citations from Le Roy's *Les Ruines* will henceforth appear in the text.
28. See Armstrong 2011 on Le Roy's philosophy of architectural time and his engagements with the picturesque.
29. Winckelmann 1952-57: 3: 38, 317, 366.
30. Winckelmann 1952-57: 2: 31; and see Haskell 1987: 32-3.
31. See Moore 2008: 148.
32. On d'Hancarville, Hamilton and their publication, see Ramage 1987; Jenkins and Sloane 1996; Lissarrague and Reed 1997; Moore 2008; Heringman 2013; and Hönes 2014.
33. On this inscription, see Orrells 2011.
34. See Braider 1999 and Marshall 1997.
35. On this publication, see Heringman 2013.

36. See also Grell 1995. On Naples in eighteenth-century antiquarianism and collecting culture, see the special issue of the *Journal of the History of Collections* 19.2 (2007) and Schnapp 2000.
37. On Hamilton's 'discovery' of Catholic phallic worship, see Rousseau 1987; Carabelli 1996; Davis 2010; Hönes 2014; and Orrells 2015.
38. See Marchand 1996; Orrells, Bhambra and Roynon 2011; and Leonard 2012.
39. See Hönes 2014; Orrells, Bhambra and Roynon 2011; and Orrells 2015.
40. Bernal 1991: 161–88.
41. Bernal 1991: 212–14.
42. Herder 1990: 2/1: 660. The translation of Herder is taken from Harloe 2013: 227.
43. See Orrells, Bhambra and Roynon 2011 on nineteenth- and twentieth-century scholarly and intellectual arguments about the importance of Egypt for writers of the black Atlantic.

CHAPTER 11
EKPHRASIS, LEO SPITZER AND THE POLITICS OF FORM[1]
Ruth Webb

This paper has a double thread. I will look at the political implications of a form of ekphrasis in the ancient world: the ekphrasis *tropou,* the account of the manner (*tropos*) in which something was done or made which crosses the formal boundary between description and narration[2] and which makes visible not just the artefact but the political power, the agency and the control of resources that enable it to come into being. The earliest surviving discussion of this category of composition is in the first-century AD *Progymnasmata* by a certain Theon who cites accounts of military stratagems and the making of weapons, including the Shield of Achilles, as examples. The ekphrasis *tropou* as defined by Theon existed before him and continued long afterwards so my examples come from a very wide range of texts from Homeric epic to the sixth century AD and describe a wide range of artefacts, from the shield made by Hephaestus to the church of Hagia Sophia in Constantinople, described in a verse ekphrasis by a court official, Paul the Silentiary.

The question of form emerges more clearly, however, in the other strand of the paper which examines the influential definition of ekphrasis as a description of a work of art (or a text on art – the ambiguity is already present) included in an article on Keats' *Ode on a Grecian Urn* by the linguist and literary historian Leo Spitzer. Form – both the form of urn and that of the poem which, according to Spitzer, echoed its circular subject – plays a central role in this interpretation and in the definition of the genre of 'ekphrasis'. And, although Spitzer distinguished his approach from that of the New Critics,[3] there are points of contact, the chief of which is the emphasis on structure and on the poem as a complex, organic whole. For Spitzer, however, the poem only reveals its meaning in the light of its place in literary history (the 'genre' of ekphrasis) and as a response to an object seen by the poet. These characteristics of Spitzerian ekphrasis can be seen in several currents of the study of ekphrasis by literary critics, historians and art historians.

I will suggest that Spitzer's construction of the genre of ekphrasis is part of the response of the German-Jewish exile scholar of Romance languages and literature to the political and cultural challenges of the Second World War. More generally, we can see underlying Spitzer's use of the idea of 'ekphrasis' a set of conceptions of subjectivity, objectivity, agency and perception that seemed natural in the mid-twentieth-century but which have come to be questioned in more recent scholarship (just as the idea of Keats as an apolitical aesthete has been challenged).[4] Moreover, the conceptions of subject and object, of the role of discourse and its relation to its subject that characterise Spitzer's ekphrasis are distinct from those underlying the ancient conception of ekphrasis as a means of creating a quasi-visual effect on the reader or listener.

As a rhetorical technique, ancient ekphrasis was itself bound up with the political, even more than with the aesthetic. Its defining function 'to place before the eyes' was aimed primarily at persuasion and implies a relationship of power between the orator and the audience whom he induces to 'see', penetrating their minds.[5] Although this effect was widespread in archaic and classical poetry it was in the context of rhetoric and rhetorical training that it was theorized using terms like *enargeia* (the quality of vividness) or ekphrasis (a passage of poetry or prose that had the power to 'bring before the eyes'). As a skill acquired in the rhetorical schools, ekphrasis was an integral part of the acculturation of the elite as they learned to exercise their voices and their authority and to distinguish the sayable from the unsayable.[6] But rhetorical discourse is not unidirectional:[7] to be effective, the orator needed to appeal to images and associations that were shared by the community, or risk failure. Moreover, in a rhetorical context the listener could, or was expected to, resist: for every evocation of a crime or other phenomenon presented by one speaker, the audience could expect to hear an opposing version from the opposition and to elaborate their own alternative readings.[8] Rhetorical ekphrasis then, was part of an argument. In most cases, this argument took place within a shared culture, defined by a common 'distribution of the sensible', but, in some cases, the practice of ekphrasis could work explicitly or implicitly to make perceptible the unspoken. If ancient ekphrasis is rooted in the various political regimes within which it was practised, the same might not seem to be the case of Spitzerian ekphrasis with its enclosed aesthetic world. However, like New Criticism itself, Spitzer's proposed definition of ekphrasis was profoundly political.[9]

Leo Spitzer's ekphrasis

Spitzer's 1955 article on Keats' *Ode on a Grecian Urn*[10] crystallized the definition of ekphrasis that has come to dominate the study of ancient and modern literature. In fact, it would be more accurate to refer to the family of definitions of ekphrasis, given that the types of referent may vary as does the relationship of the text to the referent which it describes, comments on or rivals.[11] Spitzer identifies ekphrasis as 'the genre, known to Occidental literature from Homer and Theocritus to the Parnassians and Rilke of ... the poetic description of a pictorial or sculptural work of art'.[12] Several aspects of this short definition are recognizable from subsequent studies of ekphrasis in twentieth-century literary criticism: the use of the term 'genre' with its connotations of fixity of form and function,[13] the emphasis on figural representation ('pictorial or sculptural') and on the 'work of art' as a subject.

Not surprisingly, Spitzer's definition is an almost perfect fit for Keats' poem. Although it does not exactly describe the urn, the Ode alludes to various aspects of the artefact through its account of the poet/narrator's response first to the figures engaged in scenes of revelry and sacrifice and then to the shape and matter of the urn in the fifth and final stanza. From this, it is possible for the reader to deduce that the urn of the title, the 'still unravish'd bride of quietness' of the first line, is a marble object decorated with the representations of men or gods, and of erotic pursuit in suspended animation that pose such problems of identification to the poet at the beginning of the poem (l.8: 'What men or gods are these …?'). Spitzer organises his reading around the two poles represented by the object and its decoration, noting that the moment of recognition and unity comes at the beginning of the fifth stanza when the poet's attention is drawn away from the figures and towards the form of the urn (l.41 'O Attic shape!') after all the interpretative difficulties raised by its iconography. In his reading, the poem thus echoes the shape of the urn in its circularity, opening with an address to the silent artefact and closing with an evocation of the form as a whole and with the urn's proclamation of the unchanging value of the aesthetic in the much-debated formulation, 'beauty is truth, truth beauty'.[14]

Although Spitzer presents his definition of ekphrasis as a timeless given, it is historically contingent and anything but self-evident. In placing Keats' poem into a long lineage of representatives of 'Occidental literature' that runs from Homer (treated as a person rather than as a collective tradition) to the Alexandrian poet Theocritus, nineteenth-century French literature and early twentieth-century German poetry, Spitzer was engaging in a creative act of his own and shaping a European tradition of a very particular kind. Although he does not attempt a full survey of his 'genre' of ekphrasis, elsewhere in the article he fleshes out this tradition by mentioning in passing examples of poetry on art by various representatives of Western literature: Goethe, Mörike, Schiller, Greek epigram, Neo-Latin and the French renaissance poets of the Pléiade. It is worth looking in more detail at the rhetorical manoeuvres in this article and at the context within which it was written.

In the immediate context of his article, Spitzer's delineation of ekphrasis as genre allows him to read Keats' poem as an account of the poet's response to the object as he moves from his initial aporia in the face of the ambiguous scenes, through an appreciation of the silent music of the urn ('Heard melodies are sweet, but those unheard/Are sweeter', stanza 2) and through the renewed questions raised by the scene of sacrifice in the fourth stanza to the final 'revelation of the aesthetic message of the urn' that 'beauty is truth, truth beauty'.[15] But the invocation of 'ekphrasis' also has a polemical function. Spitzer's article takes the form of a lengthy and occasionally bitter refutation of the interpretation of Keats' *Ode* proposed by Earl Wasserman, Spitzer's colleague at Johns Hopkins University, in his 1953 book, *The Finer Tone*[16] and contains several statements of Spitzer's own method, held up as a better alternative to Wasserman's.[17] Where Wasserman appeals to the wider context of Keats' writings (a practice that distinguished his approach sharply from the contemporary exponents of New Criticism), Spitzer places the *Ode* in the diachronic lineage of 'ekphrasis'. Where Wasserman proposes a metaphysical interpretation in which the claim that 'truth is beauty' is only true beyond the earth, 'at Heaven's bourne'[18], Spitzer interprets the poem as a response to an art object and thus as a claim for the accessibility of truth and beauty on earth through aesthetic experience. Placing the poem within a tradition of writing about objects and seeing it as the expression of the poet's experience of viewing thus plays an essential role in establishing his claim.

Spitzer's reading follows the unfolding of the text, with the result that his own article adopts the form of the poem, culminating in the final aesthetic message of the urn. This emphasis on the aesthetic and on the closed circuits formed by the poem itself and the scenario of the poet's response to the object tends to conceal the politics of both the *Ode* and of Spitzer's reading. And yet, at the very start of the article (p. 68), Spitzer positions Wasserman's work squarely within the cultural and academic politics of his day, praising it for its attempts to 'bridge the gap' between New Criticism, with its exclusive focus on the poem, and scholarship (meaning appeals to the biography of the author and to contemporary writings of the poet and others). Spitzer's definition of ekphrasis and the use he makes of it in the interpretation of the *Ode* play an important role in his self-presentation as a scholar. Most importantly, it is an integral part of what he presents to the reader as his distinctive approach (distinct, that is, from that of his immediate adversary, from the New Critics and from biographical readings). Spitzer identifies this as the practice of 'French *explication de texte*', a claim that carefully positions him, and his account both of Keats' *Ode* and of the Occidental tradition he placed it in, in relation to his American colleagues.[19]

Spitzer, ekphrasis and the *Ode on a Grecian Urn*

One of Spitzer's first criticisms of Wasserman is that he failed to recognize the *Ode* as an example of 'ekphrasis'.[20] The definition is often quoted out of context, as I have done above, in a form that makes it sound like an authoritative dictionary entry. However, the words immediately before and after it make clear that, far from being a detached statement of literary historical fact, it is as polemical as the rest of the article:

> Instead of beginning as Mr Wasserman does (with a symbolic interpretation of the poem's opening line), I would first ask myself, in the down-to-earth factual 'French' manner: What is this poem about, in the simplest, most obvious terms? It is first of all a description of an urn – that is, it belongs to the genre known to Occidental literature. . . .

This is the 'Content' of Spitzer's title ('Content vs Metagrammar') to be identified by the 'simple' question, 'What is the poem about?' Spitzer, the Austrian scholar of Romance languages, exiled from Germany to Istanbul in 1933 and from there to the US three years later,[21] displays his own allegiance to the European tradition through his application of the French exercise of *explication de texte*, the detailed commentary on a passage of poetry or prose that is still the mainstay of literary training in secondary and tertiary education in France. In this highly codified exercise, the identification of the genre and historical context of the text is an essential starting point,[22] as it is in Spitzer's treatment of Keats' *Ode*. The form of the *explication* is evident too in the attention to structure and the development of the thought and in the use of a commentary that demonstrates the intertwining of form and meaning on the micro-level of figures of speech and on the macro-level of the structure of the whole passage or poem.

As an exercise in close-reading, the *explication de texte* assumes a set of canonical literary texts to which it can be applied and whose qualities can be made visible through the act of commentary.²³ It is a practice with a history, developed in the mid-nineteenth century with the aim of opening up access to education for contemporary students, including women. Despite these democratizing intentions, the *explication* was heavily influenced (and remains so) by methods of interpretation developed for ancient and religious texts and this background is often evident in the praise meted out to the author and in the search for the message conveyed by the text. The latter trait is particularly noticeable in Spitzer's analysis of the *Ode*. As he writes in his methodological introduction, his aim as critic, one that distinguished him from the New Critics, is to identify the 'particular message Keats wishes us to see embodied in the urn'. Further on in the article, commenting on the final lines 'Beauty is truth, truth beauty, – that is all Ye know on earth, and all ye need to know' he describes Keats, in quasi-religious terms, as a poet 'ordained in the Platonic faith [who] could very well have postulated the absolute sufficiency "on earth" of his aesthetic religion'. Spitzer's approach is thus both idiosyncratic – particularly in the American context he was working in – and historically and culturally contingent.²⁴

Keats' *Ode* as model ekphrasis

A full assessment of Spitzer's reading of Keats' *Ode* is beyond the scope of this chapter and of my own competence but there are three aspects of his presentation of ekphrasis that have particular resonance within the wider tradition of analysis of descriptions of works of art (whether or not these are grouped together into a single 'genre') and are relevant to the politics of Spitzer's criticism. One is the status of the work of art in relation to the words of the poem and to the speaker, the other relates to the question of form that is central to this volume, and the third is the 'Occidental' genealogy that he posits for his version of ekphrasis.

To start with the status of the work of art, the definition quoted above (p. 000) continues as follows: 'the ekphrasis, the poetic description of a pictorial or sculptural work of art, which description implies, in the words of Théophile Gautier, "une transposition d'art," the reproduction, through the medium of words, of sensuously perceptible objets d'art ("ut pictura poesis")'. There is a great deal concentrated into this 'simple' statement, which repeats the connection of ekphrasis to the 'Art for Art's sake' philosophy of Gautier and the Parnassians while also invoking Horace's parallel between poetry and the visual arts.²⁵ In doing so, Spitzer juxtaposes not just different languages and traditions but also different aspects of the question: intermediality ('transposition d'art'), the supposed similarities between poetic and pictorial representation ('ut pictura poiesis') and the possibility that words might offer access to a material object ('reproduction').²⁶ The emphasis placed on this idea of *re*production is important, as is the presentation of the work of art within this ekphrastic complex: its status as *object* is stressed, as is its availability to the senses. Spitzer's ekphrasis is thus conceived as a poetic

241

response to an object existing before and outside the poem in which the word serves to release or make explicit the meaning that is locked up within the silent object ('the unravish'd bride of quietness' of the *Ode*'s first line).

At several points in his analysis, Spitzer speaks as if Keats' words are to be read as a key to his inner state and, more precisely, to his reaction as he contemplates the urn. Having established the text's genre and orientation, Spitzer begins his analysis by asking 'What exactly has Keats seen (or chosen to show us) depicted on the urn he is describing?' explaining 'The answer to this question will furnish us with a firm contour, not only of the object of his description but of this description itself, which may later allow us to distinguish the symbolic or metaphysical inferences drawn by the poet from the visual elements he has apperceived.'[27] Spitzer's interest is clearly in the second element, the 'inferences drawn by the poet', but he makes the identification of these by the critic dependent on an understanding of the object encountered by the poet. In confidently distinguishing what Keats has 'seen' on the vase from what he adduces (the detail of the town that the poet imagines deserted by its inhabitants in the fourth stanza as they gather for their mysterious sacrifice[28]) or is unable to identify ('what men or gods are these?' l. 8) Spitzer certainly speaks as if the *Ode* were a response to a real object, an actual visual and sensual experience, while leaving open the question of whether this viewer is to be thought of as the historical Keats or a persona adopted by the poet.[29] This treatment of the poem as a response to the perception of an object is, in fact, central to Spitzer's assessment of Keats' contribution to the evolution of the 'genre' of ekphrasis:[30] 'The ekphrasis, the description of an objet d'art by the medium of the word, has here developed into an account of an exemplary experience felt by the poet confronted with an ancient work of art, an experience shown in the development of the poem as Keats's purely aesthetic aspirations come to free themselves from all non-essential admixtures'.[31] Within the context of Spitzer's wider method, this search for the poet's response corresponds to his search for the individual psyche exemplified in the style and for the creative principle present in the poet's soul.[32] His linear reading of this particular poem traces the poet's changing perception and response from *aporia* to revelation, from distance in relation to the classical past whose images defy identification to proximity, in precisely the type of sequence that the *explication de texte* encourages.

Spitzer's ekphrasis, shaped by his reading of Keats' *Ode*, is devoted by definition to the object ('objet d'art'). As instantiated in Keats' *Ode*, this object is still, unchanging, enclosed within its self-sufficient world, offering itself to the poet's vision. Even if the poet finds the imagery impossible to identify with any certainty, his role remains that of subject engaged in an act of aesthetic consumption and the critic's energy in turn is devoted to following the trajectory of that subject's personal experience. It is certainly true that, in Spitzer's reading, the urn speaks the last two lines of the poem ('Beauty is truth, truth beauty, – that is all/Ye know on earth, and all ye need to know') as well as being spoken to ('thou still unravish'd bride of quietness'). However, it/she speaks through the words of the poet who is ultimately responsible for her lines.[33]

Form

The second essential aspect of Spitzer's reading is his emphasis on form: that of the urn as reflected in Keats' *Ode*. In the trajectory he traces for the poet-as-viewer in communion with the object, the realization of 'the absolute self-sufficiency of the aesthetic message' comes as the poet directs his attention from the 'non-essential admixture' of the iconography to the enduring message encoded in its form.[34] For Spitzer, it is the *form* of the vase and of the postures adopted by the figures expressed in line 41 ('O Attic Shape! Fair attitude!') with its play on the similarity in sound between 'Attic' and 'attitude' that saves the poet from the *aporia* into which his attempt to understand the scenes has led him.[35] Spitzer has already established that the urn is circular, in accordance with the tradition of what he terms 'poetic *ekphrasis*' and that ekphrastic texts tend to imitate the form of their subjects: 'Since already in antiquity the poetic *ekphrasis* was often devoted to circular objects (shields, cups, etc.), it was tempting for poets to imitate verbally this constructive principle in their ekphraseis.'[36] This principle of circularity must lie behind the genealogy proposed in his definition of ekphrasis (the Homeric Shield, Theocritus and his cup).[37] This was not the first time that Spitzer had focussed on circularity and its implications: his 1940 article 'Le style circulaire' identified a principle of circularity in European literature from ancient Greek (Heraclitus) to the Gospel of John, medieval Latin literature and the thought of Hegel, arguing that this circular form, particularly ring composition, was seen as a literary embodiment of mystical thought characterised by a circular journey from soul to body and back to soul. Here, form is held to be consubstantial with thought.

The emphasis on form here echoes that of one of the leading exponents of New Criticism, Cleanth Brooks, in his essay 'Keats' Sylvan Historian or History without Footnotes' who refers to 'the urn itself as a formed thing, as an autonomous world'.[38] Taken in one direction, which Spitzer himself would not have followed, this conception of ekphrasis as by definition an enclosed aesthetic space is developed by Murray Krieger in his first essay on the *Ode* where the circularity of referent and poem is essential to the argument that the poem's 'formal and linguistic self-sufficiency' can allow it to constitute its own poetic. Quoting Spitzer, Krieger makes use of the appeals to the circularity of the referents in order to claim that 'the spatial metaphor about the shape of the poem ... is in a sense literal ... the poem seeks to attain the 'shape' of the urn' (268–9). Thus conceived, ekphrasis becomes 'a general principle of poetics asserted by every poem in the assertion of its integrity'.[39] As Heffernan points out, in the hands of the early Krieger ekphrasis 'merely becomes a new name for formalism'.[40]

Spitzer's ekphrasis, as embodied in Keats' *Ode*, is placed firmly within the realm of the aesthetic. Unlike Brooks he does not cut the poem off from its cultural context, in the shape of its literary tradition (the Occidental genre of ekphrasis) and the general familiarity with ancient texts, objects and ideas that he attributes to the poet and his ideal readers. But he does keep it far removed both from the political and from the material. To the unchanging nature of the urn, as embodied in its form, corresponds the unchanging nature of ekphrasis. The closed circuit created by the form of the poem modelled on the form of the urn – the circularity that is central to Spitzer's conception of ekphrasis, as we have seen – is doubled by the closed circuit of communication between poet and object expressed in the poem. To consider form in its metaphorical sense, the *Ode*, appropriately uses Greek forms (ekphrasis and then the conventions of epigram in the speaking monument at the end) to express a message that transcends cultures, languages and times: the final declaration made by the urn, through the poet, that the identity of truth and beauty (the truth and beauty of the urn's form which makes redundant any historical, archaeological, interpretation of the iconography) 'is all Ye need to know'. This is the authoritative, quasi-religious message that the exercise of *explication de texte* seeks and (inevitably) finds.

And yet, this closed world of aesthetic appreciation, the timeless communion between ancient vase, Romantic poet and twentieth-century critic, is predicated upon a particular regime of the visual and a particular understanding of the relationship between subject and object which can hardly be divorced from the political. Spitzer's reading makes visible the male subject and his evolving consciousness as he contemplates an object, passively displayed to the senses, resulting in 'an exemplary experience felt by the poet confronted with an ancient work of art').[41] This reading of the poem is predicated on an understanding of description as a verbal 'reproduction' of an object, to paraphrase Spitzer's definition of ekphrasis, which Keats, in Spitzer's view, surpasses by giving an account not of the appearance of the object but of his experience of it. In Spitzer's view of both the classic ekphrasis as descriptive 'reproduction' and the Keatsian romantic, expressive development of this, the object remains inert, complete in itself, utterly distinct from the writer/viewer whose subjective experience, presented as 'exemplary', forms the content of the poem. And, rather than propose an open reading in which the poet's *aporia* about the figural decoration remains unresolved, Spitzer's reading offers a transcendent message that takes precedence, closing the circle.

The political implications of this approach to viewing and to speaking about viewing are left implicit in Spitzer's essays. But they are highly visible in the gendered conception of ekphrasis proposed by W. J. T. Mitchell 1992 (and developed by James Heffernan 1993, among others) in which the viewing poet with his control of language is 'male' and the viewed art object 'female'.[42] This gendered ekphrasis is predicated upon a series of conflicts and rivalries, between word and image, between male and female.[43] If this gendered interpretation of ekphrasis works in some cases, like Keats' *Ode* with its bride-like urn, its development into a principle is unavoidably based on a drastic selection of examples, on some questionable dichotomies, and on some stretched interpretations.[44] The status conferred on Keats' *Ode* by Spitzer as a canonical example of ekphrasis has surely played a major role in this conception of word/image relations.

Spitzer's article avoids the openly political (in common with the New Critical approaches) but (also in common with New Criticism) is highly political in the way it defines the critic's task – his foray into the cultural and academic politics of mid-twentieth-century North America was been noted above. If 'close reading is a practice of cultivation – or enculturation',[45] Spitzer was advocating the cultivation of a subject immersed in the European literary, linguistic and philosophical tradition, keenly aware of its Greco-Latin heritage and able to navigate freely around and across that domain, as if through a museum. Moreover, Spitzer's critical practice, as instantiated in his reading of Keats, is founded on a divide between subject and object and the resulting ability of the subject to tease the 'message' out of the object.

The idiosyncrasies of the cultural context that Spitzer creates for Keats the aesthete, steeped in (Neo-)Platonic ideals, are brought into sharp focus by more recent interpretations of the Ode that stress the poet's relatively humble social background and his place in the political and cultural debates of early nineteenth-century Britain. Kelley 1995, for example, has argued for Keats' engagement with the idealist vision of Greek art put forward by contemporaries like Haydon, against the background of the controversial display of the Elgin marbles. Bewell 1986 sees in Keats' *Endymion* a questioning of the very possibility of understanding the past, undertaken against the background of the Napoleonic exploration of Egyptian antiquities. It has also been suggested that the choice of a 'Grecian urn' as a subject can be seen as a way for the 'cockney poet' Keats to claim access to high culture and stake his place in the hierarchy.[46] Keats' education did not include Greek and he was dependent on secondary sources and on translations for access to Greek culture and Greek authors, as his excitement at discovering Chapman's Homer suggests.[47]

Spitzer's reading of the *Ode* bypasses the entanglement of the *poem* with questions of class, cultural capital and imperial power and he does so precisely by presenting Keats' undertaking as a self-evident gesture within this European tradition, an instance among others of a quasi-personified 'genre' that arches across the centuries to unite the Occidental, binding Keats and Rilke to Homer.[48] Significantly for a scholar of literary history like Spitzer, there is no examination of how or why Keats might have known this 'genre'.[49] The only acknowledgement of this question comes in relation to the tradition of speaking monuments in Greek epigram: citing Friedländer's study of the subject, Spitzer pulls back from a statement of influence by claiming that Keats did not need first-hand knowledge of ancient sepulchral epigrams to write his *Ode* but was 'immersed in that particular atmosphere that any museum of classic art creates'.[50] Spitzer's creative work of invention, and his tendency towards mystification, in this article are at their clearest here.

Spitzer, ekphrasis and 'Occidental literature'

Spitzer's vision of ekphrasis is based on a conception of Western literature as a unified development from ancient Greece and Rome via the Renaissance to the Western European vernaculars, including English, thanks to Keats. There is no mention of postclassical or medieval Greece, a strange absence at first sight for a scholar who had spent three years in what was once Constantinople, where the Byzantine monuments could hardly escape notice.[51] This omission, however, reflects the cultural politics of the Spitzer's period in Istanbul: Turkey in the 1930s had just seen the population exchange with Greece that followed the Greco-Turkish War of the early 1920s but the Turkish government promoted Ancient Greece in its cultural and educational policies, a paradoxical situation underlined by Kader Konuk.[52] Spitzer's period of exile in Istanbul also coincided with the 1935 Paris Congress for the Defence of Culture, which put forward the study of 'World literature' as an antidote to fascism.[53] Spitzer's own work remained firmly focused on the European and classical traditions,[54] but he saw in them instances of a global human spirit.[55] His vision of ekphrasis as an Occidental tradition springing from the very beginnings of Greek literature to encompass German, French and English poetry is therefore deeply anchored in geo- and cultural politics. The act of bringing together texts from Homer onwards in Greek, Latin, French, Italian, Spanish, English and German under the umbrella of a single 'genre' is surely part of that project.[56] His vision of Keats' struggle with the indecipherability of the urn only to arrive at a transcendent comprehension of a uniting message about truth and beauty may well spring from the same concerns.

The content of Spitzer's genre of ekphrasis may be as relevant to the mid-twentieth-century context as its form. In highlighting a variety of approaches to the visual arts in texts, he made this unifying Western tradition into a cultural phenomenon, not one confined to the domain of literature, although this is not made explicit. It is tempting to see the intermedial, boundary-crossing, nature of this ekphrasis as bearing especial resonance for the émigré scholar. As Grant Scott points out in relation to Keats' interest in the visual arts, Lessing had attempted to establish firm frontiers ('Grenzen') between literature and the visual arts.[57] Spitzer's Occidental tradition of ekphrasis triumphantly, and creatively, breaks through these boundaries to make a pluralist whole.

So, Spitzer's apparently authoritative statement of literary historical fact, as timeless as the message – in his reading – of Keats' urn, is highly contingent. Assembled for the immediate purpose of his disagreement with Wasserman, used in order to place Keats in a classical and European tradition that he surpasses, it served a particular and vitally important purpose at a particular moment in the history of criticism (the debate between 'Critics' and 'Literary Historians' and Spitzer's attempt to find a third way) and in twentieth-century culture. It belongs to its time and place also in several of its unspoken assumptions: about the subject/object divide, about the inert nature of matter – and thus of objects like Keats' urn. I will now explore these issues further in relation to some ancient examples of what was categorised as ekphrasis *tropou*, the ekphrasis of the manner in which something was made.

Ancient rhetorical ekphrasis and the power of the word

Spitzer's conception of ekphrasis was implicitly formal: the account of the circular object in a mimetically circular poem. In contrast, the ekphrasis discussed as a category by ancient rhetoricians is markedly formless, characterised by its variety in genre, subject matter, length and encompassing both freestanding works and fragments of larger prose and poetic compositions. Nor is ekphrasis confined to static entities like Grecian urns: objects (art objects or otherwise) hardly feature in the discussions and where they do it is often in the context of the ekphrasis *tropou*, the account of the making of the thing.[58] So, in contrast to the conception of the object as static, eternal and self-contained that underlies ekphrasis as defined by Spitzer, most artefacts in the ancient ekphrastic tradition have their own vitality. They are constantly coming into being in a process of collaboration with their human makers – here the New Materialism of Jane Bennett is enlightening in the absolute and in helping to reveal the political ramifications of this conception of things in which the human subject is not sharply distinguished from inert matter and in which form is not something imposed on matter from without.[59] Bennett's approach, however, has its limitations for the texts and situations that I will consider briefly below in that the human maker is almost entirely absent from her theory so it is her evocation of the maker's co-creation of the artefact with the material that is the most suggestive here.[60] Arguably, the ekphrasis *tropou* that aims to 'bring before the eyes' the ephemeral sequence of actions and gestures that gave rise to an artefact (or that are significant in themselves as actions, giving rise to nothing) is the most obviously political of all types of ancient ekphrasis. Recounting the origins of a thing necessarily involves attributing power and agency as well as the control of resources and knowledge to certain individuals or groups. It often involves, as we shall see, acknowledging the limits of human agency in the face of matter.

There is not space to consider the whole range of the *ekphrasis tropou* so I will confine myself to some general comments. The *ekphrasis tropou* can recount an action but the type that I will focus on here involves the creation of a physical entity. Theon in his definition refers to the construction of siege machines, the Shield of Achilles and fortifications as well as a military stratagem.[61] Courtney Roby (2016) has analysed its use in scientific texts, and in Late Antique and Byzantine rhetoric, accounts of construction are frequently found within encomiastic ekphraseis of churches.

In contrast to the Shield of Achilles, these other things (beds, walls, churches, machines) have human makers working in contexts where access to power, skill and resources is not unlimited, ensuring that they are tied into the political structures of their settings. This applies to the Homeric examples of entities with human makers, such as the construction of Achilles' encampment by his men in *Iliad* 24, 448–56, of Eumaeus' pigpens in *Odyssey* 14, 5–14, and of Odysseus' own constructions: the raft (*Odyssey*, 5, 228–61) and the olive-tree bed (*Odyssey*, 23, 183–204).[62] In each case the distribution of the conception and the labour is specified, as are the materials and, most importantly perhaps, their origin. Achilles' men, like Odysseus' swineherd Eumaeus, work for their respective rulers, Eumaeus spontaneously (*autos*) in his master's absence, the Myrmidons as a collective embodiment of Achilles' authority. In stating the material used in each case (stones, pine trees and reeds for Achilles' camp, stones and shaped oak-wood on Ithaka) the ekphrasis makes clear the relationship of each construction to its setting: the Myrmidons use materials gathered from the Trojan landscape around them (and, though this is not explicitly stated, establish their domination of that landscape) while Eumaeus uses wood and stone from Odysseus' domain. The difference in the use of the wood is also significant: Eumaeus shapes the Ithacan oak into defensive stakes while the Myrmidons use soft pine trunks in their raw form.

In the case of Odysseus' own constructions, the building of the olive-tree bed in the centre of his palace is essential to his identity and the telling of it serves to prove this identity to Penelope.[63] He uses a living tree within his own territory, in stark contrast to the improvised raft he builds using Calypso's trees and Calypso's tools that disintegrates at the first storm. These examples also point to the role of the material out of which these things are made and which is far from inert. In the case of Odysseus' bed, it is the olive tree that causes him to build it where he does, exerting its own agency. In the case of the raft, the assembled trees break apart, returning to their prior state as separate pieces of wood. The example of the Achaean wall, constructed in book 7 of the *Iliad* only to be washed away after the end of the war, as announced by the poet in Book 12, hints at the similar fate of Achilles' improvised quarters. Bennett's New Materialism helps to bring out the vitality of the materials in all these cases, the impermanence and flux of the raft and the Achaean constructions is in marked contrast to Spitzer's reading of Keats' urn as a closed form bearing an everlasting aesthetic message whose maker is never alluded to.[64]

The presentation of all these ekphraseis in a narrative form underlines these energies and this work. There are still important differences in the presentation. In the case of Odysseus' projects, the making is recounted step by step using the aorist and imperfect either by the poet as part of the narration of Odysseus' actions that begins in Book 5 of the *Odyssey*, or by Odysseus himself when he tells or reminds Penelope how he built the bed in order to prove his identity and to regain his status within his palace. These narratives of making not only focus on the individual maker but allow access to the thoughts and intentions that lay behind the gestures. The contrast with the acts of collective making by anonymous soldiers is striking: the work of Achilles' men and of Odysseus' swineherd is told in retrospect as a prior action that explains the appearance of the building as it is encountered by a hero: Priam or Odysseus. The status of the craftsman is thus encoded within the form of the telling.

It would be possible to trace these questions through accounts of building of fortifications in classical historiography, as Theon invites us to in his *Progymnasmata* where he cites the construction of the fortifications around Plataea as one of his examples of the *ekphrasis tropou*. Here too, the material plays a vital role, almost as an agent in its own right and, by the nature of things, the construction process is agonistic, part of the struggle between besiegers and besieged. The manner (*tropos*) in which the work is said to be carried out is also significant as the contrast between the Athenian work at Nisaia (4.69.2) and the Peloponnesian work at Plataea, shows. While the Athenians are said to work briskly and collectively,[65] Thucydides' narrative stresses the organization of the Peloponnesians at Plataea, divided into groups who alternately work, eat and rest so that the work goes on constantly, under the compulsion (*anagkazō*) of the commanders (2.75.3). The account of the Peloponnesians siege works and the Plataeans' countermeasures (building up their own walls, undermining the enemies' ramps) means that material is vital in both senses of the word. The work is done in interaction with the physical environment (the trees from Cithaeron cut down by the Peloponnesians, the bricks from houses close to the city wall used by the Plataeans) and the process involves the transfer of material from one side to the other. This account of the beginning of the siege is remarkable for its depiction of vital matter in action and of a form in constant flux. Despite the circular forms of the walls and siege works there is little closure here, apparent or otherwise, and so the passage has not tended to draw attention. It illustrates the impossibility of drawing a firm demarcation line (another form of boundary that is policed very firmly by some twentieth-century critics)[66] between ekphrasis and narration and is particularly interesting for its depiction not only of organized human action in a military setting but also of human interaction with matter.

My final example comes from the other end of antiquity, the sixth century AD. While Thucydides' passage and the Homeric shield were retrospectively classified as ekphrasis by a rhetorician of the Roman period, this example was composed within the tradition of ancient ekphrasis. This is the ekphrasis of the great church of Hagia Sophia composed and performed by Paul the Silentiary after its reconstruction by the Emperor Justinian following the earthquake of 557 and further damage to the original dome during restoration in the following year. This thousand-line poem in a mixture of iambic and hexameter verses, in Attic and Homeric dialects, also played a central role in the constitution of the modern genre of ekphrasis thanks to the comprehensive survey of Ancient texts on art and architecture that prefaced Paul Friedländer's edition and which became a standard reference on 'ekphrasis' in the sense of description of a work of art.[67] As noted above, the absence of this Late Antique ekphrasis (in both the ancient and modern senses) from Spitzer's survey is significant, given his knowledge both of Friedländer's work and of the monuments of Constantinople: the Orthodox East had no place in his carefully constructed Western tradition of ekphrasis.

The ekphrasis of Hagia Sophia is an ekphrasis of a work of art, in contrast to the utilitarian things described by Homer's Odysseus or by Thucydides, and many individual passages do evoke the light, the surfaces, the volumes, the pillars and coloured marbles.[68] To focus entirely on these parts of the poem, however, is to miss its political aspects (in the most basic sense of the term). These are evoked most explicitly in the iambic introduction in which a personified Roma (i.e. Constantinople, the New Rome) begs Justinian to repair the damage done by the earthquake.[69] But they are evident throughout, particularly in the references to the process of construction, the decisions that were made (a feature that Paul's poem shares in common with other accounts of Hagia Sophia like the one in Prokopios' *Buildings*) and the ways in which these were put into practice. Reading Paul's poem in the light of its introduction and in the light of the tradition of ekphraseis of the ways in which things were made brings out some problems and contradictions that are masked when we consider it as just another example of an ekphrasis of an art object.

In particular, the emphasis on the materials (marble, stone, gold) and the forms (the play of concave shapes – apses domes and semi-domes that rise and dance) presents several potential problems for the poet who wishes to portray Justinian as the creator. The prior collapses had shown that this matter stubbornly refused to take on a permanent form. Moreover, its reshaping into Justinian's new church demanded hard physical work – the type of action that is made explicit in the case of the bed of Odysseus, the heroic craftsman, or Thucydides' warring forces. To attribute the agency to the Emperor alone – as Paul does l. 512 in admiring the *mētis*, the cunning intelligence, that allowed him to find the architectural solution – means obliterating the role of the architects and of the craftsmen who shaped the stones, piled them up one on top of another and then provided them with their intricate decoration. Their omission is not surprising in the context of the official presentation of an imperial construction project, but such presentations always involves a fiction and a masking of aspects of society, action and matter that do not fit the dominant narrative.

Paul, in fact, does make more mention of designers and craftsmen than other authors of encomiastic ekphraseis of buildings. In one or two places they are referred to as 'wise' (*sophoi* l. 359) and 'knowledgeable' (*daēmones* l. 362) men, a move that is made possible by the use of epic verse: the borrowed archaic dialect heroizes all the human participants, transforming stonemasons and mosaicists into 'men of knowledge'. Paul's choice of Homeric dialect for what would could have been a prose performance[70] is thus more than a matter of aesthetics and more than an opportunity to display his own talent through a verbal equivalent to the technical virtuosity that created the church. Instead this choice may be a response to the inherent problems of describing a material thing known to the audience who could see and feel for themselves the traces of past actions in every stone.

One strategy used by Paul is to attribute agency not only to the Emperor but above all to the church building which is frequently personified. The Church is not only assimilated to a human body with a head and arms but is made the subject of active verbs as it is said to 'receive' the human visitor (l. 426) who is thus portrayed as anything but a distanced and empowered observer.[71] Indeed, the role constructed for the listeners on their imaginary *periegesis* of the building is not that of a unified, disembodied spectator-interpreter. Instead, the discontinuities in the virtual tour that jumps from one part of the building to another, underlined by the narrator's own expression of disorientation at lines 444–5, helps to construct a discontinuous, multifocal model of perception that serves to minimize the individual role of the viewer and to attribute agency to the building itself. Here too, the use of epic language helps to normalize this strategy of personification which is an essential part of Paul's presentation. For, like any author of epideictic, Paul was countering alternative narratives. As Peter Bell points out in his commentary, the poet-orator omits or 'spins' various events that were to Justinian's disadvantage, as his sixth-century audience would have been well aware.[72] The same audience surely knew that, for the Emperor's will to be done, a mass of workers had laboured on masses of stone and other materials, in noise and dust. This is the alternative, contradictory ekphrasis, that is implicit in Paul's text by virtue of its rhetorical nature. It seems unlikely in the context of sixth-century Constantinople that an unauthorized speaker might use the tools of rhetoric to provide a different account of the construction.[73] But the dialectical nature of ancient rhetoric meant that any encomiastic account contained in germ the possibility of its own refutation.[74] The element of the ekphrasis *tropou* in his account invites this response, as does the opening account of the catastrophic earthquake that caused the collapse of the original dome, reducing the astonishing architectural form to rubble and showing the potential power of matter and its movements over an emperor's will. It is not necessary to suggest that Paul the Silentiary was being as subversive in his verse ekphrasis as Prokopios of Caesarea dared to be in his vituperation of Justinian and Theodora in his *Secret History*. Instead it is the very form of the ekphrasis *tropou* that contains its own contradiction and the possibility of alternative narratives of the building's coming to be.[75] Its nature as an account of process also leaves open the possibility of future transmutations, of the future catastrophes and collapses that did occur over the succeeding centuries, repeating the one recounted in the introduction.

Conclusion

The ekphrasis *tropou* is just one form of ancient ekphrasis and the examples I have briefly analysed represent one type in that they recount the making of physical entities.[76] Other ekphraseis make visible to the mind's eye pure processes or behaviours, like the scandalous actions attributed to the young Timarchus by Aeschines in his accusation.[77] Each one of my examples performs a different function within its context and demands different responses from its audience but all have in common the fact that they display each thing's entanglement with its context (whether this context is fictional, historical or present to author and audience) and the sources of power. This dynamic interaction is echoed on the level of reception by the impact that the ekphrasis was understood to have on its listener. These ekphraseis also stage interactions between matter and form and between human makers or users and things that are complex and multidirectional: matter can dictate form as in the cases of Odysseus' bed or the fortifications at Plataea, or it can refuse to retain its form; the resulting entity can exert a power over its human users, as does the church of Hagia Sophia in Paul the Silentiary's telling. In the end, it is these multiple dynamics that are 'placed before the eyes', as much as, or even more than, the resultant 'object' itself.

This is perhaps the main point of contact with Keats' *Ode* which, as Spitzer points out, depicts a process, but one of a different type: the poet-viewer's struggle to understand the ancient scenes on the urn and his turn away from identification to contemplation of the object's form. For Spitzer, this focus on the poet's experience marks the *Ode* out from the tradition of ekphrasis that he identifies in Western literature, a tradition that is thus both unified and in constant evolution. In contrast to more recent readings of Keats in general and of the *Ode* in particular, Spitzer's cuts off the poem in its circular self-sufficiency from any context other than the poet's (assumed) knowledge of Antiquity and belief in the aesthetic. And yet, Spitzer's own context is omnipresent, from the immediate academic debate with Earl Wasserman on the one hand and with the New Critics on the other to the overarching desire – or need – for a unified Western tradition transcending national, linguistic, generic and medial boundaries after the tearing apart of the West in the Second World War. The construction that is Spitzer's definition of ekphrasis serves these immediate functions and, within the rhetoric of his article, its nature as assemblage is in tension with its maker's presentation of his creation as an essential, historical truth, just as the composite nature of Keats' urn is in tension with the poet's claims that this non-existent object will endure.[78] In a similar manner, Spitzer's ekphrasis, a genre existing through time and yet removed from particular historical and political events, is in tension with the dynamics that gave rise to it.

Notes

1. I would like to thank audiences in London, Ghent and Yale for their comments on different versions of this paper and Phiroze Vasunia for his suggestions.
2. See, for example, the discussion in Adam and Petitjean 1989: 153–71 who argue for the exclusion of such passages from the category of 'récit' in their classification. De Jong 2001 uses the term 'dynamic description'.
3. Spitzer cites Brooks 1947 but does not engage with his interpretation.
4. See, for example, Bewell 1986 and Bromwich 1986; Kelley 1995, Kandl 2001; and the collection of essays in Rohrbach and Sun 2011.
5. Quintilian, *Institutio oratoria*, 8.3.62. As Goldhill 2007: 5 points out, such vivid appeals constitute 'a weapon of rhetoric'.
6. See Gunderson 2000.
7. See Rancière 2004a: 18 on the constant potential for rhetoric to be used by 'unauthorized speakers on the public stage'. Even in the absence of these unauthorized voices, it is possible to see any speech as containing its opposite, in germ. On the recent history of the dialogical understanding of rhetoric see Czubaroff 2012.
8. Theon *Progymnasmata*, 120.3–8 speaks of confirmations and refutations of ekphraseis.
9. On the right-leaning politics of New Criticism and their adoption of the practice of close reading developed by Richards and Empson in a totally different spirit, see North 2017: 26–46.
10. The article originally appeared in *Comparative Literature*, 7 (1955). My quotations come from the republication in the collection *Essays on English and American Literature* (1962).
11. 'Ekphrasis' may be limited to 'verbal representations of visual representations' whether real or imaginary (as in Heffernan 1991 and 1993) or may include non-representational objects and buildings; it may be confined to attempts to describe or may encompass interpretations and responses that say little or nothing about the appearance of the object and include almost any 'words about art'. See the remarks of Bartsch and Elsner 2007 and Hollander 1995: 3–91 for a survey of the range of modern poetic 'ekphrasis'; the inclusion of descriptions of buildings reflects the ancient and Byzantine usage of the term. As I will suggest below, this variety may be at least partly attributable to Spitzer's framing of his definition.
12. Spitzer 1962: 72.
13. Spitzer 1949: 247–8 implies that the 'sub-genre' of the ode remained stable from Pindar to Whitman.
14. On the interpretations of these final lines see, for example, Wolfson 2003 as well as the discussion in Spitzer 1962.
15. Spitzer 1962: 83 cf. p. 90. I am using the typographical conventions adopted by Spitzer in his article.

16. On Wasserman's life and career see Stiller 2014. On Wasserman's criticism and its relationship to New Criticism, see Peterfreund 2006. Wasserman criticizes in particular the New Critics' aversion to reaching outside the poem and defends the practice of appealing to the poet's writings in order to find clues to interpretation. See also the interview with his student W. J. T. Mitchell, http://www.rc.umd.edu/praxis/mitchell/interview/mitch-interview.html section 5.

17. On Spitzer's polemics see Hatzfeld 1961: 57. Calin 2007: 17 notes that these sparked some of his best work.

18. The expression 'at Heaven's bourne' derives from Keats' poem *Endymion*. Spitzer objects strongly to this use of one poem to explain another and to what he sees as Wasserman's transformation of the expression into a critical term.

19. The passage reads in full 'Being no Keats scholar but only a practitioner of French *explication de texte*, I may be allowed to offer my own relatively simple explanation of the "Ode on a Grecian Urn" with the hope that the difference of method and perhaps the traditionalism of my approach may not be without value'.

20. Cf. Heffernan 1991: 297.

21. On Spitzer's life see Hatzfeld 1961. On his period in Istanbul where he laid the foundations for the department of Romance Language and Literature as part of Atatürk's reforms see Konuk 2005 and 2010 and, on the impact of these and other exiles on the creation of comparative literature as a discipline, see Apter 2003. Spitzer was replaced in Istanbul by another Jewish refugee from Nazi Germany, Erich Auerbach, who remained there until 1947. Porter 2010a and Saïd 1983 examine the impact of exile on Auerbach's vision of world literature.

22. In another demonstration of *explication de texte* applied to a poem by Walt Whitman (Spitzer 1949) the author devotes the first third of the article to a survey of the theme of birds in '1500 years of Occidental poetry', from Medieval Latin poetry through the Christian-Pythagoreanism of the Renaissance and Early modern period, the English and German romantics, including Keats' nightingale, and nineteenth-century French literature and Wagnerian opera. Only then does he make the classic first move of the *explication de texte* by dividing Whitman's poem into three sections and proceeding to a linear reading that brings out the pantheistic message of the poem. As in his analysis of Keats' *Ode*, Spitzer does not distinguish author and narrator.

23. Close reading implies a fixed and limited canon of works to analyse. See North 2017: 112 on Moretti's reaction to this. Bardon (1946) provides models of 'explication de textes' contemporary with Spitzer's work which often note the author's adherence to the canonical: his 'mastery' of the chosen form and the 'beauty' of the text.

24. The French exercise in the nineteenth and early twentieth centuries was also characterised by the requirement that students show the indefinable quality of *goût* (taste). See Ravoux-Rallo and Guichard 1996: 8. On 'taste', from a mid-twentieth-century French perspective see the works of Bourdieu, in particular (on the study of literature) Bourdieu and Fasseron 1964. Spitzer's own ideal reader was steeped in an idealizing version of the classical tradition as is clear from his claim that the Pythagorean allusions of Keats' poem should be evident to his reader (p. 78: 'I feel entitled to bring this Greek concept (which after all is familiar to any cultured reader) to bear on our poem, since it is a topos with Keats...'). Spitzer appeals without hesitation to 'taste' as a critical criterion in his article on Keats' *Ode* (p. 90). Elsewhere he relies on 'good sense' combined with intuition. See Calin 2007: 18. See also Spitzer 1967; Starobinski 1970; Karabétian 2000: 75–86.

25. Horace, *Odes* 2,10,5–8, promoting the golden mean, also provides the epigraph to Spitzer's chapter.

26. As such, it is a perfect example of an assemblage as defined by Bennett 2010: 24, put together to fulfil a specific need, more than the sum of its components, which retain their individual potency.
27. Spitzer 1962: 72–3.
28. Spitzer 1955: 81 'The "little town" with its lonely streets exists, not on the frieze, but only in the imagination of the poet.'
29. For discussion of the various candidates for identification as Keats' urn see Jack 1967: 214–24 who concludes that the poet drew on a range of visual sources. On the unspoken assumptions that guide many readings of the *Ode* as a response to an object see Roberts (1995) who emphasizes the tensions inherent in Keats' project of conveying a torus-shaped object with no beginning and no end in an ode destined to be printed on a page.
30. On the importance of genre in *explication de texte* see further Bergez 2010: 80–3. The degree to which the text adheres to the rules of its genre, departs from or develops them is one of the standard questions.
31. Spitzer 1955: 89, cf. 81: 'at this moment the poet comes to feel …'.
32. Starobinski 1970: 20–1; Calin 2007: 16.
33. Spitzer 1962: 88: 'Note that in spite of writing *on* an urn the poet has all through spoken *to* the urn ("thou") and that he may very well suggest his own conclusion by <u>words lent to the urn</u>.' (Italics in the original, my underlining.) Compare Edward Saïd's comments on the way Aeschylus lends words to the Persians (Saïd 2003: 56).
34. Spitzer 1962: 88. Cf the passage cited above: 'Keats's purely aesthetic aspirations come to free themselves from all non-essential admixtures' (89).
35. Spitzer 1962: 82: 'audible, spiritual relief comes to him [the poet] when, turning away from the detail of the three scenes, he looks at the beauty of the whole urn and of the whole frieze, "O Attic shape! Fair attitude!" the first vocative referring to the urn, the second to the persons represented on the frieze. The *archaeological* message of the urn is dead, its *aesthetic* message is alive "for ever" … Mr Wasserman seems not to have felt the sudden rise of the poet's voice in happy exaltation, the powerful upsurge of feeling marked by that magic line, "O Attic shape!..," in which the urn, after having been as it were fragmented into various divisions under the microscopic scrutiny of the curious poet, now suddenly re-assumes its unbroken flawless totality, rising again as a perfect whole!'. On Keats' wordplay here see Roberts 1995: 9–10.
36. Spitzer 1962: 73 n 5.
37. Spitzer 1962: 73 n 5 mentions a modern example of an ekphrastic poem on a circular object, Mörike's *Gedicht auf eine Lampe* to which he had devoted an article in 1951. With respect to Keats' *Ode* Roberts 1995 offers a stimulating challenge to the understanding of the urn as a circular by contrasting the non-Euclidean properties of a hollow, three-dimensional form with the linear presentation of the object in the *Ode*.
38. It is to this type of reading that Wohl 2015: 4 refers when she cites the 'Keatsian urn of New Criticism' as a counter-example. Spitzer refers in passing, and without footnotes, to Brooks' study, noting on p. 88 that they both see the attribution of speech to the urn at the end of the poem as being linked to its silence at the beginning, which for Brooks is one of the essential paradoxes of the *Ode*, while for Spitzer it is the expression of the *Ode*'s message in an appropriately Greek form, echoing not just ekphrasis but sepulchral epigrams (pp. 91–3). As mentioned above, Spitzer distinguished his method from that of the 'New Critics' in his emphasis on genre and literary history and in his appeal to the rules of linguistics which I assume were among the tools Brooks rejects as the mere 'machinery' behind the text

(cf. North 2017: 39–40 referring to 'psychological machinery'). On the affinities between New Criticism with *explication de texte* as practised in French Universities in the 1920s, see Cowley, in Barrett et al. 1950: 88.

39. Krieger 1992: 284 cited by Heffernan 1991: 298.
40. Krieger's interpretation changed later: see Kartiganer 1974, Krieger 1992 and Cosgrove 1997.
41. Spitzer 1962: 89.
42. Mitchell himself argues that the 'Otherness' of the visual arts in relation to language is partial, relating to the medium not the message. He acknowledges the effects of his selection of examples and presents the male–female dichotomy as just one 'figure of difference' out of many potential figures (1992: 717). The 1994 version of the article differs here and elsewhere.
43. See for example Heffernan 1993: 109 (in his discussion of Keats' *Ode*): 'When the conflict between [word and image] becomes a conflict between narrative and stasis, when ekphrasis converts the picture of an arrested action into a story, as it typically does, we can read this conversion in terms of gender: the male agent of narrative overcoming the female as image, as fixed and fixating object of desire.' (Heffernan's reading of Keats shows him resisting 'the impulse to narrate' and articulating his distance from the figures on the urn.) Because Heffernan's focus is on ekphrasis as verbal representation of visual representation, his analysis does not address the abstract form of the object as Spitzer does.
44. Tallon 2016 reacts against this current through a reading of the works of a female poet. See also Fisher 2006, Chapter 4, esp. p. 145 on the selective corpus of examples used by Heffernan and Mitchell. Swensen 2001 seeks to bypass the dichotomies and rivalries that underpin this gendered version of ekphrasis.
45. North 2017: 108.
46. Scott 1994: 19 citing the remarks of Levinson 1988: 3, 5 and 19 about Keats as a 'literary entrepreneur'.
47. Keats, 'On first looking into Chapman's Homer' (1816). The comparison between Chapman's concrete language and the more abstract version by Pope is discussed by Ferber 2012: 123–5.
48. In a similar way, the later approaches to ekphrasis that focus on gender and the tensions between the word and the image as its other avoid the questions of social and cultural inequality that are raised, for example, the failure to interpret the images on the urn in Keats' poem.
49. In addition to Homer, Keats may have had access to Theocritus through English translations. See Kelley 2001: 172–4.
50. Spitzer 1962: 93. Spitzer remarks in his discussion of 'le style circulaire' ' how things that are the most distant in time and place are linked together if one examines their deepest nature' ('combien les choses les plus éloignées dans l'espace et dans le temps sont reliees entre elles si l'on en scrute la nature profonde'). The same type of ahistorical affinity seems to be operative in his conception of the category of ekphrasis.
51. Keats' view of Greece from early nineteenth-century London was similarly confined to the classical (unlike that of Byron, who had the means to travel). See Scott 1994: 19–20.
52. Konuk 2010: 67.
53. Curthoys 2005.
54. He did, however, learn Turkish. See Spitzer 1934 and Atak 2011.
55. Gillman 2010: 61–2. Apter 2003 :256 notes how Spitzer 'preached a universal Eurocentrism'.
56. The context of Istanbul University in which Romance languages were taught by German émigrés, contributed to his vision of European culture. See Kader 2010: 33–5 on Spitzer's

insistence that his successor be German rather than French. Victor Klemperer was another candidate for the post.

57. Scott 1994: 36–7.
58. See Platt (forthcoming).
59. Bennett 2010: 52–61.
60. Ibid. I am grateful to Edith Hall for pointing out this limitation of Bennett's materialism.
61. Theon, *Progymnasmata*, 118.22–119.2. Text and translation in Webb 2009: 197–200; discussion ibid., 69–72. Depending on their presentation, these *ekphraseis tropou* can be said to provoke an embodied response in their audiences but I will not address this question in any detail here.
62. See Webb 2018a.
63. See Zeitlin 1996; Dougherty 2001; Webb 2018a.
64. Spitzer 1962: 82.
65. Roisman 1993: 17.
66. Genette's essay 'Frontières du récit' (originally published in 1966 and reprinted in Genette 1969) questions the strict boundary seen by these critics.
67. Friedländer 1912. Friedländer was another German-Jewish émigré who taught briefly at Johns Hopkins in 1939–40 before moving to UCLA.
68. On the aesthetics of Paul's ekphrasis see, in particular, Pentcheva 2011 and Schibille 2014.
69. On the introduction see Van Opstall 2017. Bell 2009 provides a translation and commentary of the beginning and end of the poem as part of a collection of political texts from the reign of Justinian. On the poem's interaction with its political and ceremonial context see Whitby 1985 and Macrides and Magdalino 1988.
70. See, for example, Chorikios of Gaza, *Laudatio Marciani* I; Prokopios of Caesarea, *Buildings*, I.1.17–78.
71. Webb 2018b.
72. Bell 2009: 190 n. 11 cf. p. 200 n. 53.
73. As suggested by Rancière 2004: 18.
74. See Webb 2003.
75. A Babylonian brick in the collections of the British Museum (item number 90136) stamped with the name of Nebuchadnezzar II (sixth century BC) as its political maker also bears a name in Aramaic, presumably added by the workman. See Hislop and Hockenhull 2018.
76. All of these entities have in common the fact that they would more readily be thought of as examples of 'design' than as examples of 'art'.
77. Aeschines, *Against Timarchus*, 41–3; 53–4 are examples of the *tropoi*, here meaning behaviours, attributed to Timarchus. On this speech and Aeschines' effacing of his own role as orator see Wohl 2010: 45–50.
78. On the composite nature of the urn see Jack 1967: 214–24; on the resulting tensions within the poem see Roberts 1995: 11–13.

BIBLIOGRAPHY

Names of Greek and Latin authors and texts are largely abbreviated in the style of the *Oxford Classical Dictionary* (4th edn, 2012) or given more explicitly; titles of journals are abbreviated as in *L'année philologique* or given more explicitly.

Acosta-Hughes, B. and S. A. Stephens (2012), *Callimachus in Context: From Plato to the Augustan Poets,* Cambridge: Cambridge University Press.
Adam, J.-M. and A. Petitjean (1989), *Le texte descriptif: traité d'analyse linguistique et textuelle,* Paris: Nathan.
Adam, James, ed. (1963), *The Republic of Plato.* 2nd edn, 2 vols, Cambridge: Cambridge University Press. Original edn 1902.
Adorno, T. W. (1973), *The Jargon of Authenticity,* translation of *Jargon der Eigentlichkeit* (Frankfurt: Suhrkamp Verlag, 1965) by Knut Tarnowski and Frederic Will, Evanston: Northwestern University Press.
Adorno, T. W. (1997), *Aesthetic Theory,* ed. and trans. R. Hullot-Kentor, London: The Athlone Press.
Agger, B. (2008), 'Political Sentences: Anti-Intellectualism, Obscurantism and Polymorphous Perversity', *Sociological Inquiry,* 78: 423–43.
Aghion, I., ed. (2002), *Caylus, mécène du roi: collectionner les antiquités au XVIIIe siècle,* Paris: Institut national d'histoire de l'art
Ahl, F. (1984), 'The Art of Safe Criticism in Greece and Rome', *American Journal of Philology,* 105: 174–208.
Allen, D. C. (1970), *Mysteriously Meant: The Rediscovery of Pagan Symbolism and Allegorical Interpretation in the Renaissance,* Baltimore: Johns Hopkins University Press.
Althusser, L., É. Balibar, E. Roger, P. Macherey and J. Rancière (2016), *Reading Capital: The Complete Edition,* London: Verso
Anderson, W. D. (1965), *Matthew Arnold and the Classical Tradition,* Ann Arbor: University of Michigan Press.
Apter, E. (2003), 'Global Translatio: The "invention" of Comparative Literature, Istanbul, 1933', *Critical Inquiry,* 29 (2): 253–81.
Arendt, H. (1958), *The Human Condition,* Chicago: University of Chicago Press.
Armstrong, C. D. (2011), *Julien-David Leroy and the Making of Architectural History,* London/New York: Routledge.
Armstrong, D. (1995), 'The Impossibility of Metathesis: Philodemus and Lucretius on Form and Content in Poetry,' in Obbink (1995), 210–32.
Asmis, E. (1991), 'Philodemus's Poetic Theory and *On the Good King According to Homer*', *Classical Antiquity* 10 (1): 1–45.
Asmis, E. (1992), 'Crates on Poetic Criticism,' *Phoenix,* 46 (2): 138–69.
Asmis, E. (1995), 'Philodemus on Censorship, Moral Utility, and Formalism in Poetry', in Obbink (1995), 148–77.
Assmann, J. (2014), *Religio Duplex: How the Enlightenment Reinvented Egyptian Religion,* Cambridge: Polity Press.
Atak, T. (2011), 'Learning Turkish' [English translation of Spitzer 1934], *PMLA* 126 (3): 763–79.
Austin, C. and G. Bastianini, eds (2002), *Posidippi Pellaei quae supersunt omnia,* Milan: LED.

Bibliography

Austin, N. (1975), *Archery at the Dark of the Moon: Poetic Problems in Homer's Odyssey*, Berkeley, CA: University of California Press.
Azoulay, V. (2004a), 'Exchange as Entrapment: Mercenary Xenophon?', in Lane Fox (ed.), 288–304.
Azoulay, V. (2004b), 'The Medo-Persian Ceremonial: Xenophon, Cyrus and the King's Body', in Tuplin (ed.), 147–73.
Baigrie, B. S., ed. (1996), *Picturing Knowledge: Historical and Philosophical Problems Concerning the Use of Art in Science*, Toronto: University of Toronto Press.
Bakhtin, M. M. (1981), 'Discourse in the Novel', in M. Holquist (ed.), *The Dialogic Imagination: Four Essays*, trans. C. Emerson and M. Holquist, 259–422, Austin, TX: University of Texas Press.
Bakker, E. J. (2001), 'Homer, Hypertext, and the Web of Myth', in U. Schaefer and E. Spielmann (eds), *Varieties and Consequences of Literacy and Orality / Formen und Folgen von Schriflischkeit un Mündlichkeit: Franz Bäuml zum 75 Geburtstag*, 149–60, Tübingen: Narr.
Bakker, E. J. (2005), *Pointing at the Past: From Formula to Performance in Homeric Poetics*, Washington, DC: Center for Hellenic Studies.
Bakker, E. J. (2013), *The Meaning of Meat and the Structure of the Odyssey*, Cambridge: Cambridge University Press.
Bakker, E. J. and F. Fabricotti (1991), 'Peripheral and Nuclear Semantics in Homeric Diction: The Case of Dative Expressions for Spear', *Mnemosyne* 44: 63–84.
Balling, H. and A. K. Madsen (2003), *From Homer to Hypertext: Studies in Narrative, Literature and Media*, Odense: University Press of Southern Denmark.
Barber, B. (1996), 'Misreading Democracy: Peter Euben and the *Gorgias*', in Ober and Hedrick (eds), 361–75.
Barchiesi, A. (2000), 'Rituals in Ink: Horace on the Greek Lyric Tradition' in Depew and Obbink (eds), 167–82.
Barchiesi, A. (2001), 'The Crossing' in S. Harrison (ed.), *Texts, Ideas, and the Classics: Scholarship, Theory, and Classical Literature*, 142–63, Oxford: Oxford University Press.
Bardon, H. (1946), *Explications latines de licence et d'agrégation,* Paris: Vuibert.
Barlow, M. and S. Kemmer, eds (2000), *Usage Based Models of Language*, Stanford, CA: CSLI Publications, Center for the Study of Language and Information.
Barlow, S. (1971), *The Imagery of Euripides: A Study in the Dramatic Use of Pictorial Language*, London: Methuen.
Barnes, Jonathan (2008), *Coffee with Aristotle*, London: Duncan Baird.
Barrett, H. (1987), *The Sophists: Rhetoric, Democracy, and Plato's Idea of Sophistry,* Novato, CA: Chandler & Sharp.
Barrett, W., K. Burke, M. Cowley, R.G. Davis, A. Tate and H. Haydn (1950), 'The New Criticism', *The American Scholar* 20: 86–104.
Barth, B. (1991), *Schellings Philosophie der Kunst: Göttliche Imagination und ästhetische Einbildungskraft*, Freiburg: Verlag Karl Alber.
Barthes, R. (1971), 'Style and Its Image', in S. Chatman (ed), *Literary Style: A Symposium*, Oxford: Oxford University Press.
Bartsch, S. and Elsner, J. (2007), 'Introduction: Eight Ways of Looking at an Ekphrasis', *Classical Philology,* 102 (1): i-vi.
Beard, M. (2016), 'Finley's Journalism', in D. Jew, R. Osborne and M. Scott (eds), *M I Finley: An Ancient Historian and his Impact*, 151–81. Cambridge: Cambridge University Press.
Beck, D. (2005), *Homeric Conversation*, Washington, DC: Center for Hellenic Studies.
Beck, D. (2012), 'The Presentation of Song in Homer's *Odyssey*', *Orality, Literacy and Performance in the Ancient World*, 25–53, Leiden: Brill.
Becker, A. (1995), *The Shield of Achilles and the Poetics of Ekphrasis*, Lanham, MD: Rowman & Littlefield.
Beckner, C., and J. Bybee (2009), 'A Usage-Based Account of Constituency and Reanalysis', *Language Learning,* 59: 27–46.

Bibliography

Beistegui, M. de (2000), 'Hegel: Or the Tragedy of Thinking', in M. de Beistegui and S. Sparks (eds), *Philosophy and Tragedy*, 11–37, London: Routledge.
Belfiore, E. (1984), 'Aristotle's Concept of *Praxis* in the *Poetics*', *Classical Journal*, 79: 110–24.
Belfiore. E. (1992), *Tragic Pleasures: Aristotle on Plot and Emotion*, Princeton: Princeton University Press.
Bell, P. (2009), *Three Political Voices from the Age of Justinian*, Translated Texts for Historians, 52, Liverpool: Liverpool University Press.
Bender, J. and M. Marrinan (2010), *The Culture of Diagram*, Stanford: Stanford University Press.
Benhabib, S. (1996), 'On Hegel, Women and Irony', in Mills (ed.): 25–44.
Benjamin, A. (2013), *Working with Walter Benjamin: Recovering a Political Philosophy*, Edinburgh: Edinburgh University Press.
Benjamin, A. (2016), 'Barring Fear: Philo and the Hermeneutic Project', *Epoché*, 20 (2): 307–26.
Benjamin, A. (2019), '"In an Unbounded Way": After Kant on Genius', *Research in Phenomenology*, 49 (1): 9–30.
Benjamin, W. (1994), *The Correspondence of Walter Benjamin, 1910–1940*, ed. G Scholem and T. W. Adorno, trans. M. R. Jacobson and E. M. Jacobson, Chicago: Chicago University Press.
Benjamin, W. (1996), *Gesammelte Briefe* Band II, 1919–1924, Frankfurt-am-Main: Suhrkamp.
Bennett, J. (2010), *Vibrant Matter: A Political Ecology of Things,* Durham, NC and London: Duke University Press.
Bennington, G. (2011), 'A Moment of Madness: Derrida's Kierkegaard', *The Oxford Literary Review*, 33: 103–27.
Bergez, D. (2010), *L'explication de texte littéraire*, Paris: Armand Colin.
Berlant, L. G. (2008), 'Thinking About Feeling Historical', *Emotion, Space and Society*, 1: 4–9.
Berlant, L. G. (2011), *Cruel Optimism,* Durham, NC: Duke University Press.
Bernal, M. (1991), *Black Athena: The Afroasiatic of Classical Civilization.* London: Vintage.
Bernays, J. (1863), *Die Dialoge des Aristoteles in ihrem Verhältniss zu seinen übrigen Werken*, Berlin: W. Hertz.
Bewell, A. J. (1986), 'The Political Implications of Keats's Classical Aesthetics', *Studies in Romanticism*, 25 (2): 220–9.
Bickendorf, Gabriele (1998), *Die Historisierung der italienischen Kunstbetrachtung im 17. und 18. Jahrhundert,* Berlin: Gebr. Mann.
Bierl, A. (2012), 'Orality, Fluid Textualization and Interweaving Themes: Some Remarks on the *Doloneia*: Magical Horses from Night to Light and Death to Life', in F. Montanari, A. Rengakos and C. Tsagalis (eds), 133–74.
Billig, M. (1995), 'Social critique and common-sense', *Discourse & Society*, 6: 555–7.
Bizos, M. (1971), *Xénophon. Cyropédie I,* Paris: Les Belles Lettres.
Blass, F. (1892), *Die Attische Beredsamkeit*, 11.1, 2nd edn, Leipzig: Teubner.
Blevins, J. P. and J. Blevins, eds (2009), *Analogy in Grammar: Form and Acquisition*, Oxford: Oxford University Press.
Blondell, R. (2002), *The Play of Character in Plato's Dialogues,* Cambridge: Cambridge University Press.
Blundell, M. W. (1989), *Helping Friends and Harming Enemies: A Study in Sophocles and Greek Ethics*, Cambridge: Cambridge University Press.
Boas, H. C. (2016), 'Frames and Constructions for the Study of Oral Poetics', in M. Antović and C. P. Cánovas (eds), *Oral Poetics and Cognitive Theory*, 99–124, Berlin: De Gruyter.
Boedeker, D. (2000), 'Herodotus' Genres', in Depew and Obbink (eds), 97–114.
Bol, P. C. et al., eds (1989–98), *Forschungen zur Villa Albani: Katalog der antiken Bildwerke,* 5 volumes, Berlin: Gebr. Mann.
Bopp, F. (1816), *Über das Conjugationssystem der Sanskritsprache in Vergleichung mit jenem der griechischen, lateinischen, persischen und germanischen Sprache. Nebst Episoden aus dem*

Bibliography

Ramajana und Mahabharata in genauen metrischen Übersetzungen aus dem Originaltexte und einigen Abschnitten aus den Vedas, Frankfurt.

Bourdieu, P. (1996), *The Rules of Art: Genesis and Structure of the Literary Field*, Stanford: Stanford University Press

Bourdieu, P. and J.-C. Passeron (1964), *Les héritiers: Les étudiants et la culture*, Paris: Les Éditions de Minuit.

Bouvier, D. (2015), 'Quand le concept de "formule" devient un obstacle épistémologique: la conception du stock de formules préfabriquées', *Gaia* 18: 225–43.

Bowler, P. (1989), *The Invention of Progress: the Victorians and their Past*, Oxford: Oxford University Press.

Bowra, C. M. (1961), *Heroic Poetry*, London: Macmillan.

Boyarin, D. (2009), *Socrates and the Fat Rabbis*, Chicago: University of Chicago Press.

Boyarin, D. (2012), 'Deadly dialogues: Thucydides with Plato', *Representations*, 117 (1):59–85.

Boys-Stones, G. R., ed. (2003), *Metaphor, Allegory, and the Classical Tradition*, Oxford: Oxford University Press.

Bozzone, C. (2010), 'New Perspectives on Formularity', in S. W. Jamison, H. C. Melchert and B. Vine (eds), *Proceedings of the 21st Annual UCLA Indo-European Conference*, 27–44, Bremen: Hempen Verlag.

Bozzone, C. (2014), 'Constructions: A New Approach to Formularity, Discourse, and Syntax in Homer', PhD, University of California, Los Angeles.

Bradley, P. (2001), 'Irony and the Narrator in Xenophon's *Anabasis*', in E. I. Tylawsky and C. G. Weiss (eds), *Essays in Honour of Gordon Williams*, 59–84, New Haven, CT: Henry R. Schwab Publishers.

Braider, C. (1999), 'The Paradoxical Sisterhood: "ut pictura poesis"', in Glyn Norton (ed.) *The Cambridge History of Literary Criticism, Volume 4: The Renaissance*, 168–75, Cambridge: Cambridge University Press.

Braun, T. (2004), 'Xenophon's dangerous liaisons', in Lane Fox (ed.) (2004): 97–130.

Breitenbach, H. R. (1967), *Xenophon von Athen* (Stuttgart). Reprinted from Pauly's *Realencyclopädie der classischen Altertumswissenschaft*, vol. IX.A2

Briant, P. (2017), *The First European: A History of Alexander in the Age of Empire*, trans. N. Elliott, Cambridge, MA: Harvard University Press.

Brinkema, E. (2014), *The Forms of the Affects*, Durham, NC: Duke University Press.

Brisson, L. et J.-F. Pradeau (2007), *Dictionnaire Platon*, Paris: Ellipses.

Bromwich, D. (1986), 'Keats's Radicalism', *Studies in Romanticism*, 25: 197–210.

Brooks, C. (1947), *The Well-Wrought Urn: Studies in the Structure of Poetry*, New York: Reynal and Hitchcock.

Brown, W. (1994), '"Supposing truth were a woman . . .": Plato's Subversion of Masculine Discourse', *Feminist Interpretations of Plato* ed. Nancy Tuana, 157–80, University Park, PA: Pennsylvania State University Press.

Brownson, C. L. (1998), *Xenophon, Anabasis*, revised ed. J Dillery (1st edition 1922), Cambridge, MA: Harvard University Press.

Bundy, E. L. (1986), *Studia Pindarica*, Berkeley and Los Angeles: University of California Press.

Burgess, D. L. (2004), 'Lies and Convictions at Aulis', *Hermes* 132: 37–55.

Burgess, J. S. (2001), *The Tradition of the Trojan War in Homer and the Epic Cycle*, Baltimore: Johns Hopkins University Press.

Burgess, J. S. (2006), 'Neoanalysis, Orality, and Intertextuality: An Examination of Homeric Motif Transference', *Oral Tradition*, 21: 148–81.

Burgess, J. S. (2010), 'The Hypertext of Astyanax', *Trends in Classics*, 2: 211–24.

Burgess, J. S. (2012), 'Intertextuality Without Text in Early Greek Epic', in Ø. Andersen and D. Haug (eds), *Relative Chronology in Early Greek Epic Poetry*, 168–83, Cambridge: Cambridge University Press.

Burgess, J. S. (2015), *Homer*, London: I. B. Tauris.
Burke, E. (1958 [1767]), *A Philosophical Inquiry into the Origin of our Ideas of the Sublime and the Beautiful*, ed. J. T. Boulton, London: Routledge and Kegan Paul.
Burnyeat, M. F. (1999), 'Culture and Society in Plato's *Republic*', in G. B. Peterson (ed.), *The Tanner Lectures on Human Values*, vol. 20, 215–324, Salt Lake City: University of Utah Press.
Burrow, J. (1981), *A Liberal Descent: Victorian Historians and the English Past*, Cambridge: Cambridge University Press.
Butler, J. (2000), *Antigone's Claim: Kinship Between Life and Death*, New York: Columbia University Press.
Butler, S., and A. Purves, eds (2013), *Synaesthesia and the Ancient Senses*, Durham: Acumen.
Buzzetti, E. (2014), *Xenophon the Socratic Prince*, New York: Palgrave Macmillan.
Bybee, J. (1985), *Morphology: A Study of the Relation Between Meaning and Form*, Amsterdam: J. Benjamins.
Bybee, J. (2006), 'From Usage to Grammar: The Mind's Response to Repetition', *Language*, 82: 711–33.
Bynum, D. E. (1987), 'Of Sticks and Stones and Hapax Legomena Rhemata', in J. M. Foley (ed.), *Comparative Research on Oral Traditions: A Memorial for Milman Parry*, Columbus, OH: Slavica, 93–119.
Byrne, D. and G. Callaghan (2013), *Complexity Theory and the Social Sciences*, London: Routledge.
Calame, C. (1990), 'Narrating the Foundation of a City: The Symbolic Birth of Cyrene', in L. Edmunds (ed.), *Approaches to Greek Myth*, 277–341, Baltimore: Johns Hopkins University Press.
Calin, W. (2007), *Twentieth-Century Humanist Critics: From Spitzer to Frye*, Toronto: University of Toronto Press.
Cameron, A. (1995), *Callimachus and his Critics*, Princeton: Princeton University Press.
Cánovas, C. P. and M. Antović (2016a), 'Construction Grammar and Oral Formulaic Theory', in C. P. Cánovas and M. Antović (eds), *Oral Poetics and Cognitive Science*: 79-98.
Cánovas, C. P. and M. Antović (2016b), 'Formulaic Creativity: Oral Poetics and Cognitive Theory', *Language and Communication*, 47: 66–74.
Carabelli, G. (1996), *In the Image of Priapus*, London: Duckworth.
Card, O. S. (1991), *Ender's Game*, New York: Tor Books.
Carlier, P. (2010), 'The Idea of Iimperial Monarchy in Xenophon's *Cyropaedia*', in Gray (2010): 327–66 [Reprinted in trans. from "L'idée de monarchie impériale dans la *Cyropédie* de Xénophon," *Ktema* 3 (1978): 133-163]
Carroll, J. (1982), *The Cultural Theory of Matthew Arnold*, Berkeley: University of California Press.
Carroll, M. D. (1984), 'Rembrandt's "Aristotle": Exemplary Beholder', *Artibus et Historiae* 5: 35–56.
Cartledge, P. (1987), *Agesilaos and the Crisis of Sparta*, Baltimore: Johns Hopkins University Press.
Castello, L. Á. (2008), 'Analogía y anomalía en Varrón: De lingua latina VIII-X', *Docenda Homenaje a Gerardo H Pagés* (Buenos Aires: Universidad de Buenos Aires, Facultad de Filosofía y Letras Colegio Nacional de Buenos Aires) 185–218.
Caygill, H. (1998), *Walter Benjamin: The Colour of Experience*, London: Routledge.
Caylus, A. C.-P. de Tubières de Grimoard de Pestels de Levis comte de (1752–67), *Recueil d'Antiquités Égyptiennes, Étrusques, Grecques, Romaines*, Paris: Desaint and Saillant.
Chambry, E., ed. and trans. (1967), *Platon, Oeuvres complètes*, Tome 7. 1, *La république, livres IV-VII*, Paris: Les Belles Lettres (originally published 1933).
Chant, D. (1986), 'Role Inversion and Its Function in the *Iphigeneia At Aulis*', *Ramus* 15: 83–92.
Chanter, T. (1995), *Ethics of Eros: Irigaray's Rewriting of the Philosophers*, New York: Routledge.
Chennevières, P. de (1897), 'Un amateur français au XVIIIe siècle', *L'oeuvre d'art* 5: 153-4, 170-2, 177–8, 198–200.
Chomsky, N. (1986), *Knowledge of Language: Its Nature, Origin and Use*, New York: Praeger.

Bibliography

Christensen, J. P. (2007), 'The Failure of Speech: Rhetoric and Politics in the *Iliad*', PhD thesis, New York University.

Christiansen, M. H. and N. Chater (2016), *Creating Language: Integrating Evolution, Acquisition, and Processing*, Cambridge, MA: Harvard University Press.

Chroust, A.-H. (1966), 'Eudemus, or On the Soul: A Lost Dialogue of Aristotle on the Immortality of the Soul', *Mnemosyne*, 19 (1): 17–30.

Claus, D. B. (1975), 'Αἰδώς in the language of Achilles', *Transactions of the American Philological Association*, 105: 13–28.

Čolacović, Z. (2006), 'The Singer Above Tales: Homer, Mededović and Traditional Epics', *Seminari Romani di Cultura Greca*, 9: 161–87.

Čolacović, Z. (2019), 'Avdo Mededović's Post-Traditional Epics and Their Relevance to Homeric Studies', *Journal of Hellenic Studies* 138: 1–48.

Collini, S. (1994), *Matthew Arnold: a Critical Portrait*, Oxford: Oxford University Press.

Coltman, Viccy (2009), *Classical Sculpture and the Culture of Collecting in Britain since 1760*, Oxford: Oxford University Press.

Consigny, S. (1987), 'Transparency and Displacement: Aristotle's Concept of Rhetorical Clarity', *Rhetoric Society Quarterly*, 17: 413–19.

Conte, G. B. (1994), *Genres and Readers*, Baltimore: Johns Hopkins University Press.

Coole, D. (2005), 'Rethinking Agency: A Phenomenological Approach to Embodiment and Agentic Capacities', *Political Studies*, 53: 124–42.

Cope, E. M. (1877), *Aristotle's Rhetoric*, 3 vols, ed. J. E. Sandys, Cambridge: Cambridge University Press.

Cosgrove, B. (1997), 'Murray Krieger: Ekphrasis as Spatial Form, Ekphrasis as Mimesis' in J. Morrison and F. Krobb (eds), *Text into Image: Image into Text*, 25–31, Amsterdam and Atlanta: Rodopi.

Craske, Matthew (1997), *Art in Europe 1700–1830: A History of the Visual Arts in an Era of Unprecedented Urban Economic Growth*, Oxford: Oxford University Press.

Croft, W. (2001), *Radical Construction Grammar: Syntactic Theory in Typological Perspective*, Oxford: Oxford University Press.

Crombie, Alistair (1994), *Styles of Scientific Thinking in the European Tradition*, 3 vols, London: Duckworth.

Cronk, N. and K. Peeters, eds (2004), *Le comte de Caylus: les arts et les lettres: actes du colloque international, Université d'Anvers (UFSIA) et Voltaire Foundation, Oxford, 26-27 mai 2000*, Amsterdam: Rodopi.

Crozat, P. and P.-J. Mariette (1729–42) *Recueil d'estampes d'après les plus beaux tableaux et d'après les plus beaux desseins qui sont en France*, 2 vols, Paris: Imprimerie Royale.

Csapo, E. (2004), 'The Politics of the New Music', in P. Murray and P. Wilson (eds), *Music and the Muses: The Culture of Mousike in the Classical Athenian City*, 207–48, Cambridge: Cambridge University Press.

Csapo, E. (2010), *Actors and Icons of the Ancient Theater*, Chichester: Wiley-Blackwell.

Csapo, E., H. R. Gotte, J. R. Green and P. Wilson, eds (2014), *Greek Theatre in the Fourth Century B.C.*, Berlin: De Gruyter.

Currie, B. (2016), *Homer's Allusive Art*, Oxford: Oxford University Press.

Curthoys, N. 2005, 'The Emigré Sensibility of World Literature: Historicizing Hannah Arendt and Karl Jaspers' Cosmopolitan Intent', *Theory and Event*, 8 (3).

Czubaroff, J. (2012), 'Dialogue and the Prospect of Rhetoric', *Review of Communication*, 12: 44–65.

Danek, G. (1996), 'Intertextualität in der Ilias: Intertextualität in der Odyssee', *Wiener humanistische Blätter*, 38: 22–36.

Danek, G. (1998), *Epos und Zitat: Studien zu den Quellen der Odyssee*, Vienna: Österreichische Akademie der Wissenschaften.

Danek, G. (2002), 'Traditional Referentiality and Homeric Intertextuality', in F. Montanari (ed.), *Omero tremila anni dopo*: 3–19.
Danek, G. (2005), 'Review of Čolaković and Rojc-Čolaković 2004', *Würzburger Studien zur Altertumswissenschaft*, 118: 5–20.
Daval, R. (2009), *Enthousiasme, ivresse et mélancolie*, Paris: Vrin.
Davis, W. (2010), *Queer Beauty: Sexuality and Aesthetics from Winckelmann to Freud and Beyond*, New York: Columbia University Press.
de Beistegui, M. (2000), 'Hegel: or the Tragedy of Thinking', in M. de Beistegui and S. Sparks (eds), *Philosophy and Tragedy*, 11–37, London: Routledge.
Décultot, Élisabeth (2000) *Johann Joachim Winckelmann: Enquête sur la genèse de l'histoire de l'art*, Paris: Presses Universitaires de France.
De Decker, F. (2015), 'A Morphosyntactic Analysis of Speech Introductions and Conclusions in Homer', PhD, Ludwig Maximiliansuniversität.
De Jong, I. (2001), *A Narratological Commentary on the Odyssey*, Cambridge: Cambridge University Press.
De Jong, I. (2015), 'Pluperfects and the Artist in Ekphrases', *Mnemosyne*, 68: 1–28.
de Laura, D. (1969), *Hebrew and Hellene in Victorian Britain*, Austin: University of Texas Press.
Delebecque, E. (1957), *Essai sur la vie de Xénophon*, Paris: Klincksieck.
Deleuze, G. and F. Guattari (1983), *Anti-Oedipus: Capitalism and Schizophrenia*, translated by R. Hurley, M. Seem and H. R. Lane, Minneapolis: University of Minnesota Press.
Deleuze, G. and F. Guattari (1987), *A Thousand Plateaus: Capitalism and Schizophrenia*, translated by B. Massumi. Minneapolis: University of Minnesota Press.
Deleuze, G. and F. Guattari (1994), *What is Philosophy?* (English translation of *Qu'est-ce que la philosophie?*, Paris: Les éditions de Minuit)., New York: Columbia University Press.
Demont, P. (2014), 'Remarques sur la technique du dialogue dans la *Cyropédie*', in Pontier (2014): 195–209.
Denyer, N. (2007), 'Sun and Line: The Role of the Good', *Cambridge Companion to the Republic* ed. G. R. F. Ferrari, 284–309, Cambridge: Cambridge University Press.
Depew, M. and D. Obbink, eds (2000), *Matrices of Genre*, Cambridge, MA: Harvard University Press.
de Romilly, J. (1965), 'Les *Phéniciennes* d'Euripide ou l'actualité dans la tragédie grecque', *Revue de Philologie*, 39: 28–47.
Derrida, J. (1972), 'La pharmacie de Platon', *La dissemination*, 74–196, Paris: Seuil.
Derrida, J. (1982), 'White Mythology: Metaphor in the Text of Philosophy', in *Margins of Philosophy*, 207–71, Chicago: University of Chicago Press. [Orig. 'La mythologie blanche: La métaphor dans la texte philosophique', *Marges de la philosophie*, Paris 1972: 247–324.]
Derrida, J. (1992), 'Force of Law: The "Mystical Foundation of Authority"', in D. Cornell, M. Rosenfeld, and D. G. Carlson (eds), *Deconstruction and the Possibility of Justice*, trans. M. Quaintance, 3–67. London: Routledge.
Derrida, J. (1995), *The Gift of Death*, translated by D. Willis, Chicago: University of Chicago Press.
Derrida, J. (1996), *Le Monolinguisme de l'autre*, Paris: Galilée.
Derrida, J. (1972), 'La Pharmacie de Platon', *La Dissemination*, Paris: Editions du Seuil.
Derrida, J. (1997), *The Politics of Friendship*, trans. G. Collins, London and New York: Verso.
Dickinson Classical Commentaries: the *Aetia*: http://dcc.dickinson.edu/callimachus-aetia.
Diès, A. (1965), 'Introduction', *Platon. Oeuvres complètes*, Tome 6, *La république, livres I-III* ed. E. Chambry, v-cxxxviii. Paris: Société d'Edition, Les Belles Lettres. (Originally published 1932.)
Dietz, M. (1985), 'Citizenship with a Feminist Face: the Problem with Maternal Thinking', *Political Theory*, 13: 19–37.
Dillery, J. (1995), *Xenophon and the History of his Times*, London and New York: Routledge.
Dillery, J. (2017), 'Xenophon: The Small Works', in Flower (ed.) (2017): 195–219.

Bibliography

Dirlmeier, F. (1984), *Aristoteles. Werke in deutscher Übersetzung* vol. 7.i (*Eudemische Ethik*), 4th edition, Berlin: Akademie-Verlag.

Dorion, L.-A. (2010), 'The Straussian Exegesis of Xenophon: The Paradigmatic Case of *Memorabilia* IV.4', in Gray (ed.), 281–323 [Reprinted in trans. from "L'exegèse straussienne de Xénophon", *Philosophie Antique*, 1 (2001): 87–118]

Dougherty, C. (2001), *The Raft of Odysseus: The Ethnographic Imagination of Homer's Odyssey*, New York: Oxford University Press.

Dougherty, C. and L. Kurke (1993), *Cultural Poetics in Archaic Greece: Cult, Performance, Politics*, Cambridge: Cambridge University Press.

Dover, K. (1997), *The Evolution of Greek Prose Style*, Oxford: Oxford University Press.

Dowden, K. (1989), *Death and the Maiden: Girls' Initiation Rites in Greek Mythology*, New York: Routledge.

duBois, P. (2004), 'Toppling the Hero: Polyphony in the Tragic City', *New Literary History*, 35 (1): 63–81.

Dubow, J. (2007), 'Case Interrupted: Benjmain, Sebald, and the Dialetical Image', *Critical Inquiry*, 33 (4): 820–36.

Dubrow, H. (1990), *A Happier Eden: The Politics of Marriage in the Stuart Epithalamium*, Ithaca, NY: Cornell University Press.

Ducrot, O. and T. Todorov (1972), *Dictionnaire encyclopédique des sciences du langage*, Paris: Éditions du Seuil.

Due, B. (1989), *The Cyropaedia: Xenophon's Aims and Methods*, Aarhus: Aarhus University Press.

Due, B. (2002), 'Narrator and narratee in Xenophon's *Cyropaedia*' in B. Amden et al. (eds), *Noctes Atticae: 34 Articles on Greco-Roman Antiquity and its Nachleben: Studies Presented to J. Meyer*, 82–92, Copenhagen: Museum Tusculanum Press.

Dumesnil, J. (1858), *Histoire des plus célèbres amateurs et de leurs relations avec des artistes faisant suite à celle des plus célèbres amateurs italiens, Vol 1: Pierre-Jean Mariette 1694–1774*, Paris: E. Dentu.

Düring, I. (1961), *Aristotle's Protrepticus: An Attempt at Reconstruction*, Göteborg, Sweden: Acta Universitatis Gothoburgensis.

Duso, A. (2006), 'L'analogia in Varrone', in R. Oniga and L. Zennaro (eds), *Atti della giornata di linguistica latina*, 9–20, Venice: Cafoscarina.

Dutton, D. (1999), 'Language Crimes: A Lesson in How Not to Write, Courtesy of the Professoriate', *The Wall Street Journal*, February 5.

Eagleton, T. (1975), 'Ideology and Literary Form', *New Left Review*, I/90 (March/April): 81–109.

Eagleton, T. (1981), 'The Idealism of American Criticism', *New Left Review*, 12 (1981): 53–65.

Eagleton, T. (1990), *The Ideology of the Aesthetic*, Malden, MA: Blackwell.

Eagleton, T. (2002), *Sweet Violence: The Idea of the Tragic*. Oxford: Wiley Blackwell.

Eagleton, T. (2006), *Criticism and Ideology: A Study in Marxist Literary Theory*, revised edn, London: Verso.

Easterling, P. (1993), 'The End of an Era? Tragedy in the Fourth Century', in A. Sommerstein et al. (eds), *Tragedy, Comedy, and the Polis*, 559–69, Bari: Lavante Editori.

Eckhardt, R. (2006), *Meaning Change in Grammaticalization: An Enquiry into Semantic Reanalysis*, Oxford: Oxford University Press.

Edelstein, L. (1966), *Plato's Seventh Letter*, Leiden: Brill.

Edwards, M. W. (1986), 'Homer and Oral Tradition: The Formula, Part I', *Oral Tradition*, 1: 171–230.

Edwards, M. W. (1988), 'Homer and Oral Tradition: The Formula, Part II', *Oral Tradition*, 3: 11–60.

Eichler, G. (1880), *De Cyrupaediae capite extremo*, Dissertation, Leipzig.

Elam, K. (1980), *The Semiotics of Theatre and Drama*, London: Methuen.

Bibliography

Eldredge, N. and S. J. Gould (1972), 'Punctuated Equilibria: An Alternative to Phyletic Gradualism', in T. J. M. Schopf (ed.), *Models in Paleobiology*, 82–115, San Francisco: Freeman, Cooper.

Ellis, N. C. and D. Larsen-Freeman, eds (2009), *Language as a Complex Adaptive System*, Malden, MA: Wiley-Blackwell.

Elmer, D. F. (2010), 'Oral-Formulaic Theory', in M. Finkelberg (ed.), *The Homer Encyclopedia*, II. 604–7, Malden, MA: Wiley-Blackwell.

Elmer, D. F. (2013a), *The Poetics of Consent: Collective Decision Making and the Iliad*, Baltimore: Johns Hopkins University Press.

Elmer, D. F. (2013b), 'Poetry's Politics in Archaic Greek Epic and Lyric', *Oral Tradition*, 28: 143–66.

Elmer, D. F. (2015), 'The "Narrow Road" and the Ethics of Language Use in the *Iliad* and the *Odyssey*', *Ramus*, 44: 155–83.

Else, G. F. (1938), 'Aristotle on the Beauty of Tragedy', *HSCP* 49: 179–204.

Elshtain, J. (1982), 'Antigone's Daughters', *Democracy*, 2: 46–59.

Elshtain, J. (1989), 'Antigone's Daughters Reconsidered: Continuing Reflections on Women, Politics and Power', in S. White (ed.), 222–35.

Elster, J. (2011), 'Hard and Soft Obscurantism in the Humanities and Social Sciences', *Diogenes*, 58: 159–170.

Euben, J. P. (1996), 'Reading Democracy: "Socratic" Dialogues and the Political Education of Democratic Citizens', in Ober and Hedrick (eds), 327–59.

Fantuzzi, M. and R. Hunter (2004), *Tradition and Innovation in Hellenistic Poetry*, Cambridge: Cambridge University Press.

Farness, J. (1985), 'Text and Tradition in Plato's *Ion*', *Philological Quarterly*, 64 (2): 155–74.

Fearn, D. (2007), *Bacchylides: Politics, Performance, Poetic Tradition*, Oxford: Oxford University Press.

Fenzi, Enrico, ed. (1999), *Francesco Petrarca, De sui ipsius et multorum ignorando. Della mia ignoranza e di quella di molti altri,* Milan: Mursia.

Ferber, M. (2012), *The Cambridge Introduction to Romantic Poetry*, Cambridge: Cambridge University Press.

Ferris, D. (2003), 'Benjamin's Affinity: Goethe, the Romantics, and the Pure Problem of Criticism', in B. Hanssen and A. Benjamin (eds), *Walter Benjamin and Romanticism*, London: Bloomsbury.

Festugière, A. J. (1950), *Contemplation et vie contemplative selon Platon*. 2nd edn, Paris: Vrin. (Originally published 1935.)

Ficino, M. (2008), *Commentaries on Plato*, Vol. 1, trans. M. J. B. Allen, Cambridge, MA: Harvard University Press.

Fillmore, C. J. (1977), 'The Case for Case Reopened', in P. Cole (ed.), *Syntax and Semantics 8: Grammatical Relations*, 59–81, New York: Academic Press.

Fink, B. (1995), *The Lacanian Subject: Between Language and Jouissance,* Princeton: Princeton University Press.

Finkelberg, M. (1990), 'A Creative Oral Poet and the Muse', *American Journal of Philology*, 111: 293–303.

Finkelberg, M. (2002), 'The Sources of the *Iliad*', in H. M. Roisman and J. Roisman (eds), *Essays on Homer (= Colby Quarterly 38)*: 151–61.

Finkelberg, M. (2003), 'Homer as a Foundation Text', in M. Finkelberg and G. G. Stroumsa (eds), *Homer, the Bible, and Beyond: Literary and Religious Canons in the Ancient World*, 75–96, Leiden: Brill.

Finkelberg, M. (2004), 'Oral Theory and the Limits of Formulaic Diction', *Oral Tradition*, 19: 236–52.

Finkelberg, M. (2012), 'Oral Formulaic Theory and the Individual Poet', in Montanari, Rengakos and Tsagalis (eds), 73–82.

Bibliography

Finkelberg, M. (2015), 'Meta-Cyclic Epic and Homeric Poetry', in M. Fantuzzi and C. Tsagalis (eds), *The Greek Epic Cycle and its Ancient Reception: A Companion*, 126–38, Cambridge: Cambridge University Press.

Finley, M. I. (1956), *The World of Odysseus*, London: Chatto and Windus.

Fisher, B. (2006), *Museum Mediations: Reframing Ekphrasis in Contemporary American Poetry*, New York and London: Routledge.

Fletcher, J. (2008), 'Women's Space and Wingless Words in the *Odyssey*', *Phoenix*, 62: 77–91.

Flower, M. A. (2012), *Xenophon's Anabasis or the Expedition of Cyrus*, Oxford: Oxford University Press.

Flower, M. A. ed. (2017), *The Cambridge Companion to Xenophon*, Cambridge: Cambridge University Press.

Foley, H. P. (1985), *Ritual Irony: Poetry and Sacrifice in Euripides*, Ithaca, NY: Cornell University Press.

Foley, H. P. (2001), *Female Acts in Greek Tragedy*, Princeton: Princeton University Press.

Foley, J. M. (1985), *Oral-Formulaic Theory and Research: An Introduction and Annotated Bibliography*, New York: Garland.

Foley, J. M. (1988), *The Theory of Oral Composition: History and Methodology*, Bloomington, IN: Indiana University Press.

Foley, J. M. (1991), *Immanent Art: From Structure to Meaning in Traditional Oral Epic*, Bloomington, IN: Indiana University Press.

Foley, J. M. (1999), *Homer's Traditional Art*, University Park, PA: Pennsylvania State University Press.

Foley, J. M. (2010), 'Oral Traditions', in M. Finkelberg (ed.), *The Homer Encyclopedia*, II: 607–10, Malden, MA: Wiley-Blackwell.

Ford, A. (1995), '*Katharsis*: The Ancient Problem', in A. Parker and E. K. Sedgwick (eds), *Performativity and Performance*, 109–32, London: Routledge.

Ford, A. (2002), *The Origins of Criticism: Literary Culture and Poetic Theory in Classical Greece*, Princeton: Princeton University Press.

Foucault, M. (2001), *L'Herméneutique du sujet: Cours au Collège de France, 1981–82*, ed. F. Gros, Paris: Gallimard/Seuil.

Foucault, M. (2008), *Le gouvernement de soi et des autres: Cours au Collège de France. 1982–83*, ed. F. Gros, Paris: Gallimard/Seuil.

Frampton, S. A. (2017), 'The Pre-History of the Universal Library', *Eidolon*, Dec. 22: https://eidolon.pub/alexandria-in-the-googleplex-or-the-pre-history-of-the-universal-library-cf6a2a5c3198

Frank, J. (2018), *Poetic Justice: Rereading Plato's Republic*, Chicago: University of Chicago Press.

Fraser, P. (1972), *Ptolemaic Alexandria*, 3 vols, Oxford: Oxford University Press.

Franke, W. (2000), 'Metaphor and the Making of Sense: The Contemporary Metaphor Renaissance', *Philosophy & Rhetoric*, 33 (2): 137–53.

Fränkel, H. (1975), *Early Greek Poetry and Philosophy*, Oxford: Blackwell.

Freeman, E. A. (1856), 'Grote's History of Greece', *North British Review*, 25: 141–72.

Friedländer, P. (1912), *Johannes von Gaza und Paulus Silentiarius: Kunstbeschreibungen Justinianischer Zeit*, Leipzig and Berlin: B. G. Teubner.

Friedrich, P. and J. M. Redfield (1978), 'Speech as a Personality Symbol: The Case of Achilles', *Language*, 54: 263–88.

Friedrich, R. (2007), *Formular Economy in Homer: The Poetics of the Breaches*, Stuttgart: Franz Steiner Verlag.

Friedrich, R. (2011), 'Formelsprache', in A. Regkakos and B. Zimmermann (eds), *Homer-Handbuch: Leben – Werk – Wirkung*: 45–64.

Fritzsche, P. (2011), *Stranded in the Present: Modern Time and the Melancholy of History*, Cambridge, MA: Harvard University Press.

Bibliography

Funke, H. (1964), 'Aristoteles zu Euripides' *Iphigeneia in Aulis*', *Hermes*, 92: 284–99.
Furley, D. and A. Nehamas (eds) (1994), *Aristotle's Rhetoric: Philosophical Essays*, Princeton: Princeton University Press.
Gadamer, H.-G. (1988), 'Reply to Nicholas P. White', trans. R. C. Norton and D. J. Schmidt, in Griswold (ed.), *Platonic Writings/Platonic Readings*, 258–66. New York: Routledge..
Gadamer, H.-G. (1991), *Plato's Dialectical Ethics: Phenomenological Interpretations Relating to the Philebus*, trans. R. M. Wallace, New Haven, CT: Yale University Press.
Gauthier, P. (1985), 'Xénophon et l'odyssée des "Dix-Mille"', *L'Histoire*, 79: 16–25.
Gelzer, T. (1993), 'Transformations'. in A. Bulloch et al. (eds), *Images and Ideologies: Self-Definition in the Hellenistic World*, 130–51, Berkeley and Los Angeles: University of California Press.
Genette, G. (1966), *Figures I*, Paris: Editions du Seuil.
Georges, P. (1994), *Barbarian Asia and the Greek Experience: From the Archaic Period to the Age of Xenophon*, Baltimore: Johns Hopkins University Press.
Gera, D. L. (1993), *Xenophon's Cyropaedia: Style, Genre and Literary Technique*, Oxford: Oxford University Press.
Germana, N. A. (2017a), *The Anxiety of Autonomy and the Aesthetics of German Orientalism*, Rochester: Camden House.
Germana, N. A. (2017b), 'The Colossal and Grotesque: The Aesthetics of German Orientalism in Kant and Hegel', in J. Cho and D. McGetchin (eds) *Gendered Encounters between Germany and Asia*, 23–39, Basingstoke: Palgrave Macmillan.
Gibert, J. (1995), *Change of Mind in Greek Tragedy*, Göttingen: Vandenhoeck & Ruprecht.
Gifford, T. (1999), *Pastoral*, London: Routledge.
Gillman, D. (2010), *The Idea of Cultural Heritage*, Cambridge: Cambridge University Press.
Gish, D. A. (2009), 'Spartan Justice: The Conspiracy of Kinadon in Xenophon's *Hellenika*', *Polis*, 26 (2): 339–69.
Givón, T. (1971), 'Historical Syntax and Synchronic Morphology: An Archaeologist's Field Trip', *Papers from the Regional Meetings of the Chicago Linguistic Society*, 7: 394–415.
Givón, T. (1979), *On Understanding Grammar*, New York: Academic Press.
Givón, T. (1984), *Syntax: A Functional-Typological Grammar*, vol. 1, Amsterdam: John Benjamins.
Givón, T. (1995), *Functionalism and Grammar*, Amsterdam: John Benjamins.
Goethe (2008), *Werke, Hamburger Ausgabe, Band 12: Schriften zur Kunst, Schriften zur Literatur, Maximen und Reflexionen*.
Goldberg, A. E. (2006), *Constructions at Work: The Nature of Generalization in Language*, Oxford: Oxford University Press.
Goldhill, S. (1986), *Reading Greek Tragedy*, Cambridge: Cambridge University Press.
Goldhill, S. (2000), 'Civic Ideology and the Problem of Difference: The Politics of Athenian Tragedy, Once Again', *Journal of Hellenic Studies* 120: 34–56.
Goldhill, S. (2002), *The Invention of Prose. Greece and Rome*, New Surveys in the Classics No. 32, Oxford: Oxford University Press.
Goldhill, S. (2006), 'Antigone and the Politics of Sisterhood', in Zajko and Leonard (eds), 141–62.
Goldhill, S. (2007), 'What is ekphrasis for?', *Classical Philology*, 102 (1): 1–19.
Goldhill, S. (2011), *Victorian Culture and Classical Antiquity: Art, Opera, Fiction and the Proclamation of Modernity*, Princeton: Princeton University Press.
Goldhill, S. (2012), *Sophocles and the Language of Tragedy*, Oxford: Oxford University Press.
Goldhill, S. (2014), 'The Ends of Tragedy: Schelling, Hegel and Oedipus', *PMLA*, 129 (4): 634–48.
Goldhill, S. (2020), *Preposterous Poetics: The Politics and Aesthetics of Form in Late Antiquity*, Cambridge: Cambridge University Press.
González, J. M. (2013), *The Epic Rhapsode and His Craft: Homeric Performance in a Diachronic Perspective*, Hellenic Studies Series 47, Washington DC: Center for Hellenic Studies.
Goodell, T. (1901), *Chapters on Greek Metric*, New York: Charles Scribner's Sons.

Bibliography

Gossmann, L. (1994), 'Philhellenism and Anti-Semitism: Matthew Arnold and his German Models', *Comparative Literature*, 46: 1–39.
Gould, S. J. (2002), *The Structure of Evolutionary Theory*, Cambridge, MA: Harvard University Press.
Graczyk, Annette (2015), *Die Hieroglyphe im 18. Jahrhundert: Theorien zwischen Aufklärung und Esoterik*, Berlin/Munich/Boston: De Gruyter.
Graff, R. (2001), 'Reading and the "Written Style" in Aristotle's *Rhetoric*', *Rhetoric Society Quarterly*, 21: 502–9.
Gray, V. (1981), 'Dialogue in Xenophon's *Hellenica*', *Classical Quarterly*, 31 (2): 321–34.
Gray, V. (1989), *The Character of Xenophon's Hellenica*, Baltimore: Johns Hopkins University Press.
Gray, V. (2007), *Xenophon on Government*, Cambridge: Cambridge University Press.
Gray, V. (2011), *Xenophon's Mirror of Princes: Reading the Reflections*, Oxford: Oxford University Press.
Gray, V. ed. (2010), *Xenophon: Oxford Readings in Classical Studies*, Oxford: Oxford University Press.
Green, R. (2002), 'Towards a Reconstruction of Performance Style', in P. Easterling and E. Hall eds., *Greek and Roman Actors*, 93–126, Cambridge: Cambridge University Press.
Grell, Chantal (1993), *L'Histoire entre Érudition and Philosophie: Étude sur la connaissance historique à l'âge des Lumières*, Paris: Presses Universitaires de France.
Grell, Chantal (1995), *Le dix-huitième siècle et l'antiquité en France 1680–1789*, 2 vols, Oxford: Voltaire Foundation.
Grethlein, J. (2017), *Aesthetic Experiences and Classical Antiquity: The Significance of Form in Narratives and Pictures*, Cambridge: Cambridge University Press.
Griener, Pascal (1998), *L'esthétique de la traduction: Winckelmann, les langues et l'histoire de l'art, 1755–1784*, Genève: Droz.
Griffith, M. (1995), 'Brilliant Dynasts: Power and Politics in the *Oresteia*', *Classical Antiquity*, 14 (1): 62–129.
Griffith, M. (1999), *Antigone. Sophocles*, Cambridge: Cambridge University Press.
Gros, F. (2008), 'Situation du cours', in Michel Foucault, *Le gouvernement de soi et des autres: Cours au Collège de France 1982–83* ed. Frédéric Gros, 347–62, Paris: Gallimard/Seuil.
Gruen, E. S. (2011), *Rethinking the Other in Antiquity*, Princeton and Oxford: Princeton University Press.
Gunderson, E. (2000), *Staging Masculinity: The Rhetoric of Performance in the Roman World*, Ann Arbor: University of Michigan Press.
Gurd, S. A. (2005), *Iphigenias At Aulis: Textual Multiplicity, Radical Philology*, Ithaca, NY: Cornell University Press.
Gurd, S. A. (2012), *Work in Progress: Literary Revision as Social Performance in Ancient Rome*, Oxford: Oxford University Press.
Gutzwiller, K., ed. (2005), *The New Posidippus*, Oxford: Oxford University Press.
Hacking, I. (1992), '"Style" for historians and philosophers', *Studies in History and Philosophy of Science*, 23: 1–20.
Hadot, P. (1995), *Qu'est-ce que la philosophie antique?* Paris: Gallimard.
Hall, E. (1996), 'Is There a Polis in Aristotle's *Poetics?*' in M. S. Silk (ed.), *Tragedy and the Tragic*, 295–309, Oxford: Oxford University Press.
Hall, E. (1997), 'The Sociology of Athenian Tragedy' in P. Easterling (ed.), *The Cambridge Companion to Greek Tragedy*, 93–126, Cambridge: Cambridge University Press.
Hall, E. (2006), *The Theatrical Cast of Athens: Interactions between Ancient Greek Drama and Society*, Oxford: Oxford University Press.
Hall, E. (2010), *Greek Tragedy: Suffering under the Sun*, Oxford: Oxford University Press.

Hall, E. (2012), 'The Politics of Metrical Variety in the Classical Athenian Theater', in D. Yatromanolakis (ed.), *Music and Cultural Politics in Greek and Chinese Societies,* vol. 1: *Greek Antiquity,* 1–28, Cambridge, MA: Harvard University Press.
Hall, E. (2017a), 'Master of Those Who Know': Aristotle as Role Model for the Twenty-first Century Academician', *European Review,* 25: 3–19.
Hall, E. (2017b), Review of J. Duban, *The Lesbian Lyre, TLS Times Literary Supplement* (6 January), 26–7.
Hall, E. (2018a), 'Aristotle's theory of katharsis in its historical and social contexts', in E. Fischer-Lichte and B. Wihstutz (eds), *Transformative Aesthetics,* 26–47. London: Routledge.
Hall, E. (2018b), 'Materialisms Old and New' in M. Telò and M. Mueller (eds), *The Materialities of Greek Tragedy: Objects and Affect in Aeschylus, Sophocles, and Euripides,* 203–18, London: Bloomsbury.
Hall, E. (2018c), *Aristotle's Way,* London: Penguin Random House.
Halliwell, S. (1987), *The Poetics of Aristotle: Translation and Commentary,* London: Duckworth.
Halliwell, S. (1998), *Aristotle's Poetics.* Chicago: University of Chicago Press.
Halliwell, S. (2002), *The Aesthetics of Mimesis: Ancient Texts and Modern Problems,* Pinceton: Princeton University Press.
Halliwell, S. (2011), *Between Ecstasy and Truth: Interpretations of Greek Poetics from Homer to Longinus,* Oxford: Oxford University Press.
Hamilton, C. D. (1994), 'Plutarch and Xenophon on Agesilaus', *Ancient World,* 25 (2): 205–12.
Hamilton, W. (1973), *Plato: Phaedrus and Letters VII and VIII,* London: Penguin
Hammer, D. C. (1997), '"Who shall readily obey?": Authority and Politics in the *Iliad*', *Phoenix,* 51: 1–24.
Hammer, D. C. (1998), 'The Politics of the *Iliad*', *The Classical Journal,* 94: 1–30.
Hammer, D. C. (1999), 'Homer, Tyranny, and Democracy', *Greek, Roman and Byzantine Studies,* 39: 331–60.
Hammer, D. C. (2002), *The Iliad as Politics: The Performance of Political Thought,* Norman, OK: University of Oklahoma Press.
Hampton, C. (1994), 'Overcoming Dualism: The Importance of the Intermediate in Plato's *Philebus*', in N. Tuana (ed.), *Feminist Interpretations of Plato,* 217–42, University Park, PA: Pennsylvania State University Press.
[Hancarville, Pierre d'] (1766–67), *Collection of Etruscan, Greek, and Roman Antiquities, from the Cabinet of the Hon. W. Hamilton, etc. (Antiquités Étrusques, Grecques, et Romaines, tirées du Cabinet de M. Hamilton, etc.)* Naples.
Hanink, J. (2014), *Lycurgan Athens and the Making of Classical Tragedy,* Cambridge: Cambridge University Press.
Hanssen, B. (1995), 'Philosophy at its Origin: Walter Benjamin's Prologue to the Ursprung des deutschen Trauerspiels', *MLN,* 110 (4): 809–33.
Hanssen, B. and A. Benjamin, eds (2003), *Walter Benjamin and Romanticism,* London: Bloomsbury.
Haraway, D. (1988), 'Situated Knowledges: The Science Question in Feminism and the Privilege of Partial Perspective', *Feminist Studies,* 14 (3): 575–99.
Harder, A., ed. (2012), *Callimachus, Aetia,* 2 vols., Oxford: Oxford University Press.
Harloe, K. (2013), *Winckelmann and the Invention of Antiquity: History and Aesthetics in the Age of Altertumswissenschaft,* Oxford: Oxford University Press.
Harman, R. (2012), 'A Spectacle of Greekness: Panhellenism and the visual in Xenophon's *Agesilaus*', in F. Hobden, G. Oliver and C. Tuplin (eds), *Xenophon. Ethical Principle and Historical Enquiry,* 427–53, Leiden and Boston: Brill.
Harman, R. (2013), 'Looking at the Other: Visual Mediation and Greek Identity in Xenophon's *Anabasis*', in E. Almagor and J., Skinner (eds), *Ancient Ethnography: New Approaches,* 79–96, London: Bloomsbury.

Bibliography

Harrison, B. (1999), '"White Mythology" Revisited: Derrida and His Critics on Reason and Rhetoric', *Critical Inquiry*, 25 (3): 505–34.

Hartouni, V. (1986), 'Antigone's Dilemma: a Problem in Political Membership', *Hypatia*, 1: 3–20.

Harward, J. (2014), *The Platonic Epistles: Translated with Introduction and Notes*, Cambridge: Cambridge University Press. (Originally published 1932.)

Haskell, F. (1987), 'The Baron d'Hancarville: An Adventurer and Art Historian in Eighteenth-Century Europe' in F. Haskell, *Past and Present in Art and Taste: Selected Essays*, 30–45, New Haven, CT: Yale University Press.

Haskins, E. (2000), '"Mimesis" Between Poetics and Rhetoric: Performance Culture and Civic Education in Plato, Isocrates, and Aristotle', *Rhetoric Society Quarterly*, 30 (3): 7–33.

Hatzfeld, J. (1961), 'Leo Spitzer (1887–1960)', *Hispanic Review*, 29 (1): 54–7.

Hau, L. I. (2016), *Moral History from Herodotus to Diodorus Siculus*, Edinburgh: Edinburgh University Press.

Headlam, W. (1902) 'Greek Lyric Metre', *Journal of Hellenic Studies*, 22: 209–27.

Heath, M. (2014), 'Aristotle and the Value of Tragedy', *British Journal of Aesthetics*, 54 (2): 111–23.

Heffernan, J. A. W. (1991), 'Ekphrasis and Representation', *New Literary History*, 22: 297–316.

Heffernan, J. A. W. (1993), *Museum of Words: The Poetics of Ekphrasis from Homer to Ashbery*, Chicago: University of Chicago Press.

Hegel, G. (1944), *Lectures on the Philosophy of Religion*, 3 vols, English trans., New York.

Hegel, G. (1967), *The Phenomenology of Spirit*, trans. J. Baillie, intro. G. Lichtheim, New York, NY: Harper & Row; reprint, 2nd edn, 1931.

Hegel, G. (1975), *Aesthetics: Lectures on Fine Art*, 2 vols, trans B. Knox, Oxford: Oxford University Press.

Heidegger, M. (1982), 'The Age of the World Picture', in *The Question Concerning Technology and Other Essays*, trans. W. Lovitt, 115–54, New York: Harper Torchbooks.

Heidegger, M. (1998). 'Plato's Doctrine of Truth', trans. Thomas Sheehan, in W. McNeill (ed.), *Pathmarks*, 155–82, Cambridge: Cambridge University Press.

Heikamp, D. D. and B. P. Strozzi, eds (2014), *Baccio Bandinelli: Scultore e maestro*, Firenze: Firenze Musei.

Herder, J. G. (1990), *Schriften zur Literatur*, ed. R. Otto, 3 volumes, Berlin and Weimar: Aufbau-Verlag.

Heringman, N. (2013), *Sciences of Antiquity: Romantic Antiquarianism, Natural History, and Knowledge Work*, Oxford: Oxford University Press.

Higgins, W. E. (1977), *Xenophon the Athenian: The Problem of the Individual and the Society of the Polis*, Albany: State University of New York Press.

Hinman, W. S. (1935), *Literary Quotation and Allusion in the Rhetoric, Poetics and Nicomachean Ethics of Aristotle*, Staten Island: Intelligencer Printing.

Hirsch, S. (1985), *The Friendship of the Barbarians: Xenophon and the Persian Empire*, Hanover and London: University Press of New England.

Hislop, I. and T. Hockenhull (2018), *I Object: Ian Hislop's Search for Dissent*, London: Thames and Hudson.

Hodkinson, S. (1994), '"Blind Ploutos"? Contemporary Images of the Role of Wealth in Classical Sparta', in A. Powell and S. Hodkinson (eds), *The Shadow of Sparta*, 183–222, London: Routledge/Classical Press of Wales.

Hoffmann, T. and G. Trousdale, eds (2013), *The Oxford Handbook of Construction Grammar*, Oxford: Oxford University Press.

Hogan, J. C. (1976), 'Double πρίν and the Language of Achilles', *The Classical Journal*, 71: 305–10.

Holland, C. (1998), 'After Antigone: Women, the Past, and the Future of Feminist Political Thought', *American Journal of Political Science*, 42: 1108–32.

Hollander, J. (1995), *The Gazer's Spirit: Poems Speaking to Silent Works of Art*, Chicago: University of Chicago Press.

Hönes, H.-C. (2014), *Kunst am Ursprung: Das Nachleben der Bilder und die Souveränität des Antiquars*, Bielefeld: Transcript Verlag.

Honig, B. (2010), 'Antigone's Two Laws: Greek Tragedy and the Politics of Humanism', *New Literary History*, 41: 1–38.

Honig, B. (2011), 'Ismene's Forced Choice: Sacrifice and Sorority in Sophocles' *Antigone*', *Arethusa*, 44: 29–68.

Honig, B. (2013), *Antigone Interrupted*, Cambridge: Cambridge University Press.

Hopper, P. J. and E. C. Traugott (2013), *Grammaticalization*, Cambridge: Cambridge University Press.

Humbert, J.-M., M. Pantazzi and C. Ziegler, eds (1994), *Egyptomania: l'Egypte dans l'Art occidental, 1730–1930*, Paris: Réunion des Musées Nationaux and Ottawa: Musée des Beaux-arts du Canada.

Humble, N. (2004), 'The author, date and purpose of chapter 14 of the *Lakedaimonion Politeia*', in Tuplin, 215–28.

Humble, N. (2014), 'L'innovation générique dans la *Constitution des Lacédémoniens*', in Pontier, 213–34.

Humble, N. (2018), 'Xenophon's Philosophical Approach to Writing: Socratic Elements in the Non-Socratic Works', in A. Stavru and C. Moore (eds), *Socrates and the Socratic Dialogue*, 577–97, Leiden: Brill.

Humble, N. (2020), 'True History: Xenophon's *Agesilaos* and the Encomiastic Genre', in A. Powell and N. Richer (eds), *Xenophon and Sparta*, Swansea: Classical Press of Wales.

Hunter, R. (2004), *Plato's Symposium*, Oxford: Oxford University Press.

Huntington, S. (1996), *The Clash of Civilizations and the Remaking of World Order*, New York: Simon & Schuster.

Inwood, M. (1983), *Hegel*, London: Routledge.

Irigaray, L. (1985), *Speculum of the Other Woman*, trans. C. Gill, Ithaca, NY: Cornell University Press.

Issacharoff, M. (1989), *Discourse as Performance*, Stanford: Stanford University Press.

Iversen, E. (1993), *The Myth of Egypt and its Hieroglyphs in European Tradition*, Princeton: Princeton University Press.

Jack, I. (1967), *Keats and the Mirror of Art*, Oxford: Oxford University Press.

Jackson, D. F. (2006), *The Constitution of the Lacedaimonians by Xenophon of Athens*, Lewiston, Queenston and Lampeter: The Edwin Mellen Press.

Jacob, C. (2013), 'Fragments of a History of Ancient Libraries', in J. König, K. Oikonomopoulou and G. Woolf (eds), *Ancient Libraries*, 57–84, Cambridge: Cambridge University Press.

Jameson, F. (1971), *Marxism and Form: Twentieth-Century Dialectical Theories of Literature*, Princeton: Princeton University Press.

Jameson, F. (1976), 'The Ideology of Form: Partial Systems in *La Vieille Fille*,' *SubStance*, 5 (15): 29–49.

Jameson, F. (1981), *The Political Unconscious: Narrative as a Socially Symbolic Act*, Ithaca, NY: Cornell University Press.

Jameson, F. (2007), *The Modernist Papers*, London: Verso.

Jameson, F. (2015), 'Early Lukács, Aesthetics of Politics?' *Historical Materialism* 23 (1): 3–27.

Janda, L. (2007), 'Inflectional Morphology', in D. Geeraerts and H. Cuyckens (eds), *The Oxford Handbook of Cognitive Linguistics*, 632–49, Oxford: Oxford University Press.

Janko, R. (1991), *The Iliad: A Commentary, Volume 4: Books 13–16*, Cambridge: Cambridge University Press.

Janko, R., ed. (2000), *Philodemus, On Poems: Book 1*, Oxford: Oxford University Press.

Bibliography

Jarvis, S. (2010), 'For a Poetics of Verse', *PMLA*, 125 (4), 931–5.

Jauss, H. R. (1982), *Toward an Aesthetic of Reception*, trans. T. Bahti, Minneapolis: University of Minnesota Press.

Jebb, R. C. (1900), *Sophocles: The Plays and Fragments Vol III: Antigone*, Cambridge: Cambridge University Press.

Jenkins, I. and K. Sloan, eds (1996), *Vases and Volcanoes: Sir William Hamilton and His Collection*, London: British Museum Press.

Jones, J. (1962 [1980]), *On Aristotle and Greek Tragedy*, Stanford, CA: Stanford University Press.

Jouan, F. (1983), *Euripide VII: Iphigénie à Aulis*, Paris: Les Belles Lettres.

Jowett, B. and L. Campbell (1894), *Plato's Republic: The Greek Text*. Vol. 3. *Notes*, Oxford: Clarendon Press.

Kahane, A. (1994), *The Interpretation of Order: A Study in the Poetics of Homeric Repetition*, Oxford: Oxford University Press.

Kahane, A. (2005), *Diachronic Dialogues: Authority and Continuity in Homer and the Homeric Tradition*, Lanham, MD: Rowman & Littlefield.

Kahane, A. (2007), 'Disjoining Meaning and Truth: History, Representation, Apuleius' Metamorphoses and Neoplatonist Aesthetics', in J. R. Morgan and M. Jones (eds), *Philosophical Presences in the Ancient Novel*, 245–69, Groningen: Barkhuis Publishing and Groningen University Library.

Kahane, A. (2013), 'The (Dis)continuity of Genre: A Comment on the Romans and the Greeks', in F. Montanari and A. Rengakos (eds), *Trends in Classics Supplementary Volumes 5*, 37–54, Berlin: Walter de Gruyter.

Kahane, A. (2018), 'The Complexity of Epic Diction', *Yearbook of Ancient Greek Epic* 2 (1): 78–117.

Kahane, A. (2019), 'Oral Theory and Intertextuality: The Case of the Homeric Hymns', in S. Bär and A. Maravela (eds), *Narratology and Intertextuality: New Perspectives on Greek Epic from Homer to Nonnus*, Leiden: Brill.

Kahane, A., M. Mueller, C. Berry and B. Parod, *The Chicago Homer*, http://homer.library.northwestern.edu/.

Kamuf, P. (1988), *Signature Pieces: On the Institution of Authorship*, Ithaca, NY: Cornell University Press.

Kandl, J. (2001), 'The Politics of Keats's Early Poetry' in S. J. Wolfson (ed.), *The Cambridge Companion to Keats*, 1–19, Cambridge: Cambridge University Press.

Kant, I. (2009), *Critique of the Power of Judgement* trans. P. Guyer and E. Matthews, Cambridge: Cambridge University Press.

Karabétian, E. (2000), *Histoire des Stylistiques*. Paris: A. Colin.

Kartiganer, D. M. (1974), 'The Criticism of Murray Krieger: The Expansions of Contextualism', *Boundary 2*, 2 (3): 584–607.

Kaufman, E. (1989), 'Architecture and Travel in the Age of British Eclecticism', in E. Blau and E. Kaufman (eds), *Architecture and its Image: Four Centuries of Architectural Representation*, 58–85, Montreal: Canadian Centre for Architecture/Centre Canadien d'Architecture.

Kelley, T. M. (1995), 'Keats, Ekphrasis and History' in N. Roe (ed.) *Keats and History*, 212–37, Cambridge: Cambridge University Press.

Kelley, T. M. (2001), 'Keats and "Ekphrasis"' in S. J. Wolfson (ed.) *The Cambridge Companion to Keats*, 170–85, Cambridge: Cambridge University Press.

Kelly, A. (2007), *A Referential Commentary and Lexicon to Iliad VIII*, Oxford: Oxford University Press.

Kelly, G. A. (1969), *Idealism, Politics and History: Sources of Hegelian Thought*, Cambridge: Cambridge University Press.

Kelly, J. (2009), *The Society of Dilettanti: Archaeology and Identity in the British Enlightenment*, New Haven: Yale University Press.

Kirk, G. S. (1985), *The Iliad: A Commentary. Volume I, Books 1–4*, Cambridge: Cambridge University Press.
Kitto, H. (1961), *Greek Tragedy*, London: Methuen.
Knox, B. M. W. (1964), *The Heroic Temper: Studies in Sophoclean Drama*, Berkeley: University of California Press.
Knox, B. M. W. (1966), 'Second Thoughts in Greek Tragedy', *GRBS* 7: 213–32.
Koditschek, T. (2011), *Liberalism, Imperialism, and the Historical Imagination: Nineteenth-Century Visions of a Greater Britain*, Cambridge: Cambridge University Press.
Kogan, P. (1969), *Northrop Frye: the High Priest of Clerical Obscurantism*, Montreal: Progressive Books.
Konuk, K. (2005), 'Jewish German Philologists in Turkish Exile: Leo Spitzer and Eric Auerbach' in A. Stephan (ed.), *Exile and Otherness: New Approaches to the Experience of Nazi Refugees*, Bern: Peter Lang.
Konuk, K. (2010), *East West Mimesis: Auerbach in Turkey*, Stanford, CA: Stanford University Press.
Koselleck, R. (1985), *Futures Past: on the Semantics of Historical Time*, trans. K. Tribe, Cambridge, MA: MIT Press.
Koselleck, R. (2002), *The Practice of Conceptual History: Timing History, Spacing Concepts*, trans. T. Prsener, K. Behnke and J. Welge, Stanford, CA: Stanford University Press.
Kouklanakis, A. (2001), 'Thersites, Odysseus, and the Social Order', in F. L. Lisi (ed.), *Plato's Laws and its Historical Significance*, 35–53, Baden-Baden: Academia.
Koyré, A. (1962), *Introduction à la lecture de Platon, suivi de Entretiens sur Descartes*, Paris: Gallimard.
Kramnick, J. and A. Nersessian (2017), 'Form and Explanation', *Critical Inquiry*, 43: 650–69.
Kramsch, C. (2012), 'Why is Everyone So Excited About Complexity Theory in Applied Linguistics?', *Mélanges CRAPEL*, 33: 9–24.
Kramsch, C., ed. (2002), *Language Acquisition and Language Socialization: Ecological Perspectives*, London: Continuum.
Kraus, C. S., ed. (1999), *The Limits of Historiography: Genre and Narrative in Ancient Historical Texts*, Leiden: Brill.
Krentz, P. (1995), *Xenophon: Hellenika II.3.11–IV.2.8*, Warminster: Aris & Phillips.
Krieger, M. (1992), *Ekphrasis: The Illusion of the Nnatural Sign*, Baltimore: Johns Hopkins University Press.
Kroll-Smith, S., ed. (2008), 'Special Section on Writing Sociology', *Sociological Enquiries*, 78 (3), 307–450.
Kroll, W. (1924), *Studien zum Verständnis der römischen Literatur*, Stuttgart: J. B. Metzler.
Krummen, E. (1990), *Pyrsos Hymnon: Festliche Gegenwart und mytnisch-rituelle Tradition als Voraussetzung einer Pindarinterpretation (Isthmie 4, Pythie 5, Olympie 1 und 3)*, Berlin: Walter De Gruyter. [Translated into English as *Cult, Myth, and Occasion in Pindar's Victory Odes: A Study of Isthmian 4, Pythian 5, Olympian 1, and Olympian 3*, trans. J. G. Howie, Arca 52, Prenton: Francis Cairns, 2014.]
Kullmann, W. (2015), 'Motif and Source Research: Neoanalysis, Homer and Cyclic Epic', in M. Fantuzzi and C. Tsagalis (eds), *The Greek Epic Cycle and Its Ancient Reception*, 108–26, Cambridge: Cambridge University Press.
Kunze, M. (2003), *Winckelmann und Ägypten: Die Wiederentdeckung der Ägyptischen Kunst im 18. Jahrhundert*, Stendal: Winckelmann-Gesellschaft.
Kurke, L. (1991), *The Traffic in Praise: Pindar and the Poetics of Social Economy*, Princeton: Princeton University Press.
Kuryłowicz, J. (1965), 'The Evolution of Grammatical Categories', *Diogenes*, 13: 55–71.
Kyriakou, P. (1993), 'Aristotle's Philosophical "Poetics"', *Mnemosyne*, 4th ser., 46 (3): 344–55.
Lacan, J. (1992), *The Ethics of Psychoanalysis: Seminar VII*, edited by J.-A. Miller, trans. D. Porter, London: Tavistock/Routledge.

Bibliography

Lacan, J. (2006), 'Seminar on "The Purloined Letter"', in *Écrits*, trans. B. Fink, 6–48, New York: W. W. Norton & Co.

Lada-Richards, I. (1996), 'Emotion and Meaning in Tragic Performance', in M. S. Silk (ed.), *Tragedy and the Tragic: Greek Theatre and Beyond*, 397–413, Oxford: Oxford University Press.

Laforse, B. (2013), 'Praising Agesilaus: The Limits of Panhellenic Rhetoric', *Ancient History Bulletin*, 27: 29–48.

Lakoff, G. (1987), *Women, Fire, and Dangerous Things: What Categories Reveal About the Mind*, Chicago: University of Chicago Press.

Lane Fox, R., ed. (2004), *The Long March: Xenophon and the Ten Thousand*, New Haven & London: Yale University Press.

Lang, B. (2010), 'The Ethics of Style in Philosophical Discourse', in Lavery and Groarke (eds) 21–34.

Larsen-Freeman, D. (1997), 'Chaos/Complexity Science and Second Language Acquisition', *Applied Linguistics*, 18: 141–65.

Larsen-Freeman, D. and L. Cameron (2008), *Complex Systems and Applied Linguistics*, Oxford: Oxford University Press.

Latour, B. (1996), 'On Actor-Network Theory: A Few Clarifications', *Soziale Welt*, 47: 369–81.

Latour, B. (2005), *Reassembling the Social: An Introduction to Actor-Network-Theory*. Oxford: Oxford University Press.

Lavery, J. and L. Groarke (2010), 'Introduction: genre as a tool of philosophical interpretation and analysis', in Lavery and Groarke (eds) 13–38.

Lavery, J. and L. Groarke, eds. (2010), *Literary Form, Philosophical Content: Historical Studies of Philosophical Genres*, Madison and Teaneck: Fairleigh Dickinson University Press.

Law, V. (2003), *The History of Linguistics in Europe: From Plato to 1600*, Cambridge: Cambridge University Press.

Lawrence, S. E. (1988), 'Iphigenia At Aulis: Characterization and Psychology in Euripides', *Ramus*, 17: 91–109.

Lear, J. ([1988] 1999), 'Catharsis', reprinted in *Open Minded: Working out the Logic of the Soul*. Cambridge, MA: Harvard University Press.

Lear, J. (1988), *Aristotle: The Desire to Understand*, Cambridge: Cambridge University Press.

Leca, B. (2005), 'An Art Book and Its Viewers: The "Recueil Crozat" and the Uses of Reproductive Engraving', *Eighteenth-Century Studies*, 38 (4): 623–49.

Lee, V. (1912), *Vital Lies: Studies of Some Recent Varieties of Obscurantism*, London: John Lane, The Bodley Head.

Leech, G. (1985), 'Stylistics' in T. van Dijk (ed.), *Discourse and Literature*, 39–57, Amsterdam: John Benjamins.

Lehmann, C. (2015), *Thoughts on Grammaticalization*, 3rd edn., Berlin: Berlin Language Science Press.

Leibniz, G. W. Q. (1985), *Die philosophischen Schriften*, vols. 1 & 6, Darmstadt: Olms.

Leidl, C. (2003), 'The Harlot's Art: Metaphor and Literary Criticism', in G. R. Boys-Stones (ed.), *Metaphor, Allegory, and the Classical Tradition*, 31–54, Oxford: Oxford University Press.

Leighton, A. (2007), *On Form: Poetry, Aestheticism, and the Legacy of a Word*, Oxford: Oxford University Press.

Leonard, M. (2005), *Athens in Paris: Ancient Greece and the Political in Postwar French Thought*, Oxford: Oxford University Press.

Leonard, M. (2006), 'Lacan, Irigary, and Beyond: Antigones and the Politics of Psychoanalysis', in Zajko and Leonard (eds), 121–39.

Leonard, M. (2012), *Socrates and the Jews: Hellenism and Hebraism from Moses Mendelssohn to Sigmund Feud*, Chicago: University of Chicago Press.

Le Roy, J.-D. (2004 [1770]) *The Ruins of the Most Beautiful Monuments in Greece*, trans. David Britt, Los Angeles, CA: Getty Publications.

Levine, C. (2015), *Forms: Whole, Rhythm, Hierarchy, Network*, Princeton: Princeton University Press.
Levinson, M. (1998), *Keats's Life of Allegory: The Origins of a Style*, New York and Oxford: Oxford University Press.
Levinson, M. (2007), 'What Is New Formalism?' *PMLA*, 122(2), 558–69.
Lincoln, B. (1994), *Authority: Construction and Corrosion*, Chicago: University of Chicago Press.
Lindsay, W. M., ed. (1903), *Nonii Marcelli de conpendiosa doctrina libros xx, Onionsianis copiis usus*, 3 vols., Leipzig: Teubner.
Lipka, M. (2002), *Xenophon's Spartan Constitution: Introduction, text, commentary*, Berlin: Walter de Gruyter.
Lissarrague, F. and M. Reed (1997), 'The Collector's Books', *Journal of the History of Collections*, 9 (2): 275–94.
Livingstone, N. (1998), 'The Voice of Isocrates and the Dissemination of Cultural Power', in Too and Livingstone (eds), 263–81.
Lloyd, G. E. R. (1966), *Polarity and Analogy: Two Types of Argumentation in Early Greek Philosophy*, Cambridge: Cambridge University Press.
Lloyd-Jones, H. (1962), 'The Guilt of Agamemnon', *CQ*, 12: 187–99.
Loraux, N. (2002), *The Divided City: On Memory and Forgetting in Ancient Athens*, trans. C. Pache and J. Fort, New York: Zone.
Lord, A. B. (1960), *The Singer of Tales*, Cambridge, MA: Harvard University Press.
Lord, A. B. (1995), *The Singer Resumes the Tale*, Ithaca, NY: Cornell University Press.
Lossau, M. (1990), 'Xenophons Odyssee', *Antike und Abendland*, 36: 47–52,
Lowrie, E. (1991), *Thersites: A Study in Comic Shame*, New York, NY: Garland.
Lucas, D. W. (1968), *Aristotle: Poetics*, Oxford: Clarendon Press.
Luccioni, J. (1947), *Les idées politiques et sociales de Xénophon*, Paris: Ophrys.
Lukács, G. (1963a), *Die Eigenart des Ästhetischen I* and *II*, in *Werke* Volume 10, *Ästhetik I*, Neuwied and Berlin: Luchterhand.
Lukács, G. (1963b), *Die Eigenart des Ästhetischen II*, in *Werke*, Volume 11, *Ästhetik I*, Neuwied and Berlin: Luchterhand.
Lukács, G. (1969 [1935]), 'Zur Ästhetik Schillers', in *Werke*, Volume 10, *Probleme der Ästhetik*, Neuwied and Berlin: Luchterhand.
Lukács, G. (1971), *History and Class Consciousness: Studies in Marxist Dialectics*, trans. Rodney Livingstone, Cambridge, MA: MIT Press.
Lukács, G. (1978), *The Theory of the Novel: A Historico-philosophical Essay on the Forms of Great Epic Literature*, trans. Anna Bostock, London: Merlin Press (originally published 1971; trans. of *Die Theorie des Romans*, Berlin: Cassirer, 1920).
Lukács, G. (2010), *Soul and Form*, ed. J. T. Sanders and K. Terezakis, New York: Columbia University Press.
Luschnig, C. A. E. (1988), *Tragic Aporia: A Study in Euripides' Iphigenia At Aulis*, Ramus Monographs. Berwick Victoria: Aureal Publications.
Lush, B. V. (2015), 'Popular Authority in Euripides' *Iphigenia in Aulis*', *AJP*, 136: 207–42.
Lyons, S. (2014), 'Obscurantism and the Language of Excess', *Philosophy Now*, 104, 33–5.
Maas, P. (1962), *Greek Metre*, trans. H. Lloyd-Jones, Oxford: Oxford University Press.
MacDowell, D. M. (1986), *Spartan Law*, Edinburgh: Scottish Academic Press.
MacIntyre, A. (1996), *A Short History of Ethics*, London: Macmillan.
MacKendrick, P. (1953), 'T. S. Eliot and the Alexandrians', *Classical Journal*, 49 (4): 7–13.
Mackie, H. S. (1996), *Talking Trojan. Speech and Community in the Iliad*, Lanham, MD: Rowman & Littlefield.
MacMullan, T. (2007), 'Jon Stewart and the New Public Intellectual', in J. Holt (ed.) *The Daily Show and Philosophy*, 57–68. Malden, MA: Blackwell.
Macrides, R. and P. Magdalino (1988), 'The Architecture of Ekphrasis: Construction and Context of Paul the Silentiary's Poem on Hagia Sophia', *BMGS* 12: 47–82.

Bibliography

Malkin, I. (1994), *Myth and Territory in the Spartan Mediterranean*, Cambridge: Cambridge University Press.
Marchand, S. (1996), *Down from Olympus: Archaeology and Philhellenism in Germany, 1750–1970*, Princeton: Princeton University Press.
Marchand, S. (2009), *German Orientalism in the Age of Empire: Religion, Race, and Scholarship*, Cambridge: Cambridge University Press.
Marchant, E. C. (1925), *Xenophon: Scripta minora*, Cambridge, MA: Harvard University Press.
Marcuse, H. (1964), *One-Dimensional Man: Studies in the Ideology of Advanced Industrial Society*, London: Routledge & Kegan Paul.
Mariette, P.-J. (1750), *Traité des Pierres Gravées*, Paris: L'Imprimerie De L'Auteur.
Marincola, J. (1999), 'Genre, Convention, and Innovation in Greco-Roman Historiography', in Kraus (ed.), 281–324.
Marincola, J. (2009), *The Landmark Xenophon's* Hellenika, ed. R. B. Strassler, New York and Toronto: Pantheon.
Marincola, J. (2017), 'Xenophon's *Anabasis* and *Hellenica*', in Flower (ed.), 103–18.
Markantonatos, A. (2012), 'Leadership in Action: Wise Policy and Firm Resolve in Euripides' *Iphigenia At Aulis*', in A. Markantonatos and B. Zimmermann (eds), *Crisis on Stage: Tragedy and Comedy in Late Fifth-Century Athens*, 189–218, Berlin: De Gruyter.
Marks, J. R. (2005), 'The Ongoing νεῖκος: Thersites, Odysseus, and Achilleus', *American Journal of Philology*, 126: 1–31.
Marr, J. (2005), 'Class Prejudice in the Ancient Greek World: Thersites, Cleon, and other upstarts', *Pegasus*, 48: 2–9.
Marshall, D. (1997), 'Literature and the Other Arts: (i) Ut pictura poesis', in H. B. Nisbet and Claude Rawson (eds), *The Cambridge History of Literary Criticism, Volume 4: The Eighteenth Century*, 681–99, Cambridge: Cambridge University Press.
Martin, R. P. (1989), *The Language of Heroes*, Ithaca, NY: Cornell University Press.
Martindale, C. (2005), *Latin Poetry and the Judgement of Taste: An Essay in Aesthetics*, Oxford: Oxford University Press.
Mastronarde, D. J. (2010), *The Art of Euripides: Dramatic Technique and Social Context*, Cambridge: Cambridge University Press.
McCall, M. H. (1969), *Ancient Rhetorical Theories of Simile and Comparison*, Cambridge, MA: Harvard University Press.
McCarney, J. (2000), *Hegel on History*, London and New York: Routledge.
Meillet, A. (1912), 'L'évolution des formes grammaticales', *Scientia*, 12: 130–58.
Meillet, A. (1923), *Les origines indo-européenes des mètres grecs*, Paris: Les Presses Universitaires de France.
Mellert-Hoffmann, G. (1969), *Untersuchungen zur 'Iphigenia in Aulis' des Euripides*, Heidelberg: Winter.
Melman, B. (2006), *Culture of History: English Uses of the Past, 1800–1953*, Oxford: Oxford University Press.
Messing, G. M. (1981), 'On Weighing Achilles' Winged Words', *Language*, 57: 888–900.
Michelakis, P. (2006), *Euripides: Iphigeneia At Aulis*, London: Duckworth.
Michelini, A. N. (1999), 'The Expansion of Myth in Late Euripides: *Iphigeneia At Aulis*', in M. Cropp, K. Lee and D. Sansone (eds), *Euripides and Tragic Theatre in the Late Fifth Century*, 41–57, *Illinois Classical Studies*, 24–25.
Middleton, R. (2004), 'Introduction', in Le Roy (2004 [1770]), 1–199.
Miller, P. A. (1994), *Lyric Texts and Lyric Consciousness: The Birth of a Genre from Archaic Greece to Augustan Rome*, London: Routledge.
Miller, P. A. (2007), *Postmodern Spiritual Practices: The Construction of the Subject and the Reception of Plato in Lacan, Derrida, and Foucault*, Columbus: Ohio State University Press.

Miller, P. A. (2015), 'Dreams and Other Fictions: The Representation of Representation in Republic 5 and 6', *American Journal of Philology*, 136: 37–62.

Miller, W. (1914), *Xenophon: Cyropaedia, Books I-IV*, Cambridge, MA: Harvard University Press.

Millis, B. W. and S. D. Olson (2012), *Inscriptional Records for the Dramatic Festivals of Athens: IG II² 2318–2325 and Related Texts*, Leiden: Brill.

Mills, P. (1996), 'Hegel's *Antigone*', in Mills (ed.), 59–88.

Mills, P., ed. (1996), *Feminist Interpretations of Hegel*, University Park, PA: Pennsylvania State University Press.

Minchin, E. (2006), 'Men's Talk and Women's Talk in Homer: Rebukes and Protests', *Mediterranean Archaeology*, 19: 213–24.

Missiakoulis, Spyros (2008), 'Aristotle and Earthquake Data: A Historical Note', *International Statistical Review*, 76, 130–33.

Mitchell, W. J. T. (1986), *Iconology: Image, Text, Ideology*, Chicago: University of Chicago Press.

Mitchell, W. J. T. (1992), 'Ekphrasis and the Other', *South Atlantic Quarterly*, 91: 695–719 (reprinted in *Picture Theory*, Chicago: University of Chicago Press, 1994).

Mocciaro, E. and W. Short, eds. (2018), *Toward a Cognitive Classical Linguistics: The Embodied Basis of Constructions in Greek and Latin*, Berlin: De Gruyter.

Momigliano, A. (1993), *The Development of Greek Biography*, Cambridge: Cambridge University Press.

Momigliano, A. (1950), 'Ancient History and the Antiquarian', *Journal of the Warburg and Courtauld Institutes*, 13 (3/4): 285–315.

Montanari, F., A. Rengakos and C. Tsagalis, eds. (2012), *Homeric Contexts: Neoanalysis and the Interpretation of Oral Poetry*, Trends in Classics, Berlin: De Gruyter.

Moore, J. (2008), 'History as Theoretical Reconstruction? Baron D'Hancarville and the Exploration of Ancient Mythology in the Eighteenth Century', in J. Moore, I. M. Morris and A. J. Bayliss (eds), *Reinventing History: The Enlightenment Origins of Ancient History*, 137–67, London: Centre for Metropolitan History.

Moran, R. (1989), 'Seeing and Believing: Metaphor, Image, and Force', *Critical Inquiry*, 16 (1): 87–112.

Moran, R. (1996), 'Artifice and Persuasion: The Work of Metaphor', in A. Rorty (ed.), *Essays on Aristotle's* Rhetoric, 385–98, Princeton: Princeton University Press.

Moraux, P. (1975), 'Cicéron et les ouvrages scolaires d'Aristote', in *Atti del II Colloquium Tullianum*, 81–96, Rome: Centro di Studi ciceroniani.

Mori, A. (2008), *The Politics of Apollonius Rhodius' Argonautica*, Cambridge: Cambridge University Press.

Morrow, G. R. (1962), *Plato's Epistles* Indianapolis: Bobbs-Merrill.

Most, G. W. (1985), *The Measures of Praise: Structure and Function in Pindar's Second Pythian and Seventh Nemean Odes*, Hypomnemata, 83, Göttingen: Vandenhoeck & Ruprecht.

Most, G. W. (2000), 'Generating Genres: The Idea of the Tragic', in Depew and Obbink (eds), 15–36.

Most, G. W. (2005), 'How Many Homers?', in A. Santoni (ed.), *L'Autore multiplo: Pisa, Scuola Normale Superiore, 18 ottobre 2002*, 1–14, Pisa: Scuola normale superiore.

Mouffe, C. (2013), *Agonistics: Thinking the World Politically*, London: Verso.

Nadon, C. (2001), *Xenophon's Prince Republic and Empire in the Cyropaedia*, Berkeley and Los Angeles: University of California Press.

Nagler, M. N. (1974), *Spontaneity and Tradition: A Study in the Oral Art of Homer*, Berkeley: University of California Press.

Nagy, G. (1976), 'Formula and Meter', in B. A. Stoltz and R. S. Shannon (eds), *Oral Literature and the Formula*, 239–60, Ann Arbor: Center for the Coördination of Ancient and Modern Studies, University of Michigan.

Nagy, G. (1992), *Greek Mythology and Poetics*, Ithaca, NY: Cornell University Press.

Nagy, G. (1997), *The Best of the Achaeans*, Baltimore: Johns Hopkins University Press.

Bibliography

Nagy, G. (2012), 'Signs of Hero Cult in Homeric Poetry', in F. Montanari, A. Rengakos and C. Tsagalis (eds), 27–71.

Nagy, G. (2015), 'Oral Traditions, Written Texts, and Qestions of Authorship', in M. Fantuzzi and C. Tsagalis (eds), *The Greek Epic Cycle and Its Ancient Reception*, 59–77, Cambridge: Cambridge University Press.

Nancy, J.-L. (1982), *Le Partage des voix*, Paris: Galilée.

Neer, R. T. (2002), *Style and Politics in Athenian Vase-Painting: The Craft of Democracy, ca. 530–460 B.C.E.*, Cambridge: Cambridge University Press.

Neer, R. T. (2010), *The Emergence of the Classical Style in Greek Sculpture*, Chicago: University of Chicago Press.

Nehamas, A. (1998), *The Art of Living: Socratic Reflections from Plato to Foucault*, Berkeley: University of California Press.

Newman, S. J. (2001), 'Aristotle's Definition of Rhetoric in the *Rhetoric*: The Metaphors and Their Message', *Written Communication*, 18: 3–25.

Newman, S. J. (2002), 'Aristotle's Notion of Bringing-Before-the-Eyes: Its Contributions to Aristotelian and Contemporary Conceptualizations of Metaphor, Style and the Audience', *Rhetorica*, 20 (1): 1–23.

Nicolai, R. (2014), 'At the Boundary of Historiography: Xenophon and his Corpus', in G. Parmegianni (ed.), *Between Thucydides and Polybius: The Golden Age of Greek Historiography*, 63–87, Washington, DC: Center for Hellenic Studies.

Nicolis, G. and I. Prigogine (1989), *Exploring Complexity: An Introduction*, New York: W. H. Freeman.

Nietzsche, F. (1879), 'Die Obskuranten', in *Menschliches, Allzumenschliches. Ein Buch für freie Geister*, vol. II, 1–39, 27, Chemnitz: Ernst Schmeitzner.

Nietzsche, F. (1999), *The Birth of Tragedy and Other Writings*, ed. R. Geuss and R Speirs, trans R. Speirs, Cambridge: Cambridge University Press.

Nightingale, A. (1993) 'The folly of praise: Plato's critique of encomiastic discourse in the *Lysis* and *Symposium*', *Classical Quarterly* 43: 112–130

Nightingale, A. W. (1995), *Genres in Dialogue: Plato and the Construct of Philosophy*, Cambridge: Cambridge University Press.

Nimis, S. T. (1986), 'The Language of Achilles: Construction vs. Representation', *The Classical World*, 79: 217–25.

Nisard, C., ed. (1877), *Correspondence inédite du comte de Caylus avec le Père Paciaudi, théatin (1757–1765)*, 2 volumes, Paris: Imprimé par autorisation du Gouvernement.

Noël, M. P. (2014), 'Ἐγκώμιον ou ἔπαινος? Définitions et usages de l'éloge dans *l'Évagoras* d'Isocrate et l'*Agésilas* de Xénophon', in Pontier (ed.), 253–68.

North, J. (2017), *Literary Criticism: A Concise Political History*, Cambridge, MA: Harvard University Press.

Nussbaum, M. (1986), *The Fragility of Goodness: Luck and Ethics in Greek Tragedy and Philosophy*, Cambridge: Cambridge University Press.

O'Neill, E. G. (1942), 'Word-Types in the Greek Hexameter', *Yale Classical Studies*, 8: 103–78.

Obbink, D., ed. (1995), *Philodemus and Poetry: Poetic Theory and Practice in Lucretius, Philodemus, and Horace*, New York and Oxford: Oxford University Press.

Ober, J. and C. Hedrick, eds (1996), *Dêmocratia: A Conversation on Democracies, Ancient and Modern*, Princeton: Princeton University Press.

Ollier, F. (1934), *Xénophon. La République des Lacédémoniens*, Lyon: A. Rey and Paris: F. Alcan.

Oral Traditions online Bibliography, from http://www.oraltradition.org/bibliography/.

Olson, G. and S. Copland (2016), 'Towards a Politics of Form', *European Journal of English Studies*, 20 (3): 207–21.

Orrells, D. (2011), 'Burying and Excavating Winckelmann's *History of Art*', *Classical Receptions Journal*, 3 (2): 166–88.

Orrells, D. (2015), *Sex: Antiquity and its Legacy*, New York: Oxford University Press.

Bibliography

Orrells, D., G. K. Bhambra and T. Roynon (2011), *African Athena: New Agendas*, Oxford: Oxford University Press.

Osborne, R. (2009), 'Economic Growth and the Politics of Entitlement', *Cambridge Classical Journal: Proceedings of the Cambridge Philological Society*, 55: 97–125.

Osborne, R. (2016), 'Finley's Impact on Homer', in D. Jew, R. Osborne and M. Scott (eds), *M I Finley: An Ancient Historian and his Impact*, 58–75, Cambridge: Cambridge University Press.

Osterkamp, Ernst (1989), 'Zierde und Beweis: Über die Illustrationsprinzipien von J. J. Winckelmanns Geschichte der Kunst des Alterthums', *Germanisch-romanische Monatsschrift*, 39: 301–25.

Ostwald, M. (1986), *From Popular Sovereignty to the Sovereignty of Law: Law, Society, and Politics in Fifth-Century Athens*, Berkeley: University of California Press.

Pace, N. (2009), 'La poetica epicurea di Filodema di Gadara.' *Rheinisches Museum für Philologie* 152 (3/4), 235–64.

Pangle, T. L. (1994), 'Socrates in the Context of Xenophon's Political Writings', in P. A. Vander Waerdt (ed.), *The Socratic Movement*, 127–50, Ithaca, NY: Cornell University Press.

Pappas, N. (2020), 'Plato's Aesthetics', *The Stanford Encyclopedia of Philosophy* (Fall 2020 edition), ed. E. N. Zalta, at https://plato.stanford.edu/archives/fall2020/entries/plato-aesthetics/.

Parry, A. (1956), 'The Language of Achilles', *Transactions of the American Philological Association*, 87: 1–7.

Parry, M. (1971), *The Making of Homeric Verse: The Collected Papers of Milman Parry*, Oxford: Oxford University Press.

Pelling, C. (1999), 'Epilogue', in Kraus (ed.), 325–60.

Pelling, C. (2017), 'Xenophon's Authorial Voice', in Flower (ed.), 241–62.

Penn, D. C., K. J. Holyoak and D. J. Povinelli (2008), 'Darwin's Mistake: Explaining the Discontinuity Between Human and Nonhuman Minds', *Behavioral and Brain Sciences*, 31: 109–78.

Pentcheva, B. (2011), 'Hagia Sophia and Multisensory Aesthetics', *Gesta*, 50: 93–111.

Perpillou-Thomas, F. (1993), *Fêtes d'Égypte ptolémaïque et romaine d'après la documentation papyrologique greque*. Studia Hellenistica 51, Louvain: Universitas Catholica Lovaniensis.

Peterfreund, S. (2006), 'Earl Wasserman: A critical (re-)reading', *Wordsworth Circle*, 37 (2): 64–7.

Pinkard, T. (2002), *German Philosophy 1750–1860: The Legacy of Idealism*, Cambridge: Cambridge University Press.

Pippin, R. (1988), *Hegel's Idealism: The Satisfactions of Self-Consciousness*, Cambridge: Cambridge University Press.

Pistelli, H., ed. (1888), *Iamblichi Protrepticus, ad fidem cod. Florentini*, Leipzig: Teubner.

Plato (1914), *Phaedo* in *Euthyphro, Apology, Crito, Phaedo, Phaedrus*, trans. H. N. Fowler, Loeb Classical Library, Cambridge, MA: Harvard University Press.

Plato (1925a), *Ion* in *Statesman, Philebus, Ion* ed. H. N. Fowler and W. R. M. Lamb, Loeb edn, 401–48, Cambridge, MA: Harvard University Press.

Plato (1925b), *Symposium* in *Lysis, Symposium, Gorgias*, trans. W. R. M. Lamb, Loeb Classical Library, Cambridge, MA: Harvard University Press.

Plato (1926), *Greater Hippias* in *Cratylus, Parmenides, Greater Hippias, Lesser Hippias*, trans. H. N. Fowler, Loeb Classical.

Plato (1929), *Timaeus* in *Timaeus, Critias, Cleitophon, Menexenus, Epistles*, trans. R. G. Bury, Loeb Classical Library, Cambridge, MA: Harvard University Press.

Plato (1930–35), *Republic*, 2 vols, trans. P. Shorey, Loeb Classical Library, Cambridge, MA: Harvard University Press.

Plato (1953), *Phaedo*, ed. J. Burnet. Oxford: Clarendon Press.

Plato (1991), *Gorgias*, ed. E. R. Dodds, Oxford: Oxford University Press. Reprint, corr edn, 1966.

Plato (2017), *Phaedrus* ed. H. N. Fowler (1914), in *Euthyphro, Apology, Crito, Phaedo*, ed. C. Emlyn-Jones and W. Preddy, Loeb Classical Library, 407–524, Cambridge, MA: Harvard University Press, 2017.

Bibliography

Platt, V. (2014), 'Agamemnon's Grief: On the Limits of Expression in Roman Rhetoric and Painting', in J. Elsner, and M. Meyer (eds), *Art and Rhetoric in Roman Culture*, 211–31, Cambridge: Cambridge University Press.

Platt, V. (forthcoming), *Imprint and Line: Making and Mediating between Classical Art and Text*, Cambridge: Cambridge University Press.

Pontier, P. (2010), 'L'Agésilas de Xénophon: comment on réécrit l'histoire', *Cahiers des études anciennes*, 47: 359–83.

Pontier, P., ed. (2014), *Xénophon et la Rhétorique*, Paris: Presses de l'université Paris-Sorbonne.

Popper, K. R. (1945), *The Open Society and its Enemies*. Vol. 1. London: Routledge.

Porter, J. I. (1995), 'Content and Form in Philodemus: The History of an Evasion', in Obbink (ed.), 97–147.

Porter, J. I. (2003), 'The Materiality of Classical Studies', *Parallax*, 9 (4): 64–74.

Porter, J. I. (2004), 'Homer: The History of an Idea', in R. L. Fowler (ed.), *The Cambridge Companion to Homer*, Cambridge: Cambridge University Press.

Porter, J. I. (2010a), 'Auerbach, Homer, and the Jews', in S. Stephens and P. Vasunia (eds), *Classics and National Cultures*, 235–57, Oxford: Oxford University Press.

Porter, J. I. (2010b), *The Origins of Aesthetic Thought in Ancient Greece: Matter, Sensation, and Experience*, Cambridge: Cambridge University Press.

Postlethwaite, N. (1988), 'Thersites in the *Iliad*', *Greece and Rome*, 35: 123–36.

Potts, A. (1994), *Flesh and the Ideal: Winckelmann and the Origins of Art History*, New Haven, CT: Yale University Press.

Potts, A. (2006), 'Introduction', in Winckelmann (ed.) 2006a: 1–53.

Proietti, G. (1987), *Xenophon's Sparta*, Leiden: Brill.

Pucci, P. (2016), *Euripides' Revolution Under Cover*, Ithaca, NY: Cornell University Press.

Purves, A. C. (2010), *Space and Time in Ancient Greek Narrative*, New York: Cambridge University Press.

Raaflaub, K. A. (2004), 'Aristocracy and Freedom of Speech in the Greco-Roman World', in I. Sluiter and R. M. Rosen (eds), *Free Speech in Classical Antiquity*, 41–61, Leiden: Brill.

Rabe, Hugo, ed. (1899), *Ioannes Philoponus De aeternitate mundi contra Proclumi*, Lipsiae, 1899.

Rabinowitz, N. S. (1993), *Anxiety Veiled: Euripides and the Traffic in Women*, Ithaca, NY: Cornell University Press.

Raimo, A. (2003), 'The Warp and Woof of Cognition', in B. D. Joseph and R. D. Janda (eds), *The Handbook of Historical Linguistics*, 425–40, Malden, Ma: Blackwell.

Ramage, N. (1987), 'The Initial letters in Sir William Hamilton's "Collection of Antiquities"', *The Burlington Magazine*, 129: 446–56.

Rancière, J. (1996), *La parole muette: essai sur les contradictions de la litterature*, Paris: Hachette.

Rancière, J. (2004a), *Disagreement: Politics and Philosophy*, trans. J. Rose, Minneapolis, MN: University of Minnesota Press.

Rancière, J. (2004b), *The Politics of Aesthetics: The Distribution of the Sensible*, trans. G. Rockhill, London: Continuum.

Rancière, J. (2010), *Dissensus: On Politics and Aesthetics*, trans. S. Corcoran, London: Continuum.

Rancière, J. (2011), 'The Politics of the Spider', in Rohrbach and Sun, 239–50.

Ravoux-Rallo, E. and S. Guichard (1996), *L'explication de texte à l'oral des concours*. Paris: Armand Colin.

Ready, J. (2010), 'Why Odysseus Strings His Bow', *Greek Roman and Byzantine Studies*, 50: 133–57.

Reardon, B. P. (1991), *The Form of Greek Romance*. Princeton: Princeton University Press.

Rebenich, S. (1998), *Xenophon: Die Verfassung der Spartaner*, Darmstadt: Wissenschaftliche Buchgesellschaft.

Redfield, J. M. (2011), 'The Politics of Theogony', *Archiv für Religionsgeschichte*, 13: 31–6.

Rees, J. (2006), *Die Kultur des Amateurs: Studien zu Leben und Werk von Anne Claude Philippe de Thubières, Comte des Caylus (1692-1765)*, Weimar: VDG.

Reeve, C. D., trans. (2004), *Plato: Republic*, Indianapolis: Hackett.
Reeve, M. D. (1973), 'The Language of Achilles', *Classical Quarterly*, 23: 193–5.
Rehm, R. (1994), *Marriage to Death: The Conflation of Wedding and Funeral Rituals in Greek Tragedy*, Princeton: Princeton University Press.
Reichel, M. (1995), 'Xenophon's *Cyropaedia* and the Hellenistic Novel', in H. Hofmann (ed.), *Groningen Colloquia on the Novel* vol. 4, 1–20, Groningen: Egbert Forsten.
Reinhardt, K. (1979), *Sophocles*, trans. H. Harvey and D. Harvey, New York: Barnes & Noble. (Originally published Frankfurt 1947.)
Rhodes, P. J. (2003), 'Nothing to Do with Dionysus: Athenian Drama and the Polis', *JHS*, 123: 104–19.
Richer, G. (2016), *Inheriting Walter Benjamin*, London: Bloomsbury.
Richter, D. H., ed. (1999), *Ideology and Form in Eighteenth-Century Literature*, Lubbock, TX: Texas Tech University Press.
Ricoeur, P. (1978), *The Rule of Metaphor*, trans. R. Czerny, London: Routledge. (Originally published as *Métaphore vive*, Paris 1975.)
Ritchie, Jack, ed. (2012), *Styles of Thinking* = Special Issue of *Studies in History and Philosophy of Science* 43, 595–665.
Roberts, A. (1995), 'Keats's "Attic Shape": "Ode on a Grecian Urn" and non-euclidian geometry', *Keats-Shelley Review*, 9: 1–14.
Roby, C. (2016), *Technical Ekphrasis: The Written Machine between Alexandria and Rome*, Cambridge: Cambridge University Press.
Rocheblave, Samuel (1889), *Essai sur le comte de Caylus: l'homme, l'artiste, l'antiquaire*, Paris: Hachette.
Rohrbach, E. and E. Sun (2011), 'Reading Keats, Thinking Politics: An Introduction', *Studies in Romanticism* 50 (2): 229–38.
Roisman, J. (1993), *The General Demosthenes and his Use of Military Surprise*, Stuttgart: Franz Steiner.
Rood, T. (2004), 'Panhellenism and self-presentation: Xenophon's speeches', in Lane Fox: 305–29.
Rorty, A., ed. (1992), *Essays on Aristotle's Poetics*, Princeton: Princeton University Press.
Rorty, A., ed. (1996), *Essays on Aristotle's Rhetoric*, Princeton: Princeton University Press.
Rose, P. W. (1988), 'Thersites and the Plural Voices of Homer', *Arethusa*, 21: 5–25.
Rose, P. W. (1992), *Sons of the Gods, Children of Earth: Ideology and Literary Form in Ancient Greece*, Ithaca: Cornell University Press.
Rose, P. W. (2012), *Class in Archaic Greece*, Cambridge: Cambridge University Press.
Roselli, D. K. (2007), 'Gender, Class and Ideology: The Social Function of the Virgin Sacrifice in Euripides' *Children of Heracles*', *Classical Antiquity*, 26: 81–169.
Rosen, R. M. (2007), *Making Mockery: The Poetics of Ancient Satire*, Oxford: Oxford University Press.
Rosen, R. M. and P. C. Díaz (2003), 'The Death of Thersites and the Sympotic Performance of Iambic Mockery', *Pallas*, 61: 121–36.
Rosenblum, R. (1967), *Transformations in Late Eighteenth-Century Art*, Princeton: Princeton University Press.
Rosenmeyer, T. G. (1965), 'The Formula in Early Greek Poetry', *Arion*, 4: 295–311.
Ross, W. D., trans. (1952), *Select Fragments* (= *The works of Aristotle* vol. 12), London: Oxford University Press.
Rousseau, G. S. (1987), 'The Sorrows of Priapus: Anticlericalism, Homosocial Desire and Richard Payne Knight', in G. S. Rousseau and R. Porter (eds), *Sexual Underworlds of the Enlightenment*, 101–53, Manchester: Manchester University Press.
Rousseau, P. (2015), 'War, Speech and the Bow Are Not Women's Business', in J. Fabre-Serris and A. M. Keith (eds), *Women and War in Antiquity*, 15–33, Baltimore: Johns Hopkins University Press.
Rudwick, M. (2005), *Bursting the Limits of Time: The Reconstruction of Geohistory in the Age of Revolution*, Chicago: University of Chicago Press.

Bibliography

Rudwick, M. (2008), *Worlds Before Adam: The Reconstruction of Geohistory in The Age of Reform*, Chicago: University of Chicago Press.

Rush, F. (2009), 'Literature and Politics', in R. Eldridge (ed.), *The Oxford Handbook of Philosophy and Literature*, 496–516, Oxford: Oxford University Press.

Russell, D. A. (1981), *Criticism in Antiquity*, Berkeley, CA: University of California Press.

Russell, D. A. and M. Winterbottom, eds (1972), *Ancient Literary Criticism: The Principal Texts in New Translations*, Oxford: Oxford University Press.

Russo, J. A. (1997), 'The Formula', in I. Morris and B. Powell (eds), *A New Companion to Homer*, 238–60, Leiden: Brill.

Russo, J. A. 2010. 'Formula', in M. Finkelberg (ed.), *The Homer Encyclopedia*, Malden, Mass.: Wiley-Blackwell. I: 296–8.

Rutherford, I. 2001, *Pindar's Paeans*, Oxford: Oxford University Press.

Rutherford, R. (2012). *Greek Tragic Style: Form, Language and Interpretation.* Cambridge: Cambridge University Press.

Ryholt, K. (2013), 'Libraries in Ancient Egypt', in J. König, K. Oikonomopoulou and G. Woolf (eds), *Ancient Libraries*, 23–37, Cambridge: Cambridge University Press.

Sacks, S., ed. (1978), *On Metaphor*, Chicago: University of Chicago Press.

Saïd, E. (1983), *The World, the Text and the Critic*, Cambridge MA: Harvard University Press.

Saïd, E. (2003), *Orientalism*, Harmondsworth: Penguin. (Originally published 1978.)

Salmon, F. (2006), 'Stuart as Antiquary and Archaeologist in Italy and Greece', in Soros (ed.), 103–45.

Sansone, D. (1991), 'Iphigeneia Changes Her Mind', *Illinois Classical Studies*, 16: 161–72.

Saxonhouse, A. W. (1992), *Fear of Diversity: the Birth of Political Science in Ancient Greek Thought*, Chicago: University of Chicago Press.

Saxonhouse, A. W. (1994), 'The Philosopher and the Female: The Political Thought of Plato', in N. Tuana (ed.), *Feminist Interpretations of Plato*, 67–85, University Park, PA: Pennsylvania State University Press.

Scafa, E. (2008), 'Palace Politics and Social Results', *Pasiphae: rivista di filologia e antichità egee*, 2: 707–33.

Schechner, R. (1995), 'Problematizing Jargon', *TDR*, 39, 7–9.

Schein, S. L. (2016 [1998]), 'Milman Parry and the Literary Interpretation of Homeric Poetry', *Homeric Epic and Its Reception*, 117–26, Oxford: Oxford University Press.

Schein, S. L. (2016), 'Ioannis Kakridis and Neoanalysis', *Homeric Epic and Its Reception: Interpretive Essays*, 127–37, Oxford: Oxford University Press.

Schelling, F. (1989), *The Philosophy of Art*, trans. D. Stott, Minneapolis: University of Minnesota Press.

Schibille, N. (2014), *Hagia Sophia and the Byzantine Aesthetic Experience*, Farnham: Ashgate.

Schivelbusch, W. (1980), *The Railway Journey: The Industrialization of Time and Space in the Nineteenth Century*, trans. A. Hollo, Oxford: Blackwell.

Schlegel, F. (1988), *Kritische Schrfiten und Fragment [1798–1801], Studienausgabe* Band 2, ed. E. Behler and H. Eichner, Paderborn: Ferdinand Schöningh.

Schmidt, D. (2001), *On Germans and Other Greeks: Tragedy and Ethical Life*, Bloomington, IN: Indiana University Press.

Schmidt, J.-U. (2002), 'Thersites und das politische Anliegen des Iliasdichters', *Rheinisches Museum für Philologie*, 145 (2): 129–49.

Schmitt, C. B. (1965), 'Aristotle as a Cuttlefish: The Origin and Development of a Renaissance Image', *Studies in the Renaissance*, 12, 60–72.

Schnapp, A. (2000), 'Antiquarian Studies in Naples at the End of the Eighteenth Century: From Comparative Archaeology to Comparative Religion', in G. Imbruglia, *Naples in the Eighteenth Century: The Birth and Death of a Nation State*, 154–66, Cambridge: Cambridge University Press.

Schopenhauer, A. (1965 [1891]), 'On Style', translated by T. Bailey Saunders, reprinted in *Parerga und Paralipomena* vol. 2 = *Sämtliche Werke* vol. 5, 589–650, Stuttgart: Cotta-Insel.

Schoske, S. and A. Grimm, eds (2005), *Winckelmann und Ägypten: Die Wiederentdeckung der ägyptischen Kunst im 18. Jahrhundert*, Munich: Staatliches Museum Ägyptischer Kunst.

Schütrumpf, E. (1989), 'Form und Stil aristotelischer Pragmatien', *Philologus* 133, 177–91.

Schwebel, P. (2012), 'Intensive Infinity: Walter Benjamin's Reception of Leibniz and its Sources', *MLN*, 127 (3).

Schwebel, P. (2014), 'Monad and Time: Reading Leibniz with Heidegger and Benjamin' in A. Benjamin and D. Vardoulakis (eds), *'Sparks will Fly': Benjamin and Heidegger*, Albany, NY: State University of New York Press.

Schwebel, P. (2017), 'Constellation and Expression in Leibniz and Benjamin' in C. Sauter and N. Sahraoui (eds)., *Thinking in Constellations: Walter Benjamin and the Humanities*, Newcastle upon Tyne: Cambridge Scholars Publishing.

Scott, G. (1994), *The Sculpted Word: Keats, Ekphrasis and the Visual Arts*, Hanover, NH: University Press of New England.

Scully, S. (1984), 'The Language of Achilles: The ὀχθήσας Formulas', *Transactions of the American Philological Association*, 114: 11–27.

Searle, J. R. and D. Vanderveken (1985), *Foundations of Illocutionary Logic*, Cambridge: Cambridge University Press.

Segal, C. (1981), *Tragedy and Civilization: An Interpretation of Sophocles*, Cambridge, MA: Harvard University Press.

Selden, D. L. (1998), 'Alibis', *Classical Antiquity*, 17 (2): 289–412.

Selden, D. L. (1994), 'Genre of Genre', in J. Tatum (ed.), *The Search for the Ancient Novel*, 39–64, Baltimore: Johns Hopkins University Press.

Serpieri, A. (1978), 'Ipotesi teorica di segmentazione del testo teatrale', in A. Serpieri et al. (eds), *Come comunica il teatro: dal testo alla scena*, 11–54, Milan: Edizioni il Formichiere.

Shorey, P., ed. and trans. (1935), *Plato: Republic*, Cambridge: Harvard University Press.

Siegel, H. (1980), 'Self-Delusion and the Volte-Face of Iphigenia in Euripides' *Iphigenia At Aulis*', *Hermes*, 108: 300–21.

Siegel, H. (1981), 'Agamemnon in Euripides' *Iphigeneia At Aulis*', *Hermes*, 109: 257–65.

Sifakis, G. M. (2002), 'The Actor's Art in Aristotle', in P. Easterling and E. Hall (eds), *Greek and Roman Actors*, 148–64, Cambridge: Cambridge University Press.

Sistakou, E. (2016), *Tragic Failures: Alexandrian Responses to Tragedy and the Tragic*, Trends in Classics 38, Berlin: De Gruyter.

Slings, S. R., ed. (2003), *Platonis Rempublicam*, Oxford: Oxford University Press.

Sluiter, I. (2016), 'Obscurity', in A. Grafton and G. Most (eds), *Canonical Texts and Scholarly Practices: A Global Comparative Approach*, 34–51, Cambridge: Cambridge University Press.

Smentek, K. (2014), *Mariette and the Science of the Connoisseur in Eighteenth-Century Europe*, Farnham: Ashgate.

Snell, B. (1983), 'From Tragedy to Philosophy: Iphigenia in Aulis', in E. Segal, ed., *Oxford Readings in Greek Tragedy*, 396–405, Oxford: Oxford University Press.

Söderbäck, F., ed. (2010), *Feminist Readings of Antigone*, Albany, NY: SUNY Press.

Solez, K. (2012), 'Troy as Turning-post: Chariot-racing as a Metaphor for High Stakes, Power Politics, and the Threat of Death in the "Iliad" and Aeschylus' "Agamemnon"', *Nikephoros: Zeitschrift für Sport und Kultur im Altertum*, 25: 7–17.

Soros, S. W., ed. (2006), *James 'Athenian' Stuart: The Rediscovery of Antiquity*, New Haven, CT: Yale University Press.

Sorum, C. E. (1992), 'Myth, Choice, and Meaning in Euripides' *Iphigenia At Aulis*', *AJP*, 113: 527–42.

Souilhé, Joseph, ed. and trans. (1960), *Platon: Lettres*. 3rd edn., Paris: Société d'Edition, Les Belles Lettres.

Bibliography

Sourvinou-Inwood, C. (1989), 'Assumptions and the Creation of Meaning: Reading Sophocles' *Antigone*', *Journal of Hellenic Studies*, 109: 143–8.

Spitzer, L. (1934), '*En apprenant le turc: Considérations psychologiques sur cette langue*', *Bulletin de la Société Linguistique de Paris*, 35 (1): 82–101.

Spitzer, L. (1940), 'Le style circulaire', *Modern Language Notes*, 55 (7): 495–9.

Spitzer, L. (1949), 'Explication de texte applied to Walt Whitman's poem "Out of the cradle endlessly rocking"', *ELH*, 16 (3): 229–49.

Spitzer, L. (1951), 'Wiederum Mörike's Gedicht "Auf eine Lampe"', *Trivium*, 9: 203–25.

Spitzer, L. (1962), 'The "Ode on a Grecian Urn" or Content vs. Metagrammar', reprinted in *Essays on English and American Literature*, Princeton: Princeton University Press. [Originally published in *Comparative Literature* 7 1955.]

Spitzer, L. (1967), *Linguistics and Literary History: Essays in Stylistics*, Princeton: Princeton University Press.

Squire, M. (2009), *Image and Text in Graeco-Roman Antiquity*, Cambridge: Cambridge University Press.

Squire, M. (2012), *The Iliad in a Nutshell: Visualizing Epic on the Tabulae Iliacae*, Cambridge: Cambridge University Press.

Squire, M. and J. Wienand (2017), *Morphogrammata / The Lettered Art of Optatian: Figuring Cultural Transformations in the Age of Constantine*. Morphomata, 33, Paderborn: Wilhelm Fink Verlag.

Städel Museum (2013), *Schönheit und Revolution: Klassizismus 1770–1820*, Munich: Hirmer.

Stafford, B. M. (1980), 'Beauty of the Invisible: Winckelmann and the Aesthetics of Imperceptibility', *Zeitschrift für Kunstgeschichte*, 43: 65–78.

Stafford, B. M. (1991), *Body Criticism: Imaging the Unseen in Enlightenment Art and Medicine*, Cambridge, MA: MIT Press.

Starobinski, J. (1970), 'Leo Spitzer et la lecture stylistique' in L. Spitzer, *Etudes de Style*, 7–39, Paris: Gallimard.

Steiner, G. (1961), *The Death of Tragedy*, London: Faber & Faber.

Steiner, G. (1984), *Antigones*, Oxford: Oxford University Press.

Stephens, S. A. (2003), *Seeing Double: Intercultural Poetics in Ptolemaic Alexandria*, Berkeley: University of California Press.

Stephens, S. A. (2015), *Callimachus, The Hymns*, Oxford: Oxford University Press.

Stephens, S. A. (2018), *The Poets of Alexandria*, London: I. B. Tauris.

Stern, Fritz J., ed. (1970), *The Varieties of History: From Voltaire to the Present*, London: Macmillan.

Stiller, Shale D. (2014), 'Remembering a Giant: Earl Wasserman', *Johns Hopkins Magazine* (Winter), https://hub.jhu.edu/magazine/2014/winter/remembering-earl-wasserman

Stillinger, J. 'Fifty-nine ways of reading "Ode on a Grecian Urn"', in O'Rourke (ed.) *Ode on a Grecian Urn: Hypercanonicity and Pedagogy* http://www.rc.umd.edu/praxis/grecianurn/contributorsessays/grecianurnstillinger.html (reprinted in Stillinger, *Romantic Complexity: Keats, Coleridge and Wordsworth*, Urbana-Champaign, 2006).

Stock, G. (1897), *Lectures in the Lyceum: Or, Aristotle's Ethics for English Readers*, London: Longmans, Green & Co.

Stockert, W. (1992), *Euripides, Iphigenie in Aulis*, Vienna: Die Österreichischen Akademie der Wissenschaften.

Strauss, L. (1939), 'The Spirit of Sparta or the Taste of Xenophon', *Social Research*, 6: 502–36.

Stuart, J. (1762), *The Antiquities of Athens: Measured and delineated by James Stuart F.R.S. and F.S.A. and Nicholas Revett painters and architects*, London: John Haberkorn.

Stuurman, S. (2004), 'The Voice of Thersites: Reflections on the Origins of the Idea of Equality', *Journal of the History of Ideas*, 65: 171–89.

Sünderhauf, E. S. (2004), *Griechensehnsucht und Kulturkritik: Die deutsche Rezeption von Winckelmanns Antikenideal 1840–1945*, Berlin: Akademie.

Swenson, C. (2001), 'To Writewithize', *American Letters and Commentary*, 13.
Szlezák, Thomas A. (1999), *Reading Plato*, trans. G. Zanker, London: Routledge. (Originally published 1993.)
Tallon, L. (2016), 'Ekphrasis and Gender in Anne Finch's Longleat Poems', *Eighteenth-century Life*, 40 (1): 84–107.
Tamiolaki, M. (2017), 'Xenophon's *Cyropaedia*: Tentative Answers to an Enigma', in Flower (ed.), 174–94.
Tandon, Y. (2009), 'Neoliberal Obscurantism and its Ill-fated Children', *Capitalism, Nature, Socialism*, 20: 37–40.
Tanner, S. M. (2017), *Plato's Laughter: Socrates as Satyr and Comical Hero*, SUNY Series in Ancient Greek Philosophy, Albany, NY: SUNY Press.
Taplin, O. (1999), 'Spreading the Word Through Performance', in S. Goldhill and R. Osborne (eds), *Performance Culture and Athenian Democracy*, 33–57, Cambridge: Cambridge University Press.
Tatum, J. (1989), *Xenophon's Imperial Fiction: On the Education of Cyrus*, Princeton: Princeton University Press.
Taub, L. (2017), *Science Writing in Greco-Roman Antiquity*, Cambridge: Cambridge University Press.
Taylor, C. (1975), *Hegel*, Cambridge: Cambridge University Press.
Thalmann, W. G. (1988), 'Thersites. Comedy, Scapegoats, and Heroic Ideology in the *Iliad*', *Transactions of the American Philological Association*, 118: 1–28.
Thalmann, W. G. (1998), *The Swineherd and the Bow: Representations of Class in the Odyssey*, Ithaca, NY: Cornell University Press.
Thalmann, W. G. (2011), *Apollonius of Rhodes and the Spaces of Hellenism*, Oxford: Oxford University Press.
Tigerstedt, E. N. (1965), *The Legend of Sparta in Classical Antiquity*, Uppsala: Almquist & Wiksell.
Tomasello, M. (2003), *Constructing a Language: A Usage-Based Theory of Language Acquisition*, Cambridge, Ma: Harvard University Press.
Too, Y. L. (1998), 'Xenophon's *Cyropaedia*: Disfiguring the Pedagogical State', in Too and Livingstone: 282–302.
Too, Y. L. and N. Livingstone, eds (1998), *Pedagogy and Power: Rhetorics of Classical Learning*, Cambridge: Cambridge University Press.
Torrance, I. (2013), *Metapoetry in Euripides*, Oxford: Oxford University Press.
Tsagalis, C. (2008), *The Oral Palimpsest: Exploring Intertextuality in the Homeric Epics*, Hellenic Studies Series 29, Washington, DC: Center for Hellenic Studies.
Tsagalis, C. (2011), 'Towards an Oral, Intertextual Neoanalysis', *Trends in Classics*, 3: 209–44.
Tsagalis, C. (2014), 'Γυναίων εἵνεκα δώρων: Interformularity and Intertraditionality in Theban and Homeric Epic', *Trends in Classics*, 6: 357–98.
Tuplin, C. J. (1997), 'Xenophon's *Cyropaedia*: Education and Fiction', in A. H. Sommerstein and C. Atherton (eds), *Education in Greek Fiction*, 65–162, Bari: Levante.
Tuplin, C. J. ed. (2004), *Xenophon and his World*, Historia Einzelschriften 172, Stuttgart: Franz Steiner.
Turner, F. (1981), *The Greek Heritage in Victorian Britain*, New Haven, CT: Yale University Press.
Ubersfeld, A. (1977), *Lire le théâtre*, Paris: Éditions Sociales.
Valakas, K. (2002), 'The Use of the Body by Actors in Tragedy and Satyr Play', in P. Easterling and E. Hall (eds), *Greek and Roman Actors*, 69–92, Cambridge: Cambridge University Press.
van Alstyne, Lisa (1998), 'Aristotle's Alleged Ethical Obscurantism', *Philosophy*, 73 (285), 429–45.
Van Opstall, E. (2017), 'The Works of the Emperor and the Works of the Poet: Paul the Silentiary's Ekphrasis of Hagia Sophia', *Byzantion*, 87: 387–405.
Vasiliou, I. (2011), 'Aristotle, Agents, and Actions', in J. Miller (ed.), *Aristotle's Nicomachean Ethics: A Critical Guide*, 170–90, Cambridge: Cambridge University Press.

Bibliography

Vermeulen, I. R. (2010), *Picturing Art History: The Rise of the Illustrated History of Art in the Eighteenth Century*, Amsterdam: Amsterdam University Press.

Vernant, J.-P. (1981), 'Oedipus without the Complex', in J.-P. Vernant and P. Vidal-Naquet, *Tragedy and Myth in Ancient Greece*, trans. J. Lloyd, 63–86. Brighton: Harvester.

Vernant, J.-P. (1988a), 'Intimations of the Will in Greek Tragedy', in J.-P. Vernant and P. Vidal-Naquet (eds), *Myth and Tragedy in Ancient Greece*, trans. J. Lloyd, 49–84, Brighton: Harvester.

Vernant, J.-P. (1988b), 'Tensions and Ambiguities in Greek Tragedy', in J.-P. Vernant and P. Vidal-Naquet (eds), *Myth and Tragedy in Ancient Greece*, trans. J. Lloyd, 29–48, Brighton: Harvester.

Vickery, J. B. (1993), 'Review of Krieger, Ekphrasis: The illusion of the natural sign', *Modern Fiction Studies*, 39 (2): 433–5.

Vico, G. (1985), *The New Science of Giambattista Vico*, Ithaca, NY: Cornell University Press.

Vlassopoulos, K. (2017), 'Xenophon on Persia', in Flower (ed.), 360–75.

Voigt, E.-M., ed. (1971), *Sappho et Alcaeus. Fragmenta*, Amsterdam: Athenaeum-Polak & van Gennep.

von Humboldt, W. (1825), 'Über das Entstehen der grammatischen Formen und ihren Einfluß auf die Ideenentwicklung', Gelesen in der Akademie der Wissenschaften am 17. Januar 1822, *Abhandlungen der historisch-philologischen Klasse der Königlichen Akademie der Wissenschaften zu Berlin*, Berlin: Druckerei der Königlichen Akademie der Wissenschaften zu Berlin.

von Schlegel, A. W. (1818), *Observations sur la langue et la littérature provençales*, Paris: A la Librairie grecque-latine-allemande.

Vossius, G. J. (1696), *De Artium et Scientiarum natura ac constitutione*, Amsterdam: P. & J. Blaev.

Walker, D. P. (1972), *The Ancient Theology: Studies in Christian Platonism from the Fifteenth to the Eighteenth Century*, London: Duckworth.

Walsh, G. (1974), 'Iphigeneia in Aulis: Third Stasimon', *Classical Philology*, 69: 241–8.

Wassermann, F. M. (1949), 'Agamemnon in the Iphigenia At Aulis: A Man in an Age of Crisis', *TAPA*, 80: 174–86.

Watkin, J. (2006), 'Stuart and Revett: The Myth of Greece and Its Afterlife', in Soros (ed.), 19–57.

Webb, R. (2003), 'Praise and Persuasion: Argumentation and Audience Response in Epideictic Oratory' in E. Jeffreys (ed.), *Rhetoric in Byzantium*, 127–35. Aldershot: Ashgate.

Webb, R. (2009), *Ekphrasis, Imagination and Persuasion in Ancient Rhetorical Theory and Practice*, Farnham: Ashgate.

Webb, R. (2018a), 'Odysseus' Bed: Between Object and Action', *Mètis*, 16: 65–83.

Webb, R. (2018b), 'Spatiality, Embodiment and Agency in Ekphraseis of Church Buildings', in B. Pentcheva (ed.), *Aural Architecture in Byzantium: Music, Acoustics, Literature*, 163–75, London: Routledge.

Weigel, S. (2015), 'The Flash of Knowledge and the Temporality of Images: Benjamin's Image-Based Epistemology and its Preconditions in Visual Arts and Media History', *Critical Inquiry*, 41 (2): 344–66.

Weineck, S.-M. (1998), 'Talking about Homer: Poetic Madness, Philosophy and the Birth of Criticism in Plato's Ion', *Arethusa*, 31 (1): 19–42.

Weiss, N. A. (2014), 'The Antiphonal Ending of Euripides' *Iphigeneia in Aulis* (1475–1531)', *Classical Philology*, 109: 119–29.

Whitby, M. (1985), 'The Occasion of Paul the Silentiary's *Ekphrasis* of S. Sophia', *Classical Quarterly* 35 (1): 215–28.

White, H. (1980), 'The Value of Narrativity in the Representation of Reality', *Critical Inquiry*, 7 (1), 5–27.

White, S., ed. (1989), *Life-World and Politics: Between Modernity and Postmodernity: Essays in Honor of Fred Dallmayr*, Notre Dame, Ind.: University of Notre Dame Press.

Whitford, M. (1991), *Luce Irigaray, Philosopher in the Feminine*, London and New York: Routledge.

Whitmarsh, T. (2018), *Dirty Love: The Genealogy of the Ancient Greek Novel*, Oxford: Oxford University Press.
Whitmarsh, T. and S. Thomson, eds (2013), *The Romance between Greece and the East*, Cambridge: Cambridge University Press.
Williams, B. (1993), *Shame and Necessity*, Berkeley: University of California Press.
Williams, R. (1966), *Modern Tragedy*, London: Chatto and Windus.
Williams, R. (1977), *Marxism and Literature*, Oxford: Oxford University Press.
Williams, R. (1983), *Keywords: A Vocabulary of Culture and Society*, rev. edn., London: Fontana.
Wilson, P. (1996), 'Tragic Rhetoric: The Use of Tragedy in the Fourth Century', in M. S. Silk (ed.), *Tragedy and the Tragic: Greek Theatre and Beyond*, 310–31, Oxford: Oxford University Press.
Wilson, P. (2009), 'Tragic Honours and Democracy: Neglected Evidence for the Politics of the Athenian Dionysia', *Classical Quarterly*, 59: 8–29.
Winckelmann, J. J. (1764), *Geschichte der Kunst des Alterthums*, Dresden: In der Waltherischen Hof-Buchhandlung.
Winckelmann, J. J. (1952–57), *Briefe*, ed. W. Rehm, 4 volumes, Berlin: Walter de Gruyter.
Winckelmann, J. J. (2002), *Geschichte der Kunst des Alterthums: Text: Erste Auflage Dresden 1764, Zweite Auflage Wien 1776*, ed. A. H. Borbein, T. W. Gaethgens, J. Irmscher and M. Kunze, Mainz am Rhein: Philipp von Zabern.
Winckelmann, J. J. (2006a), *History of the Art of Antiquity*, trans. H. F. Mallgrave, Los Angeles: Getty Publications.
Winckelmann, J. J. (2006b), *Geschichte der Kunst des Alterthums: Katalog der antiken Denkmäler: Erste Auflage Dresden 1764, Zweite Auflage Wien 1776*, ed. A. H. Borbein, T. W. Gaethgens, M. R. Hofter, J. Irmscher, M. Kunze, A. Rügler, Mainz am Rhein: Philipp von Zabern.
Winckelmann, J. J. (2013), *Johann Joachim Winckelmann on Art, Architecture, and Archaeology*, trans. D. Carter, Rochester, NY: Camden House.
Winnington Ingram, R. (1980), *Sophocles: an Interpretation*, Cambridge: Cambridge University Press.
Wohl, V. (2002), *Love among the Ruins: the Erotics of Democracy in Classical Athens*, Princeton: Princeton University Press.
Wohl, V. (2010), *Law's Cosmos: Juridical Discourse in Athenian Forensic Oratory*, Cambridge: Cambridge University Press.
Wohl, V. (2014), 'Play of the Improbable: Euripides' Unlikely *Helen*', in Wohl (ed.), *Probabilities, Hypotheticals, and Counterfactuals in Ancient Greek Thought*, 142–59, Cambridge: Cambridge University Press.
Wohl, V. (2015), *Euripides and the Politics of Form*, Princeton: Princeton University Press.
Wohl, V. (2018), 'Aporía y Acción en *Ifigenia en Áulide* de Eurípides', in C. N. Fernández, J. T. Nápoli and G. C. Z. D. Fasano (eds), *Una Nueva Visión de la Cultura Griega Antigua en el Comienzo del Tercer Milenio: Perspectivas y Desafíos*, 363–88, La Plata: EDULP (Editorial de la Universidad Nacional de La Plata).
Wolfson, S. J. (1997), *Formal Charges: The Shaping of Poetry in British Romanticism*, Stanford, CA: Stanford University Press.
Wolfson, S. J. (2003), 'The Know of Not to Know It: My Returns to Reading and Teaching Keats' *Ode on a Grecian Urn*' in J. O Rourke (ed.), *Ode on a Grecian Urn: Hypercanonicity and Pedagogy*, https://www.rc.umd.edu/praxis/grecianurn/index.html.
Wolfson, S. J. (2012), 'Form', in R Greene et al. (eds), *The Princeton Encyclopedia of Poetry and Poetics*, 4th edn., 497–499, Princeton: Princeton University Press.
Wolin, S. S. (1994), 'Norm and Form: The Constitutionalizing of Democracy', in J. P. Euben, J. R. Wallach and J. Ober (eds), *Athenian Political Thought and the Reconstruction of American Democracy*, 29–58, Ithaca, NY: Cornell University Press.
Worman, N. (2002), *The Cast of Character: Style in Greek Literature*, Austin, TX: University of Texas Press.

Bibliography

Worman, N. (2008), *Abusive Mouths in Classical Athens*, Cambridge: Cambridge University Press.

Worman, N. (2015), *Landscape and the Spaces of Metaphor in Ancient Literary Theory and Criticism*, Cambridge: Cambridge University Press.

Worman, N. (2020), *Tragic Bodies: Edges of the Human in Greek Drama*, London: Bloomsbury.

Wright, M. (2009), 'Literary Prizes and Literary Criticism in Antiquity', *Classical Antiquity*, 28 (1): 138–77.

Wrobel, J., ed. (1876), *Platonis Timaeus interprete Chalcidio cum eiusdem commentario*, Leipzig: Teubner.

Yates, F. A. (2002 [1964]), *Giordano Bruno and the Hermetic Tradition*, London: Routledge.

Zajko, V. and M. Leonard, eds (2006), *Laughing with Medusa: Classical Myth and Feminist Thought*, Oxford: Oxford University Press.

Zanker, P. (1987), *Augustus und die Macht der Bilder*, Munich: Beck.

Zeitlin, F. I. (1980), 'The Closet of Masks: Role-Playing and Myth-Making in the *Orestes* of Euripides', *Ramus*, 9: 51–77.

Zeitlin, F. I. (1985), 'Playing the Other: Theater, Theatricality, and the Feminine in Greek Drama', *Representations*, 11: 63–94.

Zeitlin, F. I. (1995), 'Art, Memory, and *Kleos* in Euripides' *Iphigeneia in Aulis*', in B. E. Goff (ed.), *History, Tragedy, Theory: Dialogues on Athenian Drama*, 174–201, Austin, TX: University of Texas Press.

Zeitlin, F. I. (1996), 'Figuring Fidelity in Homer's *Odyssey*', in *Playing the Other*, 19–52, Chicago: University of Chicago Press.

Zerilli, L. (1991), 'Machiavelli's Sisters: Women and the Conversation of Political Theory', *Political Theory*, 19: 252–76.

Zuckert, C. H. (1996), *Postmodern Platos: Nietzsche, Heidegger, Gadamer, Strauss, Derrida*, Chicago: University of Chicago Press.

INDEX

Academy (Plato) 140, 174
Academy of Medical Sciences 163
Achilles 16, 23–4, 26–30, 35, 37, 40–1, 68, 76, 247–8
    Shield of 237, 247
Acosta-Hughes, Benjamin 6
Acragas 94
action 65–7, 73, 76–9
Actium 204
Adam, James 137
Adeimantus 139
Adonis 92
Adorno, Theodor W. 2, 6, 13–14, 16, 162, 181
Aeschines 251
Aeschylus 9, 69–71, 73–4
    Agamemnon 68, 70
    Oresteia 68, 74, 78
aesthetics 3, 7–10, 12–16, 30, 50, 84–6, 92, 94, 128, 145–6, 153, 155, 157, 238
Agamemnon 26–7, 35, 37, 40, 68, 70–6, 78
Agathon 96, 140
agency 65–7, 69–73, 75–9, 237
Agesander 217
Agesilaus 182–6, 191–3
Aiora 96
Ajax 35, 37
Alcaeus 85
Alcibiades 77–8
Alcman 85
Alexamenos of Teos 175
Alexander of Aphrodisias 173
Alexander the Great 15, 88, 90–1, 94, 170
Alexandria 6, 16, 84–6, 89–92, 94–5
    Library 84, 89, 93
Alt-Right 161
Ammonius of Alexandria 163, 175
Amycus 91
Anacreon 8, 85
Anacyndaraxes 173
Anaxagoras 165
Anselm of Canterbury 164
Antigone 16, 49–63
Antović, Mihailo 35
Anubis 97
Apellicon of Teos 167–8
Aphrodite 72, 170
Apollo 89, 92
    Apollo Belvedere 204, 206–7

Apollonius of Rhodes 174
    Argonautica 91–2
aporia 65–79, 129–30, 243–4
Aquinas, Thomas 164
Arcadia 91
archê 26, 28–9
Arendt, Hannah 27
    Human Condition, The 26
Ares 92
Argo 91
Argos 73–4
Ariaeus 183
Arion of Lesbos 90
Aristarchus 89
Aristophanes 149–50
    Acharnians 77
    Frogs 4, 9, 77
Aristotle 5–6, 13–14, 16, 28, 52, 65–8, 72, 75–8, 86, 88–9, 145–57, 161–76, 181
    Categories 163
    Constituiton of Athens 162
    Eudemian Ethics 168, 174
    History of Animals 171
    Metaphysics 165, 170
    Nerinthus 171
    Nicomachean Ethics 169, 171, 175
    On Good Birth 173
    On Philosophy 173
    On Pleasure 171
    On Poets 175
    On the Soul 169, 174
    Poetics 5, 13, 16, 65–6, 87, 145–57
    Politics 169
    Protrepticus 171–3, 176
    Rhetoric 16, 145–57
    Topics 173
Arnold, Matthew 50
Arsinoe 90, 92
Artemis 68–9, 73, 92, 94, 204
Athenaeus
    Deipnosophistae 171, 175
Athene 27, 94
Athenodorus 216
Athens 8–9, 12, 15, 50, 65, 70, 77–9, 85, 87–90, 95, 97, 134, 141–2, 146, 149–50, 156, 167–8, 170, 183–4, 192, 207, 214, 218–22, 224, 227

Index

Attar, Farid ud-Din
  Conference of the Birds 14
Augustine 163
  Confessions 164
Augustus 204
Aulis 72
Austin, Norman 40
Averroes (Ibn Rushd) 164–5
Avicenna (Ibn Sina) 165

Bacchylides 85, 89
Bach, Johann S.
  Matthäuspassion 25
Bannon, Stephen K. 161
Barchiesi, Alessandro 93
Baudelaire, Charles
  Correspondances 14
Bakhtin, Mikhail 1, 10–12, 181, 191
Bakker, Egbert J. 34, 40
Barlow, Shirley 145
Barnes, Jonathan
  Coffee with Aristotle 176
Basil of Caesarea
  Ep. 170
Bebrycians 91
Bell, Clive 3
Bell, Peter 250
Benjamin, Walter 2, 13, 16, 103–22
  Concept of Criticism in German Romanticism, The 105, 115–16, 118–20
  On the Concept of History 121–2
Bennett, Jane 247–8
Berenice 92, 94
Berkeley, George 163
Berlant, Lauren 67
Bernal, Martin
  Black Athena 208, 233–4
Bewell, Alan 245
Bithynia 184
Blondell, Ruby 130, 140
Boas, Hans C. 35
body 2, 7, 16, 145–57
Boedeker, Deborah 181
Boeotia 184
Boyarin, Daniel 12
Bozzone, Chiara 35
Brooks, Cleanth 243
Brown, Wendy 139–40
Bruno, Giordano 209
Burke, Edmund 154
Butler, Judith 55–7
  Antigone's Claim 54
Butler, Joseph 164
Bybee, Joan 25, 32

Calchas 74
Callimachus 5–6, 85, 87, 89, 91–2, 94–7
  Aetia 5, 94, 97
  Hymns 91–2
  Pinakes 6
Calypso 248
Cameron, Alan 87
Cameron, Lynn 25, 33
Campbell, Lewis 136
Cánovas, Cristóbal 35
catharsis 5, 13–14, 154
Catholicism 208, 232–3
Caylus, Anne-Claude-Philippe de Tubières, Comte de 207, 209–30, 234
  Recueil d'Antiquités égyptiennes, étrusques, grecques, romaines et gauloises 206–7, 209–28
Chalcidius 183
Chalcis 167
Chambry, Emile 137
Chapman, George 245
Chomsky, Noam 31
Christianity 50, 88, 203, 209
Cicero 140, 164–5, 170
  De divinatione 174
  Epistulae ad Atticum 170
  Hortensius 172
  Lucullus 176
Cithaeron 248
city-state, *see* polis
class 1, 10
Clearchus 188–9
Clement of Alexandria 174
Clytemnestra 68, 73–4, 190
comedy 9, 15, 83, 87
Conon 94
Constantinople 209, 245, 249–50
Conte, Gian Biagio 181
content 1, 2, 5, 6, 7, 9, 13–15
Coole, Diana 66, 79
Corinth 90, 193, 204
Coriscus 167
Crates of Mallos 6
Crates of Thebes 171, 176
Creon 16, 49, 51–63
Crete 92
Croft, William 25, 32
Cunaxa 186, 188
Currie, Bruno 35
Cyrene 85, 91–2
Cyrus the Great 179–80, 193–4
Cyrus the Younger 186–91, 193–4

Danaus 94
Dante Alighieri 165

Index

Deleuze, Gilles 162
Delos 87, 92
Delphi 87, 90
Demeter 94
Demetrius of Phaleron 89
democracy 12, 16, 50, 66, 77–8, 127, 133–5, 142, 147–8, 150, 157, 184
Democritus 165
Denyer, Nicholas 137
Dercylidas 185–6
Derrida, Jacques 55, 68, 129, 161–2
Descartes, René 163
dialect 3, 84, 86, 89
Diès, Auguste 137
Diogenes 165, 175
Diomedes 35, 37, 40
Dion (of Syracuse) 126–9, 133, 142
Dionysius (of Syracuse) 127–8, 132, 138, 141–2
Dionysus 77–8, 89, 96, 233
  Theatre of Dionysus 155
Dioscorides 165
Dioscuri 95
Diotima of Mantinea 113
dithyramb 4, 86-7, 89-90
Doric 85-6, 220-1
Dover, Kenneth 8
drama 6–7, 9, 57, 61, 65, 68–9, 72, 74, 78, 86, 89, 92, 147–9, 152–3, 166
  Athenian 6–8
  choral 83
  Sophoclean 53
Droysen, Johann Gustav 88
Dufresnoy, Charles Alphonse 230

Eagleton, Terry 10, 13, 16, 155
Edelstein, Ludwig 140
Egypt 88–9, 96–7, 203–10, 212, 214, 215, 230, 233–4, 245
eidos 2, 11, 137
ekphrasis 17, 204, 207, 237–51
elegy 94, 97
Elias 176
Elis 185
Ellis, Nick 25
Else, Gerald 150
Empedocles 163, 165
England 1, 209
Ephesus 91
epic poetry 4, 10–11, 15, 23–4, 26, 28–9, 31, 34-5, 38, 40–1, 83, 86, 91, 94, 97
Epicureanism 6, 170
epigram 15, 90, 92–4, 97, 239
epinician 15, 97
episteme 130–1, 136
epitaph 15

epithet 28, 35, 38, 40
epos, *see* epic
Erigone 97
Eros 70, 135
Eteocles 51
ethics 5, 8–9, 13, 16, 50–3, 55, 61, 65, 67–8, 71–6, 78–9, 128, 145, 164, 169, 208
ethos 65–79
Etruscan 203–6, 208–9, 234
Euclid 165
Eudemus 174, 176
Eumaeus 247
Euripides 7, 9, 16, 66, 68, 71, 73–4, 78–9, 152
  Orestes 8
  Hippolytus 8
  Ion 10, 145
  Iphigenia in Aulis 16, 65–79
Euthycles 94
Eurydice 60–1, 63
Euthymus 94
extremism 16, 49, 53, 55–6, 60–3

Fabricotti, Florence 34
Fabris, Pietro 231
Falstaff, John 163
family 50–6, 58–9, 61–2
feminism 49–63
Festugière, André-Jean 139–40
Ficino, Marsilio 112–13, 209
Fillmore, Charles 24, 32
Finley, Moses 25–6, 42
  World of Odysseus, The 25
Flaubert, Gustave 30
formulae 10, 23, 25, 34–40
Forster, E. M. 1
  Howard's End 2
Foucault, Michel 66, 126, 128–9, 132–3, 140–2
  Le Gouvernement de soi et des autres 140
  L'Herméneutique du sujet 140
Frampton, Stephanie Ann 87
France 222
Frank, Jill 138–9
freedom 26, 28, 30, 33, 50–1
Freeman, Edward A. 50
Freud, Sigmund 9
Friedländer, Paul 245, 249
Frühromantics 104, 115–17, 120, 122
Fry, Roger 3
Frye, Northrop 8

Gadamer, Hans-Georg 140
Galen 89, 165
Gauls 92
Gautier, Théophile 241
gender 1–2, 7, 16, 40, 49, 53, 55, 62, 244 *and passim*

291

Index

genre 3, 6, 7, 9–10, 12, 15, 49, 66, 83–7, 90, 93, 97, 145–7, 164, 181–2, 184, 191, 243
Gergis 185
German Idealism 50–2, 57
Germany 209
Givón, Talmy 32, 34
Glaucon 136, 139
Godard, Jean-Luc 30
Goethe, Johann W. 104–5, 111, 115–18, 120–2, 239
Goldberg, Adelle 25, 32, 35
Goldhill, Simon 3, 6, 9
Goldman, Emma 141
Goodell, Thomas Dwight 8
Gorgias 151, 190
Gospel of John 243
Graces 94, 170
grammar 23–4, 30–5, 40
Gray, Vivienne 183
Greece 1, 3–4, 10, 12, 17, 25, 50, 73, 75–6, 78, 84, 90, 92, 98–9, 127, 134, 170, 183, 185, 190–1, 203–34, 245–6 *and passim*
Greek Anthology 25
Greenberg, Clement 3
Griffith, Mark 9
Gros, Frédéric 141
Grote, George 50
Guattari, Felix 162

Hadot, Pierre 130, 139–40
Hagia Sophia (Constantinople) 237, 249, 251
Haimon 57, 59–61, 63
Hall, Edith 6, 8–9, 12–13, 145
Hamilton, Edith 140
Hamilton, William 207–8, 227–34
Hancarville, Baron d', Pierre-François Hugues 207–8, 227–34
Haraway, Donna 152
Harward, John 128, 140
Haydon, Benjamin 245
Headlam, Walter 8
Hector 35, 37, 40
Heffernan, James 243
Hegel, Georg W. F. 3, 10, 49–63, 88, 117, 203
Phenomoenology of Spirit, The 50
Heidegger, Martin 130
Helen 70, 74
Hellenistic period 5–7, 15–16, 83–9, 94
Hephaestus 237
Hera 92, 94
Heracles 94
Hercules Torso 204, 206
Heraclitus 164–5, 243
Herculaneum 233
Herder, Johann Gottfried 233
Herippidas 183
Hermes 170–1

Herodotus 8–9, 91, 165, 181–2
heroes/heroines 16, 23, 25, 26, 28, 37–8, 41, 51–6, 62–3, 74–7, 90–1
Hesiod 90
hexameter 6, 8, 24, 28–31, 38, 91–2
Hiero of Syracuse 93
Hippias 110
Hippocrates 165
historiography 15, 49–50, 165, 180–2, 231
Homer 4, 6–7, 11–12, 15–16, 23–42, 50, 74–5, 83–4, 90–2, 113, 165, 237–9, 243, 245, 247, 249–50
  Homeric diction 23–42
  Iliad 5–6, 16, 26–7, 29, 35, 69, 74, 78, 91, 94, 165, 247–8
  Odyssey 29, 34–5, 37, 180, 247–8
Honig, Bonnie 54, 56, 57f
Hopper, William 32, 34
Horace 6, 230, 241
  Ars poetica 6, 230
Hume, David 163
Hunter, Richard 139
hymn 4–6, 86–7, 89, 91–2, 97

iambic 87, 97, 249
Iamblichus 173, 176
  Protrepticus 172
  Mysteries of the Egyptians (De mysteriis Aegyptiorum), The 209
Ibycus 85
Icarius 96–7
Icus 96
imperialism 1–2, 89
intertextuality 24, 83–4
Ion 113
Iphigen(e)ia 66, 68–9, 72–8
Irigaray, Luce 53–5
Isis 97
Ismene 54–62
Isocrates
  Busiris 190
  Helen 190
  Panathenaicus 191–2
Italy 91, 206–8, 222, 233

Jameson, Fredric 1, 13–14, 16
  Marxism and Form 2
  Modernist Papers, The 1
  Political Unconscious, The 83
Janko, Richard 15
Jason and the Argonauts 91
Jebb, Eglantine 51
Jesus 25
Jowett, Benjamin 136
Judas 25
Justinian 249–51

Index

Kahane, Ahuvia 34
Kant, Immanuel 3, 13, 50–1, 113
   Critique of Judgement 13
Keats, John 7, 240–5, 252
   Endymion 245
   Ode on a Grecian Urn 237–52
Kelly, Adrian 36–7
Kelly, Jason M. 222
Kierkegaard, Søren 68
Kircher, Athanasius 209
Konuk, Kader 246
Kosselleck, Reinhart 49
Koyré, Alexandre 139
Kramsch, Caroline 25, 33
Krieger, Murray 243
Kroll, Wilhelm 84, 88
Kronos 27
Krummen, Evelyn 15
Kurke, Leslie 15
Kyriakou, Poulheria 153

Lacan, Jacques 52, 72
Lakoff, George 24, 32
Laocoon 217
Larsen-Freeman, Diane 25, 33
late antiquity 3, 6, 249
Le Roy, Julien-David 207, 219, 222-3, 224-7
Leibniz, Gottfried W. 119
Leonard, Miriam 52
Leonidas 192
Leto 92, 204
Letter of Aristeas 89
Levine, Caroline 2, 84–5, 88, 90, 93
Libya 91
Life of Aesop 164
linguistics 16, 23–5, 30–7, 46–7, 66, 244
Linus 165
London 219
Longinus 11
Lord, Albert 34
Louis XIV 209
Lucian 170–1
   Vitarum Auctio 170
Lucretius 163
Lukács, György 1–2, 10, 12–14, 16
Luther, Martin 203, 231
Lycurgus 179–80
Lynceus 172
Lyons, Siobhan 163, 175
lyric (poetry) 4, 10, 15, 83, 90
Lysander 183
Lysimachus of Thrace 91

Maas, Paul 8
Macedon 86, 89, 170
Machiavelli, Niccolò 164
MacKendrick, Paul 85
MacMullan, Terrance 162
madness 55, 58–9, 66, 68, 70–1, 75–7
Maimonides 164
Mandeville, Bernard 164
Mania 185–6
Marcus Aurelius 164
Marcuse, Herbert 162
Martial 214
   Epigrams 213
Martin, Richard 24
Martindale, Charles 13
Marx, Karl 11, 12, 66
Marxism 2, 10, 12–13, 83, 148–9, 157
materialism, 13–16, 120–2
materiality 5, 7, 10, 104, 146, 148, 150–3, 155–7, 206, 208–9, 216, 241, 243, 248–50
Megabates 184
Meidias 185–6
Memphis 89
Mendel, Gregor 84
Menelaos 35, 37, 40, 68–72
Menippus Eudaimonides 214
Menon 188
metaphysical 3, 5
metre 3–4, 6, 7, 8, 15, 34, 38, 84, 89
   Dorian 8
   Elegiac 97
   Phrygian 8
Milesians 193
Miletus 193
Miller, Paul Allen 129
Miller, Walter 179
mimesis 4–6, 65, 68, 77, 86, 105–7, 147, 153–4
Minos 94
Mitchell, William J. T. 244
modernism 1–3
modernity 2–3, 7–8, 12, 14, 17, 30, 51, 208
Mörike, Eduard 239
Morrow, Glenn 140
Most, Glenn 15, 87
Muses 5, 26, 41, 88, 94, 113
music 7–9, 13, 25, 65, 86, 90, 114, 149–50, 168, 239
muthos 9, 16, 65–79, 153
Myrmidons 247
myth 10, 54, 67, 72–3, 91, 129, 176

Nagy, Gregory 34
Naples 207–8, 227, 231–2
Nehamas, Alexander 130, 140
Neleus 167
Neoptolemus of Parium 6
Neoplatonists 165, 245
Nero 141, 207
New Criticism 7, 237–44
New Historicism 1, 7, 83

293

Index

New Materialism 247–8
Nicomachus 176
Nietzsche, Friedrich 11, 142, 161
    Birth of Tragedy 10–11, 164
    Ecce Homo 10
Nightingale, Andrea 191
Nike 204
Nile 213
Novalis 104, 117, 121
novel 1, 10, 83, 92, 181
Nubia 234

obscurity 161–3, 176
Occident 238–46
Odysseus 11, 27–8, 35, 37, 39–41, 72, 91, 247–9, 251
Oedipus 9, 51, 54, 155
Oikos 52
Olympus 165
Optatian 15
oratory 12, 15, 145–7, 149, 151, 157
Orientalism 203, 219, 227
Orontas 189
Orpheus 165, 209
Osiris 97
Otys 182–4, 186

paean 86–7, 89, 97
Paphlagonians 182–4
Paris 70, 74, 190
Paris (France) 209
Parmenides 164
Parnassians 238, 241
Parry, Adam 23–4, 30–1
Parry, Milman 23–4, 35–7
Parthians 234
Pasion 189
pastoral (poetry) 92–3, 97
Paul the Silentiary 237, 249–51
Pausanias 183, 209
Peleus 74
Penelope 248
Pergamum 167
Periander 90
Persia 77, 165, 179–80, 182, 184–9, 192–4
Petrarch 164
Phalaris 94
Pharnabazus 183–5
Philhellenism 50
Philiscus 171
Philitas 94
Philodemus 6
philosopher-king 125–43
philosophy 5–6, 8, 10–13, 16, 24–6, 50, 86–7, 104–5, 116, 125–43, 145, 164, 169
    see also Aristotle *and* Plato

philotimia 69–70, 72
Phleius 193
Phoenicians 244
Phoenix 95
Plataea 248, 251
Plato 3–6, 8, 11–13, 16, 86, 88, 103–22, 125–43, 147–9, 154, 163, 165, 168, 170, 173–5, 184
    Apology 11, 129, 133, 140, 191, 241
    Cratylus 109
    Fifth Letter 135
    Gorgias 171
    Hippias Major 110
    Ion 106, 111–13, 140
    Laws 11, 86
    Lysis 191
    Menexenus 191
    Parmenides 140
    Phaedo 110
    Phaedrus 11, 13, 112, 129
    Republic 4–6, 12–13, 16, 105–11, 113–14, 122, 125–6, 128, 132–3, 135–9
    Seventh Letter 16, 125–43
    Sophist 130, 140
    Symposium 12–13, 96, 112, 126, 135, 139–40, 191
    Timaeus 11, 107
Platonism 105–6, 115, 209
Pléiade 239
Pliny
    Natural History 174, 217, 231
Plutarch 140, 170–1, 174
    Life of Alexander 170
    Life of Dion 174
Pilate 25
Pindar 8, 85, 91, 93
poetry 4–8, 12, 16, 83–8, 90, 93, 105–6, 116, 166 *and passim*
performance of 7, 29, 42, 83, 85–7
polis 4, 9, 12, 28, 52, 77, 86–7, 90, 105–6, 109, 115–16, 142, 145
Pollis 96
Polydeuces 91
Polydorus 217
Polyneices 51, 56–7, 60
Pompeii 232–3
Popper, Karl 125–6
Porter, James 2, 208
Posidippus of Pella 90, 92–4, 97
prattontes 65, 69, 72, 74, 76, 78–9
praxis 26, 65–79, 153, 169
Priam 35, 248
Proclus 175
Prokopios 251
    Buildings 249
    Secret History 251

prose 1–2, 4, 6, 8–10, 12, 15–16, 83, 165, 180, 182, 193, 195 *and passim*
Protestantism 25, 203, 206
Proxenus 188
Ptah 89
Ptolemy, Ptolemies 86–7, 89–92, 94, 97, 165
Pythagoras 209

Rancière, Jacques 24, 26–42, 148, 156
   Ten Theses on Politics 29
Rang, Florens Christian 115, 118
Reeve, Michael 24
Rembrandt
   Aristotle with a Bust of Homer 165
Renaissance 11, 207, 209, 233, 245
religion 3, 8, 11, 51
Revett, Nicolas 219–23, 226
rhythm 8, 86, 90–4
Rilke, Reiner Maria 238, 245
Roby, Courtney 247
Rockhill, Gabriel 29
Romanticism (German) 104, 116–17, 121
Rome 6, 84, 88, 168, 203–6, 214, 219, 222, 230–1, 233–4, 245, 249
Rose, Peter 8–10
Rosenmeyer, Thomas G. 34
Rousseau, Jean-Jacques 164
rupture 16, 30, 33–5, 38–41
Ruskin, John 49
Ryholt, Kim 89

Sallustius, Gnaeus 170
Sappho 14, 85
Sartre, Jean-Paul 2
satire 9
Saussure, Ferdinand de 31–2, 66
Saxonhouse, Arlene 139
Scepsis 167
Schelling, Friedrich W. J. 50–1
Schiller, Friedrich 239
Schlegel, Friedrich 104, 117, 121
Schopenhauer, Arthur 161
Scopadae 95
Scott, Grant 246
Second World War 26, 237, 252
Seneca the Younger 141, 164–5
Seth 97
Sextus Empiricus 164
Shklovsky, Viktor 6
Sicily 89, 91, 127–8
Silenus 174–5
Simonides 85, 94–5, 173
Skepsis 185–6
slaves 29, 149
Sluiter, Ineke 161

Socrates 4, 6, 10–12, 106, 110, 127, 129–30, 133–4, 136, 139–41, 165, 173, 175, 182, 184, 191
Solon 162
Solzhenitzen, Aleksandr 141
Sophocles 6, 155
   Ajax 57
   Antigone 16, 49–63
   Oedipus 154–5
   Trachiniae 8
Sophron 175
Souilhé, Joseph 125, 140
Sparta 50, 77, 85, 179–80, 182–6, 190–5, 214
Spithridates 182–4, 186
Spitzer, Leo 17, 237–51
Stalinism 125–6
Steiner, George 50, 51
Stephens, Susan 6
Stesichorus 85
Stobaeus 173
   Florilegium 171
Stock, George 176
Strabo 167–8
Stuart, James 207, 219–24, 227
   Antiquities of Athens, The 219–23
subjectivity 14, 237
   female 53
   poetic 24
   political 26
Sulla 167–8
Synesius
   Encomium of Calvitius 174
Syracuse 85, 93, 126–9, 138, 174
Szlezák, Thomas A. 129

Teiresias 57, 60–1
Teles of Megara 171
telos 65, 67, 73, 75, 77–8, 146, 152
Tennyson, Alfred 8
Thales 165
Thebes 60, 183–4, 193
Themistius
   Orationes 170–1
Themistocles 95
Theocritus 85, 87, 92, 238–9, 243
   Idylls 92
Theodora 251
Theognis 173
Theon 17, 237
   Progymnasmata 237, 248
Theophrastus 167, 176
Thersites 27–9, 38–9, 41
Thetis 74
Thibron 185
Thucydides 8–9, 59, 95, 165, 181, 248–50
Timarchus 251
Tissaphernes 193

Index

Tomasello, Michael 25, 32
tragedy 4–7, 9, 10, 15, 49–51, 54, 65–6, 83, 87, 90, 146, 148–9, 150, 152–4, 156
Triton 91
Trojan War 70, 74, 91
Trojans 29, 91
Troy 74, 77
Trump, Donald 161
Tullius Cicero, Quintus 170
Tyrannion 168
tyranny 53, 86,–7, 89, 90, 94, 127–8, 133, 138, 142

usage-based approach 24–5, 31–2, 34–6, 38–40

Vergil 92
  Aeneid 91
Vernant, Jean-Pierre 9, 66, 71
verse 6, 8, 12, 25, 34, 38, 41–2 *and passim*
  elegiac 5
Vesuvius 232
Vico, Giambattista 30
  Scienza Nuova 25
Victorians 3, 50–1, 53
Vitruvius 222
Vossius, Gerardus 165

Washington, D.C. 161
White, Hayden 8
White House 161

Whitmarsh, Tim 1
Williams, Raymond 148, 150, 155–6
  Marxism and Literature 148
Winckelmann, Johann J. 121, 203–9, 211, 226–7, 229–31, 233–4
  History of the Art of Antiquity 203–6, 209, 231, 233–4
Wire, The 84, 97
Wasserman, Earl 239–40, 252
  Finer Tone, The 239
Wittgenstein, Ludwig 164
Wohl, Victoria 7, 9, 10
Wolfson, S. J. 5
Wordsworth, William 8
  Ode to Duty 8
Worman, Nancy 7

Xenias 189
Xenophon 8, 16, 91, 179–95
  Agesilaus 192–3
  Anabasis 91, 180–2, 184, 186–91, 193–4
  Cyropaedia 179–82, 193–5
  Hellenica 181–6, 190–1
  Lakedaimonion Politeia 179–82, 193–5

Zeitlin, Froma I. 9
Zeno 165, 171
Zeus 26, 35, 37, 40, 69, 90–2, 165, 170
Zoroaster 209
Zuckert, Catherine 140

www.ingramcontent.com/pod-product-compliance
Lightning Source LLC
Chambersburg PA
CBHW052152300426
44115CB00011B/1632